Everyday BIBLE

CROSSWORD COLLECTION

180 PUZZLES!

BARBOUR
PUBLISHING

© 2022 by Barbour Publishing, Inc.

ISBN 978-1-63609-144-0

Crosswords were created using licensed Crossword Weaver software (www.crosswordweaver.com).

Published by Barbour Publishing, Inc., 1810 Barbour Drive, Uhrichsville, Ohio 44683, www.barbourbooks.com

Our mission is to inspire the world with the life-changing message of the Bible.

Printed in the United States of America.

Spend your down time
productively
with a **BIBLE** crossword!

Enhance your Bible knowledge and your puzzle-solving skills with the *Everyday Bible Crossword Collection*. Here are 180 clever (and occasionally confounding) puzzles covering the fascinating people and places, times and teachings, objects and oddities of the Bible. Discover

- the apostle Paul
- the parables of Jesus
- Anna the prophetess
- Bible couples
- Noah's ark
- Judas Iscariot, the betrayer
- books of the Bible
- "donkey business"
- and much more!

Perfect for puzzle lovers of all ages, the *Everyday Bible Crossword Collection* promises a Galilean fishing boat full of fun!

PARABLES OF JESUS

ACROSS

1. Turn the other one if slapped
6. "In laughter the heart may_____" (Prov. 14:13 NIV)
10. Keyboard key (abbr.)
13. Be not just this, but 25 Down also
15. Jesus anointed blind man's eyes with this
16. Golfer's need TEE SPLT / DIRT
17. Cleopatra's love ANTONY
18. "I am the _____ ye are the branches" (John 15:5)
19. La Brea pits content
20. Lydia worked with them (Acts 16) DYE
22. "_____ us our debts"
24. Thought
26. Record player HZFI
28. Mined metals ORES
29. The _____ Samaritan
30. Some rest stop rooms
31. Passes at the bull
32. "Pay back what you _____ me!" (Matt. 18:28 NIV)
33. "We have _____ his star in the east" (Matt. 2:2)
34. Deli order BLT
36. Tavern owner

37. Along 43 Across
41. "_____ your light so shine" (Matt. 5:16)
42. Sight on 43 Across
43. _____ of Galilee
44. Psychologist Sigmund FREUD FRUED
47. He builds his house on sand
48. Jesus' mom
49. Season before Easter
50. "Let these sayings _____ down into your ears" (Luke 9:44)
51. Indiana city
52. How some described Jesus GLUTTON
54. Decorative needle case
58. Female parent (var.)
57. "This night thy _____ shall be required of thee" (Luke 12:20)
59. Supple
63. Barely make it (with "out")
64. Old story TALE
65. A man "shall _____ unto his wife" (Gen. 2:24)
66. Take out (abbr.)
67. Fencer's need
68. Sharp as a two-_____ sword EDGED

DOWN

1. Repeated, a dance
2. "Even as a _____ gathereth her chickens" (Matt. 23:37)
3. Do this at a feast
4. Worn
5. Safari destination
6. Hovercraft (abbr.)
7. Dover's are white
8. Vietnamese capital
9. Ogler
10. Raiment
11. "Beware of the _____ of the Pharisees" (Mark 8:15)

12. Mother _____ of India
14. Bread choice
21. They will be separated from 23 Down
23. They will be separated from 21 Down
24. Hawkeye State
25. See 13 Across
27. 29 Across took the wounded man to one
28. Lump
30. "Bring forth. . .fruits _____ for repentance" (Matt. 3:8)
31. Ado
33. What the sower sowed
34. Plague woe

26 "Give ye _____, O house of the king" (Hos. 5:1)

27 Top notch

28 Scot topper

29 "They have heard that _____" (Lam. 1:21) (2 words)

30 Donnybrook

31 "The house of _____" (Amos 1:5)

32 "Where no oxen are, the _____ is clean" (Prov. 14:4)

33 "His soul shall dwell at _____" (Ps. 25:13)

34 Words at the first sign of trouble (2 words)

38 _____-Cone

40 "_____ why dost thou cry out aloud?" (Mic. 4:9)

41 "_____ words stir up anger" (Prov. 15:1)

44 Pushed ahead, as through a crowd

46 One who gets free

49 Subtraction answer (abbr.)

50 Aswan High Dam lake

51 Daycare denizen

54 Mark indicating text to be removed (var.)

55 "_____ of the God of Jacob" (Ps. 81:4) (2 words)

56 "Take my _____ upon you" (Matt. 11:29)

57 Girl from Green Gables

58 "_____ his own soul?" (Mark 8:36)

59 "Duke Magdiel, duke _____" (Gen. 36:43)

60 "There went _____ sower to sow" (Mark 4:3) (2 words)

61 "And find grace to help in time of _____" (Heb. 4:16)

62 _____-relief

TRUST IN WHOM?

Trust in the LORD with all thine heart. . .and he shall direct thy paths.

PROV. 3:5-6

ACROSS

1 "Thou hast asked _____ thing" (2 Kings 2:10) (2 words)
6 "Shoo!"
10 "And the _____ went forth" (Zech. 6:7)
13 First feast of the Passover
14 "Slewest in the valley of _____" (1 Sam. 21:9)
15 "He is of _____; ask him" (John 9:21)
16 "Nor could the _____ trees" (Ezek. 31:8 NIV)
17 Yorkshire river
18 "The name of the wicked shall _____" (Prov. 10:7)
19 Start of **QUOTE** from Psalm 16:1 (3 words)
22 Cold War acronym
23 Modern American furniture designer
26 "The _____ day went Jesus out of the house" (Matt. 13:1)
30 Norse thunder god
33 "Because thou didst _____ on the LORD" (2 Chron. 16:8)
34 "Is to be made _____ of rubble" (Ezra 6:11 NIV) (2 words)
36 "And Jonah _____ in the belly" (Jon. 1:17)
38 Whole lot

39 **QUOTE**, cont'd (5 words)
43 "The house of _____ in Shiloh" (1 Kings 2:27)
44 "Sinned, _____ his parents" (John 9:3)
45 "But they also have _____ through wine" (Isa. 28:7)
46 Blind part
48 Sires' mates
51 "In the thirty-sixth year of _____ reign" (2 Chron. 16:1 NIV)
52 Pepper-upper
54 "Arise and come to my _____" (Ps. 35:2 NIV)
56 End of **QUOTE** (4 words)
62 "To _____, the prophets of Israel" (Ezek. 13:16)
64 "So he _____ the fare" (Jonah 1:3)
65 "That they may be _____ we are" (John 17:11) (2 words)
67 Unreturned serve
68 Sections of the small intestine
69 Start for glycerine
70 "_____, of the Gentiles also" (Rom. 3:29)
71 "Yet will I not _____ thee" (Matt. 26:35)
72 Writer of Psalm 89

DOWN

1 "On the hole of the _____" (Isa. 11:8)
2 "Come up unto me, and _____ me" (Josh. 10:4)
3 Twelfth Jewish month (Est. 3:7)
4 Descartes
5 "And _____ it first" (1 Kings 18:25)
6 "That _____ may be made in the book" (Ezra 4:15)
7 VII x XXII
8 Swiss river
9 "Are the _____ of my song" (Ps. 119:54 NIV)
10 Weather gauges

11 "Unto him that fashioned it long _____" (Isa. 22:11)
12 "Nor _____ for your body" (Matt. 6:25)
20 "Ye shall not _____ of it" (Gen. 3:3)
21 "He that hath an _____" (Rev. 2:7)
24 Common freshwater plant
25 Church councils
26 Wisest
27 Lunar mission
28 "Because of the _____" (Judg. 6:7)
29 Leprechaun's kin
31 "Into his _____ city" (Matt. 9:1)

32 "The _____, any kind of great" (Lev. 11:29 NIV)

35 Very long time

37 "_____ obeyed not" (Zeph. 3:2)

40 "Feed thy people with thy _____" (Mic. 7:14)

41 "The sixth captain for the sixth month was _____" (1 Chron. 27:9)

42 Pitcher's stat (abbr.)

47 "Dip the _____" (Luke 16:24)

49 Vocal SOS

50 "And made them all _____ down" (Luke 9:15)

53 Amorous archer of ancient mythology

55 He bee

57 "And the _____ of the bricks" (Exod. 5:8)

58 Demeanor

59 "The body is a _____" (1 Cor. 12:12 NIV)

60 Father of Enos (Gen. 5:6)

61 O'Hara estate

62 "See thou tell no man; but go thy _____" (Matt. 8:4)

63 "He casteth forth his _____ like morsels" (Ps. 147:17)

66 "Whom if his _____ ask bread" (Matt. 7:9)

ANGELS ALL AROUND

ACROSS

1 A mule was held "with _____ and bridle" (Ps. 32:9)
4 Vineyard measures, e.g.
9 Jesus was like one without blemish (2 words)
14 "Why make ye this _____?" (Mark 5:39)
15 Steak left too long on the grill
16 An angel released him from prison
17 Sleep stage (abbr.)
18 Fallen angel
19 "Whatsoever ye shall _____ on earth" (Matt. 18:18)
20 Bethlehem angels' focus
22 Jesus came to _____ us from eternal death
24 An animal's foot
25 Caesar's twelve
27 Jerusalem to Joppa (dir.)
29 Temple's veil was rent from top to _____
32 Drives, in England
35 Western state, for short
36 Angels rolled it away
38 "Remember not the sins of my _____" (Ps. 25:7)

40 Footnote citation (Lat.) (abbr.)
42 Openings
44 Herr's wife
45 Number of angels in Rev.
47 An angel might appear in one
49 _____ of the Lord
50 Jesus cured ten
52 Melting mollusks of Psalm 58:8
54 Number of angels at 3 Down
55 List of sub-parts (abbr.)
56 "As if!"
59 Like a swallow in Psalm 84:3, e.g.
63 Holy Land tree
67 Man was made in God's _____
69 Banquet command (2 words)
71 "Mama _____!"
72 Hands out
73 Jesus died to _____ for sin
74 God's angels never do this
75 Alcohol compounds in chemistry
76 Choir section
77 KJV negative

DOWN

1 Snarky remark
2 Thought
3 See 54 Across
4 Medical research assoc.
5 _____ of God, angel reference (Ps. 68:17)
6 Manna was gathered at a daily _____
7 Distinctive times in history
8 In _____ (together)
9 God sends blessings _____
10 Lion appellation
11 18 Across took Jesus _____ the temple
12 Plateau
13 Make coffee
21 Tel. number add-on
23 Mexican "one"

26 Possessive pronoun
28 Whether in "warp, or _____" (Lev. 13:48)
29 tower
30 Gethsemane tree
31 Shapes, as potter with clay
32 Allots
33 Most of Galilee in Bible times
34 Morning _____, angel reference (Job 38:7)
35 Italian commune
37 Angels neither hunger _____ marry
39 Whir
41 Org. division
43 35 Across city (2 words)
46 "Walk in _____ of life" (Rom. 6:4)
48 Former Chinese Chairman

51 KJV "deer"
53 Naughty child
56 Rahab agreed to _____ the spies
57 King of Judah (2 Kings 21:18)
58 Angel topper
60 Ark of Covenant's mercy _____
61 London gallery

62 English school
64 Prayer ender
65 Former Italian coin
66 Gabriel appeared to her
68 Hair spiker
70 According to

FAVORITE BIBLE STORIES

ACROSS

1 Charles, for short
5 Used at Jesus' trial
9 Fish dish
14 Tramp
15 Eden's forbidden feature
16 Examine, as one's conscience
17 "The inheritance shall be ____" (Mark 12:7)
18 Prima donna
19 Spring bird
20 3 Down son
22 Makes late
24 Sleep stage (abbr.)
25 Contained, as sheep
27 Tree juices
31 "God is ____" (1 John 4:8)
32 Put on
34 Gnawer
35 Freewoman of ancient Rome
38 Female prophet suffix
40 Keeping step
42 "He shall ____ for ever" (Rev. 11:15)
44 Fr. holy woman

46 Biblical tower
47 "Take second helpings!" (2 words)
48 Water barrier
50 Meat inspection agency (abbr.)
51 Sodom sight
52 Spider's creation
55 Genesis dust of the ground
57 God ____ everything
59 5 Across result
61 Expert
64 East Asian locale
66 When Nicodemus visited Jesus
68 He denied Jesus three times
71 Last word in prayer
73 Ark man
74 "Plop!"
75 ____ of Sharon
76 Trinity, e.g.
77 Of doubtful taste
78 Nativity star locale
79 68 Across boat needs

DOWN

1 Church voices
2 "In my Father's ____ are. . .mansions" (John 14:2)
3 20 Across dad's old name
4 Former star hitter Sammy
5 UK company name ender (abbr.)
6 Describes Sinai Desert
7 "God rested" day number
8 Jesus' ____ many lepers
9 Like the lame man after Jesus' miracle
10 Golgotha sight
11 "____ not the poor" (Prov. 22:22)
12 Tokyo tie
13 Daniel and lions' space
21 Naval military rank (abbr.)

23 Flurry
26 Eden gal
28 Ishmaelites
29 Walked back and forth
30 Inscribed pillar
31 Child's building block, maybe
33 Snatch
35 Judea and Galilee, e.g.
36 "____ to do evil" (Isa. 1:16)
37 Altar offering
39 Norm (abbr.)
41 Church missionary
43 Jerusalem to Tyre (dir.)
45 Rest for the soul, e.g.
49 Dairy sound

53 OT priest

54 "_____ of false prophets" (Matt. 7:15)

56 There was no room at the _____

58 Meat for grilling

60 South Pacific nation

61 Ancient Greek marketplace

62 A throne is a fancy one

63 Church doctrine, e.g.

65 Inventive

67 "Arise. . .flee _____ Egypt" (Matt. 2:13)

68 Los Angeles winter hour (abbr.)

69 Climate org.

70 Compassion in action (abbr.)

72 68 Across fishing need

Day 7

AARON'S ERRANDS

ACROSS

1 Prejudice
5 Light greenish-blue color
9 Summer stinger
13 "Ye are _____" (Ex. 5:17)
14 Seventh commandment no-no
15 '80s shampoo brand for highlighting hair
16 "Gather a certain _____ every day" (Ex. 16:4)
17 "They shall _____ their swords into plowshares" (Isa. 2:4)
18 Flippered mammal
19 Front of church
21 Harvard's rival
23 Aaron died here (Num. 20:27–28)
24 Anointing element
25 Aaron's sister (Ex. 15:20)
29 UK time zone
30 Matron
32 Compass point (abbr.)
33 Dispute
36 Epics
37 Potter's vessel
38 Pet. compares the devil to one (1 Pet. 5:8)
39 Priestly fabric
40 Nail
41 Tire measurement (abbr.)

42 Bluish-white metals
43 Psalms, e.g.
44 "A _____ gathereth her chickens" (Matt. 23:37)
45 Egyptians would _____ the Israelites to leave (Ex. 12:33)
46 Jacob or Laban, e.g.
47 Very soft fur
49 Energy measurements (abbr.)
50 Wing
53 "He called for Moses and Aaron by night, and said, _____ up" (Ex. 12:31)
55 Navies
57 Jacob's father (Gen. 25:26)
60 "Keep it up until the fourteenth day of the _____ month" (Ex. 12:6)
62 "Hail smote. . ._____ man and beast" (Ex. 9:25)
63 Mooring
64 "Whereby we cry, _____, Father" (Rom. 8:15)
65 Canal
66 "No more give the people straw to _____ brick" (Ex. 5:7)
67 Sacred lot carried by Aaron (Ex. 28:30)
68 Eyeglass part

DOWN

1 White-barked tree
2 American state
3 Aaron ministered at one (Ex. 28:43)
4 "I have surely _____ the affliction of my people" (Ex. 3:7)
5 "The LORD saith it; _____ I have not spoken" (Ezek. 13:7)
6 Squelch
7 Uncle Sam's place (abbr.)
8 Lawyer (abbr.)
9 "This is the _____ of Meribah" (Num. 20:13)
10 Something else (abbr.)

11 Nazareth to Jericho (dir.)
12 Golfer's goal
15 Holy of _____
20 "And it shall _____ to pass" (Ex. 4:8)
22 Jordanian capital
26 Accustom
27 Sarai's spouse
28 God does this to broken spirits
29 Weapon
30 One was performed by 25 Across (Ex. 15:20)
31 Genesis 5 data
33 "I am _____ and Omega" (Rev. 1:8)

34 "He is _____" (Matt. 28:6)

35 Moses' "hands were steady until the _____ down of the sun" (Ex. 17:12)

36 "I will _____ unto the LORD" (Ex. 15:1)

39 Italian currency

40 Pharaoh's daughter found one (Ex. 2:5–6)

42 Swiss city

43 Prune beginnings

46 The Jordan, in places

48 Aaron did this better than his brother (Ex. 4:14)

49 Disney deer

50 Worship fervently

51 Language of the Vulgate

52 Burnt offering remains

54 Jacob's twin (Gen. 25:25–26)

56 First murder victim (Gen. 4:8)

57 Computer makers

58 God's people were led through the Red _____ (Ex. 13:18)

59 _____ of the covenant

61 Reduced (abbr.)

AMAZING ABIGAIL

ACROSS

1 Abigail's husband (1 Sam. 25:3)
6 Measurement replaced by hertz (abbr.)
9 Apt description of Abigail's husband
13 "Horns of ivory and _____" (Ezek. 27:15)
14 According to song, Jesus slept on it
15 "And ye have done _____ than your fathers" (Jer. 16:12)
16 "Thou art God _____" (Ps. 86:10)
17 "The birds of the _____ have nests" (Matt. 8:20)
18 Jesus does this
19 Bag
20 "An angry man stirreth up _____" (Prov. 29:22)
22 His wife was salty (Gen. 19:23–26)
23 Maybe Adam used one in Eden to till the earth
24 Distress call
25 Ark builder
27 Coarse
29 Slain with a sling
33 Spy org.
34 Abigail's servants _____ the way (1 Sam. 25:19)
35 Abigail's husband's party attitude (1 Sam. 25:36)
36 "All we like _____ have gone astray" (Isa. 53:6)
39 Noah, Jacob, Joseph, e.g.

40 What shepherds do
41 Tyre or Sidon, e.g.
42 Kitten's cry
43 "I _____ no pleasant bread" (Dan. 10:3)
44 Some say it was what Eve picked
46 Also known as Myanmar
49 Abigail gave David five measures of it (1 Sam. 25:18)
50 Recede
51 Flightless bird
53 Typing rate (abbr.)
56 "The tongue. . .is. . .full of _____ poison" (James 3:8)
58 Where Abigail and her husband lived (1 Sam. 25:2–3)
59 David, upon hearing Abigail's husband's message (1 Sam. 25:13)
61 Cow sound
62 Doctrine
63 "Noah _____ grace in the eyes of the Lord" (Gen. 6:8)
64 Prophetic gift
65 Excuse
66 Shine
67 "I was blind, now I _____" (John 9:25)
68 Perfect

DOWN

1 Under (poet.)
2 Like Eden
3 Infant's sock
4 Mary's mother, traditionally (var.)
5 Caustic substance
6 Talks with
7 Set of ark animals
8 Medicine deliverers
9 David was one to Abigail's husband (1 Sam. 25:13)

10 Voiced
11 Norwegian capital
12 "Shall bear thee up. . ._____ thou dash thy foot" (Ps. 91:12)
15 Wale
20 Member of the legume family
21 Abigail's husband refused this to David's men (1 Sam. 25:11)
24 "My feet did not _____" (2 Sam. 22:37)
26 "Friend, go up _____" (Luke 14:10)
28 Vinegar's acid

30 Abigail's husband had too much of this, perhaps (1 Sam. 25:36)

31 Herbal beverage

32 Abigail "bowed herself on _____ face" (1 Sam. 25:41)

34 The Ten Commandments, e.g.

36 Place of ahhhs

37 Jump

38 Make a mistake

39 Affectionate monikers (2 words)

40 Hurt one's toe

42 Abigail "told him nothing, less or _____, until the morning light" (1 Sam. 25:36)

43 Subject of this puzzle, familiarly

45 Encrypted

47 Someone not nice

48 One-celled water creature (var.)

50 To escape secretly to marry

52 "Wait upon the LORD our God, _____ that he have mercy" (Ps. 123:2)

53 Abigail became David's (1 Sam. 25:39)

54 High school event

55 Aloha place

57 Medicine amount

58 Blend

60 Dynamite (abbr.)

62 _____ chi

FIRST CHRISTIANS

ACROSS

1 Hair locale
6 Volcano spew
10 Data storage devices (abbr.)
13 Made neater
15 Car rental agency
16 Sower's need
17 One devil possessed, biblically
18 Scam
19 Take flight
20 Do not do this concerning good works
22 24 Across mentor
24 Former persecutor of Christians
26 Dr. Zhivago's love
28 Norwegian capital
29 Prays
30 Bethany follower of Jesus
31 Church table
32 Miner's find
33 Place for hats, maybe
34 Sports ministry org.
35 Wind-powered apparatus
37 "Thou shalt be his _____ unto all men" (Acts 22:15)

41 Long, long time
42 Trespasses
43 _____ Grande
44 Emission
47 Turfs
48 Eutychus' seat (Acts 20:9)
49 You can whistle a happy one
50 Late-night host Jay
51 "My people are _____ to backsliding from me" (Hos. 11:7)
52 Aaron's son
54 "Faith cometh by hearing, and hearing by the _____ of God" (Rom. 10:17)
56 Watchdog agency (abbr.)
57 Humorist Bombeck
59 Do not let your faith do this
63 Insult, slangily
64 Good fight of faith, e.g.
65 In Jerusalem were "devout men, out of every _____ under heaven" (Acts 2:5)
66 Hog's home
67 "I have neither _____ on usury" (Jer. 15:10)
68 Compact

DOWN

1 Bible scholar's degree, maybe (abbr.)
2 Spy org.
3 Sum up
4 Edge in science
5 Do not cast one before swine
6 Ten Commandments, e.g.
7 Bird sanctuary
8 Lithuanian capital
9 24 Across often went there
10 _____ died for us
11 Cameroon seaport
12 Detector
14 Genetic code (abbr.)
21 Frozen dessert

23 "Ryan Express" baseballer
24 South American nation
25 Teen suffix
27 Noah's float
29 Automated tasker, for short
30 German novelist Thomas
31 Bible book written by Luke
33 Response to 24 Across preaching, often
34 Fish features
36 City of studious Christians (Acts 17:10–11)
37 Often neglected woman in Acts 6:1
38 Ireland
39 Nile Delta element
40 Sun (Lat.)

42 "He...spared not his own _____" (Rom. 8:32)

44 "Harness the horses, mount the _____!" (Jer. 46:4 NIV)

45 Pastor's place

46 Fearful

47 Sunday morning oration

48 Stately

50 24 Across audience size, often

51 Communion element

53 Missionary need

55 "Considerest not the beam that is in thine _____ eye?" (Matt. 7:3)

58 "Go to the _____, thou sluggard" (Prov. 6:6)

60 Relation

61 VW model

62 SSW opposite

NEW TESTAMENT MEN

ACROSS

1 "_____, our eye hath seen it" (Ps. 35:21)
4 Governing group
9 "We spend our years as _____ that is told" (Ps. 90:9) (2 words)
14 9 Down daily task
15 "Not _____ your liberty for a cloke of maliciousness" (1 Pet. 2:16)
16 One returned to thank Jesus
17 Anger
18 The Nile has one
19 Unite
20 Winter storm need
22 Plant fiber
24 Sicilian spewer
25 Self-satisfied
27 _____ priest, 67 Across position
31 Italian duke
32 Definitely not cool
33 Flapper's accessory
34 Caleb, for one
36 Disgust
38 Place of prayer
40 Confront
42 Grasslands

43 Greek philosopher
44 "The wise took _____ in their vessels" (Matt. 25:4)
45 "Seest thou a man that is _____ in his words" (Prov. 29:20)
47 Dart
51 Black gem
53 "Jesus...went up _____ a mountain to pray" (Luke 9:28 NIV)
54 Opera solo
55 What Caleb did in the Promised Land
57 Pet.'s brother
59 Car make
62 Segment
65 The New Testament is one
66 Simon of Cyrene's son
67 See 27 Across
68 _____ Lanka
69 66 Across' dad bore it for Jesus
70 "My wife well stricken in _____" (Luke 1:18)
71 Elephant's name

DOWN

1 Stayed with
2 David's "tomb is _____ this day" (Acts 2:29 NIV) (2 words)
3 Graying
4 New Testament book writer
5 Consumer
6 Nada
7 Explosive (abbr.)
8 Prophet in Acts 11:28
9 "He...sat for _____ at the Beautiful gate" (Acts 3:10)
10 Gnashing of _____
11 Easter month sometimes
12 Lower limb

13 "Sir, come down _____ my child die" (John 4:49)
21 Roman ruler
23 "He is of _____; ask him" (John 9:23)
25 Paul's former name
26 Arizona winter hour (abbr.)
28 Wading bird
29 Inflammatory disease
30 Noah's son
32 "Tell-Tale Heart" writer
35 US Census data (abbr.)
36 Fall month
37 Thingamabob
38 A mite, e.g.

39 _____ Spirit
40 Choir section
41 Sandy island (var.)
42 Cow sound
43 Oregon winter hour (abbr.)
45 Bunny move
46 "Don't let anyone deceive you in _____"
(2 Thess. 2:3 NIV) (2 words)
48 Soldiers came to _____ Jesus
49 _____ Nevada range
50 Pacific state

52 African ground squirrel
56 Talk back
57 Seaweed substance
58 Loch _____ monster
59 Spark
60 Mutt
61 Alien's craft (abbr.)
63 Compass point (abbr.)
64 Biological instructions carrier (abbr.)

THE LORD'S ASSURANCE

Moses said to the LORD, ". . .let me know whom you will send with me. . . ."
The LORD replied, "My Presence will go with you, and I will give you rest."
EX.33:12, 14 NIV

ACROSS

1 "____ from the east came" (Matt. 2:1 NIV)
5 "Drew to the ____" (Mark 6:53)
10 Taj Mahal site
14 "Become ____ of robbers in your eyes?" (Jer. 7:11) (2 words)
15 Ear-related
16 Thailand, once
17 Start of **QUOTE** from Matt. 11:28 (5 words)
20 "The ____ of thy strength" (Ps. 132:8)
21 Slippery swimmer
22 Very long time
23 Native-born Israeli
26 A son of Jether (1 Chron. 7:38)
28 Transaction (abbr.)
30 **QUOTE**, cont'd (3 words)
33 "Love no false ____" (Zech. 8:17)
34 "The pin of the beam, and with the ____" (Judg. 16:14)
35 Part of 22 Across
36 Ad-less network
37 "He entered into a ship, and ____ in the sea" (Mark 4:1)
38 ____ Cruces, NM

39 "On the hole of the ____" (Isa. 11:8)
42 Ohs' partners
43 "They ____ him away" (Matt. 27:2)
44 Actress Hayworth
45 **QUOTE**, cont'd (3 words)
48 "Though it ____ him all the wealth" (Prov. 6:31 NIV)
50 Blacksburg, VA., school (abbr.)
51 "To hear what your ____ are" (Acts 28:22 NIV)
52 Chinese Muslim
53 Currency of Macao
55 Apple pie maker
56 **QUOTE**, cont'd (5 words)
63 Frosts
64 "He put ____ over his face" (Ex. 34:33 NIV) (2 words)
65 "So is good ____ from a far country" (Prov. 25:25)
66 End of **QUOTE**
67 "The upper ____ also is square" (Ezek. 43:17 NIV)
68 "When the desire cometh, it is a ____ of life" (Prov. 13:12)

DOWN

1 Windows rival
2 "Why make ye this ____" (Mark 5:39)
3 "The way a ____ cutter engraves" (Ex. 28:11 NIV)
4 "Thy will be done ____" (Matt. 6:10) (2 words)
5 "They ____ into the bottom as a stone" (Ex. 15:5)
6 "It sways like a ____ in the wind" (Isa. 24:20 NIV)
7 Pizarro's gold (Sp.)
8 French composer

9 General Robert (2 words)
10 Voiceless talking (abbr.)
11 "Is there no balm in ____?" (Jer. 8:22 NIV)
12 Synthetic fabric
13 Words at the end of Rev. 1:6, 7 (pl.)
18 ____ Mountains (European-Asian boundary)
19 "Ye shall throw down their ____" (Judg. 2:2)
23 "All iniquity shall ____ her mouth" (Ps. 107:42)
24 King of Samaria (1 Kings 21:1)
25 "Moles and to the ____" (Isa. 2:20)

26 Help a crook
27 "Will a man _____ God?" (Mal. 3:8)
29 Genetic carrier (abbr.)
31 Partly submerged
32 "_____ to die" (Luke 7:2)
37 "When _____ Peter" (Acts 9:40) (2 words)
38 "Of _____ he said" (Deut. 33:8)
39 "Set out with Joshua his _____"
   (Exo. 24:13 NIV)
40 "The _____ was poured out"
   (2 Kings 4:40 NIV)
41 "Baked it in _____" (Num. 11:8)
42 "I know thee who thou _____"
   (Mark 1:24)
43 "The lot is cast into the _____"
   (Prov. 16:33)
44 "Thy _____ waxed not old upon thee"
   (Deut. 8:4)
45 Actors' words to their audiences

46 Develop slowly
47 Ukrainian city
48 "A _____ and a lamp for him"
   (2 Kings 4:10 NIV)
49 437.5 grains troy
54 "Then Samuel took a _____ of oil"
   (1 Sam. 10:1)
55 "Shall compel thee to go a _____"
   (Matt. 5:41)
57 One who specializes in a skill (suffix)
58 "He hath _____ me" (Lam. 3:2)
59 Two-wheeled cart
60 "_____ fadder's mustache!"
61 "_____ no man any thing" (Rom. 13:8)
62 "The _____ of the bow" (2 Sam. 1:18)

Day 12

OUR NOW AND FUTURE HOPE

"For I know the plans I have for you," declares the LORD, "plans to prosper you and not to harm you, plans to give you hope and a future."

JER. 29:11 NIV

ACROSS

1 Where the Mets met
5 Room at the casa
9 Urbanity
14 Alabama neighbor (abbr.)
15 "And _____ for a burnt offering" (Lev. 9:2) (2 words)
16 "Unto him that _____ to be feared" (Ps.76:11)
17 "It goes through _____ places" (Luke 11:24 NIV)
18 A discontinuity in geology (abbr.)
19 "And it shall rise up wholly like a _____" (Amos 9:5)
20 Start of **QUOTE** from Psalm 46:1 (4 words)
23 Redactors, briefly
24 "Then who _____ hinder him?" (Job 11:10)
25 Fury
26 **QUOTE**, cont'd (2 words)
32 "Bless all his _____, O LORD" (Deut. 33:11 NIV)
36 Jazz guitarist Montgomery
37 Spanish surrealist artist Joan
38 "Which _____ him in the killing of his brethren" (Judg. 9:24)
39 Nitrous, e.g.

40 Partial to (2 words)
41 Phone or photo prefix
42 Former union of Egypt and Syria (abbr.)
43 Stewing
44 **QUOTE**, cont'd (3 words)
47 "O LORD _____ Lord" (Ps. 8:1)
48 Paradigm of simplicity
49 "_____ to teach" (1 Tim. 3:2)
52 End of **QUOTE** (3 words)
56 "The LORD caused the _____ go back" (Ex. 14:21) (2 words)
58 Fern spore producers
59 "The _____ which is lent to the LORD" (1 Sam. 2:20)
60 "And on _____ of the temple" (Dan. 9:27 NIV) (2 words)
61 Familiar DC office
62 "I went down into the garden of _____" (Song 6:11)
63 "Thou shalt not _____ to offer the first of thy ripe fruits" (Ex. 22:29)
64 Neck part
65 "To _____" (perfectly) (2 words)

DOWN

1 "Ran at flood _____ as before" (Josh. 4:18 NIV)
2 "Days of _____ the king" (Matth. 2:1)
3 Oklahoma city and wife of Geraint (pl.)
4 "Thine eyes are upon me, _____ am not" (Job 7:8) (2 words)
5 South Pacific islanders
6 "Thy navel is like _____ goblet" (Song 7:2) (2 words)
7 Bert, the Oz lion
8 Promised Land inhabitants (Deut. 7:1)

9 Word with break or cake
10 Humdinger
11 Gung ho
12 "So he drew off his _____" (Ruth 4:8)
13 Standard (abbr.)
21 Burn with water
22 Goofs up
27 "As the LORD _____ unto them" (Deut. 2:14)
28 University in Socorro, NM (abbr.)
29 Leslie Caron title role
30 1982 Disney film

31 Precedes Kong

32 "And there _____ certain man at Lystra" (Acts 14:8) (2 words)

33 Capital of Ukraine

34 "That every _____ word that men shall speak" (Matt. 12:36)

35 Eye amorously

39 "And the men of the _____ answered Jonathan" (1 Sam. 14:12)

40 Popular dice game

42 "_____, and away!" (Superman's cry) (2 words)

43 Feverish

45 Ichth follower (it does sound fishy)

46 Each one answered to Dan. (Dan. 6:1–2 NIV)

49 An outbreak of disease (2 words)

50 "He put the golden _____" (Lev. 8:9)

51 Edgy

52 "He gave them _____ for rain" (Ps. 105:32)

53 Sicilian volcano

54 _____ Scotia

55 It's parallel to the radius

56 "Behold, they were _____" (Gen. 40:6)

57 "Save one little _____ lamb" (2 Sam. 12:3)

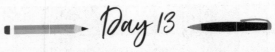

BIBLE-INSPIRED MOVIES

ACROSS

1 "Oh! Susanna" instrument
6 OT prophet is called a ____
10 Fastener
14 Way to go in Bible times
15 "Pharisees began to ____him vehemently" (Luke 11:53)
16 Eastern ruler
17 52 Down source of strength
18 Apostle Paul's way to go
19 "Thou shalt not!" (hyph.)
20 "____of his foot unto his crown" (Job 2:7)
21 Geological formation
23 Seize
24 God has a good one for you
26 "____ Tales", kid's video
28 Louise Lombard Bible character
31 ____Lamarr played 52 Down opposite
32 Noah's ark was like one
33 1960 Paul Newman movie
36 Gregory ____, David and Bathsheba star
40 The Story of ____, 1960 biblical romance
42 Buddy

43 KJV measure
44 Bible balm ingredient
45 Set out to a battleground
48 ____de la Cité, Paris
49 Lord's Prayer ender
51 52 Down asset
53 Form from clay, stone, or wood
56 Follows "fa" (2 words)
57 Keyboard key (abbr.)
58 Charlton____, The Ten Commandments star
61 ____Hill, Paul's Athens pulpit
65 Civic duty
67 What fire and brimstone did to Sodom
68 Neckwear
69 The Greatest Story title word
70 See 69 Across
71 Punctuation pause
72 Like a desert
73 What God does in the heart
74 What a Pharisee would do

DOWN

1 Cave dwellers
2 Hairdo
3 Christmas
4 Wearer of Technicolor Dreamcoat
5 Bible sections (abbr.)
6 ____Hayward, 36 Across star
7 Bible times, e.g.
8 Shield or breastplate (var.)
9 Reviews in memory
10 "A ____doth gather her brood"(Luke 13:34)
11 "Some fell ____thorns" (Matt. 13:7)
12 Moses' mountain
13 Examine deeply
21 Karl ____, philosopher
22 "I have ____you with milk" (1 Cor. 3:2)

25 Gen. Robert E. ____
27 Cheats
28 OT temple builder
29 "My ____is exceeding sorrowful" (Mark 14:34)
30 Dorothy's dog
31 Casing or covering
34 Like Easter morning tomb
35 Form of handshake or friendly greeting
37 Bible movie, usually
38 "Thou shalt ____his name Jesus" (Matt. 1:21)
39 "Every ____shall bow" (Isa. 45:23)
41 "I will ____him" (Isa. 57:19)
45 Discovers
46 Yemen neighbor

47 ____Brynner, *Solomon and Sheba* star
50 Driver's stat
52 See 31 Across
53 "Jesus ____," neon sign, maybe
54 Garlic section
55 "Lips shall ____ praise" (Ps. 119:171)
56 "Lord of ____"
59 Mary Jane

60 Movie story, often
62 Peak
63 Paul's destination
64 Magi's light
66 Bard's "before"
68 Medical research orga.

Day 14

NOAH'S ARK

ACROSS

1 Noah's ark, at times
6 Guitar accessory
10 NT epistle
13 Friendly Ghost name
15 Canaan spies hid under it
16 Gaza to Jerusalem (dir.)
17 End, as a time limit
18 Plague insects
19 Commercials, for short
20 Noah's bird
22 The Flood book
24 First critter habitat
26 ___wear, store section
28 David slew one (1 Sam. 17:34)
29 "Give to the ___" (Matt. 19:21)
30 Samson's swarm
31 Sole sores
32 Industrious insect (Prov. 6:6)
33 Unable to make a decision
34 Put on, as clothing
35 It will lie with the kid (Isa. 11:6)
37 Two-wheeler

41 Ark sea bird
42 Woe for the ark!
43 Olive product
44 Chattering bird (Isa. 38:14)
47 38 Down youngster
48 Hymn book notation
49 38 Down need, perhaps
50 Bible times money holders
51 Ballet costume
52 Paint type
54 Level
56 Liveliness
57 Ark white wader
59 "Tree...whose seed is in ___" (Gen. 1:11)
63 Solomon's exotic critter (1 Kings 10:22)
64 Fake butter
65 Smoothed
66 Number of commandments
67 "Makest thy ___ in the cedars" (Jer. 22:23)
68 Fervent love for God

DOWN

1 Expert
2 "___ melteth before the fire" (Ps. 68:2)
3 Snake in the ark
4 Ark webmaster
5 Ark long-legged bird
6 Northern athletic assn.
7 Adjusts, as wheels
8 Steps
9 Ark plow pullers
10 Movie attraction
11 Tribe member
12 Ark males, e.g.
14 Pulpit orator, for short
21 Correct
23 Black

24 1999 desktop computer flop
25 "As ye would...men should ___ you" (Luke 6:31) (2 words)
27 Diagnostic test (abbr.)
29 Buddy
30 What OT sacrifices did
31 Ark hen's mate
33 Ark tortoise racer, maybe
34 Soap brand
36 Cent
37 Ark denizen
38 Jesus' ride into Jerusalem
39 In ___ of (instead)
40 Yule-time toymaker
42 Noah's building need

44 Tie
45 Mrs. Noah's need, maybe
46 Aviators
47 Appearance, in biology
48 Computer screen sight
50 The Good Book
51 Ark swimmer

53 King of the ark?
55 Caesar's three
58 Heavy drinker
60 ____ Times, Rev. topic
61 Name for 53 Down
62 New Deal president

ABRAHAM: A MAN OF FAITH AND ACTION

ACROSS

1 Six-pack muscles (abbr.)
4 Walk on Mt. Sinai, perhaps
8 Lease giver
14 It's put in a horse's mouth (James 3:3)
15 Eve's garden
16 Take a deep breath, then _____
17 "Deliver thyself as a _____" (Prov. 6:5)
18 God promised it to Abraham
19 The Israelites _____ Egypt
20 Progressive decline
22 Ishmael to Abraham (Gen. 17:23)
23 1960s skirt
24 Did Noah use these?
27 Abraham's grandfather (Gen. 11:24–26)
31 Abraham received one from God
33 Pixie
35 Flightless bird
36 Greek goddess of dawn
38 _____ Schwarz, NYC toy store
39 Hagar was one (Gen. 16:1)
40 Describes the rock in the wilderness struck by Moses (Num. 20:11)
44 Chemist's tube
46 James the _____, son of Alphaeus (Mark 15:40)

47 Conger
49 What Israelites were with God's Commandments
50 Unrefined metal
51 "Ye shall not surely _____" (Gen. 3:4)
52 Huff
55 "Offer him there for a _____ offering" (Gen. 22:2)
58 Jerusalem to Babylon (dir.)
61 Marrow
63 Lord's Prayer opener
65 Neglected
67 Abraham was rich in these (Gen. 13:2)
70 Condiment
71 Flavor enhancer
72 "I lift up my hands toward thy holy _____" (Ps. 28:2)
73 Swiss mountains
74 A Pharisee might consider himself this in religious law
75 Abraham built an altar between here and Hai (Gen. 12:8)
76 Prophecy is not this (2 Pet. 1:21)
77 "Arise, lift up the _____" (Gen. 21:18)

DOWN

1 Abraham's former name
2 Relating to life
3 Relating to Eve's origins
4 "He is our _____ and our shield" (Ps. 33:20)
5 Gem State
6 African nation
7 "The _____ of all flesh is come before me" (Gen. 6:13)
8 "Moab. . .hath settled on his _____" (Jer. 48:11)
9 Gas company

10 Indo-Aryan language
11 "She _____ over against him, and. . .wept" (Gen. 21:16)
12 Grand _____ Opry
13 Israelites crossed the _____ Sea
21 Lubricators
25 The Lord acted as one between Laban and Jacob (Gen. 31:49)
26 Portion of meat
28 "Cold and _____. . .day and night shall not cease" (Gen. 8:22)

29 We may not _____ any part of God's Word (Rev. 22:19)

30 Describes Nabal (1 Sam. 25:3)

32 Abraham's nephew (Gen. 11:27)

34 "My face is _____ with weeping" (Job 16:16)

37 "Unto thy _____ will I give this land" (Gen. 12:7)

39 Tijuana's country

40 Slovenly person

41 South American country

42 Exploiter

43 Tack

45 Sacrificed instead of Isaac (Gen. 22:13)

48 Downwind

53 Ceremonious

54 Soft drink brand

56 Tally marker

57 Net fabric

59 Onion roll (var.)

60 Famine drove Abraham here (Gen. 12:10)

62 "Sharper than any two- _____ sword" (Heb. 4:12)

64 Pet. fished with a net instead of this

66 Eat

67 Male swan

68 "_____ sure that thou art that Christ" (John 6:69)

69 Make lace

70 Form of address (var.)

ADAM: THE FIRST DUDE

ACROSS

1 British cop
6 Wound healer
10 UAE native
14 "Oh, come, let us _____ Him!" Christmas refrain
15 Knitting stitch
16 Painter of melting clocks
17 "This is now bone of my _____" (Gen. 2:23)
18 One of the Great Lakes
19 "Grievous words _____ up anger" (Prov. 15:1)
20 Space
21 Adam felt this when hiding from God
23 "With you. . .unto the _____ of the world" (Matt. 28:20)
24 Adam was to do this to the garden
26 Makes noise during sleep
28 Delineated
31 God gave Adam "every herb bearing _____" (Gen. 1:29)
32 "There you are!"
33 They of Tyre did this (1 Chron. 22:4)
36 Jacob's description of Leah, maybe (Gen. 29:17)
40 Soda
42 God "drove _____ the man" (Gen. 3:24)

43 "Man became a living _____" (Gen. 2:7)
44 May be part of Noah's ark
45 What broke out when Samson brought the house down
48 When Eve offered, Adam did this
49 Adam's second son (Gen. 4:1–2)
51 Herb
53 "_____ is the ground for thy sake" (Gen. 3:17)
56 Half
57 Adam's helpmeet
58 You can tiptoe through them
61 "Male and female created he _____" (Gen. 1:27)
65 "God formed man of the _____ of the ground" (Gen. 2:7)
67 "The LORD is on my _____" (Ps. 118:6)
68 Leather
69 Choir member
70 "Been faithful over _____ things" (Matt. 25:21) (2 words.)
71 Small knife
72 Grate upon
73 "Fill the waters in the _____" (Gen. 1:22)
74 "Not good that the man should be _____" (Gen. 2:18)

DOWN

1 Ali _____
2 Isaac was fooled with this (Gen. 27:27)
3 God used one of Adam's
4 God gave Adam the _____ of life (Gen. 2:7)
5 Adam did not say this to God's question (Gen. 3:11)
6 What a foolish man will do with his treasure (Prov. 21:20)
7 Jesus is the _____ for Adam's sin
8 Opera solo
9 "Created he them; and _____ them" (Gen. 5:2)
10 Spots

11 A judgmental Pharisee is one
12 Dress style (hyph.)
13 Adam named these
21 "I will _____ all that afflict thee" (Zeph. 3:19)
22 Egypt to Canaan (dir.)
25 Snakelike fish
27 Chances of winning
28 Tongues of fire "sat upon _____ of them" (Acts 2:3)
29 "Where art _____?" (Gen. 3:9)
30 "To see what he would _____ them" (Gen. 2:19)
31 Adam's third son (Gen. 4:25)

34 Paul had one (Phil. 3:14)
35 Adam, e.g.
37 "The young lions _____ after their prey" (Ps. 104:21)
38 Accord not meant in Acts 1:14
39 "After one day the south wind _____" (Acts 28:13)
41 Alack's partner
45 Snake-haired women
46 Forbidden fruit was pleasant to these (Gen. 3:6)
47 Member of Mayan people
50 Wager
52 Jewish ceremonial law directed this

53 Solomon's Temple wood (1 Kings 5:10)
54 Throat dangler
55 God does this on the seventh day
56 What God does to the lukewarm (Rev. 3:16) (var.)
59 Tree of _____, the other tree in the garden (Gen. 2:9)
60 Adam's bite of the fruit was a bad one
62 Abel is a _____ of the faith (Heb. 11)
63 Adam called this home
64 Scant
66 A tower "whose _____ may reach unto heaven" (Gen. 11:4)
68 Relaxing tub

BOOK OF REVELATION

ACROSS

1 Church bell sound
5 "_____ of every unclean...bird" (Rev. 18:2)
9 Location of seven churches
13 Pathway
14 Worthy is the _____
15 Connect, in a way
16 "Partridge sitteth on _____" (Jer. 17:11)
17 "Fire was cast _____ the sea" (Rev. 8:8)
18 Navy's place (2 words)
19 "_____ is he that readeth" (Rev. 1:3)
21 Nothing
23 Conger
24 Ephesus to Troas (dir.)
25 *Phantom of the Opera* author
29 Laodiceans weren't this
30 "Jesus _____" (John 11:35)
32 SSW opposite
33 Tool shop element
36 Not lows
37 "_____, thou knowest" (Rev. 7:14)
38 "Even to _____ hairs will I carry you" (Isa. 46:4)

39 Italian city
40 Jesus' disciple, familiarly
41 Tidal movement
42 National symbols
43 34 Down tokens, perhaps
44 Time period
45 40 Across work need
46 Point
47 Where John received his vision
49 "I make all things _____" (Rev. 21:5)
50 Horse food
53 "I _____ overcame" (Rev. 3:21)
55 In abundance
57 Censer's emission
60 What gold bricks in heaven do
62 Over
63 Bound
64 First garden
65 Pitch
66 Four beasts were full of them
67 See 29 Across
68 Rushed

DOWN

1 Trainee
2 One of the beasts was like this
3 Messenger to John
4 "Who am _____ than the least of all saints" (Eph. 3:8)
5 Patron
6 Root beer brand (3 words)
7 UK time zone
8 Black
9 John saw a gold one
10 Mary to Martha, for short
11 Sorbet
12 Wanted poster letters
15 Police academy enrollees
20 Jesus' head compared to this

22 "I am _____ and Omega" (Rev. 1:8)
26 Beginning
27 "_____ my heart to fear thy name" (Ps. 86:11)
28 Former name of Jerez
29 "A golden cup in _____ hand full of abominations" (Rev. 17:4)
30 Angels' features
31 Many celebrities have big ones
33 God's flock
34 Indian snake
35 Moroccan capital
36 If you have ears, do this
39 "Sea of _____ like unto crystal" (Rev. 4:6)
40 Revelation's bottomless _____
42 Scammed

43 Plague dispenser in Rev.
46 Require
48 Orders
49 Innie or outie locale
50 "Jacob took the stone...and poured oil _____ of it" (Gen. 28:18 NIV) (2 words)
51 Compensate for, as sins
52 Used a keyboard

54 Oil cartel (abbr.)
56 Jesus does this with sinners
57 Teresa, Clare, or Anne (abbr.)
58 Mother's Day month
59 Unlocked (poet.)
61 Hoopla

PAUL'S LETTERS

ACROSS

1 What a gossip does
5 Eye infection
9 Certain groundhog
13 "We...should walk in newness of _____" (Rom. 6:4)
14 "Redeem them _____ were under the law" (Gal. 4:5)
15 Where Paul left Titus
16 Leave out
17 "I had no _____ in my spirit" (2 Cor. 2:13)
18 Cleanse, in a way
19 He was saved by faith
21 Rock of _____
23 Digit
24 "If the whole body were an _____" (1 Cor. 12:17)
25 Pauline epistle
29 Booking (abbr.)
30 "I press on toward the _____" (Phil. 3:14 NIV)
32 Opposed to Gospel, in Paul's epistles
33 Strong rope fiber
36 Support
37 Even score
38 "As in _____ all die" (1 Cor. 15:22)
39 Wooden box

40 Subject of 1 Cor. 13
41 Weekday (abbr.)
42 "Ye heard the word of _____" (Eph. 1:13)
43 Paul's preaching did this to some people
44 "_____ things are passed away" (2 Cor. 5:17)
45 Small particle
46 Gray sea eagle
47 Equity
49 Irritate (slang)
50 Montana winter hour (abbr.)
53 "We _____ should walk in newness of life" (Rom. 6:4)
55 Religious recluse
57 "Are you not _____ of what the law says?" (Gal. 4:21 NIV)
60 Convex shape
62 Actor Alda
63 "Diversities of _____, but the same Spirit" (1 Cor. 12:4)
64 Chicken house
65 Job's clothes, at one time
66 Inscribe
67 One of three in 1 Cor. 13
68 "At the name of Jesus every _____ should bow" (Phil. 2:10)

DOWN

1 Swell
2 State of uncertainty
3 Hell is said to be this
4 Greek letter
5 Drifts away
6 Subject matter
7 Affirmatives (slang)
8 Gospel singer James
9 Rainbow maker
10 "As a _____ gathereth her chickens" (Matt. 23:37)
11 "The world through _____ wisdom did not know him" (1 Cor. 1:21 NIV)

12 Downwind
15 Some Louisianans
20 "Thou shalt bruise his _____" (Gen. 3:15)
22 "The _____ of our Lord Jesus Christ" (Rom. 16:20)
26 Choir section
27 Gullible
28 "We are unto God a _____ savour of Christ" (2 Cor. 2:15)
29 Sacrificed instead of Isaac
30 Persona non _____
31 God swore one to Abraham
33 South Pacific island nation

34 Paul condemned these

35 _____ of time

36 Men's fragrance

39 Paul preached the _____ of Christ

40 Medical caregiver (abbr.)

42 "I know not to give flattering _____" (Job 32:22)

43 Strongly encourage

46 Vacation destination, maybe

48 "Things above, not on things on the _____" (Col. 3:2)

49 Jazz style

50 Italian city

51 Sermon site, maybe

52 Taut

54 "That hurts!"

56 Paul's once-rejected companion

57 This present _____

58 Clever fellow

59 Athletic group (abbr.)

61 Pasture sound

Day 19

BOOKS OF THE BIBLE

Theme answers 20, 37, and 52 Across and 4, 7, and 10 Down are each the names of three Bible books (minus "1", "2" or "3" where it applies).

ACROSS

1 Silver salmon
6 Right now, in ICU
10 "Which is the king's _____" (Gen. 14:17)
14 One of the Leeward Islands
15 One in Bonn (Ger.)
16 "And _____ of oil" (Lev. 14:21) (2 words)
17 *For Me and* _____ (1948 Judy Garland film) (2 words)
18 It goes into a slot (2 words)
19 "Where are the _____?" (Luke 17:17)
20 **THREE BIBLE BOOKS**
23 "The one _____ is the man; arrest him" (Matt. 26:48 NIV) (2 words)
24 "In the fig _____ her first time" (Hos. 9:10) (2 words)
25 "He would not let me _____ my breath" (Job 9:18 NIV)
28 "_____ weeping for her children" (Jer. 31:15)
30 Esau's first wife (Gen. 36:2)
31 R to L on a map (3 words)
33 What a fighter pilot in trouble may do

DOWN

1 "It _____ to pass" (Isa. 37:1)
2 Gemsbok is one
3 French author Victor
4 **THREE BIBLE BOOKS**
5 Greyhound relative
6 "The Lamb opened one of the _____" (Rev. 6:1)
7 **THREE BIBLE BOOKS**
8 Father of giants in the Promised Land (Num. 13:33)
9 Tenth Hebrew month (Est. 2:16)
10 **THREE BIBLE BOOKS**
11 "With _____ of flax in his hand" (Ezek. 40:3) (2 words)
12 "After so _____ time" (Heb. 4:7) (2 words)

37 **THREE BIBLE BOOKS**
40 "Gold in a swine's _____" (Prov. 11:22)
41 Rhine feeder (Swiss)
42 Butte kin
43 "Sharper than a _____ hedge" (Mic. 7:4)
45 Government operation at Bikini Island (var.)
47 Irish clergyman who determined the date of creation to be 4004 BC
50 Satisfies fully
52 **THREE BIBLE BOOKS**
57 County seat of Martin County, KY
58 "Grace to thy _____" (Prov. 3:22)
59 May be part of change in Russia
60 Twelfth Jewish month (Est. 3:7)
61 "Son of man, record this _____" (Ezek. 24:2 NIV)
62 "Stop on _____" (very quickly) (2 words)
63 Cry from a crib
64 Relative of an organization (abbr.)
65 "Caught in a cruel _____ birds are taken in a snare" (Eccl. 9:12 NIV) (2 words)

13 The opposite of "take in" or "swallow"
21 "Thy neck is an iron _____" (Isa. 48:4)
22 Krooked _____, where the Keystone Kops kaught katfish
25 Stadium cries
26 Location to the west of Nod (Gen. 4:16)
27 Russian-born American sculptor Naum
29 "Do not give _____ cry, do not raise" (Josh. 6:10 NIV) (2 words)
32 Romanov ruler of yesteryear
34 Jewish word for "complete truth"
35 "Counteth the _____" (Luke 14:28)
36 Relatives of IRAs
38 "Libnah, and _____, and Ashan" (Josh. 15:42)

39 Spanish lasso
44 Berkeley, CA, suburb
46 Capital of Iran
47 "He said, I will go _____ as thou art" (2 Kings 3:7) (3 words)
48 "I will _____ lad" (1 Sam. 20:21) (2 words)
49 Kind of engine

51 1930 Pulitzer Prize poet Conrad
53 "Whatsoever passeth through the paths of the _____" (Ps. 8:8)
54 Brief last "writes" (abbr.)
55 Roper of the polls
56 Ogle lecherously

BIBLICAL MOUNTS

And when he had sent them away, he departed into a mountain to pray.

MARK 6:46

ACROSS

1 "For as in _____ all die" (1 Cor. 15:22)

5 "And great _____ the Jews" (Est. 10:3)

10 "I _____ dream which made me afraid" (Dan. 4:5) (2 words)

14 "Not of works, _____ any man should boast" (Eph. 2:9)

15 **MOUNT** from which Barak was victorious (Judg. 4:6–16)

16 "The high places also of _____" (Hos. 10:8)

17 Laban's tender-eyed daughter (Gen. 29:16–17)

18 African pachyderm

19 "Never _____ of doing what is right" (2 Thess. 3:13 NIV)

20 Memory losses

22 **MOUNT** from which Jesus ascended (Acts 1:9–12)

24 "For my flesh is _____ food" (John 6:55 NIV)

25 "And to morrow is cast into the _____" (Luke 12:28)

26 **MOUNT** where Elijah called down fire from heaven (1 Kings 18:20–38)

29 "And they filled them up to the _____" (John 2:7)

30 Time in Chicago (abbr.)

33 Sometimes it's double-stuffed

34 "For he is _____, as he said" (Matt. 28:6)

35 Follows tee

36 **MOUNT** of _____, where Jesus met Moses and Elijah (Matt. 17:1–8)

40 "Give _____ to my words" (Ps. 5:1)

41 "Which is by the river _____" (Deut. 3:12)

42 Flightless birds down under

43 Used to copy system files in DOS

44 "Ye _____ be born again" (John 3:7)

45 "Who go to _____ bowls of mixed wine" (Prov. 23:30 NIV)

47 To a slight degree, in music

48 Fool

49 **MOUNT** where Noah parked (Gen. 8:4)

52 **MOUNT** where Saul was defeated (1 Sam. 31:1–8) (2 words)

56 "I will _____ Sisera" (Judg. 4:7 NIV)

57 "Or loose the bands of _____?" (Job 38:31)

59 Snaky fish

60 "Everything goes _____ it has since" (2 Pet. 3:4 NIV) (2 words)

61 **MOUNT** where God gave Moses the two tablets (Ex. 31:18)

62 Sobriety org.

63 "Their _____ shall not become garments" (Isa. 59:6)

64 "And as soon as I had _____ it" (Rev. 10:10)

65 Threesome

DOWN

1 "_____ man's ways seem right to him" (Prov. 21:2 NIV) (2 words)

2 Judge

3 "And _____ old lion" (Gen. 49:9) (2 words)

4 **MOUNT** on Israel's northern border (Deut. 4:48) (2 words)

5 "Because it is _____" (Ezek. 21:13) (2 words)

6 Taj _____

7 Japanese sashes

8 "_____ his son, Jehoshua his son" (1 Chron. 7:27)

9 More "hip"

10 "And _____ ashes" (Jon. 3:6) (2 words)

11 Tel _____

12 "Though I _____ perfect" (Job 9:21)

13 "Casting _____ into the sea" (Mark 1:16) (2 words)

21 "They shall _____ God" (Matt. 5:8)

23 Duckweed genus

25 "The scorching heat ____"
(Isa. 49:10 NASB) (2 words)

26 "____ for flocks" (2 Chron. 32:28)

27 "Or costly ____" (1 Tim. 2:9)

28 Raises

29 Racist

30 Simian, briefly

31 South Korean capital

32 Past or present

34 Oxydol competitor

37 Polynesian islands

38 Fruit sugar

39 **MOUNT** Moriah (2 Chron. 3:1) (2 words)

45 Register (2 words)

46 "____ my brother's keeper?" (Gen. 4:9)
(2 words)

47 "For the ____ is full" (Joel 3:13)

48 Athenian porticos

49 "And the city shall be low in ____ place"
(Isa. 32:19) (2 words)

50 Old Germanic alphabet character

51 "And Geshem the ____ heard about it"
(Neh. 2:19 NIV)

52 "Ye tithe ____ and rue and all manner of
herbs" (Luke 11:42)

53 "I am one that ____ witness of myself"
(John 8:18)

54 "In days of ____ planned it"
(Isa. 37:26 NIV) (2 words)

55 "To fear thee, ____ thy people Israel"
(1 Kings 8:43) (2 words)

58 Estuary

APOSTLES

ACROSS

1 13 Across part, maybe
5 Ladder dreamer
10 Blot
13 Singers
15 Italian affection
16 "_____these things shall be added" (Matt. 6:33)
17 Church feature
18 City transit
19 Maker of Cadenza and Soul
20 KJV "deer"
21 To bend
23 Apostles' job
25 65 Across fishing needs
26 Clings
28 To manage to pay for
31 Ezek. vision element
32 Calvary sight
33 "To _____ hairs will I carry you" (Isa. 46:4)
34 Gaping hole
37 KJV weed, sometimes with wheat
38 Pink _____, rock band
40 Nativity visitors

41 Fr. holy woman
42 Film spool
43 Matt. collected them
44 Tenth century English magnate
45 Scorners would _____ apostles
46 Huge statues
49 "Thou didst _____ on the LORD" (2 Chron. 16:8)
50 Caribbean country
51 Calvary descriptor
52 Keyboard key
55 "Pray, _____ not vain repetitions" (Matt. 6:7)
56 Apostle Paul's companion
59 Funny bone site
61 46 Across descriptor
62 Jesus' _____ was ascribed above the cross
63 "_____, thou art the Son of God" (John 1:49)
64 Joppa to Jerusalem dir.
65 _____ Pet.
66 "It hath _____ said" (Matt. 5:31)

DOWN

1 A Passover lamb must not have one
2 Buckeye State
3 "He shall not _____ his reward" (Mark 9:41)
4 Anointing need
5 Zebedee's apostle son
6 Credit card choice
7 Portable bed
8 "_____ Father"
9 5 Down to apostle John
10 Senegal's capital
11 Wonderland girl
12 Blues, with "the"
14 To set up connections
22 London company ender (abbr.)

24 Conger
25 Jewel site of Isa. 3:21
26 Sailor's greeting
27 Resurrection of the _____
28 Apostles' book
29 College house, for short
30 Golf cry
31 "Faith hath made thee _____" (Matt. 9:22)
34 Long skirt
35 "Grayheaded and very _____ men" (Job 15:10)
36 40 Across descriptor
38 Charges
39 Son of Jacob
40 Martha's sister

42 Avoids temptation
43 Bank worker
44 "Name of the wicked shall _____"
   (Prov. 10:7)
45 Editor's notation, for short
46 Freshwater fishes
47 Welcome Sinai sight
48 A subject owing allegiance
49 "He is _____!"

51 Angel glower
52 French monastic title
53 Earring location
54 Apostle Thomas was known as
57 Caesar's three
58 Period to evaluate financial results (abbr.)
60 Family dog, for short

Day 22

BLESSINGS

ACROSS

1 Examine, as one's conscience
6 Vane direction
10 Jesus, _____ of God
14 Tigris or Euphrates
15 Firm, tight
16 White House office
17 Large body of water
18 "After three days, I will _____ again" (Matt. 27:63)
19 "The _____ draweth near" (Luke 21:8)
20 South American nation
21 "Abba, _____!"
23 Body builder's pride (abbr.)
24 Snare of the wicked
26 They often accompany the choir
28 "I _____ unto the Lord" (Dan. 9:4)
31 At Jesus' trial, they would _____ Him
32 Eye not seen, "nor _____ heard" (1 Cor. 2:9)
33 Jesus came to save all _____
36 Like Easter morning tomb
40 "_____ boy!"
42 Feathered fashion accessory
43 "_____ us...our daily bread" (Matt. 6:11)
44 Parable sower's need
45 Finder, per Matthew 7:7
48 Church bench
49 _____ Spirit, the Comforter
51 Boring tools
53 Noah's need, perhaps
56 Noted volcano
57 Tokyo tie
58 Stickers
61 Huff go-with
65 "Places. . .men were _____ to haunt" (1 Sam. 30:31)
67 Jar
68 Type of cotton fabric
69 "_____ the winds. . .obey him!" (Matt. 8:27)
70 Little Mermaid's love
71 Result
72 "Flesh shall _____ in hope" (Acts 2:26)
73 Judgment _____
74 Water bird

DOWN

1 Support
2 Asian "daily bread"
3 "My cup runneth _____" (Ps. 23:5)
4 "Praise the _____ of holiness" (2 Chron. 20:21)
5 Sea bird
6 Disciple's sandal part
7 "_____ upon the Lord" (Ps. 37:9)
8 Moses' burner
9 Church feature
10 Sodom fleer
11 Like birds
12 Cuban dance
13 "Lord _____ thee, and keep thee" (Num. 6:24)
21 "We all do _____ as a leaf" (Isa. 64:6)
22 "River" in Mexico
25 Agent, for short
27 Eager, full of excitement
28 Pod dwellers
29 Offerings, "a _____ year by year" (2 Chron. 9:24)
30 Commedia dell'_____, Italian theater
31 Guff
34 "Blessing, if ye _____ the commandments" (Deut. 11:27)
35 Poet Edgar Allen
37 KJV "flute"
38 "God blessed for _____" (Rom. 9:5)
39 Good _____, the Gospel
41 Childhood affliction (abbr.)
45 Garment sections

46 Eve _____ forbidden fruit

47 "Let us _____ with patience the race" (Heb. 12:1)

50 _____ Testament

52 Wide open

53 Through " _____ of the Holy Ghost" (Rom. 15:13)

54 God grants gifts from heaven _____

55 Attends parable wedding banquet

56 God will "gather together his _____" (Mark 13:27)

59 We should "_____ one for another" (1 Cor. 12:25)

60 Paul's mission field

62 Former nation (abbr.)

63 Smoke duct

64 Beautiful "_____ of them that preach" (Rom. 10:15)

66 TV network

68 Downwind

ANNA: THE PROPHETESS

ACROSS

1 City in Judah (Josh. 15:26)
5 One who builds a house on sand, e.g.
10 What the Gardener will do with non-fruitful branches
13 Kind of woman Anna was
14 ___ protector
15 State of unconsciousness
16 Final word in prayer
17 Agitator does this to crowd, as at Jesus' trial (Mark 15:11–13)
18 Feature of God's sign to Noah after the Flood (Gen. 9:16)
19 Winglike part
21 The Garden of Gethsemane and the Temple in Jerusalem, e.g.
23 Anna "served God. . .night and ___" (Luke 2:37)
26 Conger
28 Fish tank growth
29 ___ steroids
32 Ranch guy
33 Man with unclean spirit (Mark 5:4–5) (coll. Sp.)
34 Anna's piety, perhaps
36 Murky

37 Holy ___, source of Anna's inspiration
38 Bearer of the ark of the covenant (2 Sam. 6:3)
42 Hanger-on-er, e.g.
43 Certain idol in Sinai
44 String section instrument
46 Cloth put over Jesus' face in the tomb (John 20:7)
49 Sew with a gathering stitch
51 How you might get across the Sea of Galilee
52 Format for delivering web content (abbr.)
53 Sign shoppers love to see
57 Sock
59 It's often upped
60 San ___, CA
62 Prophet from Tekoa (Amos 1:1)
66 "Play skilfully with a ___ noise" (Ps. 33:3)
67 Gen. 1:1 gives this of life as we know it
68 Promissory notes
69 What Job's comforters do
70 What God does on the seventh day
71 It happens to manna kept overnight (Ex. 16:20)

DOWN

1 When Anna saw Jesus, it was this kind of moment (Luke 2:38)
2 Mary was one
3 The glutton's partner has too much of this (Prov. 23:21)
4 Chatty bird
5 Anna and Simeon waited "for the consolation of ___" (Luke 2:25)
6 Paul and Silas, e.g.
7 Flower with a beard, often
8 David did this when he saw Bathsheba bathing (2 Sam. 11:2)
9 What a God-sent challenge might be
10 Settee

11 "I am Alpha and ___" (Rev. 1:8)
12 So yesterday
15 One presented to the Lord (Luke 2:21–22)
20 Name for tamed beast in Isa. 11:6
22 Tight
23 Painter of melting clocks
24 "And ___ they tell him of her" (Mark 1:30)
25 We should not do this when we pray (Matt. 6:7)
27 Supple
30 One called holy to the Lord (Luke 2:23)
31 Story from Job's comforters, e.g.
32 Morse code element

35 Anna's tribe (Luke 2:36) (var.)
37 Harden
38 Exclamation in Munich
39 Samson was not to cut this (Judg. 13:5)
40 French islands
41 David ___ Goliath with a stone (1 Sam. 17:49) (coll.)
42 Anna "gave thanks. . .unto the ___" (Luke 2:38)
44 Anna's faithfulness was one
45 Saul felt this way when the women praised David (1 Sam. 18:7–8)
47 Mechanical agents
48 Top-ranking corporate webmaster

49 "They had a few ___ fishes" (Mark 8:7)
50 Vietnam capital
54 Jacob fooled Isaac with this (Gen. 27:27)
55 Last Supper beverage
56 Loch ___ monster
58 "___ of turtledoves," sacrifice choice (Luke 2:24)
61 "___ thee behind me, Satan" (Luke 4:8)
63 Pasture sound
64 "Gracious words which proceeded ___ of his mouth" (Luke 4:22)
65 Sound from the tree in the midst of Eden, perhaps (Gen. 3:1–4)

BARNABAS:
BEARER OF GOD'S WORD

BY PATRICIA MITCHELL

ACROSS

1 Barnabas treated people with this
4 "Like ___ that find no pasture" (Lam. 1:6)
9 Jostle
14 Slithery fish
15 God set ___ Barnabas for His work (Acts 13:2)
16 Theologians do this to Bible phrases
17 ___ Maria
18 Barnabas laid this at the apostles' feet (Acts 4:37)
19 Paul and Barnabas discussed these with the apostolic council (Acts 15:20)
20 "Unworthy of everlasting ___" (Acts 13:46)
22 Braces oneself
24 Barnabas was not one of these
25 Prime Meridian clock reading (abbr.)
27 "___ a small world!"
29 "Barnabas. . .___ go as far as Antioch" (Acts 11:22)
32 Barnabas took this to Christians in Judea (Acts 11:29–30)
35 Spy org.
36 After a stoning, Paul went here with Barnabas (Acts 14:20)
38 North Pole workshop workers
40 "Hold up my goings. . .that my footsteps ___ not" (Ps. 17:5)
42 24 Across had too much of this

44 "I will perform the ___ which I sware" (Gen. 26:3)
45 Barnabas ___ Mark when Paul refuses (Acts 15:39)
47 Rebekah's husband (Gen. 24:67)
49 "I am ready. . .to ___ at Jerusalem" (Acts 21:13)
50 Grand Turk
52 The disciples did this, then ordained Barnabas as a missionary (Acts 13:3)
54 Farm org.
55 Before (prefix)
56 What Saul hoped to do to David with his javelin (1 Sam. 18:11)
59 Barnabas went to one in Antioch (Acts 11:26)
63 Paul's former name
67 In a tilted position
69 Athenian lawmaker and poet
71 Campus ministry org.
72 "Ye are of more ___ than many sparrows" (Matt. 10:31)
73 The Colosseum in Rome was one
74 ___ Baba
75 Because of Barnabas, "much people was ___ unto the Lord" (Acts 11:24)
76 Old ___ (stubbornly old-fashioned person)
77 Hip

DOWN

1 Greenish blue
2 Barnabas's tribe (Acts 4:36)
3 Notation in music
4 Noah's son (Gen. 5:32)
5 Those who named Barnabas (Acts 4:36)
6 Jer.'s preaching, to a scorner
7 Mid-Eden feature
8 Eye infection

9 Barnabas took one to Antioch (Acts 15:30)
10 Bearer of barley loaves and fish (John 6:9)
11 James and John, e.g. (Matt. 4:21) (abbr.)
12 Capital of Norway
13 Wild ___
21 Self
23 Ananias and Sapphira told one (Acts 5:3, 8)
26 Wet dirt

28 What a foolish man would fill with grain (Luke 12:16–20)

29 A man chosen along with Barnabas (Acts 15:22)

30 17-syllable poem

31 Run off

32 Summary

33 Jesus did this to those wanting to make Him king (John 6:15)

34 Manna would be this if kept overnight (Ex. 16:20)

35 Kansas City winter hours (abbr.)

37 Vehicle

39 Mourners showed Pet. garments Dorcas had made "while ___ was with them" (Acts 9:39)

41 You can't serve God and this

43 Radio receiver

46 Joshua did this with twelve stones in the Jordan (Josh. 4:9)

48 Vehicle

51 It became a boil on man and beast (Ex. 9:10)

53 Barnabas said this to God's call

56 Morning beverage

57 School (abbr.)

58 "Paul and Barnabas waxed ___" (Acts 13:46)

60 Mil. branch

61 Vehicle-accommodating ship

62 Horsefly

64 "All that are ___ off" (Acts 2:39)

65 CA university

66 They "___ their hands on" Paul and Barnabas (Acts 13:3)

68 Jewish opposition was Barnabas and Paul's ___ to preach to the Gentiles

70 "By what law? of works? ___: but by the law of faith" (Rom. 3:27)

GOSPEL OF MATTHEW

ACROSS

1 What Jesus calmed in Matt. 8
5 Fake chocolate
10 Pay __
13 Where Paul preached in Greece, often
15 Auto make
16 __ Baba
17 "__ of me" (Matt. 11:29)
18 "I send you forth as __ in the midst of wolves" (Matt. 10:16)
19 Swine
20 They "__ him away to crucify him" (Matt. 27:31)
21 Enter at the straight __
23 "Go...and __ all nations" (Matt. 28:19)
25 One descended at Jesus' baptism
26 Fryer
28 Changeable
31 Rationalism
32 *Phantom of the* __
33 "Come unto me...and I will give you __" (Matt. 11:28)
34 Gravestone letters
37 Paul would have made one

38 What 52 Across does
40 "His __ did shine as the sun" (Matt. 17:2)
41 The __ of the world, Matthew 24 subject
42 Tropical bird
43 Strongly suggests
44 Oregon capital
45 Bogus
46 Snacks for 9 Down
49 Fool built a house on it
50 Where Mary and Joseph fled
51 Bog
52 "Ears to hear, __ him hear" (Matt. 11:15)
55 Gentleness (abbr.)
56 Anesthetic
59 "Ye __ the violence of your hands" (Ps. 58:2)
61 Hair product
62 Recycle
63 "When Cyrenius was governor of __" (Luke 2:2)
64 "__ to Joy"
65 Jesus' tempter
66 Star position

DOWN

1 Offered to Jesus on the cross
2 *African Queen* screenwriter James
3 "Each one should carry their own __" (Gal. 6:5 NIV)
4 Fall into sin
5 Social position
6 Hurt
7 Herb Pharisees would tithe
8 Unrefined metal
9 John the __
10 Of the Vatican
11 Wonderland girl
12 Don't hide yours under a bushel
14 African nation
22 "__ Maria"

24 Tree
25 "I did cast them out as the __ in the streets" (Ps. 18:42)
26 What the sower sows
27 Judas betrayed Jesus with one
28 What we see in our brother's eye
29 Jesus' tomb on the third day
30 Flex
31 "Being warned of God in a __" (Matt. 2:12)
34 Prego's competition
35 57 Down choice
36 Mexican money
38 "How long __ ye between two opinions?" (1 Kings 18:21)
39 "Their __ were opened" (Matt. 9:30)

40 Flintstone man

42 You can't serve two

43 __ World Report

44 "I will come in...and will __ with him" (Rev. 3:20)

45 Average, on the golf course

46 Free (2 words)

47 Eyed

48 Rotation

49 Signal

51 Plateau

52 Old Italian money

53 Sponsorship

54 "Where is he __ is born King of the Jews?" (Matt. 2:2)

57 Beverage

58 Hovel

60 The light of the body, in Matthew 6:22

Day 26

GOSPEL OF MARK

ACROSS

1 What multitudes sat on in Mark 6
6 Pre-K lessons
10 Relaxation site
13 IRS cases
15 "Peace of God ___ in your hearts" (Col. 3:15)
16 Shade tree
17 Ridges
18 "Learn a parable of the fig ___" (Mark 13:28)
19 Music genre
20 Preach the Good ___
22 What John did to Jesus
24 They "rolled a stone unto the ___ of the sepulchre" (Mark 15:46)
26 Potter's oven
28 "This is my beloved Son: ___ him" (Mark 9:7)
29 "First the blade, then...the full ___ in the ear" (Mark 4:28)
30 Adorable
31 Trench
32 Angelus word
33 What Jesus forgave
34 Jesus "put forth ___ hand" (Mark 1:41)
35 Request a favor, maybe
37 Tangled

DOWN

1 Mary or Martha (slang)
2 Regret
3 Who "can ___ one cubit unto his stature?" (Matt. 6:27)
4 Join (2 words)
5 Drive
6 KJV verb
7 Brook sound
8 "Thou canst make me ___" (Mark 1:40)
9 Leak slowly
10 The World ___
11 Fountain sites, often
12 Current unit
14 Opposite of NNE

41 Lion name
42 One might be drawn in the sand
43 Noah's craft
44 Tapestry
47 Wide road (abbr.)
48 Former Russian ruler
49 It will not give light at End Times (Mark 13:24)
50 Game cubes
51 Rents to
52 "No man putteth new wine into old ___" (Mark 2:22)
54 Paper package
56 Behind
57 "Take thine _____, eat, drink" (Luke 12:19)
59 Attach
63 Exclamation of wonderment
64 "My beloved is like...a young ___" (Song 2:9 NIV)
65 Secret revealer
66 Gray sea eagle
67 One who accosted the traveler in Luke 10
68 Southpaw

21 Smelly mammal
23 "It came to pass in ___ days" (Mark 1:9)
24 It descended from heaven when 22 Across took place
25 Mined metals
27 If salt "loses ___ saltiness" (Mark 9:50 NIV)
29 Semi feature
30 "See ya later!"
31 Number loaves when 1 Across took place
33 Blind man does this after Jesus heals him
34 "Kingdom of God is at ___" (Mark 1:15)
36 "Sow the fields, and ___ vineyards" (Ps. 107:37)
37 The Jordan ___

38 ___ Days, subject of Mark 13
39 Time periods
40 Danish currency (abbr.)
42 Business ending (abbr.)
44 Winding path
45 Shingler
46 "The seed is ___ under their clods" (Joel 1:17)
47 Guinea-___, West African nation
48 Where Jesus cast out moneychangers
50 "My soul is exceeding sorrowful unto ___"
(Mark 14:34)

51 Place for a boutonniere
53 "Take heed ___ any man deceive you"
(Mark 13:5)
55 John "did ___ locusts and wild honey"
(Mark 1:6)
58 Omelette ingredient
60 Santa's helper
61 Need for Pet. and Andrew in Mark 1
62 "They passed through the Red sea as by ___
land" (Heb. 11:29)

IMPROBABLE ENCOUNTERS

These highly unlikely confrontations might elicit some strong reactions.

ACROSS

1 "What have _____ do with thee" (Mark 1:24) (2 words)
5 Cheese with red wax
9 "I _____ ease" (Job 16:12) (2 words)
14 "He built up the _____ around it" (2 Sam. 5:9 NIV)
15 19th-century popular dancer _____ Montez
16 Jung: the inner self
17 "She _____ at the door of her house" (Prov. 9:14 NIV)
18 "_____ come unto Judah" (Mic. 1:9) (2 words)
19 "This man is a _____" (Acts 22:26)
20 What Goliath (1 Sam. 17:4) did when he went to the house of Zacchaeus (Luke 19:2–3) (4 words)
23 Luster on cloth
24 "With that same _____ pottage" (Gen. 25:30)
25 Letters on some ships
28 "That _____ their tongues" (Jer. 23:31)
29 Swiss river
30 It helps the little entrepreneurs (abbr.)
33 He was an Elkoshite (Nah. 1:1)
35 "Saddled his _____" (Num. 22:21)
36 "Chased you, as _____ do" (Deut. 1:44)
37 What Zacchaeus (Luke 19:3–4) did when he went to the house of Rahab (Josh. 2:1–15) (3 words)

41 "Thy word is a _____ unto my feet" (Ps. 119:105)
42 "Ye shall not surely _____" (Gen. 3:4)
43 Speak pompously
44 They review manuscripts (abbr.)
45 Soviet fighter
46 "They do always _____ in their heart" (Heb. 3:10)
48 Followed FDR
49 "The lapwing, and the _____" (Lev. 11:19)
50 "The swallow _____ for herself" (Ps. 84:3) (2 words)
52 What Hiram, David's builder, (2 Sam. 5:11), did when he went to the house where Jesus healed the palsied man (Mark 2:1–5) (4 words)
59 "He answered her not _____" (Matt. 15:23) (2 words)
60 "Jacob _____ his clothes" (Gen. 37:34 NIV)
61 Florence's river
62 Swamp plant
63 "Who is lord _____ us?" (Ps. 12:4)
64 "The fallow _____" (Deut. 14:5)
65 Primp
66 "I have no _____ of thee" (1 Cor. 12:21)
67 "Or _____ he will hold to the one" (Matt. 6:24)

DOWN

1 "_____ away thy sins" (Acts 22:16)
2 Pennsylvania port
3 Word following Ps. 119:64 NIV
4 Watering hole
5 Upper crust
6 "I will surely _____ good" (Gen. 32:12) (2 words)
7 "I am an _____ in their sight" (Job 19:15)
8 Not fem. or neut. (abbr.)
9 More cautious

10 "For he was _____ man" (1 Sam.l 4:18) (2 words)
11 _____ Valley, CA
12 "Every way of _____ is right in his own eyes" (Prov. 21:2) (2 words)
13 Sharp taste
21 "Upon the _____ of his right hand" (Lev. 8:23)
22 Expunge
25 "Saul's _____ said, Tell me" (1 Sam. 10:15)

26 Chef or Waldorf

27 Leveling devices

29 "Lifts the needy from the _____ heap" (Ps. 113:7 NIV)

30 Word found seventy-one times in the Ps.s

31 "No money in your _____" (Mark 6:8 NIV)

32 "Such _____ their hearts to seek the LORD God" (2 Chron. 11:16) (2 words)

34 Referee's kin (abbr.)

35 "_____ it up" (Rev. 10:10)

36 "Shut the doors, and _____ them" (Neh. 7:3)

38 Prepares for publication

39 "I cannot _____" (Luke 16:3)

40 "Is _____ than an infidel" (1 Tim. 5:8)

45 "The _____ pleased him" (Est. 2:9)

46 Main dish

47 Round up again

49 Canal craft

50 "Oh that I had wings like _____!" (Ps. 55:6) (2 words)

51 "As many as _____ by sea" (Rev. 18:17)

52 Padlock's location

53 Fancy pitcher

54 "He _____ upon a cherub" (2 Sam. 22:11)

55 School on the Thames

56 City on the Oka

57 "Every _____ bands were loosed" (Acts 16:26)

58 Precedes arm or cast (prefix)

BEGINNINGS AND END

Here is a quip based on John 3:3; 1 Pet. 1:23; and Rev. 20:6 and 21:8. Read them to help figure out the quip.

ACROSS

1 "That which groweth of _____ own" (Lev. 25:5)
4 "Pierce his ear with an _____" (Ex. 21:6 NIV)
7 "Come _____, and I will show you" (Rev. 4:1 NIV) (2 words)
13 Sixth-century Chinese dynasty
14 "With cords of human kindness, with _____ of love" (Hos. 11:4 NIV)
16 "To _____ the night" (Acts 16:9) (2 words)
17 Start of scripture-based **QUIP** (see above) (2 words)
19 "Also _____ past, when Saul was king over us" (2 Sam. 5:2) (2 words)
20 "And likewise a _____" (Luke 10:32)
21 "Five gold tumors and five gold _____" (1 Sam. 6:4 NIV)
23 "And for his _____" (Jer. 52:34)
24 "And Joseph _____" (Ex. 1:6)
26 "There he _____ Jew named Aquila" (Acts 18:2 NIV) (2 words)
30 City on the Ruhr
32 **QUIP**, cont'd (2 words)
35 "They were _____ in two" (Heb. 11:37 NIV)
37 "Hither, _____ of the bread" (Ruth 2:14) (2 words)
38 "The _____ of the bow" (2 Sam. 1:18)

41 GE or IBM, e.g. (abbr.)
42 "Ye not eat of them that chew the _____" (Lev. 11:4)
43 Sudbury Neutrino Observatory (abbr.)
44 Famous canal
46 Wooden shoe
48 **QUIP**, cont'd (2 words)
50 "He is not here: for he is _____" (Matt. 28:6)
54 "David said to Ittai, 'Go ahead, march _____.' Ittai the Gittite" (2 Sam. 15:22 NIV) (2 words)
55 Sow wild _____
57 What genera are
58 "That the _____ men be sober" (Titus 2:2)
60 "As sheep in the midst of _____" (Matt. 10:16)
62 Familiar one-celled animal (var.)
66 End of **QUIP** (2 words)
68 "_____ up and go" (Acts 9:6 NIV) (2 words)
69 "And _____ through the streams" (Isa. 47:2 NIV)
70 Opposite of haw
71 Hang loosely
72 "My _____ shall comfort me" (Job 7:13)
73 Sounds of hesitation

DOWN

1 Tristan's beloved
2 "Know what _____ being played" (1 Cor. 14:7 NIV) (2 words)
3 Sifters
4 "Ye have snuffed _____" (Mal. 1:13) (2 words)
5 Hyper
6 "Ears to hear, _____ him hear" (Matt. 13:9)
7 "And shut _____ that hath the plague" (Lev. 13:50) (2 words)
8 "And baked it in _____" (Num. 11:8)
9 "It sways like a _____ in the wind" (Isa. 24:20 NIV)

10 Hophni's father (1 Sam. 1:3)
11 "The _____ of a cup" (2 Chron. 4:5 NIV)
12 Compass point (abbr.)
15 "A very _____ man" (2 Sam. 13:3 NIV)
18 "In the end it _____" (Prov. 23:32 NIV)
22 "Why make ye this _____" (Mark 5:39)
25 Newspaper article
26 "Have I need of _____ men" (1 Sam. 21:15)
27 Parisian "summers"
28 "My punishment is greater _____ I can bear" (Gen. 4:13)
29 "Leisure so much _____ eat" (Mark 6:31) (2 words)

31 "And _____ said, Turn again" (Ruth 1:11)

33 "Say unto them which _____ it" (Ezek. 13:11)

34 "Hath a familiar spirit at _____" (1 Sam. 28:7)

36 "The waters _____ the stones" (Job 14:19)

38 "Behold, we go _____ Jerusalem" (Mark 10:33) (2 words)

39 "They were _____ asunder" (Heb. 11:37)

40 "And Seth. . .begat _____" (Gen. 5:6)

42 "And into the fire" (Luke 3:9)

45 Landsteiner blood group (abbr.)

46 "The valley of the _____ of death" (Ps. 23:4)

47 "This _____ then read many of the Jews" (John 19:20)

49 Digit

51 "_____ beasts from the land" (Lev. 26:6 NIV)

52 Town in southeast New Hampshire

53 Kelvinator's cars of the 1940s

56 Nobel, for e.g.

58 "From the blood of _____" (Luke 11:51)

59 "Which was before the king's _____" (Est. 4:6)

61 "Azariah the son of _____" (2 Chron. 15:1)

62 "Is subverted, _____ sinneth" (Titus 3:11)

63 Extinct New Zealand bird

64 "His _____ hands shall bring" (Lev. 7:30)

65 "In the white of an _____?" (Job 6:6)

67 Seize

PSALMS

ACROSS

1 Bread bits Jesus gave Judas
5 Declare one's beliefs, e.g.
9 Lock
13 "Messiah" song
14 Comedian Jay
15 "Mark them which _____ divisions" (Rom. 16:17)
16 Missionary's needs, _____, maybe
17 "He causeth his wind to _____" (Ps. 147:18)
18 "He shall _____ before God for ever" (Ps. 61:7)
19 "_____ be the Lord" (Ps. 28:6)
21 "Thou wilt _____ the afflicted" (Ps. 18:27)
23 KJV donkey
24 Rescued "out of an horrible _____" (Ps. 40:2)
25 Speak, and God will _____
29 To _____, KJV "to know"
30 "_____ out my transgressions" (Ps. 51:1)
32 KJV art
33 "One _____ of ten shekels" (Num. 7:14)
36 Gummy, sticky
37 Post opposite
38 Heavenly _____, eternal abode

39 "Cut...with pruning _____" (Isa. 18:5)
40 "I will take _____ to my ways" (Ps. 39:1)
41 23rd Ps. shepherds' concern
42 Dugout
43 Lengthy sermon characteristic
44 Medical test
45 They flattered and "_____ unto him" (Ps. 78:36)
46 Upward barrier
47 Many a Ps.
49 Luau dish
50 Knock lightly
53 "His soul shall dwell at _____" (Ps. 25:13)
55 Suitable to partake of
57 Roman soldier's arm
60 Swiss mountains
62 Maine water bird
63 "Sow in _____. . .reap in joy" (Ps. 126:5)
64 Labor Day mo.
65 KJV "soon"
66 Knitter's need
67 Playthings
68 Go against, as God's will

DOWN

1 Brazilian dance
2 College exams, maybe
3 KJV "flutes"
4 Back talk
5 Even though
6 South African grassland
7 English musician Brian
8 What Pet. does on Sea of Galilee
9 "Out of the mouth of _____" (Ps. 8:2)
10 Paris affirmative
11 Hallucinogen (abbr.)
12 Shirt sort

15 Hole
20 Lilies neither toil nor _____ (Matt. 6:28)
22 Biblical healing ingredients
26 Candle
27 Sinned
28 "I am poor and _____" (Ps. 40:17)
29 "_____ is me!" (Ps. 120:5)
30 Jesus shed His _____ for us
31 Acts writer
33 See 41 Across
34 "_____ belongeth unto God" (Ps. 62:11)
35 Jesus is the Alpha and _____

36 "Rain is over and _____" (Song 2:11)
39 He Num. them on our heads
40 Hare's action
42 Absolves, as of sin
43 "_____ on the Lord" (Ps. 27:14)
46 Tyre and Sidon features
48 Earnestly desire, as for God's presence
49 Energetic
50 Steakhouse choice

51 They "stand _____ from my sore" (Ps. 38:11)
52 Widow's mite
54 Nativity star locale
56 Fish, barley loaves bringer (2 words)
57 Prodigal son's living quarters
58 Carrot go-with
59 The high priest's servant's was cut off
61 Constellation name

PROVERBS

ACROSS

1 Foolish people fall into these
7 "_____ is not to the swift" (Eccl. 9:11)
11 British org. ender
14 Ankle-to-knee legging
15 "Hey!" at sea
16 KJV "art"
17 "Soul shall dwell _____" (Ps. 25:13) (2 words)
18 "Good _____ [better than] riches" (Prov. 22:1)
19 Musical style
20 "_____ be filled with plenty" (Prov. 3:10)
22 At a slow tempo
24 Sun
27 "Who _____ ears to hear"
29 Pre-Easter season
30 Egg-shaped
32 Liquor
35 "_____ from the snares of death" (Prov. 14:27)
37 Door handle
38 Ship section
41 "Soft _____ turneth away wrath" (Prov. 15:1)
42 Propeller cap

44 Egypt to Sinai (dir.)
45 Good Samaritan _____ wounded man
48 Pearl maker
49 Shocks
51 "_____...is fire and much wood" (Isa. 30:33)
52 First murder victim
55 Wicked "prepared a _____ for my steps" (Ps. 57:6)
56 Bank products
57 "Let her own works _____ her" (Prov. 31:31)
60 Sodom sight
64 Mandatory negative particle in French
65 Tel _____, Israel
67 Accustoms, as to evil
71 "Faithful witness will not _____" (Prov. 14:5)
72 Loose kind of talk
73 Pilot
74 "World without _____"
75 "Thine _____ may be in secret" (Matt. 6:4)
76 Grammar

DOWN

1 Accountant (abbr.)
2 Jonah's Nineveh dwelling
3 "I _____ no pleasant bread" (Dan. 10:3)
4 Soldier would _____ Jesus' side
5 Plateau
6 OT prophet is a _____
7 Rifle through
8 "Gotcha!"
9 State of unconsciousness
10 "Leah was tender _____" (Gen. 29:17)
11 God "set me in a _____ place" (Ps. 118:5)

12 "_____ up a child in the way" (Prov. 22:6)
13 Station
21 Pro Sports org.
23 Trust God "with _____ thine heart" (Prov. 3:5)
24 Fizzy drinks
25 OT meat offering bakers
26 Backslide, as into sin
28 Solomon to David
31 "Forget not my _____" (Prov. 3:1)
32 Journey (2 words)
33 Tramps

34 31 Down advice to wise

36 "Soweth iniquity shall _____ vanity" (Prov. 22:8)

38 Fool's prank

39 A wise woman "considereth a _____" (Prov. 31:16)

40 Muscle of the human forearm

43 Egypt viper

46 Israelite tribe

47 Shirt parts

49 _____ Baba

50 Time to evaluate financial results (abbr.)

52 31 Down as "_____ of thine eye" (Prov. 7:2)

53 Wise person uses his

54 Unburdened of guilt, e.g.

58 Long story

59 "Remove thy foot from _____" (Prov. 4:27)

61 Slant

62 Do not _____ sinners

63 "Flattering mouth worketh _____" (Prov. 26:28)

66 Big Blue org.

68 Unclean rodent

69 LAX screen information

70 Gender

BATHSHEBA: THE BEAUTIFUL

ACROSS

1 "He. . .put them under___" (2 Sam. 12:31)
5 Black
9 Samson's riddle was this (Judg. 14:12–13)
14 Noted persecutor of early Christians
15 Opera solo
16 David and Bathsheba found they were not ___ God's law
17 Mil. branch
18 Careen
19 Bathsheba bore Solomon, "and the Lord ___ him" (2 Sam. 12:24)
20 Terra-___ (type of clay)
22 "___, thou desirest truth" (Ps. 51:6)
24 UK driver's concern
25 Beetle
27 Time periods
31 Opposite of David's attitude when accused of sin
32 Zero
34 A Psalm, perhaps
35 A prophet accused David of this (2 Sam. 12:9)
38 Movie bio with Will Smith
40 Israel's enemy (2 Sam. 11:1)
42 Uriah ___ his life in battle (2 Sam. 11:17)
44 "Little ___ lamb" (2 Sam. 12:3)
46 "A thousand ___ in thy sight are but as yesterday" (Ps. 90:4)

47 David was this while his men went off to war (2 Sam. 11:1)
48 The rich man had many, the poor man had ___ (2 Sam. 12:3)
50 Prophetess at the Temple (Luke 2:36) (var.)
51 Pseudonym (abbr.)
52 Roman trio
55 Adultery is this
57 Bathsheba to Solomon (2 Sam. 12:24)
59 Metal
61 Corn holder
64 Relating to the brain
66 Bathsheba's baby would ___ her guilt
68 Joab would ___ the men to put Uriah up front (2 Sam. 11:15–16)
71 Sinai's Peninsula
73 Musical composition
74 Cabled
75 Nathan's story had David on the ___ of his seat
76 ___ Accords, 1993 agreement
77 David ___ as Bathsheba bathes
78 David tried to cover up his guilt, so he did this (2 Sam. 11:25)
79 David to Uriah: "Go. . .wash thy ___" (2 Sam. 11:8)

DOWN

1 David and Bathsheba had done this while Uriah was gone
2 "Ant and Grasshopper" author
3 David and Bathsheba brought about God's ___ (2 Sam. 11:27; 2 Sam 12:7–12)
4 David's accuser was not this (2 Sam. 12:1–7)
5 David would not do this while Bathsheba's son lay dying (2 Sam. 12:17)
6 Joab knew the truth, but was probably this
7 Tanker
8 Accused David (2 Sam. 12:1)
9 "They would shoot from the ___?" (2 Sam. 11:20)

10 "Uriah ___ in Jerusalem that day" (2 Sam. 11:12)
11 State official (abbr.)
12 She talked to a serpent
13 David's face may have been this when he recognized his sin
21 Communication method (abbr.)
23 Kimono sash
26 Spy org.
28 Paul's citizenship (Acts 22:25)
29 A bride may ___ herself with jewels (Isa. 61:10)

30 "They read. . .distinctly, and gave the ___ " (Neh. 8:8)

31 Gaiety

33 David took Bathsheba, and "he ___ with her" (2 Sam. 11:4)

35 Bathsheba's dad (2 Sam. 11:3)

36 Popular spirit in Russia

37 Religion promulgated in the 7th century

39 ___ Jima

41 David prepared this for Uriah (2 Sam. 11:8)

43 ___ Lanka

45 Preservation by silo storage

49 Flightless bird

53 Rich man could give one of these to poor man (2 Sam. 12:4) (abbr.)

54 Uriah said: "___, and Judah, abide in tents" (2 Sam. 11:11)

56 Referee

58 "David's ___ was greatly kindled" (2 Sam. 12:5)

60 ___ Gras

61 Thicket

62 Plant seed

63 Bathsheba's beauty would do this to David (2 Sam. 11:2)

65 Tails

67 Where Bathsheba bathed

68 Punching tool

69 Uriah would not ___ with his wife (2 Sam. 11:11)

70 David's feelings for the rich man (2 Sam. 12:5)

72 "David arose from off his ___ " (2 Sam. 11:2)

Day 32

ATTITUDE OF GRATITUDE

ACROSS

1 Banquet in heaven, perhaps
5 What God may heal
9 Gamaliel to student Paul, for short (Acts 5:34)
13 "_____ is mount Sinai" (Gal. 4:25)
14 God is potter, we are _____
15 "Grace...able to _____ you up" (Acts 20:32)
16 _____ the time, wait patiently
17 "Thy kingdom _____"
18 Sodom burner
19 "_____ are the meek" (Matt. 5:5)
21 It cannot wash away sin
23 Longing
24 Home page spots, for short
25 Martha _____ over kitchen duties
29 He gives us "meat in _____ season" (Ps. 104:27)
30 Heaviness
32 Moses to "_____two tables of stone" (Ex. 34:1)
33 Strong fiber from a tropical plant
36 Small flock
37 KJV "art"
38 _____ Spirit, Trinity member

39 Embarrassing error
40 "What _____ hath he done?" (Luke 23:22)
41 _____ Jima
42 Swiss mathematician
43 Galilee fisher's basket, maybe
44 Snooze
45 Type of wagon
46 Dedicated data storage network (abbr.)
47 Navy rank
49 Sun
50 Desktop component (abbr.)
53 Refer to Bible verse, e.g.
55 "I am filled with _____" (2 Cor. 7:4)
57 "Throne was _____ heaven" (Rev. 4:2) (2 words)
60 Vending machine coin taker
62 Do not _____ prayers of thanksgiving
63 Is reaching "threescore years and ten"
64 Winnie the _____
65 "Call his _____ Jesus" (Matt. 1:21)
66 Hymn
67 "No way!"
68 Former Russian ruler

DOWN

1 Angel Gabriel, to friends
2 Like lame man healed by Jesus
3 "Ye that...are heavy _____" (Matt. 11:28)
4 One of the twelve Greek Olympians
5 Give in, as to temptation
6 Dirt clumps
7 Noah's son
8 "Mine _____ have seen thy salvation" (Luke 2:30)
9 Removes water
10 Eve: Adam's _____
11 Stadium cheer

12 New Deal initials
15 "Behold the _____ of the Lord" (Ps. 27:4)
20 Israel's first king
22 "_____ the gift Moses commanded" (Matt. 8:4)
26 Samson was not to _____ off his hair
27 Spooky
28 "Spirit of God _____ in you" (Rom. 8:9)
29 This is the "_____ the Lord hath made" (Ps. 118:24)
30 Satisfies "with _____ out of the rock" (Ps. 81:16)
31 "Let them _____ shout for joy" (Ps. 5:11)

33 "Lord make his face _____ upon thee" (Num. 6:25)

34 Des Moines resident

35 Spills

36 Soda

39 OT _____ offerings

40 Sea flyer

42 Inching closer to sin, perhaps

43 "He maketh the storm a _____" (Ps. 107:29)

46 He will _____ the sorrowing heart

48 It's on the cake

49 Newscaster's breaking story

50 Unconscious states

51 First

52 "My lips shall _____ knowledge" (Job 33:3)

54 Sports channel

56 Church's baptismal _____

57 Scandinavian airlines

58 Sinful pride

59 OT cheap metal

61 London bathroom

Day 33

GOSPEL OF LUKE

ACROSS

1 Slightly open
5 School groups (abbr.)
9 "Your feet __ with the preparation of the gospel" (Eph. 6:15)
13 "Though I be __ in speech" (2 Cor. 11:6)
14 The __ Supper
15 "Son of man cometh at an hour when ye __ not" (Luke 12:40)
16 Citrus drinks
17 Shaft
18 Jesus changed it into wine
19 What John came to do
21 "Blessed are ye that __ now" (Luke 6:21)
23 Former speedy transport (abbr.)
24 Wicked
25 Ruffles
29 Sneer at
30 Tel __
32 Lion moniker
33 Goliath's foe
36 God's freely given mercy
37 The Ten Commandments, e.g.
38 Opposed to (dial.)
39 Christian symbol

40 Jesus' foster dad (Sp.)
41 Tax agency (abbr.)
42 Oozy substance
43 "His word was with __" (Luke 4:32)
44 "__ us now go even unto Bethlehem" (Luke 2:15)
45 Abba
46 Mother's Day month
47 Easter celebrations, e.g.
49 Jesus, __ of God
50 "__ brought forth a son" (Luke 1:57)
53 Serpent sound
55 Dealt with
57 Shiny fabric
60 "What's the bright __?"
62 "Let him impart to him that hath __" (Luke 3:11)
63 Bias
64 Pinches
65 Standard
66 "Who can __ war against it?" (Rev. 13:4 NIV)
67 "Your Father, who __ what is done in secret" (Matt. 6:4 NIV)
68 Capital of Western Samoa

DOWN

1 Many in the Middle East
2 Jesus' betrayer
3 Skillful
4 "Come unto me...I will give you __" (Matt. 11:28)
5 Public squares
6 "All the world should be __" (Luke 2:1)
7 Certain communication (abbr.)
8 What Jacob fed his famished brother
9 Form
10 "Prophesy! Who __ you?" (Luke 22:64 NIV)
11 Three Persons, __ God
12 Danish currency (abbr.)
15 Disciple number

20 Footnote abbreviation (Lat.)
22 Long stories
26 "Ye bear witness that ye __ the deeds of your fathers" (Luke 11:48)
27 Taunt
28 Parable subject with seeds
29 Great noise
30 Pleasant smell
31 Flower holder
33 Our __ bread
34 "__ with thine adversary quickly" (Matt. 5:25)
35 Former Microsoft product
36 Certain stagehand
39 Potter's needs

40 "Good tidings of great __" (Luke 2:10)
42 Treatment for a broken bone
43 Window feature
46 Mire
48 European river
49 Cliff (arch.)
50 "Latchet of whose shoes I am not worthy to __ down and unloose" (Mark 1:7)
51 ___ Matisse, painter

52 Swelling
54 "Thy ___ are forgiven thee" (Luke 5:20)
56 She saw baby Jesus in the temple
57 Compass dir.
58 Pie __ mode (2 words)
59 Name in a photo
61 What Jesus does on Calvary

GOSPEL OF JOHN

ACROSS

1 Prayer word
5 Gulf war missile
9 Sinai landscape descriptor
13 Chocolate candy name
14 Trial situation
15 Fashion
16 Paul's missionary destination
17 Flair
18 Easter morning messenger
19 Where Jesus raised Lazarus from death
21 Community org.
23 Caesarea to Jerusalem (dir.)
24 King (Lat.)
25 Caesarea has one
29 Sneer at (slang)
30 Lazarus "had __ in the grave four days" (John 11:17)
32 Climate watchdog group (abbr.)
33 "I am the __ of life (John 6:35)
36 Paul, "the __ of sinners" (1 Tim. 1:16 NIV)
37 "I saw thee under the __ tree" (John 1:50)
38 "Behold the __ of God" (John 1:29)
39 Toss out

40 What Jesus changed water into
41 "__ to a Grecian Urn"
42 Some UK dwellers
43 Musical tones
44 Peter's trade tool
45 Slimy
46 Manna came with it
47 Wood nymphs
49 Toddler
50 See 44 Across
53 Payment option
55 Bring into bondage
57 Tempter
60 Lazarus's tomb, probably
62 Maintain
63 "He that is without sin. . .let him first cast a __ at her" (John 8:7)
64 Ointment brought to Jesus' tomb
65 Not women's
66 "__ of this body" (2 Pet. 1:13 NIV)
67 Jesus' mom
68 "Or __ believe me for the very works' sake" (John 14:11)

DOWN

1 Many Holy Land dwellers
2 Law-giver of old
3 Scribes and Pharisees in Jesus' time, e.g.
4 OT ship builder
5 Easter play sections
6 Sepals of a flower
7 Red, white, and blue nation (abbr.)
8 What Peter did three times
9 Measuring instrument
10 "If he...ask an __, will he offer him a scorpion?" (Luke 11:12)
11 What Peter would do after 8 Down
12 Conger
15 Empty

20 Sinai descriptor
22 Carry off (with "away")
26 Be suitable for
27 Speak your mind
28 What a storm does
29 Little bit
30 Terrible
31 Monumental gateway
33 "Born, not of __ but of God" (John 1:13)
34 Meteorologist's tool
35 Nail filing board
36 Ace
39 One of three on Calvary
40 "Wonderful!"

42 Salt addition

43 They "left their ___, and followed him" (Matt. 4:20)

46 Jesus rode into Jerusalem on one

48 ___-garde

49 Certain choir member

50 Belly feature

51 Makes fair

52 Brief

54 First man

56 Jesus healed many who were this

57 Former fast flier

58 What they did at the Last Supper

59 2,000 pounds

61 Pie ___ mode (2 words)

Day 35

DONKEY BUSINESS

ACROSS

1 "Without an inhabitant, _____ this day" (Jer. 44:22) (2 words)
5 "As it _____ we had not delayed" (Gen. 43:10 NIV) (2 words)
9 "He shall gather the _____ with his arm" (Isa. 40:11)
14 "The Jews of _____ sought to stone thee" (John 11:8)
15 "How _____ dispossess them?" (Deut. 7:17) (2 words)
16 "There shall be _____ of Jesse" (Rom. 15:12) (2 words)
17 What Samson used to kill a thousand men (Judg. 15:16 NIV) (3 words)
20 Presbyterian parsonage
21 "They _____ not, they spin not" (Luke 12:27)
22 "Sing unto him _____ song" (Ps. 33:3) (2 words)
23 Follows *printemp* (Fr.)
24 Caesar's "I"
26 "He planteth an _____" (Isa. 44:14)
28 _____-cone
29 "I cannot find one _____ man among you" (Job 17:10)
31 "Why make ye this _____, and weep?" (Mark 5:39)
34 Formerly Siamese
37 "But as my beloved sons I _____ you" (1 Cor. 4:14)
39 "The law is not _____ on faith" (Gal. 3:12 NIV)
41 What happened when Balaam saw the angel? (Num. 22:27–28) (3 words)

44 "Watch ye and pray, lest ye _____ into temptation" (Mark 14:38)
45 "There was one Anna. . .of the tribe of _____" (Luke 2:36)
46 "Because I am a man of unclean _____" (Isa. 6:5)
47 European theater of operations (abbr.)
48 "He _____ save himself!" (Mark 15:31 NIV)
50 "Give _____ king" (1 Sam. 8:6) (2 words)
52 "Under your arms to _____ the ropes" (Jer. 38:12 NIV)
53 Metro maker
54 "Thou sayest that I _____ king" (John 18:37) (2 words)
57 "Do not give _____ cry" (Josh. 6:10 NIV) (2 words)
60 "By this time there is a bad _____" (John 11:39 NIV)
63 Where Moses saw the burning bush (Ex. 3:1–2)
65 Jesus entered Jerusalem this way (Matt. 21:4–5 NIV) (4 words)
68 "Beast had _____ as a man" (Rev. 4:7) (2 words)
69 Hoodwink
70 Giant Mel's family
71 "When _____ with us" (Acts 20:14) (2 words)
72 "Their throat is an _____ sepulchre" (Rom. 3:13)
73 Flag-maker Betsy

DOWN

1 "A blind man, or _____" (Lev. 21:18) (2 words)
2 "He was _____ that saying" (Mark 10:22) (2 words)
3 "Slain by him _____ time" (1 Chron. 11:11) (2 words)
4 "Captains over _____" (Deut. 1:15)
5 "He casteth forth his _____ like morsels" (Ps. 147:17)
6 "Thus shall ye _____ David" (1 Sam.l 18:25) (2 words)
7 "Give him drink: for _____ doing" (Rom. 12:20) (2 words)

8 South Pacific country of 320 islands
9 "The _____ of the LORD is perfect" (Ps. 19:7)
10 Another name for *Hebron* (Gen. 35:27)
11 "Nor the _____ by night" (Ps. 121:6)
12 "A _____ of him shall not be broken" (John 19:36)
13 "Some bread and some lentil _____" (Gen. 25:34 NIV)
18 "This man Dan.. . .was found to have a _____ mind" (Dan. 5:12 NIV)
19 "_____ for the day!" (Joel 1:15)
25 "Her _____ is interwoven with gold" (Ps. 45:13 NIV)

27 First son of Cush (Gen. 10:7)

28 "A thousand shall fall at thy _____" (Ps. 91:7)

29 "Every day they _____ my words" (Ps. 56:5)

30 "Them that were entering _____ hindered" (Luke 11:52) (2 words)

31 "Whatever you _____ will give you" (Mark 6:23 NIV) (2 words)

32 "I sink in _____ mire" (Ps. 69:2)

33 Chances

34 "Make _____ an ark of gopher wood" (Gen. 6:14)

35 "Not be even a _____ of sexual immorality" (Eph. 5:3 NIV)

36 "I speak _____ wise men" (1 Cor. 10:15) (2 words)

38 A son of Ezer (Gen. 36:27)

40 "_____ man's ways seem right to him" (Prov. 21:2 NIV) (2 words)

42 Free Willy, e.g.

43 "That was the _____ Light" (John 1:9)

49 "As _____ lappeth" (Judg. 7:5) (2 words)

51 Fashionable London district

52 "Her _____ is far above rubies" (Prov. 31:10)

53 "The vines with the tender _____" (Song 2:13)

54 "Prepared an _____ the saving of his house" (Heb. 11:7) (2 words)

55 "The church that _____ at their house" (1 Cor. 16:19 NIV)

56 "Darkened by the smoke from the _____" (Rev. 9:2 NIV)

57 First son of Ulla (1 Chron. 7:39)

58 "But his _____ looked back" (Gen. 19:26)

59 "As in _____ all die" (1 Cor. 15:22)

61 "And whatsoever ye _____ it heartily" (Col. 3:23) (2 words)

62 "He went _____ the mountain" (Ex. 24:18 NIV) (2 words)

64 _____ about (approximately) (2 words)

66 "He hath spread a _____ for my feet" (Lam. 1:13)

67 "Ye have made it a _____ of thieves" (Luke 19:46)

Day 36

GOD'S REQUIREMENT

ACROSS

1 "And with the one _____ tenth deal of flour" (Ex. 29:40) (2 words)
6 "Shew I unto you _____ excellent way" (1 Cor. 12:31) (2 words)
11 "There _____ man in the land of Uz" (Job 1:1) (2 words)
15 "Even upon _____ by the wall" (1 Sam. 20:25) (2 words)
16 Third son of Micah (1 Chron. 8:35)
17 "And the _____ arose" (Job 29:8)
18 Start of **ANSWER** to the question in the quote from Micah 6:8 (above) (5 words)
21 _____ -cone
22 "Lead _____ Benjamin" (Hos. 5:8 NIV) (2 words)
23 Chinese general of chicken fame
24 Baton Rouge school (abbr.)
25 Copiers' needs
28 "They are as a _____" (Ps. 90:5)
30 **ANSWER**, cont'd (2 words)
33 "From wing _____ wing tip" (1 Kings 6:24 NIV) (2 words)
36 "So long" in Lyon
37 "Great is _____ of the Eph." (Acts 19:28)
39 "A _____ of horses" (Isa. 21:9 NIV)

43 "Attack them and _____ them open" (Hos. 13:8 NIV)
44 **ANSWER**, cont'd (2 words)
47 Org. of attorneys
48 "Though you _____ me" (Ps. 17:3 NIV)
50 What Jefferson was
51 Playful swimmer
53 Uncle Tom's creator
55 **ANSWER**, cont'd (2 words)
56 Extent
59 "That they which _____ race run all" (1 Cor. 9:24) (3 words)
62 Clumsy fellow
63 Morning hours (abbr.)
66 "_____ his son" (1 Chron. 7:27)
67 "Why make ye this _____" (Mark 5:39)
70 End of **ANSWER** (4 words)
75 "And when _____ the blood" (Ex. 12:13) (2 words)
76 Spokes
77 He played Superman
78 "Even so _____ I you" (John 20:21)
79 "_____ from the blue" (2 words)
80 Exceptional mount

DOWN

1 Retrieving dogs, e.g.
2 "God is _____ and shield" (Ps. 84:11) (2 words)
3 "And shaken _____ pieces" (Job 16:12) (2 words)
4 "The lapwing, and the _____" (Lev. 11:19)
5 From _____ Z (2 words)
6 "Is taken _____ end" (Jer. 51:31) (2 words)
7 "Every _____ town" (2 Kings 3:19 NIV)
8 Tulsa school (abbr.)
9 "I will give you _____" (Matt. 11:28)
10 "He who _____ meat" (Rom. 14:6 NIV)
11 "I am the _____" (John 14:6)
12 "Like chaff swept away by _____?" (Job 21:18 NIV) (2 words)

13 "Where would the _____ of smell be?" (1 Cor. 12:17 NIV)
14 Make sense (2 words)
19 "If I have _____ this" (Ps. 7:3)
20 "That remain, that nothing be _____" (John 6:12)
25 "The great _____ of his right foot" (Lev. 14:14)
26 Egg
27 "And two lions standing by the _____" (2 Chron. 9:18)
29 Abram's nephew (Gen. 12:5)
30 Acidy
31 Garfield's friend
32 "My _____ shall praise thee" (Ps. 63:3)
34 "Enter ye _____ the strait gate" (Matt. 7:13) (2 words)

35 "And she took a _____" (2 Sam. 13:9)

37 "He _____ out his sword" (Acts 16:27)

38 More wintry

40 "That they may _____ whole month" (Num. 11:21) (2 words)

41 "Where is _____ thy brother?" (Gen. 4:9)

42 "They _____ my steps" (Ps. 56:6)

45 Former name of Tokyo

46 "Not lawful to _____ the sabbath days?" (Luke 6:2) (2 words)

49 Recipe measurement (abbr.)

52 Hughes' airline

54 Small duck

55 Slight hair alteration

56 "_____ strength was not known" (Judg. 16:9) (2 words)

57 "Whether we be sober, it is for your _____" (2 Cor. 5:13)

58 "Was it from heaven, or _____?" (Luke 20:4) (2 words)

60 "_____ I make thy foes thy footstool" (Acts 2:35)

61 Kind of ball game pitchers dream of (2 words)

64 British pianist Dame _____ Hess

65 Q-tip, e.g.

67 Shammah's father, one of David's mighty men (2 Sam. 23:11)

68 "I did mourn as a _____" (Isa. 38:14)

69 Azariah's father (2 Chron. 15:1)

71 "A man sick of the palsy, lying on a _____" (Matt. 9:2)

72 "_____ set my bow in the cloud" (Gen. 9:13) (2 words)

73 Points of days (abbr.)

74 "It is _____ high day" (Gen. 29:7)

NUMBERS

ACROSS

1 Parable sower's goal
5 Paul and Silas, informally
9 "Walked on," KJV-style
13 Messala in "Ben-Hur," for example
14 Bread spread
15 European river
16 Pharisees would _____ love, mercy, faith
17 Distort, as the facts
18 Delilah _____ Samson to tell his secret
19 Large number of disciples Jesus sent out
21 "Ninety and _____ which went not astray" (Matt. 18:13)
23 Egypt to Mt. Sinai direction
24 Good Samaritan would _____ wounded man
25 Number Israelite tribes
29 Quantity (abbr.)
30 Type of type
32 Horse food
33 "For _____ is the kingdom"
36 Abraham's eyebrows might have been _____
37 Desktop element (abbr.)
38 Numerous angels
39 "_____ of fools is deceit" (Prov. 14:8)
40 "God _____, Let there be light" (Gen.1:3)
41 Southern constellation
42 "Carry neither _____, nor scrip" (Luke 10:4)
43 Spanish punctuation mark
44 Polish river
45 St. _____, Mary's mom, traditionally
46 Cereal choice
47 Evening and morning, the _____ day
49 Transplantable soil and grass
50 Health treatment resort
53 "I will give you _____" (Matt. 11:28)
55 Toy construction set
57 Southeast Asian plant
60 Act like Gadarene madman
62 Aviation prefix
63 Means "character" in Greek
64 Judea or Galilee, for example
65 Andrew's fishing needs
66 Jesus fasted forty _____
67 The Prodigal son lived in pigs' _____
68 Church part

DOWN

1 "Take up his _____, and follow" (Mark 8:34)
2 Paul's house arrest city, and namesakes
3 Holy Land oil
4 Andrew's brother, for short
5 "Put it on Facebook!" (2 words)
6 Synthetic resin
7 Downwind
8 "Light is _____ for the righteous" (Ps. 97:11)
9 Trinity number
10 Big truck
11 God number
12 _____ Moines, IA
15 Tarmac
20 "Call his _____ Jesus" (Matt. 1:21)
22 Impatient
26 In the area
27 Lacking liveliness or animation
28 Church music selection, maybe
29 Proverbs' industrious insect
30 Tactile arterial palpitation
31 Patmos, for one
33 Defrosts

34 Large group of people
35 Abraham's son
36 Jesus was _____ in Bethlehem
39 42 Across not to contain _____
40 Number days of creation
42 Section of fence or railing
43 Rise and fall of sea levels
46 Asian peninsula nations
48 Don't fiddle with their middles
49 Number of loaves that fed a multitude

50 "_____ places shall fall" (Ezek. 38:20)
51 Tyre and Sidon, e.g.
52 "He _____ and followed him" (Mark 2:14)
54 Don't fall into one
56 Jesus' first miracle town
57 "Arise, take up thy _____" (Matt. 9:6)
58 Airport data (abbr.)
59 "_____ kingdom come"
61 "We _____ the children of God" (Rom. 8:16)

BIBLE KIDS

ACROSS

1 Seize
5 "I will _____ all that afflict thee" (Zeph. 3:19)
9 Anointing substances
13 "Sun to _____ by day" (Ps. 136:8)
14 Ark grouping
15 "Delete that!" (2 words)
16 Give off
17 Nazareth for child Jesus
18 Solomon "had _____ a navy of Tharshish" (1 Kings 10:22) (2 words)
19 David's disloyal son
21 Ruth's little one
23 Make lace
24 Priest to boy Samuel
25 Crustacean related to shrimp and crab
29 One bringing loaves, fishes to Jesus
30 Information
32 First mom
33 Where 20 Down walks
36 Andrew's brother
37 Summer mo.
38 Like Esau's meat
39 What magi brought baby Jesus
40 LA school

41 Progressive party member (abbr.)
42 Like Swiss cheese
43 Forgiveness _____ the soul from guilt
44 Stretch to make do
45 Cana water container, perhaps
46 Prohibit
47 Headdress
49 "It shall be _____ with" the wicked (Isa. 3:11)
50 What God feels toward sin
53 "There is none _____ beside him" (Deut. 4:35)
55 David's wise son
57 To get by begging
60 Blue hue
62 Having a common boundary
63 "_____ not, nor be dismayed" (1 Chron. 22:13)
64 "It shall bruise thy _____" (Gen. 3:15)
65 Devilish tactic
66 Paul, a _____ maker by trade
67 Christ "hath _____ suffered for sins" (1 Pet. 3:18)
68 Samuel, for one

DOWN

1 Herod the _____
2 Ballroom dance
3 Favored-guests (2 words)
4 Alpha follower
5 "_____ me with thy free spirit" (Ps. 51:12)
6 Obed's grandmother (Ruth 4:17)
7 "Eyes of Israel were _____ for age" (Gen. 48:10)
8 Black-and-white snack
9 Beat, win
10 Common contraction
11 "Faithful witness will not _____" (Prov. 14:5)

12 Depot (abbr.)
15 _____ Augustus
20 "Little child shall _____ them" (Isa. 11:6)
22 What a mosquito does
26 Jesus, Prince of _____
27 Small egg
28 Ballerina painter
29 "_____ up...treasures in heaven" (Matt. 6:20)
30 Submit, as to God's wil
31 Was missing at Jesus' trial (abbr.)
33 Plastic piece at the end of shoelace
34 Japanese poem

35 Sodom remain
36 Stack, as of wood
39 Choir robes
40 See 45 Across
42 Jesus _____ Jairus' daughter
43 Eden event, with "The"
46 Fair-haired girl (var.)
48 "Fathered", KJV-style
49 Abraham's boy
50 Permeate

51 Elijah would _____ Zarephath widow's son (1 Kings 17)
52 "_____ into the kingdom of God"
54 Alpine sound
56 36 Across needs
57 Omaha summer hour (abbr.)
58 "Blessed _____ the merciful" (Matt. 5:7)
59 Dan.'s temporary abode
61 Desire

CAIN: FIRST BORN

ACROSS

1 "Began ___ to call upon the name of the LORD" (Gen. 4:26)
4 Cain did not feel this as a vagabond (Gen. 4:14)
8 Meat stew
14 Battle tool in 1 Sam. 13:20 (var.)
15 Off-Broadway award
16 Acceptance of Abel's gift would do this to Cain (Gen. 4:5)
17 Owner of the Technicolor Dreamcoat, familiarly
18 "If haply they might ___ after him" (Acts 17:27)
19 First name in mysteries
20 Cain may have felt like one among other men
22 God ___ Cain live
23 God told Cain to "___ over" temptation (Gen. 4:7)
24 Cain was banished east of here (Gen. 4:16)
27 Files
31 Peasant
33 Distress call
35 Forbidden to a Nazarite (Judg. 13:7)
36 God said to Cain's father, "In the sweat of thy face shalt thou ___ bread" (Gen. 3:19)
38 Long time
39 What a student might do the night before a test

40 Adam ___ the blame to Eve for their sin
44 An Iraqi's southern neighbor
46 Wise men came from this direction (Matt. 2:1)
47 Cain's dwelling place (Gen. 4:16)
49 Oxygen
50 Form of communication (abbr.)
51 ___ Giovanni, Mozart opera
52 Dish at many Thanksgiving feasts
55 Cain's brother kept these (Gen. 4:2)
58 "The ___ is not to the swift" (Eccl. 9:11)
61 "There was a swarm of ___ and honey" (Judg. 14:8)
63 ___ Lanka
65 Italian dish
67 Eli was this to Samuel
70 Wrap a flag, e.g.
71 Pastor, familiarly
72 One-celled water creature (var.)
73 Soft white cheese
74 Winter hazard
75 God said to Cain, "Now art thou ___ from the earth" (Gen. 4:11)
76 What Gomorrah might have looked like
77 Eve said of Cain, "I have gotten a ___ from the LORD" (Gen. 4:1)

DOWN

1 Isa. is considered a ___ prophet
2 Second book of the Bible
3 "Eye of a ___" (Mark 10:25)
4 Living room furniture piece
5 White poplar
6 Site of Abel's death (Gen. 4:8)
7 Conger
8 Cain's fear of God's punishment was this
9 God expressed this toward Cain (Gen. 4:10)
10 Persona non ___
11 Horse morsel

12 Good reaction to sin
13 Can be made with a bag
21 Cain felt ___ of hope (Gen. 4:14)
25 Tel Aviv to Jerusalem (dir.)
26 Cranny partner
28 Eastern garment
29 Perhaps what Cain farmed
30 Very large truck
32 Abel gave his best beast "and of the ___ thereof" (Gen. 4:4)
34 How a bug in a rug feels

37 Cain would do this to his crops

39 Sweet melon

40 "Waters called he ___" (Gen. 1:10)

41 Discuss with, over

42 Paphos is on one

43 God warned Cain, "sin lieth at the ___" (Gen. 4:7)

45 Woe to those who "have gone in the ___ of Cain" (Jude 11)

48 Genetic code (abbr.)

53 Dizziness

54 Roman statesman

56 ___ Park, CO destination

57 God would do this to Cain concerning Abel (Gen. 4:9)

59 There are these on this page

60 Cain said, "Thou hast driven me out. . .from the face of the ___" (Gen. 4:14)

62 Multiple of punishment due a killer of Cain (Gen. 4:15)

64 Cain's grandson (Gen. 4:18)

66 "Every one that findeth me shall ___ me" (Gen. 4:14)

67 Apple computer

68 Flightless bird

69 "Remember not the sins. . .___ my transgressions" (Ps. 25:7)

70 Org. of aspiring tillers of the field

PROPHETS AND PROPHECIES

ACROSS

1 Festival or feast
5 "Be not _____ with thy mouth" (Eccl. 5:2)
9 Samuel foretold his kingdom's loss
13 Nobleman
14 Sandwich spread
15 Obstruct, as wicked scheme
16 _____ will flourish during last days
17 Gush out
18 Paris pancake
19 OT judge and prophetess
21 "Elder…serve the younger" elder son (Gen. 25:23)
23 Caesarea to Jerusalem (dir.)
24 Distinctive period of time
25 Inviolate
29 "_____ of the Lord will come" (2 Pet. 3:10)
30 Agabus tied himself with Paul's to prophesy
32 Menu term (2 words)
33 "Time to awake out of _____" (Rom. 13:11)
36 Jesus' betrayer
37 "_____ flesh is unclean" (Lev. 13:15)
38 Lunch order, maybe (2 words)
39 Jesus' would not be broken (Ps. 34:20)
40 Jesus would be _____ in Bethlehem (Mic. 5:2)

41 Sunbeam
42 Put in sync
43 Quirky
44 Rambunctious toddler
45 Beginning of Belshazzar's message on the wall
46 Soldiers took Jesus, "_____ him away" (John 19:16)
47 Big snake
49 Do not _____ for highest place (Luke 14:10)
50 "Gotcha!"
53 Creative
55 Narrow strip of land
57 "I make _____ enemies thy footstool" (Luke 20:43)
60 Wise men came from there
62 Congers
63 "My _____ shall not pass away" (Matt. 24:35)
64 Healthy food choice
65 "Who shall be _____ to stand?" (Rev. 6:17)
66 Everyone _____ God thanks and praise
67 God has good one for you
68 "I am...the first and the _____" (Rev. 22:13)

DOWN

1 Jesus _____ 5,000
2 Roof overhangs
3 Dan or Asher, e.g.
4 Cockney greeting
5 Prayer beads
6 "I am _____ and Omega" (Rev. 22:13)
7 "We shall _____ him as he is" (1 John 3:2)
8 Sewing machine inventor
9 Prideful prance
10 Yes vote
11 Sports official, for short
12 Soap substance
15 Form of undergarment for men

20 Sow goodness, "_____ in mercy" (Hos. 10:12)
22 Paul's companion
26 Israel's first priest
27 Actor Gable
28 Brownish-orange color
29 "Gloria in Excelsis _____"
30 Cask stoppers
31 First home
33 Soldiers would _____ Jesus of his clothes
34 Soil descriptor
35 From "_____ have I called my son" (Matt. 2:15)

36 "Let us _____ ourselves" to God (Jer. 50:5)
39 Combined (arch.)
40 "Israel shall blossom and _____" (Isa. 27:6)
42 Italian loves
43 Prophesied pierced in Ps. 22:16
46 KJV's "hearken"
48 See 43 Down
49 Scenic view, as from Temple Mount
50 One-celled animal

51 Outer shells
52 Good characteristic
54 Dog's sound
56 Jesus would _____ the sick
57 "Sharp sword with _____ edges" (Rev. 2:12)
58 "_____ long, O Lord?" (Rev. 6:10)
59 Anger
61 Suffer

Day 41

GIFTS OF THE SPIRIT

ACROSS

1 "Power of Christ may __ upon me" (2 Cor. 12:9)
5 Prominent fellow
10 Vane dir.
13 Dole out
15 Where many martyrs died
16 Haw's partner
17 It justifies believers
18 Swine "ran violently down a __ place into the sea" (Mark 5:13)
19 Jesus began His ministry at about thirty years of __
20 Explosive (abbr.)
21 "Envy __ the bones" (Prov. 14:30 NIV)
23 Creatures "hath been __ of mankind" (James 3:7)
25 We are "baptized into one __" (1 Cor. 12:13)
26 Holy threesome
28 Holy Spirit "__ you by our gospel" (2 Thess. 2:14)
31 KJV "Spirit"
32 Columbia, Cornell, and Dartmouth, for short
33 Pack of paper
34 Curtsy

37 Health food store staple
38 Wishy-washy
40 Former Italian currency
41 Poor man had "one little __ lamb" (2 Sam. 12:3)
42 Voting group
43 Hand lotion brand
44 Fruit of the Spirit
45 Spirit-given insight
46 Classic TV detective
49 "I __ up by Revelation" (Gal. 2:2)
50 Paris "bye"
51 "If ye __ and devour one another" (Gal. 5:15)
52 Airport info (abbr.)
55 French possessive
56 Converted by the Spirit
59 "Blessed are they that __" (Matt. 5:4)
61 Before (poet.)
62 Have being
63 Moses' brother
64 Hallucinogenic drug (abbr.)
65 Spiritual result of disbelief
66 Mariana "Peaceful Island"

DOWN

1 Huckleberry Finn's ride
2 Dash
3 Needle's eye, for one
4 Little one
5 Abhorrent to the Spirit
6 Satanic __, forbidden by the Spirit
7 Garden buzzer
8 Three Persons, __ God
9 Sacrament
10 Indian lamb kebab
11 Sire
12 Like a field sown with sin, according to parable

14 "I'm in the __ of death" (2 Sam. 1:9 NIV)
22 Strange
24 "Go to the __, thou sluggard" (Prov. 6:6)
25 Sky shade (Fr.)
26 "If children, __ heirs" (Rom. 8:17)
27 Spirit keeps you on the right one
28 Refer to
29 Declare
30 Spirit's gift to you
31 God's mercy
34 Holy Spirit symbol
35 Don't fiddle with its middle
36 Is there none in Gilead?

38 Yap
39 Insane (Sp.)
40 Spirit's no-no
42 Bewildered
43 Movie theater
44 Poet Edgar Allen
45 Like the Sea of Galilee
46 Sinai sight
47 Bad smells
48 Wrinkled

49 Measurement for Noah's ark
51 "Covet earnestly the __ gifts" (1 Cor. 12:31)
52 Vacation money, perhaps
53 Horse's gait
54 Spirit-filled temple prophetess
57 "The __ is laid unto the root of the trees" (Luke 3:9)
58 Through
60 Peter's need

Day 42

GOD'S PROMISES

ACROSS

1 Sicilian volcano
5 Paul's travels, often (2 words)
10 Wheel's tooth
13 Book holder
15 Musician/poet Leonard
16 Tokyo tie
17 God promises you this to do great things
18 Foot parts
19 Sports figure, for short
20 Holy Land edible
21 "John and...Pharisees __ to fast" (Mark 2:18)
23 "Every day they __ my words" (Ps. 56:5)
25 At Jesus' trial, a soldier __ Him
26 "Hast thou not poured me out...and curdled me like __?" (Job 10:10)
28 God promises you this as you walk His way
31 Hymn sound
32 Mirror shapes, often
33 Intones a rhyming patter, e.g.
34 Make taboo
37 Frolic

38 Gain a point
40 God promises you this always
41 Psalm 23 creature
42 Sin, e.g.
43 Author Carroll
44 God promises comfort when you do this
45 Sinner __ to temptation
46 Princess dress, e.g.
49 King David's dad, familiarly
50 Repeal
51 God promises you this when you're burdened
52 Offense against God
55 River (Sp.)
56 Crete and Cyprus, e.g.
59 Bring joy
61 Put treasures "where neither moth __ rust doth corrupt" (Matt. 6:20)
62 God promises to provide these
63 God promises to __ leave you
64 GPS letters
65 They come in gaggles
66 New product ad, perhaps

DOWN

1 Sports channel
2 KJV pronoun
3 Salamander
4 Brew
5 God's comfort soothes these
6 Has digits
7 Mary or Martha, e.g.
8 Conger
9 God promises these when you pray
10 Apples have them
11 Extremely heavy
12 Spirit's favors
14 "Bring forth...__ worthy of repentance" (Luke 3:8)
22 Pigpen
24 "Behold a great __ dragon" (Rev. 12:3)

25 God's assistance
26 What fire and brimstone do
27 We have this for the future
28 Lazarus's affliction
29 Declare
30 Jesus' "__ spread abroad" (Mark 1:28)
31 Heavenly promise
34 One of seven poured out in Rev.
35 Passionate
36 Loch __ monster
38 Ghetto
39 God promises that He will __ about you
40 Dregs
42 Hitting player while they're shooting
43 God promises to do this when you pray

44 Computer data handler (abbr.)
45 "Amen!"
46 Chili con __
47 Hamburger enhancement, maybe
48 Sleep sound
49 Jesus, Root of __
51 Color wheel section

52 God promises to __ those who believe
53 Detail
54 Roman persecutor of Christians
57 God promises to __ you wherever you are
58 Downwind
60 "They had bound him, they __ him away" (Matt. 27:2)

Day 43

"SIMON, SIMON. . ."

ACROSS

1 An early city of the tribe of Judah (Josh. 15:26)
5 "Behold the _____ of God!" (John 1:36)
9 A **SIMON** who had an infamous son named _____ (John 13:26)
14 "Nothing" in Nogales
15 A grandson of Esau (Gen. 36:10–11)
16 "We spend our years as _____ that is told" (Ps. 90:9) (2 words)
17 "_____ with joy receiveth it" (Matt. 13:20)
18 "Change my _____, because I am perplexed" (Gal. 4:20 NIV)
19 Faux silk
20 A **SIMON** from Samaria who practiced _____ (Acts 8:9, 11 NIV)
22 Ukrainian capital
24 "_____ God blessed them" (Gen. 1:22)
25 Short literary pieces
27 A **SIMON**, one of the twelve, called _____ (Luke 6:15)
30 Canadian First Nation member
32 City in Harar province, Ethiopia
33 "Stand in _____, and sin not" (Ps. 4:4)
36 "They may _____ whole month" (Num. 11:21) (2 words)
38 "O God, do not _____ my plea" (Ps. 55:1 NIV)

42 A **SIMON** as Jesus addressed him (John 21:15) (4 words)
45 Artist's workplace
46 Lute, harp, and piano ensemble
47 "Neither hath the _____ seen" (Isa. 64:4)
48 "_____ my Father are one" (John 10:30) (2 words)
50 "Keep a tight _____ on his tongue" (James 1:26 NIV)
52 A **SIMON** who lived by the sea and was _____ (Acts 10:6) (2 words)
55 Epitomes of slowness
59 "_____ his son" (1 Chron. 7:27)
60 "Some would even _____ to die" (Rom. 5:7)
63 One of the seven first deacons (Acts 6:5)
64 Dizzy with joy
67 "God _____ the increase" (1 Cor. 3:6)
69 Bathe
70 "Death will _____ them" (Rev. 9:6 NIV)
71 "An _____ for every man" (Ex.16:16)
72 "Had no _____ who it was" (John 5:13 NIV)
73 A **SIMON** living in Bethany who was a _____ (Matt. 26:6)
74 "Where are the _____?" (Luke 17:17)
75 Social misfit

DOWN

1 "He had _____ written" (Rev. 19:12) (2 words)
2 "I said, Should such a _____ I flee?" (Neh. 6:11) (2 words)
3 "Am I _____ head" (2 Sam. 3:8) (2 words)
4 "The inspired man a _____" (Hos. 9:7 NIV)
5 "From the _____ of our inheritance" (Num. 36:3)
6 "Sallu, _____, Hilkiah" (Neh. 12:7)
7 "What a wretched _____ am!" (Rom. 7:24 NIV) (2 words)

8 "A passing _____ that does not return" (Ps. 78:39 NIV)
9 "With her _____ on her shoulder" (Gen. 24:45 NIV)
10 Actress Hagen
11 "Then the same _____ evening" (John 20:19) (2 words)
12 "He _____ on the land" (Mark 6:47)
13 "He _____ you abundant showers" (Joel 2:23 NIV)
21 A **SIMON** who bore the cross for Jesus and was a _____ (Mark 15:21)

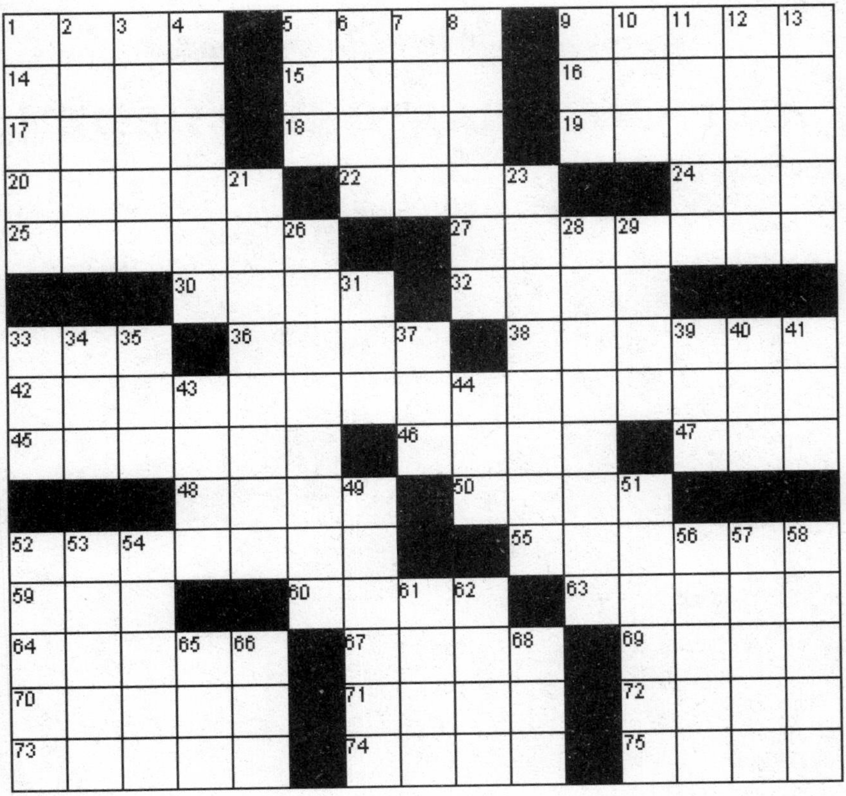

23 Substantiates

26 "Wherewith shall it be _______?" (Luke 14:34)

28 Knee (2 words)

29 "Whether he be a sinner _______, I know not" (John 9:25) (2 words)

31 Arena where 65 Down commanded (abbr.)

33 "The foal of an ______" (Matt. 21:5)

34 "To _______, Israel" (Neh. 11:3)

35 Australian big bird

37 "Go to the _______, thou sluggard" (Prov. 6:6)

39 "Love _______ another" (1 John 3:23)

40 "Without a _______ of brightness?" (Amos 5:20 NIV)

41 NNE + 90 degrees

43 Viking's Zeus

44 Hockey's Bobby

49 "Wounded the _______?" (Isa. 51:9)

51 "To give us a _______ his holy place" (Ezra 9:8) (2 words)

52 "It is his _______" (Acts 12:15)

53 Sheer fabric

54 "On to Daberath _______ to Japhia" (Josh. 19:12 NIV) (2 words)

56 "Which _______ before Titus" (2 Cor. 7:14) (2 words)

57 "A _______ of good men" (Titus 1:8)

58 Golfer Sammy

61 "The two-horned _______ had seen" (Dan. 8:6 NIV) (2 words)

62 "And, behold, I, ______ I" (Gen. 6:17)

65 WWII general (initials)

66 "Your" to a hillbilly

68 "_______ the lamp of God went out" (1 Sam. 3:3)

BIBLICAL BEASTS OF BURDEN

ACROSS

1 "To whom I shall give _____" (John 13:26) (2 words)
5 "They made a calf in _____" (Ps. 106:19)
10 "For thou art my _____" (Ps. 71:5)
14 "With the _____ grain offering" (Num. 28:12 NIV) (2 words)
15 "But I am afraid that just _____ was deceived" (2 Cor. 11:3 NIV) (2 words)
16 "_____ when we were dead in sins" (Eph. 2:5)
17 "Throughout all _____, world without end" (Eph. 3:21)
18 Doomed one
19 "And they were _____ before the king" (Est. 6:1)
20 **BEAST** and burden referred to in Jer. 51:21 NIV (3 words)
23 Office of Natural Resources (abbr.)
24 Classical Portuguese writer _____ Miranda (2 words)
25 "_____ na na"
28 "And what _____ this day unto these" (Gen. 31:43) (3 words)
31 "Give everyone what you _____" (Rom. 13:7 NIV) (2 words)
33 Prince Valiant's son
34 **BEAST** of burden prophesied in Zech. 9:9 (4 words)
37 Nugget source
39 "I wouldn't do that for all the _____ in China!"
40 "In the _____ of the land of Edom" (Num. 33:37)

41 **BEAST** carrying "Faithful and True" found in Rev. 19:11 (3 words)
46 "Went Jesus _____ of the house" (Matt. 13:1)
47 "Into the _____ one of them survived" (Ex.14:28 NIV) (2 words)
48 "Their dead were _____ along the Shaaraim road" (1 Sam. 17:52 NIV)
50 "Wherewith the _____ number of them is" (Num. 3:48)
51 Expression of resignation (2 words)
54 "Four days _____ I was fasting until this hour" (Acts 10:30)
55 **BEAST** with a question (Num. 22:28 NIV) (2 words)
61 Former boxer Max
63 "Sat like a _____ in the desert" (Jer. 3:2 NIV)
64 "Seeing _____ stranger?" (Ruth 2:10) (3 words)
65 Part of a list
66 "All her vows, _____ her bonds" (Num. 30:14) (2 words)
67 "And Anab, and Eshtemoh, and _____" (Josh. 15:50)
68 "Lest ye _____ your God" (Josh. 24:27)
69 Column of items in Paris
70 "Mending their _____" (Matt. 4:21)

DOWN

1 "The children of _____, six hundred fifty and two" (Neh. 7:10)
2 Asian palm tree
3 "An _____ for every man" (Ex.16:16)
4 "After that ye shall _____" (Gen. 18:5) (2 words)
5 "What is the matter, _____ not be afraid" (Gen. 21:17 NIV) (2 words)
6 "But thou, _____ of man" (Ezek. 3:25) (2 words)

7 Tears
8 "For Hiram was _____ lover of David" (1 Kings 5:1) (2 words)
9 "Your houses may _____ the frogs" (Ex.8:9 NIV) (3 words)
10 "_____ am I; send me" (Isa. 6:8)
11 "The power of the Highest shall _____ thee" (Luke 1:35)
12 It's split in soup

13 "An _____ is come" (Ezek. 7:6)
21 Star in Pegasus
22 "Out the _____ bowlful of water" (Judg. 6:38 NIV) (2 words)
26 A policeman's defense (2 words)
27 "And I _____ in my ward whole nights" (Isa. 21:8) (2 words)
28 "Immediately a rooster _____" (Matt. 26:74 NIV)
29 "Alive, _____ seen of her" (Mark 16:11) (3 words)
30 "And his _____ unto Isaac" (Ps. 105:9)
32 Halfway between due east and northeast (abbr.)
33 "And Josh. said, _____ Lord GOD" (Josh. 7:7) (2 words)
35 Baseball's Durocher
36 "Wherein shall go no galley with _____" (Isa. 33:21)

38 "One" in Essen (Ger.)
42 "For if thou lift up thy _____ upon it" (Ex. 20:25)
43 Gasoline additive
44 Hay platform
45 Consequently
49 Pertaining to a very long time
52 New Zealand native
53 Namesakes of Ms. Lazarus
56 "An exceeding great _____" (Ezek. 37:10)
57 "Ye are the _____ of the earth" (Matt. 5:13)
58 Welles's citizen
59 Give off
60 Sweet potatoes down South
61 "For me, except I _____ thee" (2 Kings 4:24)
62 "And _____ it up" (Rev. 10:10)

JOURNEYS

ACROSS

1 Concepts
6 "Ponder the _____ of thy feet" (Prov. 4:26)
10 Jazz style
13 Landing strip
15 Double reed instrument
16 Important baseball stat
17 Prawn
18 Writer Bombeck
19 TV network
20 32 Across home
22 He went from Ur to 48 Down
24 Water (Sp.)
26 Paul was "beaten with _____" (2 Cor. 11:25)
28 Nix
29 Tekoa prophet
30 "_____ not thy face from me" (Ps. 102:2)
31 Blanches
32 "_____ doth gather her brood" (Luke 13:34)
33 "God is _____" (1 John 4:8)
34 Sea bird
35 God reacts _____ to evil
37 32 Across feature

41 "_____ Maria"
42 _____ Spirit, the Counselor
43 In the past
44 Like Prov. fool
47 _____ Hill, Paul's Athens destination
48 Place for baby Jesus
49 John _____, Barnabas' travel companion
50 "Ye are the _____ of the earth" (Matt. 5:13)
51 Lions are big ones
52 God's people in _____ of peace (Ps. 34:14)
54 It comes in a skein
56 Old Glory's nation (abbr.)
57 Ghetto
59 Lad brought five to Jesus
63 _____ lepers healed, one gave thanks
64 Fiery weapon of wicked (Eph. 6:16)
65 OT prophet
66 "Man did _____ angels' food" (Ps. 78:25)
67 Like Paul Ephesus-bound
68 "Fall into...the _____ of the devil" (1 Tim. 3:7)

DOWN

1 "_____ raining!"
2 Dit partner
3 Sin
4 _____ curiae not at Jesus' trial
5 South Pacific nation
6 "Raven" author
7 Scrape
8 Where Jesus laid, and others
9 God will _____ you wherever you are
10 Jacob's ladder dream site
11 Gothic church descriptor
12 John's exile island
14 Naval military rank (abbr.)
21 In the loop, with "to"
23 _____-garde

24 Our Father ender
25 Asian sound maker
27 Ps., maybe
29 "Gotcha!"
30 Fox has one, per Luke 9:58
31 Talk to God
33 "He shall _____ for ever" (John 6:51)
34 Snaky fish
36 Crowd "sat down in _____" (Mark 6:40)
37 Years Israelites wandered in desert
38 KJV "deer"
39 Sponsorship (var.)
40 Bandits would often _____ travelers
42 *Space Odyssey* computer
44 "Lord will not _____ sin" (Rom. 4:8)

45 67 Across common ailment
46 Without moderation; out-and-out
47 Faithful people _____ spiritually
48 Israelites' destination
50 Paul's traveling companion
51 Jesus' Calvary destination
53 National food organization

55 _____ Baba
58 NYC transit org.
60 _____ Dolorosa, Jesus' route
61 "Give _____ to his commandments" (Ex. 15:26)
62 Pronoun for Mary

RIGHT LIVING

ACROSS

1 Follows "forever and ever"
5 Book holder
10 A pastor must be "_____to teach" (1 Tim. 3:2)
13 Title for Jesus
15 Moral no-no
16 London cuppa
17 God will "Give thee a _____ of life" (Rev. 2:10)
18 A shelter of vines or branches
19 You must sit to have one
20 As a "_____ gathereth her chickens" (Matt. 23:37)
21 "_____ of my bones" (Gen. 2:23)
23 "Continue in the _____ of God" (Acts 13:43)
25 Graph feature
26 Wanted poster data
28 Jacob's new name
31 His disciples were _____ to Jesus' words
32 Cookbook direction
33 The world is _____ with wickedness
34 Truthful person's no-no
37 "The greatest of these" in 1 Corinthians 13

38 Do not turn _____ from God's commandments
40 Manna for Israelites
41 Ps. 23 concern
42 _____ & Span cleaner brand
43 Delight
44 "Let your light _____!"
45 Logger
46 Tropical fruit
49 Brightness or warmth of color
50 To position rightly, as with God's will
51 Regretted, as misdeed
52 Give God "glory _____ unto his name" (1 Chron. 16:29)
55 _____ Commandments
56 Moderator
59 Flip over
61 36 Down figure
62 Twelve were sent into Canaan
63 Firm, as God's promises
64 Moses parted the _____ Sea
65 KJV commandment word
66 Have "_____ upon the poor" (Prov. 19:17)

DOWN

1 Jerusalem pass-through
2 Stallion's ark partner
3 Black
4 Sinai to Egypt (dir.)
5 "Foolish shall not _____" before God (Ps. 5:5)
6 OT unclean animal
7 Flow's partner
8 Old card game
9 We must _____ others their misdeeds
10 Map book
11 A clear conscience means _____ of mind
12 Scotch products
14 Present from birth
22 Olive _____, a Holy Land product

24 Sunbeam
25 Galilee storm maker
26 Like the Sinai Desert
27 Jesus gave His _____ for us
28 Patmos descriptor
29 Flat-bottomed boat
30 What the Gergesene madman would do
31 Jesus paid the _____ of sin
34 Parable sower's favorite soil
35 Small amount
36 61 Across garden
38 Samoan capital
39 Commits wrongs
40 What angels did
42 Timidity

43 The Commandments book
44 Droop
45 Brew
46 _____ Noster, Lord's prayer
47 Pain reliever brand
48 Longed, with "for"
49 Parable wedding attender

51 Rod partner
52 Sandwich purveyor
53 Bible study section, e.g.
54 Whirlpool
57 Dashboard information
58 Clandestine org.
60 What balloons do

DANIEL: THE LION TAMER

Day 47

ACROSS

1 Daniel chose the ___ of righteousness
5 What Daniel heard as the door to the lions' den closed, maybe
9 Daniel's face was not this after refusing the king's food
13 Great Lake
14 "Take thee a ___, and lay it before thee" (Ezek. 4:1)
15 Painting prop
16 Daniel was given a new one of these (Daniel 1:7)
17 "___, Father" (Mark 14:36)
18 Plant part
19 Daniel and his friends "had ___ in them" (Dan. 1:4)
21 Subject of Nebuchadnezzar's dream (Dan. 4:10)
23 Hallucinogen (abbr.)
24 Spy guys' org.
25 Daniel would do this from the lions' den
29 Luke, familiarly (Col. 4:14)
30 Nick
32 "Do they not ___ that devise evil?" (Prov. 14:22)
33 Adam and Eve each made one (Gen. 3:7)
36 Nathan may have done this as he said, "Thou art the man" (2 Sam. 12:7)
37 Man has dominion "over the fowl of the ___" (Gen. 1:26)
38 Subject of Daniel's vision (Dan. 8:5)
39 "He sent divers ___ of flies among them" (Ps. 78:45)
40 Dog food brand
41 Actress MacGraw
42 Daniel's pussycats
43 Marcel Marceau, for one
44 "Prove thy servants. . .___ days" (Dan. 1:12)
45 Sight the king expected would be left in the fiery furnace
46 Where Nebuchadnezzar dreamed (Dan. 2:29)
47 Compositions
49 Beige
50 Tweak
53 "___ of the kingdom" (Matt. 16:19)
55 Daniel could not have this on him (Dan. 1:4)
57 Burnt color
60 Asian country
62 For sure, Daniel was not this (Daniel 1:4)
63 Wall word (Daniel 5:28)
64 Volcano
65 Guards probably did this to the lions' den
66 Psalmist's bed did this (Ps. 6:6)
67 Daniel would ___ it wrong to eat the king's food (Daniel 1:8)
68 Humorist Bombeck

DOWN

1 Inability to interpret the king's dreams was a ___ offense (Daniel 2:5)
2 Persians' neighbors
3 Stepping forward to interpret the king's dreams, Daniel was not this (Dan. 5:17)
4 "Thou shalt bruise his ___" (Gen. 3:15)
5 Lions were this with Daniel
6 African nation
7 Clerical garment
8 "In it was ___ for all"(Daniel 4:12)
9 Recipient
10 Form of communication
11 Downwind
12 Idols were worshipped under this (Hos. 4:13)
15 Daniel was not ___ from the king's decree (Dan. 6:13)
20 Saintly image of sorts
22 "Try my ___" (Ps. 26:2)
26 Darius set Daniel "over the whole ___" (Dan. 6:3)

27 Even Job did this at times
28 Concerning Daniel, there wasn't "any ___ or fault found in him" (Dan. 6:4)
29 Morse code mark
30 Kansas in August descriptor, according to song
31 Wallops
33 Syrian merchandise (Ezek. 27:16)
34 Sticks
35 Blessings are like these in Ezekiel 34:26
36 What Daniel could have said to the king's magicians
39 No one could call Daniel this
40 Assist
42 Tiers

43 Wall word (Dan. 5:25)
46 Ointment
48 '80s pro-wrestler, ___ the African Dream
49 Steak
50 African country
51 Muslim religion
52 Animal kingdom division
54 Snow vehicle
56 "I ___ on the work of thy hands" (Ps. 143:5)
57 Down's partner
58 What the lions may have said to Dan.
59 Undergarment
61 Daniel never ___ the king's food

DAVID: THE GREAT KING

ACROSS

1 Javelin's results, if David hadn't ducked (1 Sam. 18:11)
6 Essence
10 Saul was more than a ____ jealous of David (1 Sam. 18:8)
13 Balloon filler, often
15 Scandinavian capital
16 See 42 Across
17 Saul's changing moods made him one to David
18 "They. . .burn incense unto their ____" (Hab. 1:16)
19 Might accompany "snow, and vapours," as in Psalm 148:8
20 David's strings (1 Sam. 16:23)
22 David's son (2 Sam. 13:37)
24 Describes the scope of David's experiences
26 "Moab. . .hath settled on his ____" (Jer. 48:11)
28 Jonathan's feelings toward David (1 Sam. 18:1)
29 "Fiddlesticks!"
30 David's popularity was ____ for Saul's jealousy
31 Nathan ____ David's guilt (2 Sam. 12:7)
32 Samuel anointed David with it (1 Sam. 16:13)
33 Absalom gathered one to run ahead of him (2 Sam. 15:1)
34 Min. part
35 Shelve again

37 A hose with a hole is ____
41 Gardener's tool
42 Beverage in the hand of a drunkard, perhaps (Prov. 26:9)
43 Snaky scarf
44 The rich man "____ sumptuously every day" (Luke 16:19)
47 "The Philistines. . .____" (1 Sam. 17:51)
48 Because of David and Bathsheba's sin, "the child ____" (2 Sam. 12:18)
49 Greek god of war
50 Campus military org.
51 David's dad, for short (Ruth 4:17)
52 Saul's jealousy would ____ David's life (1 Sam. 18:11)
54 Joseph's coat had many (Gen. 37:3)
56 Battle with no winner
57 Opposing (dial.)
59 Absalom set himself up as a ____ ruler (2 Sam. 15:2–4)
63 "As a ____ doth gather her brood" (Luke 13:34)
64 "Git!"
65 Web cruiser
66 Booming transport (abbr.)
67 Battlefield casualty, often
68 David's weapon (1 Sam. 17:49)

DOWN

1 Referring to Michal (1 Sam. 14:49)
2 "Ascribed unto David ____ thousands" (1 Sam. 18:8)
3 ____ Baba
4 David was one with the crowds (1 Sam. 18:8) (2 words)
5 Berried shrub, often poisonous
6 "Defy the armies of the living ____?" (1 Sam. 17:26)
7 "Established him king over ____" (2 Sam. 5:12)
8 Thick slices

9 Jonathan gave David his (1 Sam. 18:4)
10 Dorcas was one (Acts 9:39)
11 Shelf for a religious object, perhaps
12 Saul ____ David too young to challenge Goliath (1 Sam. 17:33)
14 Priests' advice: "Make. . .images of your mice that ____ the land" (1 Sam. 6:5)
21 Sound of Goliath when he fell, maybe (1 Sam. 17:49)
23 Alas! partner
24 Great Lakes city
25 Describes David and Jonathan (1 Sam. 18:1)

27 Brain wave tracker (abbr.)
29 Conquered by Josh. (Josh. 12:23)
30 David's plea to God: "Hide thy ___ from my sins" (Ps. 51:9)
31 "Thy servant kept his father's sheep" from one (1 Sam. 17:34)
33 "He hath requited me evil for ___" (1 Sam. 25:21)
34 Jonathan to David: "The LORD be between me and thee, and between my ___ and thy seed for ever" (1 Sam. 20:42)
36 "David laid up ___ words in his heart" (1 Sam. 21:12)
37 Hanger-on
38 Wading bird
39 Responses to Saul's order to kill David (1 Sam. 19:1-2)
40 David's seer's name (2 Sam. 24:11)

42 Bacon-lettuce-tomato sandwich
44 In Athens, Paul found many (Acts 17:22-23)
45 "The God of the ___ of Israel" (1 Sam. 17:45)
46 What Nathan's story led David to do (2 Sam. 12:13)
47 Folded sheets of paper
48 David's cry: "Render to them their ___" (Ps. 28:4)
50 "David did that which was ___ in the eyes of the LORD" (1 Kings 15:5)
51 David's kingly descendent (Matt. 1:1)
53 Grating sound
55 FedEx competitor
58 East of Eden land (Gen. 4:16)
60 Suspicious aircraft (abbr.)
61 Where Dan. spent time with lions (Dan. 6:16)
62 Silver or gold, e.g.

CHRISTIAN LIFE

ACROSS

1 People salute them
6 Slumps
10 Christian __ of heaven
14 Juliet's love
15 Christians __ others
16 Be "perfect, __ as your Father...is perfect" (Matt. 5:48)
17 Where grasses of fields go, according to Jesus
18 What lionlike adversary does, according to Peter
19 Sea of Galilee transport
20 Lady's man, for short
21 Sabbath Day
23 Winter hazard
24 "I Am Jesus' Little __"
26 Metal joiner
28 Lesotho capital
31 Choir section
32 Joppa to Jerusalem (dir.)
33 Herons
36 Dog's breakfast, maybe
40 Former New York stadium

42 Bishop must be "__ to teach" (1 Tim. 3:2)
43 Steadfast, as in faith
44 Sabbath song
45 Christian talk with God
48 Old evil __
49 Christian should not tell one
51 High church service, often
53 __ song, contemporary worship music
56 Fencing sword
57 Desire, with "for"
58 Played (2 words)
61 Tap in lightly
65 Drags
67 Christian cares for body and __
68 First name in cosmetics
69 Nobel Prize city
70 "Repent; or __ I will come" (Rev. 2:16)
71 Marketplace where Paul spoke
72 Christian might ask God for this
73 KJV "hart"
74 Lassos

DOWN

1 Plague pest
2 What fills Christian's heart
3 Final word for 45 Across
4 Ideal Christian words and actions
5 Steelwool soap pad brand
6 Banished Hagar laid her child under one
7 Billions of years
8 "Rejoice and be __"
9 Spreads out
10 NT book after Philemon (abbr.)
11 Elliptic
12 "__ be with you"
13 "__ not into temptation" (Matt. 26:41)
21 Christian should not be this
22 Pet. drew in great catch, "__ was not the net broken" (John 21:11)

25 KJV "art"
27 While away the time
28 Web
29 Sodom, after fire and brimstone fell
30 "If any man __ to be contentious" (1 Cor. 11:16)
31 Court counselor (abbr.)
34 "Lips that speak knowledge are a __ jewel" (Prov. 20:15 NIV)
35 Climate watchdog group (abbr.)
37 Christian's have eternal __
38 Teen dance event
39 Bad one means trouble ahead
41 Against (prefix)
45 "My beloved Son, in whom I am well __" (Matt. 3:17)

46 Sports channel
47 KJV "antelope"
50 17 Across remains
52 Christian ___ of bitterness (2 words)
53 Tall post
54 Recyclers do this
55 Point of view
56 Swiss mathematician

59 Portion, with "out"
60 Christian should not have a short one
62 At the peak of
63 Christians know they are a ___ human
64 Green legumes
66 Lawn
68 "First the blade, then the ___" (Mark 4:28)

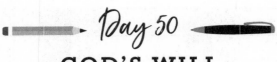

Day 50

GOD'S WILL

ACROSS

1 Carpet choice
5 Former Russian ruler
9 Psalm, e.g.
13 "Moses made a serpent...put it upon a __" (Num. 21:9)
14 Bruins' home (abbr.)
15 God's will: not your weakness, but His __
16 Knows about (2 words)
17 Campus mil. unit
18 What steeple bell does
19 God's will: be __ with what you have
21 Style
23 Work unit
24 Former military, for short
25 Not two masters, "for __ he will hate the one..." (Matt. 6:24)
29 God's will: bring this to those who need help
30 Cloaks and togas, e.g.
32 KJV "art"
33 "__ to the glory of God" (1 Cor. 10:31) (2 words)
36 Mealtime no-no
37 Israelite tribe
38 God's will: be a __ steward

39 Mentions certain authorities
40 Foolish remark, sometimes
41 __ Baba
42 God's will: be harmless as __
43 Gardeners' needs
44 Bible land sea
45 Detail
46 God's will: be courageous, not __
47 One most liberated from sin, e.g.
49 Angel's halo, for one
50 Jesus ascended and __ at God's right hand
53 Campus locale, for short
55 Portliness
57 God's Son
60 Humorist Bombeck
62 "Rejoice...__ for joy" (Luke 6:23)
63 Eagle's nest
64 Crucifixion need
65 Gawk
66 Stumble, as into sin
67 Community org.
68 Wickedness, in parables

DOWN

1 Myrrh
2 God's will: __ parents
3 God's will: get __ with others
4 Fellow, for short
5 "Ye __ to God from idols" (1 Thess. 1:9)
6 Composer Francis __ Key
7 Keyboard key (abbr.)
8 God's will: run the __ set before you
9 God's will: __ others toward Him
10 God's will: cast the beam out of your __ eye
11 Brainwave meas. (abbr.)
12 Priscilla to Aquila, today
15 God's will: __ Him with songs of thanksgiving
20 God's will: avoid this!

22 Hosiery choice
26 Hell
27 God's forgiveness will __ guilt
28 "Tears," KJV style
29 Brew
30 OT idolatrous emblem
31 Miners' quests
33 Snow White friend
34 Tanker
35 God's will: do not lay __ His commandments
36 God's will: __ cheerfully
39 Terra __, patio decor
40 God's will: let Him fill your heart with __
42 Neglect

43 God's will: have __ for the future
46 Secret rabbinical doctrines
48 God's Spirit will __ you to do His will
49 Very funny
50 "Set thy face toward the __ of Jerusalem" (Ezek. 4:7)
51 Dickens's __ of Two Cities (2 words)
52 Used a keyboard

54 God's will: __ yourself
56 God's will: be __ to speak
57 James (abbr.)
58 Conger
59 __ Lanka
61 Uncooked

Day 51

SALVATION INSTRUCTIONS

ACROSS

1 "Look from the top of _____" (Song 4:8)
6 He sold his soul
11 "The head of the _____" (Lev. 8:22)
14 French painter
15 "_____ also is joined with them" (Ps. 83:8)
16 "His mother's name also was _____" (2 Kings 18:2)
17 Start of **QUOTE** from Acts 2:21 NIV (2 words)
19 "_____ of renown" (Gen. 6:4)
20 Cowardly lion
21 It may be humble
22 One kind of value
24 Ike's command (abbr.)
25 "Of oil olive an _____" (Ex.30:24)
26 They may be put on
27 **QUOTE**, cont'd (4 words)
33 "This _____ your health" (Acts 27:34) (2 words)
35 "_____ the nations be glad" (Ps. 67:4) (2 words)
36 "The _____ appeareth" (Prov. 27:25)
37 "Casting all your _____ upon him" (1 Pet. 5:7)
38 Low, heavy carts
40 "Never _____ of doing what is right" (2 Thes. 3:13 NIV)

41 "They had a great while _____ repented" (Luke 10:13)
42 "As a _____ offering" (Lev. 5:13)
43 "Then appeared the _____ also" (Matt. 13:26)
44 **QUOTE**, cont'd (4 words)
48 Sandusky's lake
49 "The grove of _____ trees" (Song 6:11 NIV)
50 "Eat not of it _____" (Ex.12:9)
53 "I will _____ the dawn" (Ps. 57:8 NIV)
56 "Unto me men gave _____" (Job 29:21)
57 Actress Hayworth
58 "He said, _____ is a lion's whelp" (Deut. 33:22)
59 End of **QUOTE** (3 words)
62 "I said in my haste, All men _____ liars" (Ps. 116:11)
63 It may surround a lagoon
64 "Jesus saw that a crowd was running to the _____" (Mark 9:25 NIV)
65 "Against her; and she _____ them" (1 Sam. 25:20)
66 Utilize again
67 Edible Asian tubers

DOWN

1 "If it be _____" (Lev. 27:7) (2 words)
2 "Stood every _____ his tent door" (Ex.33:8) (2 words)
3 "_____ infancy you have known the holy Scriptures" (2 Tim. 3:15 NIV) (3 words)
4 At no time (poet.)
5 Four-wheeler (abbr.)
6 Finely milled grain for cooked cereal
7 "As long _____ do well" (1 Pet. 3:6) (2 words)
8 "Not unto _____ Lord" (Ps. 115:1) (2 words)

9 "As surely as the _____" (Hos. 6:3 NIV) (2 words)
10 Silvan fungal infestation (2 words)
11 "In _____ was there a voice" (Matt. 2:18)
12 Cain's brother
13 "I will lift up _____ eyes" (Ps. 121:1)
18 Big heroic tale
23 Familiar US ID
25 "Came unto mount _____" (Num. 20:22)
26 "The Lord's chosen _____" (Isa. 48:14 NIV)
28 "Once cultivated by the _____" (Isa. 7:25 NIV)

29 Reluctant
30 "The name of the _____ is Hiddekel" (Gen. 2:14) (2 words)
31 "The _____, because he cheweth" (Lev. 11:6)
32 "Lift up now thine _____" (Gen. 13:14)
33 "_____ do all things through Christ" (Phil. 4:13) (2 words)
34 A long story about past events or people
38 "I have nothing _____ to write to His Majesty" (Acts 25:26 NIV)
39 "A daily _____ for every day" (2 Kings 25:30)
40 "Coated it with _____ and pitch" (Ex. 2:3 NIV)
42 "There was no _____" (2 Chron. 15:19) (2 words)
43 Toddler

45 Response to a mouse?
46 "To _____ us to serve him" (Luke 1:74 NIV)
47 "I will _____ Sisera" (Judg. 4:7 NIV)
51 "I _____ pleasant bread" (Dan. 10:3) (2 words)
52 Walks in water
53 "For as in _____ all die" (1 Cor. 15:22)
54 "_____ no clothes" (Luke 8:27)
55 "As a wild bull in _____" (Isa. 51:20) (2 words)
56 Right-angle pipes
57 "Whosoever shall say to his brother, _____" (Matt. 5:22)
60 Bud's comic pal in early films
61 Mach 2 flier (abbr.)

SNAKE IN THE GRASS

PUZZLE QUOTE RUNS FORWARD & BACKWARD, UP & DOWN

ACROSS

1 Start of **QUOTE** from Gen. 3 (see note above)

5 Part of **QUOTE**

9 Part of **QUOTE**

14 "And _____ bare Jabal" (Gen. 4:20)

15 "_____ abhor me" (Job 30:10)

16 Wealthy or powerful person

17 "Or clothe his neck with a flowing _____?" (Job 39:19 NIV)

18 Negative replies

19 Recover metal by heating ore

20 "The LORD shall judge the _____ of the earth" (1 Sam. 2:10)

21 Charlotte Brontë's Jane and family

23 Asian inland sea

24 Part of **QUOTE**

25 Oklahoma town

27 Avenue crossers (abbr.)

30 "_____ to your faith virtue" (2 Pet. 1:5)

32 Part of **QUOTE**

36 "Round about the _____ thereof" (Ex. 28:33)

37 "I know it _____ of a truth" (Job 9:2) (2 words)

39 "For whether is _____" (Matt. 9:5)

40 Ecology watchdog group (abbr.)

41 Part of **QUOTE**

43 "They _____ the ship aground" (Acts 27:41)

44 "Now learn this _____ from the fig tree" (Matt. 24:32 NIV)

46 "Ye shall find a colt _____" (Mark 11:2)

47 "We _____ many" (Mark 5:9)

48 Part of **QUOTE**

49 "Jerusalem, _____, she is broken" (Ezek. 26:2)

50 Manuscripts (abbr.)

51 "As it had been the face _____ angel" (Acts 6:15) (2 words)

53 Part of **QUOTE**

55 "_____ do all things through Christ" (Phil. 4:13) (2 words)

58 "Who will _____ us?" (Isa. 6:8) (2 words)

61 Expression of annoyance

65 Natives of northern Ohio, once

67 Friskies rival

68 "Why should _____ with thee?" (2 Sam. 13:26) (2 words)

69 "Get a new _____ on life" (start over)

70 Afrikaans, language of South Africa

71 Swiss river

72 Part of **QUOTE**

73 Part of **QUOTE**

74 Part of **QUOTE**

DOWN

1 "He shall have no _____ in the street" (Job 18:17)

2 "Thy god, _____, liveth" (Amos 8:14) (2 words)

3 Baton

4 Part of **QUOTE**

5 Part of **QUOTE**

6 Nautical greeting

7 "O thou _____, go, flee thee away" (Amos 7:12)

8 "That thou wilt not cut off _____ after me" (1 Sam. 24:21) (2 words)

9 _____ and offs

10 Southwestern covered porches

11 Salah's son (Gen. 10:24)

12 "Alone" (Sp.)

13 Part of **QUOTE**

22 Tin in Chemistry 101

26 "Shall go _____ out" (John 10:9) (2 words)

27 Off-the-_____ (not custom-made)

28 Conical abode

29 "_____ her jugs" (Jer. 48:12 NIV)

30 Abijam's son (1 Kings 15:8)

31 "This man _____ many miracles" (John 11:47)

33 "Solomon sent to _____, saying" (1 Kings 5:2)

34 "They that sow in _____ shall reap in joy" (Ps. 126:5)

35 Sea eagles

37 "Let them break _____" (Ex. 32:24) (2 words)

38 Nine-digit ID (abbr.)

39 "Mine _____ is consumed because of grief" (Ps. 6:7)

42 US Native American agency

45 "Over these _____ have buried here" (Jer. 43:10 NIV) (2 words)

49 "As he that feareth _____" (Eccl. 9:2) (2 words)

52 Ashcroft, e.g. (abbr.)

53 Part of **QUOTE**

54 Part of **QUOTE**

55 Part of **QUOTE**

56 "Immediately the cock _____" (Matt. 26:74)

57 Rizpah's mother, Saul's concubine (2 Sam. 3:7)

59 "The wall of the city shall fall down _____" (Josh. 6:5)

60 Colorful tropical fish

62 Quantity of paper

63 Taj Mahal site

64 Having pedal digits

66 "In just a _____" (very shortly)

MERRY CHRISTMAS!

ACROSS

1 Noah's son
4 Electrical power measures
9 Shepherds would _____ to see Jesus
12 First man
14 Atmosphere layer
15 Gruesomeness
16 "Why do the heathen _____?" (Ps. 2:1)
17 _____ray, shark cousin
18 There appeared a heavenly _____
19 Like baby Jesus
21 Camel kin
23 Three Persons, _____ God
24 "Unto us a _____ is given" (Isa. 9:6)
25 God "exalted _____ of low degree" (Luke 1:52)
28 "_____Maria"
31 "It came to _____"
34 Document releasing a right or claim
36 OT seer's gift
38 Barely make do
40 Zacharias not _____to speak
41 "On _____peace" (Luke 2:14)

43 Esther was "_____and beautiful" (Est. 2:7)
44 US workforce agency
45 Luke and others (abbr.)
46 Caesar Augustus sent one out
48 Scandinavian capital
51 A senior school in Brooklyn (abbr.)
53 Mary, e.g.
54 Santa's helper
56 KJV "donkey"
58 Jesus' crib
61 Christmas month
66 Like Christmas Eve shepherds
67 Blot out, as sins
69 Jesus came to _____us
70 Jerusalem, e.g.
71 African nation
72 Dell
73 Gaza to Bethlehem dir.
74 Mary "pondered. . .in her _____" (Luke 2:19)
75 _____Times

DOWN

1 Angelic instrument
2 Purim month
3 They went home a different way
4 "Blessed art thou among _____" (Luke 1:28)
5 Rhododendron
6 Broadway award
7 Explosive
8 Book "sealed with seven _____" (Rev. 5:1)
9 No _____for them at the inn
10 _____Minor (Little Dipper)
11 Galilee fishermen's needs
13 "Good will toward _____" (Luke 2:14)
15 African nation
20 "O _____, All Ye Faithful"
22 Prune

25 Moral no-no
26 Where shepherds watched sheep
27 12 Across spouse
29 Bible passage
30 New York winter hour (abbr.)
32 Scorches
33 Where 18 Across appeared
34 Bundle
35 The color of Christmas
37 Advanced degree (abbr.)
39 "Come..._____my child die" (John 4:49)
42 God showed "strength with his _____" (Luke 1:51)
43 Interdenominational sports org.
47 "There is none _____beside him" (Deut. 4:35)

49 Like spiders

50 Madrid stadium shout

52 Roman ruler

55 "No fountain. . .yield salt water and _____" (James 3:12)

57 Smell

58 Spice

59 Contrary to (dial.)

60 Bible margin entry, perhaps

61 Art movement

62 Brief communication (abbr.)

63 Sheaf

64 Let's "go _____ unto Bethlehem" (Luke 2:15)

65 "Time to _____, and. . .to sew" (Eccl. 3:7)

68 Herb Pharisees tithed

Day 54

EASTER

ACROSS

1 Rights org.
5 To make bare
10 Woman "taken...in the very _____" (John 8:4)
13 The condemned Jesus to _____
15 Choir accompanier
16 Expert, for short
17 Bye-bye
18 Small choral group, maybe
19 Sports official, for short
20 Pill, for short
21 Gospel writer
23 One on cross with Jesus
25 _____ Supper
26 In theory
28 Resurrection would _____ false accusations
31 Jesus calmed one on the Sea of Galilee
32 Gethsemane disciples could not stay _____
33 Bible book
34 Mexico Mrs.
37 They cast lots for His _____
38 Machine tool

40 Believer _____ along God's path
41 Barely make do
42 Moist, as in the morning
43 Scrap
44 Sound navigation technique
45 Jesus was betrayed for _____ pieces silver
46 School group
49 "We have _____ the Lord" (John 20:25)
50 Flee to wed
51 "Father, forgive _____" (Luke 23:34)
52 Agricultural youth org.
55 Pen point
56 Nebraska city
59 Swiss mathematician
61 Electronics device (abbr.)
62 _____ Room, 25 Across site
63 They "mocked him, and _____ him" (Luke 22:63)
64 ____ of Galilee
65 He rose after _____ days
66 Pod pals

DOWN

1 Eden tender
2 Give up or grant
3 They _____ Him in a tomb
4 North American Indian
5 Soldiers made _____ of Him
6 Tock preceder
7 Gnawer
8 Chemistry suffix
9 Judas' coins bought _____ field
10 Easter month, often
11 64 Across fisherman's need
12 Caramelized sugar candy (var.)
14 Godly people are _____ toward others
22 "_____, and ye shall receive" (John 16:24)
24 Noah's son

25 33 Across writer
26 Lice plague sufferer's problem
27 Pamper, with "on"
28 "Some would even _____ to die" (Rom. 5:7)
29 *Star Wars* furry bipeds
30 Bethlehem Holy One
31 Greek mythology creature
34 To "mount up with wings" (Isa. 40:31)
35 "I will give you _____" (Matt. 11:28)
36 Like Sodom, after brimstone fell
38 Pre-Easter season
39 At Gethsemane, they led Him _____
40 Mocker's Calvary smirk
42 Give away (2 words)
43 Sermon topics, e.g.

44 Jesus would _____ in 62 Across
45 Golf course need
46 Wards off
47 "He is _____!"
48 Hooded snake
49 Believers _____ the Good News
51 KJV "you"

52 Arctic sight
53 Greek cheese
54 Greek god of war
57 Traffic cop's concern (abbr.)
58 10 Down (abbr.)
60 Game official, for short

DEBORAH: THE JUDGE

ACROSS

1 Queen of ___, Solomon's visitor (1 Kings 10:1)
6 Abel's portions offered to the Lord (Gen. 4:4)
10 Deborah's song: "They rehearse the righteous ___ of the Lord" (Judg. 5:11)
14 "Blessed above ___ shall Jael. . .be" (Judg. 5:24)
15 Off-Broadway award
16 "Shall ye not eat of them that ___ the cud" (Lev. 11:4)
17 This does not exist between Deborah and Sisera (Judg. 4:11–17)
18 Cincinnati baseball team
19 Companion of harp, viol, tabret, and wine (Isa. 5:12)
20 The Baptizer's mom, familiarly
21 Barak's response to Deborah would ___ to his fear (Judg. 4:8)
23 Pan mate
24 Jael would go out of her tent and ___ Sisera (Judg. 4:18)
26 Iodine compound
28 Succoth shelters (Gen. 33:17)
31 Barak would not go unless Deborah did this (Judg. 4:8)
32 "They chose new gods; then was ___ in the gates" (Judg. 5:8)
33 Noble's attendant
36 Dutch cheese
40 Highest point
42 "They that handle the ___ of the writer"

(Judg. 5:14)
43 God to Gideon: "The people are yet too ___" (Judg. 7:4)
44 Children's love
45 Jael covered Sisera with this (Judg. 4:18)
48 Deborah to Barak: "Take with thee ___ thousand men" (Judg. 4:6)
49 Herod's brother, familiarly (Matt. 14:3)
51 Capital of Canada
53 Jael to Sisera: "___, my lord" (Judg. 4:18) (2 words)
56 God will be there you when your hair turns this (Ps. 71:18) (var.)
57 "___ Maria"
58 Matt. thru Acts, e.g.
61 Food for your printer
65 Adam and Eve, originally
67 "Out of Ephraim was there a ___ of them" (Judg. 5:14)
68 Priest in Toledo
69 Margarine
70 Wager
71 "Curse ye Meroz, said the ___ of the Lord" (Judg. 5:23)
72 A woman of Deborah's wisdom and courage is this
73 Jabin, king of Canaan, suffered this (Judg. 4:24)
74 Jesus stood in yours

DOWN

1 You might do it to the deck
2 "That disciple took her unto his own ___" (John 19:27)
3 Give off
4 Deborah dwelt "between Ramah and ___" (Judg. 4:5)
5 "Is there ___ man here?" (Judg. 4:20)
6 "Shield or spear seen among ___ thousand in Israel?" (Judg. 5:8)
7 Sisera hoped Jael would ___ his escape (Judg. 4:18)
8 Wave word

9 Meeting
10 Med. org.
11 Hot stuff
12 Barak was this about fighting Sisera (Judg. 4:8)
13 Scandinavian
21 Sanctuary section
22 Doubting disciple, familiarly
25 Jael was this with Sisera (Judg. 4:17–21)
27 Deborah would ___ Barak's request with disfavor (Judg. 4:9)
28 Jael did more than this to Sisera

29 Folded Mexican sandwich
30 Sisera, captain of Jabin's ___ (Judg. 4:7)
31 Barak basically said to Deborah, "I ___!" (Judg. 4:8)
34 October birthstone
35 Deborah and Jael outshine these in this story
37 Book of Num. contains these
38 After victory, Israel had peace ___ (Judg. 5:31)
39 Loud bird
41 Sports channel
45 Lot's wife turned to one (Gen. 19:26)
46 "The children of Israel again did evil in the sight of the ___" (Judg. 4:1)
47 LAX info
50 Deborah and Jael were this

52 Herod the Great was this
53 "Go and draw toward mount ___" (Judg. 4:6)
54 Screamer's throat dangler
55 Deborah's song would ___ to the Israelite's victory
56 "People of the LORD go down to the ___" (Judg. 5:11)
59 A commandment might be this
60 Jesus welcomed them (Matt. 19:14)
62 Sisera's soldiers "fell upon the ___ of the sword" (Judg. 4:16)
63 Israel is one
64 Israelites were not to do this with heathen peoples
66 Sisera was Deborah's (Judg. 4:14)
68 Abraham, Isaac, and Jacob, for short

ELI: THE GREAT PRIEST

ACROSS

1 Sheep's clothing wearer
5 Nebuchadnezzar's nail resembled this (Dan. 4:33)
9 You can chart Paul's missionary journeys on these
13 The ark sat on the "great stone of ___" (1 Sam. 6:18)
14 Fruit
15 Upon
16 "Hannah ___ up after they had eaten" (1 Sam. 1:9)
17 Blend
18 "Hophni and Phinehas, are ___" (1 Sam. 4:17)
19 Eli, Hophni, Phinehas, and Samuel, e.g. (abbr.)
21 18 Across to Eli (2 words)
23 Arizona Indian
25 Needs of the "ready writer" in Psalm 45:1
26 What the messenger may have put on himself (1 Sam. 4:12)
29 Part of offering Eli's sons took for themselves (1 Sam. 2:15)
31 Eli's sons' behavior did not ___ God's will for priests
34 Officer in US Armed Forces (abbr.)
35 Gem State
37 Asian country

39 As priest, Eli wore this
41 Shape of God's sign to Noah
42 IHOP condiment
43 "Eli. . . sat ___ a seat by a post of the temple" (1 Sam. 1:9)
44 Terra-___ (type of clay)
46 Tire wall letters
47 Altar builders do this
50 "Spear was like a weaver's ___" (1 Sam. 17:7)
51 Philistines took the ark "and ___ it by Dagon" (1 Sam. 5:2)
52 Eli ___ his sons' disobedience (1 Sam. 23–24)
54 In a parade, but not the Bible
56 Man with the unclean spirit, e.g. (Mark 5:2)
59 Gomer's appearance, perhaps (Hos. 1:2–3)
63 Soft drink
64 Most of the Bible is written in this
66 Eli presided over the Temple ___
67 Stave
68 Jael ___ ___ Sisera (Judg. 4:18) (2 words)
69 European river
70 No one could do this to 56 Across (Mark 5:4)
71 Biblical paradise
72 Sunday song

DOWN

1 "How can one be ___ alone?" (Eccl. 4:11)
2 In orchestra, but not the Bible
3 "Knew nothing of all this, ___ or more" (1 Sam. 22:15)
4 "Give ___ to roast for the priest" (1 Sam. 2:15)
5 "Whatsoever. . .cheweth the ___" (Lev. 11:3)
6 Samuel's offering (1 Sam. 7:9)
7 20 Down descriptor
8 Eli's "eyes began to ___" (1 Sam. 3:2) (2 words)
9 Eli's sons did not behave this way

10 The Holy Spirit makes hearts ___
11 Parents' school groups (abbr.)
12 Third day creation (Gen. 1:11)
14 At first, Eli ___ to see Hannah (1 Sam. 1:13–14)
20 Fifth day creation (Gen. 1:20)
22 Basketball assoc.
24 Almost sacrificed (Gen. 22:9–12)
26 National rights org.
27 Eli's sons would ___ what they wanted (1 Sam. 2:16)

28 Eli gave more ___ to his sons than to God (1 Sam. 2:29)

30 Heart's motion

32 See 20 Down

33 Eli served in the Lord's ___

36 Musical group, perhaps

38 "Then did they ___ in his face" (Matt. 26:67)

40 Eli's sons were this

42 Dance

45 To make firm

48 Eli took a ___ from Hannah's behavior (1 Sam. 1:13)

49 "The lamp of God went out in the ___" (1 Sam. 3:3)

53 Eli's sons ___ dishonor the Lord

55 Hannah was ___ in grief (1 Sam. 1:7)

56 Fizzy beverage

57 Christ was the second (1 Cor. 15:22)

58 Eli's life ends on a sad ___

60 Hauling cart

61 Printer need

62 "Solomon had horses. . .and linen ___" (1 Kings 10:28)

63 Sound barrier breaker

65 "If a man ___ against the Lᴏʀᴅ, who shall intreat for him?" (1 Sam. 2:25)

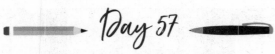

JESUS CHRIST

ACROSS

1 Make taboo
4 Spirit "__ light on one's inmost being" (Prov. 20:27 NIV)
9 "Blessed __ the poor in spirit" (Matt. 5:3)
12 Some churchgoers, e.g.
14 Disciple
15 "He that ploweth should __ in hope" (1 Cor. 9:10)
16 Bitterness
17 Heavyset
18 "Or __ believe me for the...works' sake" (John 14:11)
19 Eternity
21 The Lord's __
23 __ Baba
24 Twitch
25 Stolen property
28 Cell card
31 Half (prefix)
34 Dance to music
36 He came to __ for sin
38 John, the voice of __ crying in the wilderness
40 Hairdo

41 He came from David's __ line
43 Bruins' school (abbr.)
44 Length meas.
45 Guy's partner
46 __, Son, and Holy Spirit
48 Eden name
51 Jesus gave people this (abbr.)
53 Nifty
54 They are "as the early __ that passeth away" (Hos. 13:3)
56 Keyboard key (abbr.)
58 Graduates
61 Mary "__ the feet of Jesus" (John 12:3)
66 Greek second letter
67 Capital of Senegal
69 Western treaty group (abbr.)
70 Bible times edible
71 Christ "shall rise the __ day" (Mark 9:31)
72 Flightless birds
73 Bible land tree
74 Jesus laid __ on the sick
75 Apple or peach, maybe

DOWN

1 Jesus, __ of Bethlehem
2 Tel __, Israel
3 Pharaoh's river
4 Thread holder
5 Ego
6 Fencing sword
7 Snub, for short
8 Risen Christ, "firstfruits of them that __" (1 Cor. 15:20)
9 Supportive friend
10 Christ __ Easter morning
11 Pitcher
13 German article
15 Christ, Prince of __
20 Christ's gift bringers

22 Christ came to __ us of guilt
25 Hagia __, former Istanbul cathedral
26 Christ came to save the __
27 "They would have repented long __ in sackcloth" (Matt. 11:21)
29 Song of Solomon, e.g.
30 "Mama __!"
32 Barista specialty
33 Bay
34 Comics sound
35 Work unit
37 Storybook character
39 Christ restored the high priest servant's
42 Horse tidbit
43 Southwestern Indian

47 Against (prefix)
49 Publicist
50 Pet., James, and John, e.g.
52 Fabrication
55 Temple or ark measurement
57 Christ, Lord of __
58 Christ invites us to call our Father this
59 Dregs

60 Salt Lake state
61 Related
62 Gaza to Joppa (dir.)
63 Pat down lightly
64 Decorative needle case
65 Med measurement
68 Expression of surprise

HOLY SPIRIT

ACROSS

1 "While we ___ yet sinners, Christ died" (Rom. 5:8)
5 Pseudo chocolate
10 Toast go-with
13 Japanese poem
15 Sporty car brand
16 Prideful person has a big one
17 Birchlike tree
18 Spirit never does this
19 Mary ___ at Jesus' feet
20 Greens need
21 Sky color (Fr.)
23 When "the Spirit of ___, is come, he will guide you" (John 16:13)
25 Spirit ___ inside the heart
26 Forger might have many
28 God-given gift
31 KJV "Spirit"
32 Where Spirit lives in you
33 What the sower of parable sowed in
34 Phone greeting, slangily (var.)
37 Great Lake
38 Architect Frank ___ Wright

40 Sermon delivery, usually
41 Land east of Eden
42 Sullen
43 Pie serving
44 Spirit's compassion
45 When it's hard to pray, Spirit ___ for us
46 Funnel-shaped fish
49 Angel's topper
50 Island greeting
51 Central points
52 Legume
55 "Grieve not the holy Spirit of ___" (Eph. 4:30)
56 Whining voice type
59 Shy, cheerful, or friendly, e.g.
61 Gaza to Bethlehem (dir.)
62 "Who has insulted the Spirit of ___?" (Heb. 10:29 NIV)
63 Holy person
64 Devil's color, popularly
65 "Rich he hath sent ___ away" (Luke 1:53)
66 "Lions roar after their ___" (Ps. 104:21)

DOWN

1 "___ saith the scripture?" (Rom. 4:3)
2 Spiritual comfort, e.g.
3 Do not "delay to offer the first of thy ___ fruits" (Ex. 22:29)
4 Make do (with "out")
5 54 Down projects
6 Freedom org.
7 Herb tithed by Pharisees
8 Lode yield
9 Spirit's water
10 Like a dove, Spirit descended on Him
11 Multicolored rock
12 "Treasures in heaven, where ___...do not destroy" (Matt. 6:20 NIV)

14 Straight
22 "___ your light so shine" (Matt. 5:16)
24 OT unclean rodent
25 Like Sinai Desert
26 Sailor's call
27 "Each one should carry their own ___" (Gal. 6:5 NIV)
28 "Art thou ___ the Son of God?" (Luke 22:70)
29 Aircraft (prefix)
30 "There is ___ up for me a crown of righteousness" (2 Tim. 4:8)
31 "Happy are ye; for the spirit of ___. . .resteth upon you" (1 Pet. 4:14)
34 Church solo, maybe

35 "Walk honestly. . .that ye may have __ of nothing" (1 Thess. 4:12)

36 Madrid stadium sounds

38 Apocryphal story, e.g.

39 Ricky's partner on classic TV

40 Sandwich spread

42 Unsettle

43 Leaves, informally

44 Dashboard reading (abbr.)

45 Joey's home

46 Brew

47 "Neither pray I for these __" (John 17:20)

48 Out-__, old fashioned

49 Perforated

51 Bible truth, e.g.

52 Animal combo for Noah's ark

53 "__ Kleine Nachtmusik" (Ger.)

54 Court figure (abbr.)

57 "To whom hath the __ of the Lord been revealed?" (John 12:38)

58 Maple syrup

60 Music genre

BIBLICAL WARRIORS

ACROSS

1 San _____, Italian resort city
5 "Eli _____ unto her" (1 Sam. 1:14)
9 "This man is a _____" (Acts 22:26)
14 Famous cookie
15 Madrid paintings
16 "To _____ harnessed" (Song 1:9 NIV) (2 words)
17 "At that day shall the heart of the _____ be as the heart of a woman in her pangs" (Jer. 49:22) (4 words)
20 City SW of Honshu, Japan
21 "They _____ my path" (Job 30:13)
22 Decorate again
23 This creature should be the sluggard's role model (Prov. 6:6)
25 "Eat not of it _____" (Ex.12:9)
27 "Wake up _____ all the men of war draw near" (Joel 3:9) (4 words)
36 "Lest he _____ thee to the judge" (Luke 12:58)
37 "_____, I have no man" (John 5:7)
38 Amoz's son (2 Kings 20:1)
39 Blue pencils
41 Old horse
43 Lowest deck of seats in a stadium

44 Where Jethro lived (Ex.3:1)
46 Spanish sun
48 "I cast my _____ against them" (Acts 26:10 NIV)
49 "He had slain Gedaliah the son of Ahikam, _____ war" (Jer. 41:16) (4 words)
52 "One beka _____ person" (Ex.38:26 NIV)
53 "I am as _____ mocked" (Job 12:4)
54 "Passeth through the paths of the _____" (Ps. 8:8)
58 "To a point below Beth _____" (1 Sam. 7:11 NIV)
60 "Thou didst _____ the earth with rivers" (Hab. 3:9)
65 "Pass before your brethren armed, _____ of valour" (Josh. 1:14) (4 words)
68 Proportion
69 Sit for an artist
70 "_____ your heart, and not your garments" (Joel 2:13)
71 Inactive
72 "I will give him the morning _____" (Rev. 2:28)
73 Cainan's father (Gen. 5:9)

DOWN

1 Tomato variety
2 Composer Satie
3 Vast
4 _____ and aahs
5 "Their dark _____" (Prov. 1:6)
6 "As a seal upon thine _____" (Song 8:6)
7 Object
8 Tenfold
9 UK fliers (abbr.)
10 "An _____ for every man" (Ex.16:16)
11 "All things were _____ by him" (John 1:3)
12 "It became _____ in his hand" (Ex.4:4) (2 words)

13 Captain of the Nautilus
18 Formerly Siamese
19 "_____ trying to please men?" (Gal. 1:10 NIV) (3 words)
24 "Behold, seven _____ ears and blasted" (Gen. 41:6)
26 "This shall be your _____ border" (Num. 34:6)
27 Student paper
28 If Ovid had II eggs for breakfast and Nero had II, together they _____ (2 "words")
29 Skip or slur over a syllable, as "ma'am"
30 "The law might be fully _____ us" (Rom. 8:4 NIV) (2 words)

31 Worthless stuff

32 "They deceive the minds of _____ people" (Rom. 16:18 NIV)

33 "The camps that _____ the east" (Num. 10:5) (2 words)

34 "Give _____ my words" (Ps. 5:1) (2 words)

35 "The _____ cometh in" (Hos. 7:1)

40 Cornmeal mush in New England

42 "_____ the pool of Siloam" (John 9:11) (2 words)

45 Dinah, to Esau (Gen. 25:25–26; Gen. 34:1)

47 Illegal hangman

50 Daddy's dad

51 "Our hearts did _____" (Josh. 2:11)

54 Rani's gown

55 Enthusiasm

56 "Old ones" (Ger.)

57 "Grievous words _____ up anger" (Prov. 15:1)

59 "Children not accused of _____ or unruly" (Titus 1:6)

61 *Jane* _____

62 "These things saith the _____" (Rev. 3:14)

63 _____-vein

64 "The four _____ of the grate of brass" (Ex.38:5)

66 "When it is _____" (Job 6:17)

67 Org. founded by Juliette Gordon Low

Day 60

BIBLICAL PAIRS

ACROSS

1 "If an ox _____ a man or a woman" (Ex.21:28)
5 "With the _____ facing Joppa" (Josh. 19:46 NIV)
9 Olympic gymnast Comaneci
14 "An _____ for every man" (Ex.16:16)
15 "Or clothe his neck with a flowing _____?" (Job 39:19 NIV)
16 "One for _____" (Matt. 17:4)
17 **BIBLICAL PAIR** from 1 Sam. 17 (3 words)
20 "At whom do you _____" (Isa. 57:4 NIV)
21 "No one _____ a patch" (Matt. 9:16 NIV)
22 "Passed to the _____ of Cyprus" (Acts 27:4 NIV)
23 "Thou anointest my head with _____" (Ps. 23:5)
24 "Saddled his _____" (Num. 22:21)
27 A very long time
29 **BIBLICAL PAIR** from Ruth 1
34 "In wrath they _____ me" (Ps. 55:3)
37 "Thou art _____ sister" (Gen. 24:60)
38 "I will break off a tender _____" (Ezek. 17:22 NIV)
39 Memo notation, meaning "to hurry" (abbr.)

40 Greek philosopher
43 "With a _____ of blue" (Ex.28:28)
44 Violin forerunner
46 "Judas had the _____" (John 13:29)
47 Israeli Red Sea port
48 **BIBLICAL PAIR** from Acts 15–17 (3 words)
52 Blackthorn
53 Moon explorer (abbr.)
54 "The _____ isn't there! Where can I turn now?" (Gen. 37:30 NIV)
57 Father of Cush (Gen. 10:6)
60 "In the cities of the _____" (Jer. 33:13)
62 "Fine linen, and coral, and _____" (Ezek. 27:16)
64 **BIBLICAL PAIR** from 2 Kings 2 (3 words)
68 Ocean vessel
69 "No, _____ you will be condemned" (James 5:12 NIV) (2 words)
70 Sterling (abbr.)
71 First to reach the North Pole
72 "As he saith also in _____" (Rom. 9:25)
73 "Restore all that was _____" (2 Kings 8:6)

DOWN

1 "For _____ loved the world" (John 3:16) (2 words)
2 Man from Muscat
3 Jump for joy
4 One of the Great Lakes
5 "I _____ brother to dragons" (Job 30:29) (2 words)
6 "He _____ before, and climbed up into a sycomore tree" (Luke 19:4)
7 "All the _____ of the earth shall see the salvation of our God" (Isa. 52:10)
8 Sea between Greece and Turkey
9 Wrestling holds
10 Mr. Baba

11 "By which it had gone down in the _____ of Ahaz" (2 Kings 20:11)
12 "When your words came, _____ them" (Jer. 15:16 NIV) (2 words)
13 "Now _____ was speaking with me" (Dan. 8:18) (2 words)
18 Danube feeder (Ger.)
19 "Fellowservants, which _____ him an hundred pence" (Matt. 18:28)
25 "Get thee down, that the rain _____ thee not" (1 Kings 18:44)
26 Synagogue, to a Jew
28 Major Italian port
29 Wards off

30 "Cretans and _____—we hear them" (Acts 2:11 NIV)

31 Type of exam

32 "_____, Rehob, Hashabiah" (Neh. 10:11 NIV)

33 "Where can _____ meat for all these people?" (Num. 11:13 NIV) (2 words)

34 "David took an _____" (1 Sam. 16:23)

35 "I saw as it were _____ of glass" (Rev. 15:2) (2 words)

36 Prohibition (var.)

41 "He is the _____" (Isa. 9:15)

42 Stare amorously

45 "Which is called _____" (Luke 23:33)

49 Father of Shem (Gen. 5:32)

50 Part of FDR

51 A son of Helem (1 Chron. 7:35)

54 Sew temporarily

55 "Worship no _____ god" (Ex.34:14)

56 "A thousand _____ as one day" (2 Pet. 3:8)

57 "A very present _____ in trouble" (Ps. 46:1)

58 "That they should believe _____" (2 Thes. 2:11) (2 words)

59 "Here is your _____" (Luke 19:20 NIV)

61 Grandson of Adam (Gen. 5:6)

63 Silent star Lillian

65 Follows Isa. (abbr.)

66 "A loving _____" (Prov. 5:19 NIV)

67 "Between their teeth, _____ it was chewed" (Num. 11:33)

THE GOSPEL

ACROSS

1 Slightly open
5 Snitch
9 Gospel writer, for short
13 Jesus' ride
14 Round, caramel-centered candy
15 Thief on cross, e.g.
16 First garden
17 Greetings (Lat.)
18 Israelites in Egypt brick product
19 John would _____ Jesus in Jordan
21 Good Samaritan took _____ of victim
23 Sodom remain
24 "_____ me come unto thee" (Matt. 14:28)
25 Prayer place in Jerusalem
29 Nada
30 It was fatted for a feast
32 Cleric, for short
33 Gospel: _____ of Life
36 Jesus' body would not _____
37 16 Across woman
38 Star shone there
39 About 66 from Nazareth to Jerusalem
40 Prophet Eli, e.g.
41 Not "_____ for the kingdom of God" (Luke 9:62)

42 "Shepherds abiding in the _____" (Luke 2:8)
43 John's dinner: locusts and wild _____
44 "There cometh _____ mightier than I" (Mark 1:7)
45 Bullets
46 "Let us _____ with patience" (Heb. 12:1)
47 Rotate
49 NT writer
50 16 Across devilish figure
53 Break up wood
55 Plague pests
57 Chatter "like a _____ or a swallow" (Isa. 38:14)
60 KJV woeful cry
62 Like Galilee or Judea, e.g.
63 Disciple
64 Wheel covering
65 Window part
66 Solomon's menagerie animals
67 Thorn crown put on Jesus' _____
68 Dutch cheese

DOWN

1 One-celled water animal
2 Jesus' betrayer
3 Hebrew letter
4 Temple veil was _____ in two
5 South American nation
6 "God so _____ the world"
7 Brew
8 Pear variety
9 Computer part
10 Bible times, bygone
11 Bath
12 Ball holder
15 Make less dense

20 Footnote abbreviation
22 Bible lands map book, for example
26 Groom like an eagle
27 Dike
28 "Preach gospel to _____ creature" (Mark 16:15)
29 Disciple, for short
30 Church orchestra string, maybe
31 Did well
33 Confuse
34 Weather for Noah
35 OT queen (var.)
36 Carpe _____

39 Old printer, for short

40 Jesus, _____ of God

42 "Abba, _____!"

43 Sings with closed mouth

46 Sins _____ clean in Jesus' blood

48 Blemish conditions

49 Princess headwear

50 Like church incense, maybe

51 Inscribed stone

52 Bible hymn

54 "Thy word. . .light unto my _____" (Ps. 119:105)

56 "Soul shall dwell at _____" (Ps. 25:13)

57 Tax time worker (abbr.)

58 Agent, for short

59 Jesus _____ Last Supper with disciples

61 "Before God, I _____ not" (Gal. 1:20)

CONVERSIONS

ACROSS

1 "Sin shall have great _____" (Ezek. 30:16)
5 Declare beliefs, e.g.
9 Believer _____ where God leads
13 Lord, "there is none _____" (Isa. 45:5)
14 "Hi" in Rome
15 Extinguish
16 "Sinners sat _____...with Jesus" (Mark 2:15)
17 Scoffer's prefix for "Christian"
18 Main artery
19 Believing, Abram left his _____
21 God has "given you the _____" (Josh. 2:9)
23 "Beam is in thine own _____" (Matt. 7:4)
24 Olive _____
25 Expel from law practice
29 Soil, turf
30 Chimney
32 Stadium shout
33 Gen.
36 Ogre
37 Dad _____ to meet prodigal son
38 "With what measure ye _____" (Mark 4:24)
39 God gives believer a new _____

40 Ancient Athens suburb
41 _____-Jima
42 Samuel anointed him king
43 Zarephath believer
44 Number lepers healed
45 Conversion turns one from _____
46 Repeated, a chocolate treat
47 Robe part
49 Lust will "_____against the soul" (1 Pet. 2:11)
50 Berlin exclamation
53 Negative (dial.)
55 Believer strives for _____conduct
57 "_____of great price" (Matt. 13:46)
60 Ark of Covenant feature
62 Carpe _____
63 Burnt offering leavings
64 Women's magazine
65 Sports channel
66 Jesus rose from the _____
67 Jordan River sight, perhaps
68 Peter and Andrew's fishing needs

DOWN

1 Faith brings _____to the soul
2 Metal
3 Woman had "an _____of blood" (Luke 8:43)
4 "Jesus Saves" sign, maybe
5 Many a plague insect
6 Bible cover, maybe
7 "Take, _____: this is my body" (Mark 14:22)
8 Waters _____in Galilee storm
9 KJV "possessions"
10 "_____Father"
11 Miami winter hour (abbr.)
12 _____of Galilee
15 Lion's den man
20 Honk

22 Grown-up
26 Child _____during long sermon, perhaps
27 Texas historical site
28 "_____a right spirit" (Ps. 51:10)
29 "Taste and _____" (Ps. 34:8)
30 I know "how _____I am" (Ps. 39:4)
31 Title for Jesus
33 Neglects, as a commandment
34 Stairway post
35 Meaning of Pet.'s name
36 _____Troy, author and commentator
39 God's presence, safe _____for believers
40 Racket
42 Jesus cast out _____

43 God's _____ has power to convert
46 Mayberry's Fife
48 Golden-_____corn
49 Jesus came to save the whole _____
50 "_____, and make thy bed" (Acts 9:34)
51 To name (arch.)
52 Sunday songs

54 KJV "you"
56 Gen. paradise
57 Cat's paw feature
58 Joppa to Jerusalem (dir.)
59 "Found it!"
61 _____ Testament

ELIJAH HEARD IT

ACROSS

1 Elijah's disciple (1 Kings 19:19)
7 Elijah "____ slain all the prophets" (1 Kings 19:1)
10 Abba, familiarly
14 Cowboy shows
15 Lyric poem
16 Actor Alda
17 Elijah suggested the prophets' idol was this (1 Kings 18:27)
18 Associated with 17 Across
19 Ding's partner
20 "A rod out of the ____ of Jesse" (Isa. 11:1)
21 Singing cowboy Autry
22 "Who may stand. . .when ____ thou art angry?" (Ps. 76:7)
23 Elijah's nemesis
25 Moray
26 Sound from bird Noah sent out (Gen. 8:8)
29 Elijah was not this to Jezebel
30 Popular tape
34 Asian plum
36 Many boomers now
39 Where Elijah discovered God (1 Kings 19:12) (3 wds.)
42 Least fresh
43 The widow's never emptied (1 Kings 17:16)

44 Elijah would do this from Jezebel (1 Kings 19:3)
45 Sports org.
46 Thanks to Elijah, the widow and her son did this (1 Kings 17:15)
47 Place of ahhhs
50 "All the ____ of the earth shall fear him" (Ps. 67:7)
51 God's Commandments are one of these to us
53 George Bernard
55 Girl
59 Opera offering
60 The God that sends fire, "____ him be God" (1 Kings 18:24)
61 Highest
63 Plateau
64 "Dress it first; for ye ____ many" (1 Kings 18:25)
65 "O LORD, ____" (1 Kings 18:37) (2 words)
66 Rind
67 Yearning
68 Elijah and the heathen prophets ____ to a contest (1 Kings 18:24)

DOWN

1 Time periods
2 The prodigal son was this
3 The heathen prophets' idol was this
4 "If it ____ good to thee, I will give" (1 Kings 21:2)
5 Used by Cain, perhaps
6 Forbidden fruit offerer
7 Elijah went "unto ____ the mount of God" (1 Kings 19:8)
8 Yemini city
9 Districts of ancient Attica
10 Pedestal part

11 Elijah felt this way (1 Kings 19:10)
12 Herodias's daughter did one (Matt. 14:6)
13 Who told Elijah, "Arise and eat" (1 Kings 19:5)
21 Guy's partner
23 Roman god
24 Gretel's sibling (abbr.)
26 Bank products
27 Horse chow
28 Leave out
30 Eastern state (abbr.)
31 Disarm a gun

32 Social science

33 Pliers, e.g.

35 Part of Elijah's and the prophets' altars

36 Elijah "came and ___ down under a juniper" (1 Kings 19:4)

37 Omani town

38 "Beat it!"

40 Colorado Springs zone (abbr.)

41 Before (poet.)

45 Mt. Carmel to Zarephath (dir.)

47 Classic comics pooch

48 Mash

49 God to Elijah: "___, get thee to Zarephath" (1 Kings 17:9)

50 Man of God had done this, and he shouldn't have (1 Kings 13:22)

52 He had no ability to send fire to his altar

53 Widow to Elijah: "Art thou come. . .to ___ my son?" (1 Kings 17:18)

54 "God Was ___," title for 39 Across

55 When he spoke, Elijah was not one of these

56 Land for the two altars, perhaps

57 Elijah proved God was not the ___ as a heathen idol

58 Snow goer

61 Elijah's response to 39 Across?

62 Place to hang Elijah's mantle

ELISHA: MAN OF GOD

ACROSS

1 "___ of lions" (Dan. 6:16)

4 Moses' burning sight (Ex. 3:2)

9 Pump

14 Cain's mom

15 Naaman "stood at the door of the ___ of Elisha" (2 Kings 5:9)

16 Gehazi made a serious one (2 Kings 5:20)

17 Fluffy's doc

18 Naaman's letter caused the king of Israel this (2 Kings 5:7)

19 Elisha to Gehazi: "Is it a time to receive ___?" (2 Kings 5:26)

20 God is always this (Heb. 10:37) (2 words)

22 Candy bar choice

24 Elisha healed many of these

25 Ahaz worshipped "under every green ___" (2 Kings 17:10)

27 Community org.

31 Lydia needed one (Acts 16:14)

32 A "corruptible crown," perhaps (1 Cor. 9:25)

33 A long time

34 Fabled fabler

36 Epistle of Paul, in a way

38 They go along with a Day 3 creation (Gen. 1:10)

40 Gehazi did not tell Naaman the ___ story (2 Kings 5:22)

42 Stones of the altar will become like this (Isa. 27:9)

43 Relating to what Pet. cut off Malchus's head (John 18:10)

44 Charged particle

45 Gehazi could have used one to haul his loot (2 Kings 5:23)

47 Elisha's question proved one to Gehazi (2 Kings 5:25)

51 Naaman does this to Gehazi's request (2 Kings 5:23)

53 Gehazi's was a bad one (2 Kings 5:20)

54 Hearing what Elisha said, Naaman "went away in a ___" (2 Kings 5:12)

55 Dueling sword

57 Legendary lady of soul

59 Tylenol's competitor

62 Part of Gehazi's loot (2 Kings 5:26)

65 Conversational computer of film

66 Naaman was one (2 Kings 5:1)

67 Lover's voice was like this (Song 2:14)

68 Samaria to Gilgal (dir.)

69 Bingo

70 How Naaman felt when he heard Elisha's orders (2 Kings 5:12)

71 Business org. ending

DOWN

1 The slothful man is ___ of understanding (Prov. 24:30)

2 Smoothly

3 You'll find one in 1 Down's field (Prov. 24:31)

4 Gehazi's story to Naaman was this (2 Kings 5:22)

5 Under Elijah, Elisha could ___ his skills

6 On the floor of a Syrian's tent, perhaps (2 Kings 7:8)

7 *Missouri* letters

8 "___ than all the waters of Israel?" (2 Kings 5:12)

9 Interstate sight

10 Elisha sent one to Naaman (2 Kings 5:10)

11 The widow may have borrowed one (2 Kings 4:3)

12 "Beloved is like a ___" (Song 2:9)

13 Naaman's servants wanted him to ___ Elisha's instructions (2 Kings 5:13)

21 Where Naaman's wife's maid came from (2 Kings 5:2)

23 The couple in Cana did this (John 2:1)

25 Num. in which Naaman measured payment (2 Kings 5:23)

26 Music style

28 Costa ___, CA

29 One was kindled by God's fire (2 Sam. 22:9)

30 Widow to Elisha: "Thine handmaid hath not ___ thing in the house" (2 Kings 4:2)

32 Handy communication

35 Deer cousin

36 La Guardia message (abbr.)

37 Summer in Samaria, sometimes

38 "___ thee with badgers' skin" (Ezek. 16:10)

39 Naaman thought Elisha should "strike his ___ over" his scars (2 Kings 5:11)

40 Manner

41 The widow would do this to Elisha (2 Kings 4:1)

42 Hush-hush org.

43 Elisha: "They that be with us ___ more than they that be with them" (2 Kings 6:16)

45 Elisha heard one (2 Kings 5:25)

46 Ukrainian city

48 Wept for her kids (Matt. 2:18)

49 How Syrians felt to hear "noise of a great host" (2 Kings 7:6)

50 Pared

52 How many times the child sneezed (2 Kings 4:35)

56 Caffeine-free beverage brand

57 Fruit

58 Elisha was this until his death (2 Kings 13:19–20)

59 Church garb

60 Downwind

61 Gov. agency

63 Attila was one

64 Would dad offer son a scorpion instead of this? (Luke 11:12)

SYMBOLS OF THE CHURCH

ACROSS

1 Cheat
5 Treaty
9 Bible legume
13 1813 Battle of Lake __
14 Winglike
15 "I will __ on you no longer" (Jer. 3:12 NIV)
16 Measuring instrument (var.)
17 Choir piece, maybe
18 Church feature
19 Race-runner, as Christ's Church
21 Church __, cemetery site sometimes
23 James or John's need
24 Storm on Galilee call, maybe
25 Martha's worries at Lazarus's tomb
29 Easter month, often (abbr.)
30 Plague pests
32 "__, Lord: I believe" (John 11:27)
33 Affliction of many Jesus healed
36 Ado
37 Mary "__ at Jesus' feet" (Luke 10:39)
38 Reveal a secret
39 Resign
40 Face a camera, perhaps

41 "He has performed mighty deeds with his __"
(Luke 1:51 NIV)
42 What the healed lame man does
43 "No bread, no bag, no money in your __"
(Mark 6:8 NIV)
44 Family member, for short
45 Affectations
46 What James and John might do
47 Several gentlemen, for short
49 East of Eden land
50 Delivery service
53 Church song
55 Like ocean bottom
57 Enlarge
60 Church section
62 Currency in Paris or Rome
63 Append
64 "They that __ soft clothing are in kings'
houses" (Matt. 11:8)
65 Sound croaky
66 Shirt clasp
67 Church is the "__ of the earth" (Matt. 5:13)
68 "Resist the devil, and he will __ from you"
(James 4:7)

DOWN

1 "Eternal life...promised before the world __"
(Titus 1:2)
2 Very angry
3 Church, __ in world of darkness
4 Boat element
5 Church pulpit occupier
6 They were brought to Jesus' tomb
7 Nutritionist's concern (abbr.)
8 Helen of __
9 Church, the __ of Christ
10 Greek mythological figure
11 Punching tool
12 Vane reading (abbr.)
15 "The __ sows the word" (Mark 4:14 NIV)

20 Catch sight of
22 Tie choice
26 Household cleaner brand
27 Mustard seed "the __ of all seeds"
(Matt. 13:32)
28 Fills
29 "__, and it shall be given you" (Luke 11:9)
30 Little leaven leavens many __
31 29 Across bloom, perhaps
33 Blood element
34 Eagle's nest
35 Church is as "__ among wolves" (Luke 10:3)
36 "__ not, little flock" (Luke 12:32)
39 Natural belief in God

40 Church seat

42 Vocal cord locale

43 Church, "the ___ of Christ" (1 Cor. 12:27)

46 Former Crystal Cathedral Schuller

48 Christ "giveth his life for the ___" (John 10:11)

49 Adenoidal

50 Typical

51 Analyze syntactically

52 Mount of Olives feature, e.g.

54 Negatives, slangily

56 Vassal

57 God is, ___, and ever shall be

58 No room for Mary and Joseph here

59 Genetic code (Abbr.)

61 Pot dweller

GIFT OF FAITH

ACROSS

1 Faith helps us"___ how wide...deep is" Christ's love (Eph. 3:18 NIV)
6 Spigots
10 Athletic group (abbr.)
13 Harvest, e.g.
15 "Thy ___ be done"
16 Corp. honcho
17 "___ the sincere milk of the word" (1 Pet. 2:2)
18 Black-and-white snack
19 NT epistle
20 Orange peel
22 "One Lord, one faith, one ___" (Eph. 4:5)
24 ___ Reaper, symbol of death
26 Conversion spot for 54 Across
28 Wine skin
29 Judgment ___ of Christ
30 Judas would ___ himself
31 Frozen pizza brand
32 Lame man's afflicted appendage
33 Faith's gift, ___ of heaven
34 Roman Catholic sister
35 Island music maker

37 Ennui
41 Not clerical, in church
42 Times Square feature
43 Pride
44 If salt loses its ___, what good is it?
47 Printer ink color
48 Old McDonald had one
49 Serving dish
50 Hockey player's focus
51 Faith's gift, new ___ in Christ
52 Flyer's gift, perhaps
54 See 26 Across
56 Tire inflator's concern (abbr.)
57 Star Wars forest creature
59 Winter eave clinger
63 Downwind
64 "___ all that thou hast" (Luke 18:22)
65 Sketch artist
66 Omega
67 Trolley
68 Thrill

DOWN

1 Have faith in ___
2 Regret
3 O'Hare people-mover (abbr.)
4 With 30 Down, faith-giver
5 Jewish festival
6 19 Across epistle number
7 Auto safety device
8 Beg, as for forgiveness
9 Prodigal son longed to eat some
10 Gift of faith, not just words but ___
11 Lively
12 Punctuation marks
14 Commandment number
21 Window treatment
23 Steak

24 Computer expert, slangily
25 Spaghetti sauce choice
27 By faith, we are ___ body in Christ
29 Missouri Jesuit school (abbr.)
30 See 4 Down
31 Convert, e.g.
33 "How shall they ___ without a preacher?" (Rom. 10:14)
34 When darkness fell at Jesus' crucifixion
36 Architect Frank ___ Wright
37 Birds' features
38 Jesus healed many who were ___ and mute
39 Scary creature
40 Mary to Jesus
42 42 Across locale
44 Basic food

45 "Christ has __!"
46 Diverse, as spiritual gifts
47 Certain church feature
48 Family tie
50 Faith's gift, __ to do right
51 Filthy __, miser's obsession
53 Faith's gift, __ for weary soul

55 Help
58 Dutch airlines
60 EPA legislative concern
61 "__ your light shine!"
62 Bard's contraction

PREPAID

ACROSS

1 Cellular blueprints (abbr.)
5 Buncos
10 "Fools, yea, children of _____ men" (Job 30:8)
14 "The harvest is _____" (Joel 3:13)
15 "As for Saul, he made _____ of the church" (Acts 8:3 NKJV)
16 "The sons of Dishan; Uz, and _____" (1 Chron. 1:42)
17 "Even in laughter the heart may _____" (Prov. 14:13 NIV)
18 Athenian market
19 "I am _____ also" (2 Cor. 11:21)
20 Start of **QUOTE** from Rom. 5:8 (4 words)
23 Passover feast
24 Racing craft
25 "Will live, even though he _____" (John 11:25 NIV)
28 "Below the _____ of Pisgah" (Deut. 3:17 NIV)
32 "Ye shall eat the _____ of the land" (Gen. 45:18)
35 "One for _____" (Matt. 17:4)
38 "_____ went forth, and his sons" (Gen. 8:18)
39 "Let us make man in _____ image" (Gen. 1:26)

DOWN

1 "Now the reaper _____ his wages" (John 4:36 NIV)
2 Hole in the wall
3 Plant pest
4 Stitched closed the eyes of a falcon
5 Pygmalion writer
6 "As a _____ is full of birds" (Jer. 5:27)
7 Asserts
8 "Sichem, unto the plain of _____" (Gen. 12:6)
9 Shakes up

40 **QUOTE**, cont'd
43 "When ye pray, _____ not vain repetitions" (Matt. 6:7)
44 "No _____ will pitch his tent there" (Isa. 13:20 NIV)
46 "Will you not _____ them?" (Isa. 48:6 NIV)
47 "_____ skins of rams" (Ex.35:23)
48 "That thou _____ the burden of all this people upon me?" (Num. 11:11)
51 "What profit is _____ we slay our brother" (Gen. 37:26) (2 words)
53 "Thou shalt not _____" (Ex.20:15)
56 "His wrath can _____ up in a moment" (Ps. 2:12 NIV)
60 End of **QUOTE** (4 words)
65 "Whither have ye made a _____ to day?" (1 Sam. 27:10)
66 Type of musical composition
67 Gypsy men
68 Sheriff Andy's boy
69 "They _____ gods?" (Jer. 16:20) (2 words)
70 "I was blind, now _____" (John 9:25) (2 words)
71 "He who _____ souls is wise" (Prov. 11:30 NIV)
72 Four-door auto
73 "His _____ with ravin" (Nah. 2:12)

10 Cyrus's domain (Ezra 5:13)
11 "My beloved is like _____" (Song 2:9) (2 words)
12 "Nibshan, and the city of _____" (Josh. 15:62)
13 "What is mine _____" (Job 6:11)
21 The canal, the lake, and its port
22 Right-angle pipe fitting
26 "He ran unto _____, and said" (1 Sam. 3:5)
27 "Made them _____ great sin" (2 Kings 17:21) (2 words)

29 "In those days will I _____ out my spirit" (Joel 2:29)

30 "I was at _____" (Job 16:12)

31 "Which is _____ for you" (Luke 22:20)

32 "Binding his _____ unto the vine" (Gen. 49:11)

33 Emanation

34 Serving aid

36 "_____ it came to pass" (Ex.1:21)

37 Highway rig

41 Home dye brand

42 "Speak not with a _____ neck" (Ps. 75:5)

45 "Hast thou here any _____?" (Gen. 19:12)

49 Avenue crossers (abbr.)

50 Tropical fish

52 Quite flushed

54 "How right they are to _____ you!" (Song 1:4 NIV)

55 "He _____ its interior walls with cedar boards" (1 Kings 6:15 NIV)

57 "Jesus _____" (Matt. 9:19)

58 Cud reservoir

59 Slalom tracks

60 "The cock shall not _____" (John 13:38)

61 Arizona tribe

62 "That there be no _____" (Deut. 11:17)

63 Author Ferber

64 "To _____ the sabbath days?" (Luke 6:2) (2 words)

Day 68

THERE'S NOTHING LIKE THIS PRESENT!

ACROSS

1 "He _____ it" (Matt. 8:9 NIV)
5 "_____ prophets no harm" (1 Chron. 16:22) (2 words)
9 "Shall lead _____ with the voice of doves" (Nah. 2:7) (2 words)
14 Formerly Christiana
15 Nabisco treat
16 "How right they are to _____ you!" (Song 1:4 NIV)
17 Start of a grateful **VERSE** from 2 Cor. 9:15 (4 words)
20 "Bread _____ in secret is pleasant" (Prov. 9:17)
21 "Zion: retire, _____ not" (Jer. 4:6)
22 Phoenix suburb
23 "I said unto him, _____, thou knowest" (Rev. 7:14)
25 "Rat-_____-tat"
27 "It had _____ horns" (Dan. 7:7)
28 "The foal of an _____" (Zech. 9:9)
31 "Coated it with _____ and pitch" (Ex.2:3 NIV)
33 "Their calls will _____ through the windows" (Zeph. 2:14 NIV)
35 "Know that it is _____, even at the doors" (Matt. 24:33)
37 **VERSE**, cont'd
39 Aikido relative
43 "As Baalath Beer (Ramah in the _____)" (Josh. 19:8 NIV)

45 "Cast the _____ away" (Matt. 13:48)
47 Absalom's sister (2 Sam. 13:1)
48 Positive poles
50 **VERSE**, cont'd
52 Droop
53 "Out of the _____ of Jesse" (Isa. 11:1)
55 Land east of Eden (Gen. 4:16)
57 "That they may _____ your good works" (Matt. 5:16)
58 Bit of current
61 "_____ Bravos in Baja"
63 "Under your arms to _____ the ropes" (Jer. 38:12 NIV)
65 Constricting snakes
67 "They _____ man from Cyrene" (Matt. 27:32 NIV) (2 words)
69 "Then appeared the _____ also" (Matt. 13:26)
73 End of **VERSE** (2 words)
76 Sioux tribe branch
77 Stare amorously
78 Bony beginning (prefix)
79 "All my _____ shall Tychicus declare unto you" (Col. 4:7)
80 "Go and _____ them" (Gen. 29:7)
81 "That he may set his _____ on high" (Hab. 2:9)

DOWN

1 "They shall _____" (Jer. 50:36)
2 US industrial safety watchdog
3 Israeli Red Sea port
4 Loudness units
5 Bill Gates created this while working for IBM
6 Sun and moon
7 "Her whelps _____ man" (Prov. 17:12) (2 words)
8 "_____ no bread" (Deut. 29:6 NIV) (2 words)
9 Fedora, e.g.

10 "Esau, who is _____" (Gen. 36:1)
11 Thesaurus man
12 "When they _____ early" (1 Sam. 5:4)
13 Kind of Ford
18 "Mine heart shall be _____ unto you" (1 Chron. 12:17)
19 Village on the Hudson
24 Opposite of *plaintiff* (abbr.)
26 "In the corners of the streets, (26) they may be (29) of men" (Matt. 6:5)
28 Daughter of Phanuel (Luke 2:36)

29 See 26 Down

30 Starch-bearing palm

32 "Will a man _____ God?" (Mal. 3:8)

34 Speech-related

36 Carmine and cinnabar

38 Stadium cry

40 Follows Joel

41 "The _____ of the bricks" (Ex.5:8)

42 Agatha's colleague

44 Put the kibosh on

46 "He will silence her noisy _____"
(Jer. 51:55 NIV)

49 Alabama civil rights march town

51 "He it is, to whom I shall give a _____"
(John 13:26)

54 "All ye _____ the earth"
(Zeph. 2:3) (2 words)

56 "Son of man, record this _____"
(Ezek. 24:2 NIV)

58 Adjoins

59 Impressionism founder

60 "In times _____ people great" (Deut. 2:10)
(2 words)

62 "Ran at flood _____ as before"
(Josh. 4:18 NIV)

64 "Set it by _____" (1 Sam. 5:2)

66 "There is no _____ in thee" (Song 4:7)

68 "I have wounded them that they were not (68)
to (70)" (Ps. 18:38)

70 See 68 Down

71 Small newts

72 "Let it stand!"

74 Compass point midway northeast and east

75 "Even as ye were _____" (1 Cor. 12:2)

COUPLES

ACROSS

1 29 Across wife
6 49 Across husband
10 Cathedral dome sound, maybe
14 Kitchen by-product
15 Woman's title in England
16 "First the blade, _____ the ear" (Mark 4:28)
17 Jesus would willingly _____ the cross (2 words)
18 "My cup runneth _____" (Ps. 23:5)
19 God comforts hearts that _____
20 Disciples watch Jesus' _____ into heaven
22 Ancient Indian
24 Like Noah's ark, for sure
25 Ps.ist _____ his soul to God
27 Homeric epic
29 1 Across husband
32 6 Across did _____ forbidden fruit
33 6 Across need, maybe
34 Zipporah's leader-husband
37 Wife "Leah was tender _____" (Gen. 29:17)
41 Black-and-white cookie
43 Road sealant

44 Joseph's wife
45 "They shall _____ as lions' whelps" (Jer. 51:38)
46 Terminal
48 Ananias, Sapphira told a big one
49 6 Across wife
51 Augustus _____ a world tax
54 Sewer's need
56 Baseball's Yogi
57 "They shall not hunger _____ thirst" (Isa. 49:10)
58 Solomon descriptor
60 7 Down wife
64 Revise text
66 Brand icon
68 British county
69 Caesar's place
70 Magi came from _____
71 Spooky
72 Sign
73 Do not _____ enemies
74 Snow sliders

DOWN

1 Long story
2 Mythical son of Zeus
3 Student mil. group
4 Single-celled organism (var.)
5 Elkanah's prayerful wife
6 Fuss
7 60 Across husband, king
8 "Our Father" conclusion
9 "Let thy tender _____ come" (Ps. 119:77)
10 KJV verb ending
11 Jesus-follower Joanna's husband
12 Herodias' husband
13 Husband, wife hold _____ each other
21 Streetcar
23 Menu designation (2 words)

26 Dramatically express emotion
28 Object
29 Dockside "Hey!"
30 5 Down _____ Samuel
31 Fishing need
35 Lord's trees "full of _____" (Ps. 104:16)
36 Eat away
38 Harvard rival
39 Pennsylvania city
40 Bible princes loved _____ garments
42 Tub spread
46 Samson's wife
47 Time in office
50 Husband, wife "I do"
52 Turning point

53 Jacob's favored wife
54 Lot and wife fled from there
55 Best
56 KJV "sired"
57 Early Church persecutor
59 Settee

61 Worker "worthy of his _____" (Luke 10:7)
62 Like Sinai Desert
63 Dregs
65 One of _____ healed men thanked Jesus
67 Lode yield

Day 70

BIBLE FOODS

ACROSS

1 Baseball stat
5 Went fast
9 What Jacob served famished Esau
13 Jesus said, "Come and _____" (John 21:12)
14 The mother of Jesus
15 Sinai food
16 Many a biblical narrative
17 The grandmother of Jesus, traditionally
18 "_____into the kingdom of God"
19 Small seed compared to faith
21 "Ye are the _____of the earth" (Matt. 5:13)
23 Monkey in Solomon's collection
24 Botswana honorific
25 Five fed five thousand
29 Casual "Behold!"
30 Black
32 Meal morsel
33 Par _____, mail choice (Fr.)
36 Butcher selections
37 Spy org.
38 Herb Pharisees tithed
39 Diamond measure

40 Coat hanger
41 Denver winter hour (abbr.)
42 Eve "took of the _____thereof" (Gen. 3:6)
43 Throbbing
44 Jesus _____with sinners
45 Jesus _____on a colt into Jerusalem
46 "Raven" author
47 Stay on the _____way
49 _____Testament
50 Youth agricultural org.
53 Disciple, familiarly
55 Lariats
57 KJV "cloven"
60 Bible study section, maybe
62 Jesus heals them
63 OT legumes
64 "God is _____"
65 River where baby Moses was found floating
66 Breakfast food
67 42 Across locale
68 OT edible meat

DOWN

1 Swelling
2 Shred (2 words)
3 See 38 Across
4 Pharisee or Sadducee, e.g.
5 Unctuous
6 Black-and-white bear
7 Sea bird
8 Lydia's pigments, for example
9 _____Ana, CA
10 TV network
11 Egypt to Canaan (dir.)
12 Lusts "_____against the soul" (1 Pet. 2:11)
15 Yearned for by freed Israelites

20 Prayer ender
22 Heaven's position
26 Choir descriptor
27 Little Mermaid's love, and others
28 Ante
29 "_____out of the oven"
30 Weird
31 Ruth would _____out gleaned barley
33 Jordan capital
34 Seen from Temple Mount, e.g.
35 Followers would _____Jesus' body
36 Pulses per second
39 One often followed Jesus
40 See 38 Across

42 Facades
43 Pea places
46 Roller of a typewriter or printer
48 Noah's weather forecasts
49 Holy Land tree
50 Manuscript term
51 Peter or Andrew, slangily

52 Beneficial supply of something
54 Christmas season
56 "_____ unto the Lord" (Ex. 15:1)
57 Joppa to Jerusalem (dir.)
58 Hook
59 Fall back
61 East of Eden land

ELISABETH'S JOY

ACROSS

1 "Are heavy ___" (Matt. 11:28)
6 Flows partner
10 Two cups make one
14 Greek marketplace in Paul's day
15 The sluggard might do this (Prov. 6:9)
16 Galilee, Samaria, or Judea
17 Breastplate stone (Ex. 28:17)
18 Mary "entered ___ the house of Zacharias, and saluted Elisabeth" (Luke 1:40)
19 The Ten Commandments
20 Caesarea to Nazareth (dir.)
21 Educational inst.
23 Polish port
25 Experts, for short
26 Fido's org.
27 Zacharias felt this way to see Gabriel (Luke 1:12)
30 Judgment, council, and hell fire (Matt. 5:22)
34 Hairdo no-no (1 Pet. 3:3)
35 Coastal hazes
36 Climate and natural resources org.
38 "Yuck!"
39 Bard's "before"
40 What you want to be when 59 Across
42 Elisabeth and Zacharias, e.g.

43 "Till thou hast ___ the very last mite" (Luke 12:59)
44 Spirits
45 Warriors of 1 Chronicle 12:2, perhaps
48 Twain's Tom
49 Elisabeth "brought forth a ___" (Luke 1:57)
50 Je ne ___ quoi (Fr.)
51 "No child, because that Elisabeth was ___" (Luke 1:7)
54 Bethsaida native, familiarily (John 1:44)
55 Large tree
58 Samoan capital
59 Paul was this from Seleucia to Cyprus (Acts 13:4)
61 Ahasuerus reigned from here to Ethiopia (Est. 1:1)
63 Paul's destination in 59 Across (Acts. 13:4)
64 "Then drew ___ unto him all the publicans and sinners" (Luke 15:1)
65 Simeon's sobriquet (Acts 13:1)
66 No doubt Elisabeth couldn't wait to ___ Mary what happened
67 Zacharias couldn't do this for a while (Luke 1:22)
68 Dales

DOWN

1 People wondered why Zacharias was this (Luke 1:21)
2 Dramatic conflict
3 Did Zacharias feel like one to argue with Gabriel? (Luke 1:18)
4 Epoch
5 Where Gabriel went after visiting Zacharias (Luke 1:26)
6 Elisabeth's son would have "power of ___" (Luke 1:17)
7 Paul was in one (Acts 26:29)
8 Deli order (abbr.)
9 Mottos

10 Caiaphas had one (Matt. 26:3)
11 Modern Persia
12 What Gabriel brought (Luke 1:13)
13 Brick making, e.g. (Ex. 5:14)
22 Fish
24 10 grams (abbr.)
25 One with a haughty spirit, e.g. (Prov. 16:18)
27 Laban and Jacob had one (Gen. 31:49–50)
28 Nebuchadnezzar's nails (Dan. 4:33)
29 Elisabeth's tribe (Luke 1:5)
30 Actress Day
31 Both Elisabeth and Zacharias were this (Luke 1:7)

32 Elisabeth's baby would "make ___ a people" (Luke 1:17)

33 Jael's weapon (Judg. 4:21)

35 Gabriel to Zacharias: "___ not" (Luke 1:13)

37 Like a wing

40 Helping

41 Among those devils entered (Matt. 8:31)

43 Team flag

46 Elisabeth's child preached to this people (Luke 1:80)

47 Edgar Allen ___

48 Okinawan weapon

50 Day 5 creation (Gen. 1:21)

51 Judah took Tamar's (Gen. 38:15)

52 Church section

53 The Jordan River in some places today

54 Church bell might do this

55 Gabriel's appearance put Zacharias on it (Luke 1:12)

56 "One of the people might lightly have ___ with thy wife" (Gen. 26:10)

57 Hill site of Paul's sermon (Acts 17:22)

60 Where 41 Down ran (Matt. 8:32)

62 Our righteousness is this (Isa. 64:6)

ESAU'S ERROR

ACROSS

1 Jacob and Esau had one, big-time (Gen. 27:41)
5 Top story
10 Women's magazine
14 Rebekah was one to Jacob in trickery (Gen. 27:8)
15 Animals in a region
16 Genesis includes these for Esau and Jacob
17 Esau sold it (Gen. 25:33)
19 Orchestra voice
20 Cry softly
21 What Christ did for your sins (Rom. 5:11)
23 Esau's father had lost this sense (Gen. 27:22)
26 Esau's father ___ for Jacob's impersonation of Esau (Gen. 27:27)
28 Esau "came out ___, all over like an hairy garment" (Gen. 25:25)
31 Charged particle
32 What Jesus does (Luke 1:68)
33 Jacob drew this from Esau (Gen. 27:41)
34 Jacob ___ gifts to Esau to appease him (Gen. 32:20)
37 Esau's dad (Gen. 25:26)
39 Crucifix
40 What Jacob told his father was not this

42 Asian capital
45 Incense descriptor
49 Winter river sight, at times
50 Camera stand
53 Computing phrase
54 "Thy dwelling shall be. . .of the ___ of heaven" (Gen. 27:39)
55 "I mean not that other men be ___" (2 Cor. 8:13)
56 Frothy
58 Power controlling device, for short
60 How Esau and Jacob may have addressed their father
61 "___ before men" (Matt. 6:1)
63 Frogs, toads, e.g.
69 What a 63 Across might do
70 Jacob wanted to ___ ___ Esau's inheritance (Gen. 25:31) (2 wds.)
71 Scat!
72 Ezek.'s vision (Ezek. 37:1)
73 Psalmist asks God to do this to his transgressions (Ps. 51:1)
74 Esau does this when Jacob gave him stew (Gen. 25:34)

DOWN

1 Charge
2 Roman count
3 Presidential initials
4 Fido's activity
5 Hairdo
6 Chinese ethnic group
7 Tower
8 Breathe in
9 "Lead on softly, according as the ___" (Gen. 33:14)
10 Black
11 West African country
12 London WC
13 Joppa to Jerusalem (dir.)

18 The meat Jacob served his father, perhaps
22 Element
23 Esau's niece Dinah to his nephew Zebulun, for short (Gen. 30:20–21)
24 Jacob's debt to Esau, e.g.
25 Economic measure (abbr.)
26 Esau to Jacob: "___ me, I pray thee" (Gen. 25:30)
27 "The LORD shall ___ to me another son" (Gen. 30:24)
29 When the patriarchs lived, e.g.
30 Noel mo.
32 2016 Games city, for short
35 At trickery, Jacob was this

36 Mill about
38 ___ of Galilee
40 Feet did this, KJV-style
41 Aaron's budded (Num. 17:8)
42 Jacob ___ from Esau (Gen. 27:43)
43 Whiz
44 Walter Cronkite, e.g.
45 Jacob would ___ Esau (Gen. 27:15–16)
46 Sticky black substance
47 Computer corp.
48 Esau emitted an "exceeding bitter ___"
   (Gen. 27:34)
51 Esau might ___ Jacob's family in revenge
   (Gen. 32:6)
52 Chemical compound

56 Nursery item
57 Esau: "Let my father ___, and eat"
   (Gen. 27:31)
59 Rebekah would ___ her husband's plans to
   bless Esau (Gen. 27:5)
60 Mount Sinai, e.g.
61 Mass garment
62 MGM's Lion
64 School org.
65 KJV "hast"
66 What Esau might have said when he realized
   what Jacob did (Gen. 27:34)
67 Commandment word
68 Distress call

LOVE IS. . .

ACROSS

1 Swing around
5 Fundamental
10 Hebrew letter
13 Winter jacket
15 Methuselah's dad
16 John took the book "and __ it up" (Rev. 10:10)
17 Theme: slow to __
18 Paul's woes, "in danger __" (2 Cor. 11:26 NIV) (2 words)
19 9 Down book (abbr.)
20 Ball holder
21 Evil in a field, parable-speak
23 Track features
25 Fish hands
26 19 Across, e.g.
28 Last Supper, a spiritual __
31 Theme: not easily brought to this
32 Sever
33 Like an angel, maybe
34 Repeated, word of disapproval
37 __ scallopini, Italian dish
38 Kick out

40 Indonesian island
41 "Tongue is the __ of a ready writer" (Ps. 45:1)
42 Car rental agency
43 Authoritative list, as Bible books
44 "As water ____ on the ground" (2 Sam. 14:14)
45 Garaged the car
46 A __, choir with accompaniment
49 "Like a __ or a sword...is one who gives false witness" (Prov. 25:18 NIV)
50 Egg-shaped
51 Attention-getting calls
52 Before faith, we're under the __
55 Jesus, true God, true __
56 Caffeine pill brand
59 Philippine dish
61 Average
62 Cow's belly
63 Organ setting device
64 Pie __ mode (2 words)
65 Arabian peninsula nation
66 Join together

DOWN

1 Row
2 Path
3 "I __ you to imitate me" (1 Cor. 4:16 NIV)
4 Make do
5 Theme: __ things patiently
6 Wager
7 Distress call
8 Frost
9 Theme, KJV-style
10 Implied
11 Coral reef
12 Bible book section
14 Creator
22 "Go to the __, thou sluggard" (Prov. 6:6)
24 Brimstone leaving

25 Theme: It will never __
26 Little Mermaid's love
27 Theme: now we know in __
28 Invitation request (abbr.)
29 Fencing sword
30 God has a good __ for you
31 Keep belt of truth around your __
34 Chariot descendant, maybe
35 __-eyed, almond-shaped feature
36 Theme: is __ to others
38 Theme: thinks no __
39 Bob __, home improvement man
40 Sharp point
42 Theme: joy __ (in abundance)
43 Instrumental

44 "City that is ___ on an hill cannot be hid" (Matt. 5:14)
45 Layer
46 Punctuation mark
47 Reward
48 Chinese bamboo eater
49 Cheat
51 Theme: one of three that remain

52 Modern 9 Down
53 First murder victim
54 Theme: gentle in ___ and deed
57 Lode yield
58 "Eyes of Israel were ___ for age" (Gen. 48:10)
60 Manna came with it

Day 74

ALL IN A BIBLE DAY

ACROSS

1 Chew
6 Fine wood
10 Modern-day help for Levi (Mark 2:14) (abbr.)
13 Cameroon seaport
15 Former Guinean currency
16 Some were masters of decorative __
17 Coiled
18 NT fisherman, for short
19 Fibber's forte
20 Joseph and Zebedee
22 Workbench tool
24 Mary and Joanna
26 Manna measure
28 False front
29 Heaps
30 Hit
31 Book title start, maybe (2 words)
32 Abraham's nephew
33 "Mine eyes have __ thy salvation" (Luke 2:30)
34 Levi's levy
35 Bishop's staff

37 Where chickens gather (2 words)
41 Brain and spinal cord combo (abbr.)
42 Herod was one
43 Owner of vineyard today, perhaps (abbr.)
44 Samuel, Gad, and Zadok
47 Saucy
48 "Father knoweth __ things ye have need of" (Matt. 6:8)
49 Writer Bombeck
50 Former Venetian magistrate
51 21 Down need
52 John the Baptizer, for one
54 Input
56 Body design, for short
57 Choir section
59 Uniform
63 Parisian summer (Fr.)
64 Mason's project, maybe
65 Lack of iron
66 Little bit
67 "Mary hath chosen that good __" (Luke 10:42)
68 Complainer

DOWN

1 Omaha summer hour (abbr.)
2 "__ great a matter a little fire kindleth" (James 3:5)
3 French "yes"
4 "Melts in your mouth" candy brand
5 Beggar's cries
6 Kitchen meas.
7 Fancy fabric
8 "I will not...__ what my lips have uttered" (Ps. 89:34 NIV)
9 Ukrainian capital
10 Candle maker's need
11 Eli, Zacharias, or Caiaphas
12 Record player
14 "__ to your faith virtue" (2 Pet. 1:5)

21 Farmer
23 Synthetic resin
24 Dock a boat
25 Jesus "went up __ a mountain to pray" (Luke 9:28 NIV)
27 God's creation
29 God's compassionate way, for short
30 God "__ what is done in secret" (Matt. 6:18 NIV)
31 "Law and the Prophets __ on these two commandments" (Matt. 22:40 NIV)
33 What Jesus forgives
34 Product of Paul's trade
36 Remnant
37 What owner of vineyard did

38 Jesus would soothe it

39 "Did ye never __ in the scriptures...?" (Matt. 21:42)

40 Dab

42 Vineyard need, perhaps

44 Choral group

45 List of boo-boos

46 Displayed feeling

47 Clay handler

48 Cloth maker

50 Nile area

51 "O death, where is thy __?" (1 Cor. 15:55)

53 Fastener

55 Similar to (2 words)

58 Choose

60 Flightless bird

61 Cusp

62 Blabbermouth would do this

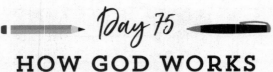

HOW GOD WORKS

ACROSS

1 "I watched the _____ he charged" (Dan. 8:4 NIV) (2 words)
6 Numerical science
10 Josip Broz
14 One-celled animal (var.)
15 "Ta-ta" in Rome
16 "Neither pray _____ these alone" (John 17:20) (2 words)
17 Start of **QUOTE** from Zech. 4:6 (3 words)
19 "For her grapes are fully _____" (Rev. 14:18)
20 Tempe, Arizona school (abbr.)
21 Major ingredient of air
23 "And she took a _____" (2 Sam. 13:9)
26 Mork's home
28 Speaker of **QUOTE**
29 Very small matter
31 "Give yourself no ____" (Lam. 2:18 NIV)
33 "Lord, I am ready _____ with thee" (Luke 22:33) (2 words)
34 "As _____ my fathers were" (Ps. 39:12)
35 "Teachers, having itching _____" (2 Tim. 4:3)
39 **QUOTE**, cont'd (4 words)

43 A son of Mushi (1 Chron. 23:23)
44 Hankering
45 "This drove which _____?" (Gen. 33:8) (2 words)
47 "I warn you, _____ before" (Gal. 5:21 NIV) (3 words)
50 "Do violence _____ man" (Luke 3:14) (2 words)
51 "The LORD _____" (Isa. 54:5) (2 words)
55 "The name of the wicked shall _____" (Prov. 10:7)
57 "Set them in two rows, six on a _____" (Lev. 24:6)
58 "Then _____ soon as she heard that Jesus was coming" (John 11:20) (2 words)
60 "To _____, Jerusalem" (Jer. 25:18)
62 It maintains highways in the Grand Canyon State (abbr.)
63 End of **QUOTE** (3 words)
68 Whirlybird (abbr.)
69 "The singers sang _____" (Neh. 12:42)
70 "Leave not thy _____" (Eccl. 10:4)
71 Pooch's remarks
72 Locomotive drivers (abbr.)
73 "_____ of Athens" (Acts 17:22) (2 words)

DOWN

1 "He _____ and worshipped him" (Mark 5:6)
2 Latin 101 word
3 "The LORD _____ Balaam" (Num. 23:16)
4 "He said, _____ Father" (Mark 14:36)
5 "Let not the king _____" (2 Chron. 18:7) (2 words)
6 AT&T rival
7 "Champ" or "camp" conclusion
8 One of the Society Islands
9 "Exceeding _____ flame of the fire" (Dan. 3:22) (2 words)
10 A scenic region of the Alps
11 "_____ and prepare a place for you" (John 14:3) (3 words)

12 Sot
13 "Beginning of days _____ of life" (Heb. 7:3 NIV) (2 words)
18 Washington's Senator Patty
22 "I _____ to those whose sin" (1 John 5:16 NIV)
23 Singer Boone
24 "He slew _____ time" (2 Sam. 23:8) (2 words)
25 "There is _____ beside me" (Isa. 45:5) (2 words)
27 Brown seaweed
30 "He giveth _____ grace" (James 4:6)
32 Frank _____ Wright

36 "The jaws of the peoples _____ that leads them astray" (Isa. 30:28 NIV) (2 words)

37 "One _____ comes this year" (Jer. 51:46 NIV)

38 Dictation taker, for short

40 Audacious

41 Kind of dam

42 Bestows

46 "As a thread of _____ is broken" (Judg. 16:9)

48 "The world also shall be _____" (1 Chron. 16:30)

49 "Wait, _____ the Lord" (Ps. 27:14) (3 words)

51 City on the Missouri River

52 Volume control

53 First duke of Normandy

54 Preminger and namesakes

56 Like some canoes

59 Narcissistic

61 "Take thee a _____, and lay it before thee" (Ezek. 4:1)

64 Gridiron gains (abbr.)

65 "A _____ without blemish" (Ezek. 46:4)

66 "Out of whose womb came the _____?" (Job 38:29)

67 "It came to pass after _____ days" (Jer. 42:7)

BIBLICAL WATERS

ACROSS

1 "Whereby we cry, _____, Father" (Rom. 8:15)
5 "Shouted _____ if they were thieves" (Job 30:5 NIV) (2 words)
9 "When I looked, behold _____ in the wall" (Ezek. 8:7) (2 words)
14 Liquid food
15 "A dead _____ flea?" (1 Sam. 24:14 NIV) (2 words)
16 "You were the _____ of perfection" (Ezek. 28:12 NIV)
17 **BIBLICAL WATER**: "Go, wash in _____" (John 9:7) (4 words)
20 "Thy want as an _____ man" (Prov. 6:11)
21 "The land of Nod, on the east of _____" (Gen. 4:16)
22 Bond foe (2 words)
23 "The twelfth month, which is the month _____" (Est. 8:12)
25 Follows Monday (abbr.)
27 "For this _____ is mount Sinai in Arabia" (Gal. 4:25)
30 **BIBLICAL WATER**: "Now _____ was there" (John 4:6) (2 words)
35 Halfway
36 "Reprove _____ scorner, lest he hate thee" (Prov. 9:8) (2 words)
37 Paper fastener
38 "Save the beast that _____ upon" (Neh. 2:12) (2 words)
40 Reputed sixth sense (abbr.)

DOWN

1 Nick and Nora's pooch
2 Danish physics Nobelist Niels
3 Ethnic group in Ghana whose language is Lelemi
4 "He shall _____ in his glory" (Ps. 102:16)
5 "Why make ye this _____; and weep?" (Mark 5:39)
6 "You cannot _____ wrong" (Hab. 1:13 NIV)
7 "Am I _____ at hand" (Jer. 23:23) (2 words)
8 "They escaped all _____ land" (Acts 27:44) (2 words)

42 "In a moment, in the twinkling of an _____ the last trump" (1 Cor. 15:52) (2 words)
43 "He saw the _____ of linen lying there" (John 20:6 NIV)
45 Greek god of love
47 British record label
48 **BIBLICAL WATER**: "Their south border was from the shore of _____" (Josh. 15:2) (3 words)
50 "For, behold, the day cometh, that shall burn _____ oven" (Malachi 4:1) (2 words)
51 "Pitched by the valley of _____" (1 Sam. 17:2)
52 "Don't change it" (on a manuscript)
54 Davenport location
57 Malayan sailing outrigger
59 "Who will _____ the battle?" (1 Kings 20:14 NIV)
63 **BIBLICAL WATER**: "Jesus, walking by _____" (Matt. 4:18) (4 words)
66 Tangy apple juice
67 "He hath spread _____ for my feet" (Lam. 1:13) (2 words)
68 "They put on him a purple _____" (John 19:2)
69 "The _____, and the vails" (Isa. 3:23)
70 "Temple of Baal and _____ it down" (2 Chron. 23:17 NIV)
71 "Dwelt in the top of the rock _____" (Judg. 15:8)

9 "He answered, Here _____" (1 Sam. 3:4) (2 words)
10 "To _____ over the trees?" (Judg. 9:9 NIV) (2 words)
11 "By this time there is a bad _____" (John 11:39 NIV)
12 "Yet will they _____ upon the LORD" (Micah 3:11)
13 Sesame Street character
18 "The _____ number of them is to be redeemed" (Num. 3:48)
19 Ignores
24 Town in SW Arizona

26 _____ Park, CO

27 "But there went up _____ from the earth" (Gen. 2:6) (2 words)

28 Circumference

29 "How right they are to _____ you!" (Song 1:4 NIV)

31 "Is not under bondage in such _____" (1 Cor. 7:15)

32 Pointless weapons

33 Andean ruminant

34 Admit (2 words)

36 Its capital is Katmandu

39 "He was _____ in his feet" (1 Kings 15:23)

41 Prophet of doom

44 "_____ fine on" (to hand down an abrupt sentence)

46 Cereal grain plant

49 "Took him by the _____" (Matt. 18:28)

50 "Or a bride her _____?" (Jer. 2:32)

53 Immigrants' class (abbr.)

54 "Hair has grown in it, the _____ is healed" (Lev. 13:37 NIV)

55 Mississippi feeder

56 "What shall _____ then?" (Luke 3:10) (2 words)

58 "To speak evil _____ man" (Titus 3:2) (2 words)

60 "There was also _____ for the rest" (Josh. 17:2) (2 words)

61 "_____, five kings of Midian" (Num. 31:8)

62 "The Nile will _____ with frogs" (Ex.8:3 NIV)

64 Hesitation sounds

65 "_____ it up" (Rev. 10:10)

OUR FATHER

ACROSS

1 Smooth, talkative
5 Bruins' university (abbr.)
9 Souse
13 "Third day he shall _____ again" (Matt. 20:19)
14 "Draw _____ to God" (Ps. 73:28)
15 Drink noisily
16 Gelatinous material derived from marine algae
17 _____ of Bethlehem
18 "_____ is the Lord's" (Ps. 24:1)
19 God never _____
21 "Declare thy mighty _____" (Ps. 145:4)
23 List ender (abbr.)
24 Jerusalem to Nineveh (dir.)
25 "Day of the Lord is _____" (Isa. 13:6) (2 words)
29 Loaves-and-fishes bringer
30 Survey
32 Digit
33 "Eat _____ like an ox" (Isa. 11:7)
36 Russian currency
37 Samaria to Moab (dir.)

38 Forward most part of ship's bow
39 Tires of
40 South Asian flour
41 Carry a burden
42 "Father of _____" (Eph. 1:17)
43 God _____ us on His path
44 Jesus _____ with sinners
45 Galilee fishing needs
46 Jesus, God's _____
47 Agonizing struggle, as of guilt
49 Hovercraft (abbr.)
50 Lord's trees are "full of _____" (Ps. 104:16)
53 Jonah swallower
55 God, _____ of all
57 "Forgive us our _____"
60 Christ died _____ for sins
62 Indian garment
63 Constellation
64 "Deliver me out of the _____" (Ps. 69:14)
65 Jesus born _____ humanity
66 Compass point (abbr.)
67 Eagerness
68 Purim month

DOWN

1 "Continue in the _____ of God" (Acts 13:43)
2 "God said, Let there be _____" (Gen. 1:3)
3 Abraham's son
4 Swiss capital
5 Straighten
6 "_____ from strife" (Prov. 20:3)
7 Big dog, for short
8 Judea or Galilee, and others
9 Cut, gash
10 "_____ Father..."
11 "...who _____ in heaven"
12 European speedometer reading (abbr.
15 May "God...strengthen, _____ you" (1 Pet. 5:10)
20 Chew like a rat

22 God _____ each person by name
26 Solomon "had _____ a navy" (1 Kings 10:22) (2 words)
27 Edged in
28 "Signs...wonders...and mighty _____" (2 Cor. 12:12)
29 Ten Commandments, e.g.
30 Cat sounds
31 Do what we're told
33 "Plop!"
34 "Thy word is _____" (John 17:17)
35 CB radio talk
36 Jesus, "_____ of David" (Rev. 5:5)
39 God desires to _____ you
40 "As a _____ doth gather her brood" (Luke 13:34)

42 Type of rock

43 "God is _____"

46 Part of door or window

48 "As _____ as ye eat this bread" (1 Cor. 11:26)

49 Ghana capital

50 "Who may _____ in thy sight?" (Ps. 76:7)

51 Artery

52 Before, earlier

54 Our heavenly _____

56 Paul's mission territory

57 Israelite tribe

58 "Come..._____ my child die" (John 4:49)

59 Baby need

61 Nada

Day 78

JESUS' MINISTRY

ACROSS

1 Queen of _____ visited Solomon
6 Gospel book, for short
10 Youth agricultural org.
13 Jesus' claims would _____ Pharisees
15 Winds and sea would _____ Jesus
16 Particle
17 Sour ale
18 Jesus decried the _____ of the Pharisees
19 Pull, as at heartstrings
20 1960s skirt
22 One of Jesus' twelve
24 Tribe
26 "Waters cast up mire and _____" (Isa. 57:20)
28 "Thou shalt bruise his _____" (Gen. 3:15)
29 When darkness fell on Calvary
30 One _____, one Shepherd
31 "Look well to thy _____" (Prov. 27:23)
32 Mischievous one
33 Jesus "in whom I am _____ pleased" (Mark 1:11)
34 Jesus made the blind to _____
35 Renters
37 Centuries _____ between Testaments
41 Feline
42 Early Church missionary
43 Pod dweller
44 "Thou canst make me _____" (Mark 1:40)
47 Devil would _____ Him to jump from temple
48 Jesus said _____ Spirit would come
49 Nonstandard negative
50 Celestial _____ announced Jesus' birth
51 Collections
52 Jesus _____ little children
54 2 Down welcoming dance, maybe
56 "Birds of the _____ have nests" (Matt. 8:20)
57 Labels
59 Cruel, brutish
63 Dawdle
64 Snack cookie
65 Flyer Earhart
66 "If _____ man come to me" (Luke 14:26)
67 GI's diagnosis
68 Garment closers

DOWN

1 _____ of Galilee
2 Hawaii airport letters
3 KJV "before"
4 NT tax collector (slang.)
5 Jesus would rise _____
6 Swab
7 "We went _____, and set forth" (Acts 21:2)
8 Lure, entice
9 Misprint
10 More suitable
11 Evil _____ God's perfect world
12 50 Across members
14 Sea eagle
21 Baal and others
23 30 Across members
24 "Thy kingdom _____"
25 Cuts off
27 "Love worketh no _____" (Rom. 13:10)
29 Zilch
30 Worshipers fell at Jesus' _____
31 Jesus came to _____ our wounds
33 Halt, with "off"
34 To swing around
36 Dashes away
37 You are "salt of the _____" (Matt. 5:13)
38 Perfect Lamb, without _____
39 Snaky fish
40 "Give us this _____ our daily bread"
42 Dance step (Fr.)
44 Jewish mystical writings

45 Mystery writer _____ Jackson Braun
46 Vigor, vitality
47 Eludes
48 Where Jesus came from
50 "I am. . .lowly in _____" (Matt. 11:29)
51 Closes loudly, as a door

53 Devil couldn't _____ Jesus' work
55 America (abbr.)
58 Turf
60 Menu term (2 words)
61 4 Down would _____ others
62 Public warning program (abbr.)

ESTHER: THE BLESSED QUEEN

ACROSS

1 Concorde, e.g.
4 British WC
7 Shushan to 22 Across (dir.)
10 Jews may have used one in defense (Est. 8:11)
12 Tool of trade, perhaps, for Andrew and Peter (Matt. 4:18)
13 Esther's appearance (Est. 2:7)
14 Leah to Joseph and Rachel to Reuben (Gen. 35:23–24)
16 Ahasuerus's exclamation to find Haman at Esther's couch (Est. 7:8)
17 Ahasuerus to Esther: "___ ye also for the Jews" (Est. 8:8)
18 Description of Esther (Est. 2:7) (2 words)
21 Ahasuerus's calls for young virgins, for short
22 Abraham's native place (Gen. 11:27–28)
23 Esther may have felt this when urged to intercede (Est. 4:16)
26 Chemical symbol
27 Esther was one (Est. 2:7)
31 Scooby-___
32 Skunklike African animal
35 Haman would ___ the king's decree to destroy Jews (Est. 3:8–9)

36 Mordecai to Esther "Who knoweth whether thou art come to the kingdom for ___" (Est. 4:14) (5 wds.)
41 Esther's pronoun
42 Fern seed
43 Haman had a lot of it (Est. 6:6)
44 Esther was given Haman's (Est. 8:7)
47 Spielberg's alien
48 Esther must not be this (Est. 4:8)
49 Mordecai acted as this to Esther (Est. 2:7)
50 "Go to the ___, thou sluggard" (Prov. 6:6)
51 Where Haman ended up (Est. 7:10) (4 words)
61 Mordecai sent letters to the Jews "with words of ___ and truth" (Est. 9:30)
62 Hospital patients do this
63 Haman's plans could be called this (Est. 3:8–9)
64 63 Across homonym
65 Jerusalem to Damascus (dir.)
66 "Singin' in the Rain" Kelly
67 "They shall not hunger ___ thirst" (Isa. 49:10)
68 Esther asked the Jews not to do this for three days (Est. 4:16)
69 Comprehensive dictionary

DOWN

1 Wound cap
2 Skid
3 Charlie's sort
4 What a sluggard does
5 Honolulu's island
6 The king's command to his servants was this (Est. 1:10)
7 "Cause Haman to make haste, that he may do as Esther hath ___" (Est. 5:5)
8 Shushan is one
9 One might be among those singing (Song 2:12)
11 Energy measurement (abbr.)
13 TGI day (abbr.)

15 A Psalm often has one
17 Haman's mind did this, perhaps
19 Haman was one, in the foolish sense
20 Austrian river (var.)
23 Passports are these
24 Particle of dust turned to one under Aaron's rod (Ex. 8:16)
25 Ness and Lomond
27 Bread spread
28 Sukkot shelter
29 Sackcloth partner
30 Mr. Ed's negative, perhaps
33 Jesus would do this on the third day

34 Elf

37 Excited (with "up")

38 Christians were martyred in one, at times

39 Ahasuerus would not ___ for Vashti's refusal

40 Chinese sauce

45 Church part

46 Chinese philosophical concept

50 Ornamental stud

51 "I stand. . .and knock: if any man. . .___ the door, I will come in" (Rev. 3:20)

52 Christians' nemesis in Rome

53 Esau had a lot of this (Gen. 27:11)

54 Often in cubes

55 Wax mate

56 One of Columbus' ships

57 In the king's dream, one of these was iron (Dan. 2:33)

58 Black-and-white treat

59 Ahasuerus enjoyed too much of this (Est. 1:10)

60 "If Mordecai be of the ___ of the Jews" (Est. 6:13)

GABRIEL: THE ARCHANGEL

ACROSS

1 Never say this to Gabriel!
6 Investment choices (abbr.)
9 It's for lovers (abbr.)
11 Rights org.
12 Downwind
13 Tramps
16 Temptation, often
17 Gabriel to Mary: "Elisabeth, she hath also conceived a son in her old ___" (Luke 1:36)
18 How Gabriel might respond if you said 1 Across
19 **GABRIEL'S MESSAGE**, Part 1 (Luke 1:28) (3 words)
23 It came to ___: KJV for "when"
24 "Fear not" are words Gabriel would use and ___
25 Pasty glue
29 13th letter of the Greek alphabet
30 **GABRIEL'S PROMISE**: "The Lord ___" (Luke 1:28) (3 wds.)
33 ___ voyage
36 Mary and Joseph would ___ Jesus (Luke 1:80)

37 Sports org.
38 Press
40 After His resurrection, Jesus did this with His disciples (Luke 24:43)
41 Design process (2 words)
44 Fashionable
45 Post-jail sentence
46 **GABRIEL'S MESSAGE**, Part 2 (Luke 1:28)
50 Car rental agency
52 Joseph might have been doing this during Jesus' birth if Nikon had been around (2 words)
58 Cuisine choice
59 Parents should not be this (Prov. 23:13)
60 Connection
61 Wildebeest location
62 Kind of messenger Gabriel was
63 Herodias's daughter needed one (Matt. 14:6)
64 Grizzly bear state (abbr.)
65 Dan. and lions met here (Dan. 6:16)
66 **GABRIEL'S MESSAGE**, Part 3 (Luke 1:28)

DOWN

1 Never do this to Gabriel!
2 Astronomer Sagan
3 "Jealousy is the ___ of a man" (Prov. 6:34)
4 Card series
5 U.K. politician (abbr.)
6 "Puts on," KJV-style
7 Impressionist painter
8 Huldah was one (2 Kings 22:14)
9 Popularity
10 Sackcloth mate
13 "We should be saved. . .from the hand of all that ___ us" (Luke 1:71)
14 Pacific tourist destination
15 Reuben, Judah, and Simon (abbr.)
20 "They ___ upon him" (Matt. 27:30)

21 "The charity of every one of you all toward ___ other aboundeth" (2 Thess. 1:3)
22 God's Word is this
25 Space station
26 Paul and shipmates were this in a storm (Acts 27:15)
27 Pakistani valley in the news
28 A good soldier of Christ does not do this (2 Tim. 2:3)
29 Rebekah put goat skins on Jacob's (Gen. 27:16)
31 Jacob to Esau
32 Movie *2001*'s talking computer
33 100 cents in Ethiopia
34 You can fiddle with its middle
35 Gabriel's time in France

39 Bethlehem to Jerusalem (dir.)

41 Angel to shepherds: "This shall be a ___ unto you" (Luke 2:12)

42 ___ Span cleanser

43 Mary "___ in her mind what manner of salutation this should be" (Luke 1:29)

46 "The king had ___ a navy of Tharshish" (1 Kings 10:22) (2 words)

47 What place God needs to have in your life (Matt. 6:33)

48 Mary was this with Gabriel's message (Luke 1:38)

49 Little girl in Cancun

50 "Kings of armies did flee ___" (Ps. 68:12)

51 Harpy

53 Gabriel's tidings (Luke 1:19)

54 Gabriel was "sent to speak ___" Zacharias (Luke 1:19)

55 Range

56 "They shall fall by the ___ of the sword" (Luke 21:24)

57 "We have ___ his star in the east" (Matt. 2:2)

58 Fido's org.

63 Jericho to Jerusalem (dir.)

Day 81

BAPTISM

ACROSS

1 Ship's letters
4 Shrine item, perhaps
9 Shining, like angels
14 Salon feature, often
15 OT or NT time period
16 "__ we were yet sinners, Christ died" (Rom. 5:8)
17 Devil might __ fiery darts
18 He baptized Cornelius
19 Seeped
20 Web action
22 Evils
24 Devil descriptor
25 Church feature
27 27th US president
31 Sicilian erupter
32 Composer Francis __ Key
33 Bible metal
34 Angry
36 End
38 Arrangements
40 Speaker setting
42 "Now are ye __ in the Lord" (Eph. 5:8)
43 Kinder
44 Expert, for short
45 "Word was made flesh, and __ among us" (John 1:14)
47 Scorch
51 Loch __ monster
53 Hawkeye State
54 Mother of Mary, traditionally
55 Baptism ending
57 John the Baptizer's river
59 "No longer a __, but God's child" (Gal. 4:7 NIV)
62 Take exception to
65 Baptized are __ body in Christ
66 Tanker
67 Baptism will __ guilt from soul
68 Gossip
69 Garden tool
70 Tears
71 Joppa to Hebron (dir.)

DOWN

1 Functioning
2 Modern 10 Down
3 South Pacific island dweller
4 Agents, for short
5 Fencing sword
6 Sodom fleer
7 Cube cooler
8 Messiah
9 Unauthorized mil. leave
10 "Baptizing them in the name of...the Holy __" (Matt. 28:19)
11 Screen star Taylor
12 Madrid cheer
13 Say "I do"
21 Apparition
23 "__ us...cast off the works of darkness" (Rom. 13:12)
25 Bible book of many baptisms
26 Poet Edgar Allan __
28 Molecule
29 Pentecost's tongues of __
30 Explosive (abbr.)
32 Maple tree product
35 Trail feature
36 Lager
37 Disciple Judas acted as one
38 Beget
39 Some people have huge ones
40 Handyman Bob
41 Reformation Day mo.

42 Caregiver's certificate (abbr.)

43 With 64 Down, what baptized believers put on

45 "Live after the flesh, ye shall __" (Rom. 8:13)

46 Many looked at Jesus with awe and __

48 Baptism __ us with 10 Down

49 Pineapple (Ger.)

50 God will never __ on His promises

52 "Believe and be __" (Luke 8:12)

56 Mary to Jesus (Fr.)

57 "The __ shall live by faith" (Rom. 1:17)

58 Mined metals

59 Steel wool pad brand

60 Mouth part

61 Chicken __ king (2 words)

63 Poetic preposition

64 See 43 Down

APOSTLE PAUL

ACROSS

1 Paul's missionary focus
5 Former Russian ruler
9 Opaque gem
13 Twin Cities state (abbr.)
14 Rant's partner
15 Where Paul left Titus
16 I "am not __ to be called an apostle" (1 Cor. 15:9)
17 Madrid cheers
18 Cut down
19 King who invited Paul to speak (Acts 26)
21 Edible root
23 Peter would cast it into the sea
24 Paul's son in faith, for short
25 Ananias had one concerning Paul
29 Computer choice
30 "Spirit of truth... __ out from the Father" (John 15:26 NIV)
32 Caleb, for one
33 Some Southeast Asians
36 Speak suddenly
37 Retention problem (abbr.)
38 Paul taught "in the lecture __ of Tyrannus" (Acts 19:9 NIV)
39 I "am less than the __ of all saints" (Eph. 3:8)

40 Funny saying
41 Card game
42 I am "the __ of sinners" (1 Tim. 1:16 NIV)
43 Bloodsucker
44 French possessive
45 Has
46 Seafood choice
47 Peter, in France
49 Corp. department
50 Recipe measure (abbr.)
53 Vegetable
55 Lasagna spice
57 "I have made myself a __ to everyone" (1 Cor. 9:19 NIV)
60 Stylish
62 Black
63 With cupbearer in Joseph's prison
64 Garden chore
65 Paul on the road: "Who art thou, __?" (Acts 9:5)
66 Pre-K lessons
67 Eye infection
68 Those Jesus invited to come to Him

DOWN

1 Jordan capital
2 Blockade
3 Static
4 Against
5 __ of Capricorn
6 Arabic peace (var.)
7 "__ Maria"
8 "Power of Christ may __ upon me" (2 Cor. 12:9)
9 Black-and-white snack
10 Church chair
11 Jesus __ with sinners
12 "As many as are __ by the Spirit of God" are

His (Rom. 8:14)
15 Paul, a servant of Jesus __
20 School-year groups (abbr.)
22 Prevent
26 Problem, in modern parlance
27 Concerning an eye
28 Forest dweller of myth
29 Unit of length (abbr.)
30 "We see through a __, darkly" (1 Cor. 13:12)
31 Kick out
33 Wallop
34 Vietnamese capital

35 "Man shall not live by bread __" (Matt. 4:4)
36 Swiss capital
39 "Thou madest him a little __ than the angels" (Heb. 2:7)
40 It is proven (abbr.)
42 Philemon, Paul's dear friend and fellow __
43 "Who shall separate us from the __ of Christ?" (Rom. 8:35)
46 "He sits enthroned above the __ of the earth" (Isa. 40:22 NIV)
48 Wanders

49 Crocheted table topper
50 No-no
51 Swine sound
52 Frogs' homes
54 Book written by Luke
56 Money (Ger.)
57 Govt. agency
58 Popular dog, for short
59 58 Down registry (abbr.)
61 Smack

Day 83

THE HALL OF FAITH

ACROSS

1 London transport
5 Tall ornamental grasses
10 "Horns of ivory and _____" (Ezek. 27:15)
15 "Saw that their _____ was dead" (1 Sam. 17:51 NIV)
16 "A blind man, or _____." (Lev. 21:18) (2 words)
17 Fracas
18 "Cast him into _____" (Gen. 37:24) (2 words)
19 "_____ flood stage as before" (Josh. 4:18 NIV) (2 words)
20 "If I make my _____ hell" (Ps. 139:8) (2 words)
21 Three names from the biblical **HALL OF FAITH** (Heb. 11) (3 words)
24 Plant trunks
25 Painted metalware
26 "Such as he _____ get" (Lev. 14:30)
29 GI's duds
30 Cuckoo pint genus
31 Sauce or bean
34 "There was _____" (Luke 8:24) (2 words)
36 "Lying on _____" (Matt. 9:2 NIV) (2 words)
37 "_____ ghost" (Matt. 14:26 NIV) (2 words)
38 Three more from the **HALL OF FAITH** (3 words)

42 Chow
43 Alamo rival
44 "_____ like stallions" (Jer. 50:11 NIV)
5 GM or IBM (abbr.)
46 "Ye _____ chosen generation" (1 Pet. 2:9) (2 words)
47 "As though I shot _____ mark" (1 Sam. 20:20) (2 words)
49 "As a wild bull in a _____" (Isa. 51:20)
50 Middle Eastern chief (var.)
51 "Behold a great _____" (Dan. 2:31)
53 Three more from the **HALL OF FAITH** (3 words)
59 Kind of energy
60 "With eyes _____" (Ps. 17:11 NIV)
61 "I will give unto _____, and to thy seed" (Gen. 17:8)
62 Japanese port
63 Rachel, to Rebekah (Gen. 27:42–43; 29:10)
64 "Both the _____ of it" (Ezek. 15:4)
65 German city NW of Essen
66 "Azal: _____ shall flee" (Zech. 14:5) (2 words)
67 "By the _____, and by the hinds" (Song 2:7)

DOWN

1 "More _____ the first" (Rev. 2:19)
2 Result of payment default (abbr.)
3 La Scala solo
4 "The _____ will eat them up" (Isa. 50:9 NIV)
5 Dressed (poetic)
6 Tocsins
7 "Should such a _____ I flee?" (Neh. 6:11) (2 words)
8 Oriental nanny
9 "They _____, they catch men" (Jer. 5:26) (3 words)

10 "To _____ his father" (Gen. 50:2)
11 Bathysphere man
12 Ye _____ Shoppe
13 First moon walker _____ Armstrong
14 Appetite
22 "Laid it in _____" (Mark 6:29) (2 words)
23 "Out of the _____ of God" (Matt. 4:4)
26 "Our ship was to unload its _____" (Acts 21:3 NIV)
27 "Those who pass by without _____" (Micah 2:8 NIV) (2 words)

28 Book after Micah

30 Iowa State locale

31 "I will _____ all my raiment" (Isa. 63:3)

32 Native American tribe originally from Missouri

33 Pleasure craft

35 Assaying place

36 Location of the seven churches (Rev. 1:11)

37 Follows "expert" (suffix)

39 A leader under Ezra's direction (Ezra 8:16)

40 "Cause them to rule _____" (Dan. 11:39) (2 words)

41 "Stricken _____" (Josh. 23:1) (2 words)

46 Espousing neither the upright nor the debauched

47 "Thou shalt make _____ seat of pure gold" (Ex.25:17) (2 words)

48 Soft ice cream franchise: _____-Freez

50 "To every one _____ of bread" (2 Sam. 6:19) (2 words)

51 "As he came, and said, _____ company" (2 Kings 9:17) (3 words)

52 "_____ into the rock" (Isa. 2:10)

53 Son of Eliezer (Luke 3:29)

54 "_____ for the day!" (Joel 1:15)

55 *Rolie Polie* _____ (children's TV show)

56 Cry of disbelief (2 words)

57 Yield

58 Noted pianist Dame Myra

59 "They _____ not, neither do they reap" (Matt. 6:26)

BLESSED ASSURANCE

ACROSS

1 He wrote, "Never send to know for whom the bell tolls; it tolls for thee"
6 Actor who played the title role in *The Thief of Baghdad*
10 Verne's captain
14 "Love" in Lyon (Fr.)
15 Ku Klux _____
16 Withdraw (abbr.)
17 Beginning of some assuring **WORDS** of Jesus (John 14:1) (4 words)
20 Historical period
21 "And after that also King of _____," (Heb. 7:2)
22 Singer Fisher
23 Swiss speciality chemical company
24 Least active
25 **WORDS**, cont'd (3 words)
30 "I have been an _____ in a strange land" (Ex.18:3)
31 "For to come to him with _____" (Acts 17:15) (2 words)
35 "Have I _____ of mad men" (1 Sam. 21:15)

36 _____-Davis, pharmaceutical company
38 River in France
39 Ridiculing
41 Wash cycle
42 **WORDS**, cont'd (3 words)
45 Pre-Roman Italian
48 Formerly (arch.)
49 PhD hurdle
50 "Make thy face to _____ upon thy servant" (Ps. 31:16)
52 "Finally, brothers, good-by. _____ for perfection" (2 Cor. 13:11 NIV)
55 End of **WORDS** (4 words)
58 "A man that flattereth his neighbour spreadeth _____ for his feet" (Prov. 29:5) (2 words)
59 One of the Guthrie boys
60 "Was there _____ the death of Herod" (Matt. 2:15)
61 Small fishing boat
62 Adolescent
63 Contaminate

DOWN

1 "The valley of Shaveh, which is the king's _____" (Gen. 14:17)
2 "Now an _____ is the tenth part of an ephah" (Ex.16:36)
3 "For there is _____ just man upon earth" (Eccl. 7:20) (2 words)
4 Josh.'s father (Ex.33:11)
5 Farmer's bane
6 First US space station
7 It's good for burns
8 Author of *The Wonderful Wizard of Oz*, L. Frank
9 Reno school (abbr.)
10 Grandma's fine, decorative stitchery
11 Get out of through clever deceit
12 Slugger Roger

13 Double quartet
18 Superstitious or social prohibition (var.)
19 Actress Lamarr and namesakes
23 A good reputation depends on it
24 "And their words seemed to them as _____ tales" (Luke 24:11)
25 "Against the _____ of the rovers" (1 Chron. 12:21)
26 Civil War general Robert _____ (2 words)
27 Layer of a wedding cake
28 "Now the city was _____ and great" (Neh. 7:4)
29 Wapiti
32 Follows *ti* or *ty*
33 Amoco rival, once upon a time

34 "What _____ is this that ye have done?" (Gen. 44:15)

36 "I will even make the _____ for fire great" (Ezek. 24:9)

37 Black cuckoos in warmer parts of America

40 "Wail, oaks of Bashan; the _____ forest has been cut down!" (Zech. 11:2 NIV)

41 "When ye see a cloud _____ of the west" (Luke 12:54) (2 words)

43 "He would put the _____ again" (Ex.34:33 NLT) (2 words)

44 European sea eagles

45 "Could not be eaten, they were _____" (Jer. 24:2) (2 words)

46 "Now therefore ye _____ more strangers" (Eph. 2:19) (2 words)

47 Piece of farm equipment

50 Withered and dry

51 "Lest he _____ thee to the judge" (Luke 12:58)

52 Opposed to (prefix)

53 "_____ love with Tamar" (2 Sam. 13:4 NIV) (2 words)

54 "All the hills shall _____" (Amos 9:13)

56 "When anyone went to a wine _____ to draw fifty" (Hag. 2:16 NIV)

57 "And by night _____ pillar of fire" (Ex.13:21) (2 words)

Day 85

HEAVENLY BITS

ACROSS

1 "_____ are they that keep" God's laws (Rev. 14:12)
5 Florida city
10 Lydia's purple, e.g.
13 Verdi wrote more than one
15 Jesus would rise _____
16 King (Lat.)
17 "_____ of me" (Matt. 11:29)
18 Parisian topper
19 Hard worker, per Proverbs
20 Slang affirmative
21 Heaven's streets, per Revelation
23 God knows _____ save you (2 words)
25 Give over
26 Heaven means _____ life
28 Easily altered
31 Vertical line
32 Bible study sections, perhaps
33 Our righteousness is "as filthy _____" (Isa. 64:6)
34 Zealous admirer
37 We will be given a resurrected _____

38 Easter morn, an angel _____ Jesus' tomb
40 Roman Catholic pontiff
41 Gaza to Jerusalem (dir.)
42 Earth will pass _____
43 Calvary sight
44 "_____, and curse not" (Rom. 12:14)
45 Island on Paul's journey
46 No "slumber to mine _____" (Ps. 132:4)
49 We will not _____ in heaven
50 "Divine Comedy" author
51 Jesus came to _____ the lost
52 Airline regulatory agency (abbr.)
55 Delivery truck letters (abbr.)
56 In a stately way
59 Heaven: Celestial _____
61 Desktop component (abbr.)
62 "We have _____ and drunk" with you (Luke 13:26)
63 Entire desktop, e.g.
64 "Every _____ shall see him" (Rev. 1:7)
65 Church organ piece, maybe
66 Heaven's wall garnished with many

DOWN

1 Heaven, the _____ Jerusalem
2 Fencing sword
3 "Thrust...thy sickle, and _____" (Rev. 14:15)
4 Sin
5 Heaven's banquet _____
6 KJV "senior citizen"
7 Deface
8 Mom's apple, e.g.
9 Songs or hymns
10 Lovingly "have I _____ thee" (Jer. 31:3)
11 Old gossip (Yiddish)
12 "I will _____ thee, O LORD" (Ps. 30:1)
14 Heavenly singers
22 Many a psalm
24 Sun or moon

25 Heaven, _____ of God
26 Vivacity
27 Pulls
28 Auto job
29 KJV "soon"
30 Wait, tarry
31 Hunted ones
34 Bread
35 Church section
36 Monster's loch
38 Parable debtors _____ their creditor
39 "It came to _____..."
40 Stage element
42 Property recipient, in court
43 Shouts of praise

Down (continued)

44 Deli choice, for short
45 Pulpit occupier (abbr.)
46 To draw out, obtain
47 Like a little dog
48 Follow
49 Actor John _____
51 Snow slider

52 Unbeliever's future decider
53 School graduate, for short
54 Noise increasers, for short
57 Horse morsel
58 Energy unit
60 Medical diagnostic test (abbr.)

POTPOURRI

ACROSS

1 Winds cannot _____ a house built on rock
6 Green gem
10 Tax collector Mathew's concern (abbr.)
14 Hermit's house, maybe
15 Friend
16 Had on one's body
17 Bread bakers
18 "Many _____ false witness against him" (Mark 14:56)
19 OT shepherd prophet
20 Join metal
21 Indefinitely long period of time
22 Least covered
24 Tidy
26 Swords
27 "His anger endureth but a _____" (Ps. 30:5)
30 Moses put a serpent "upon a _____" (Num. 21:9)
31 Bottomless pit
32 Sandwich sweetener
33 Praying publican stood "afar _____" (Luke 18:13)
36 Washer cycle
37 LAX screen information

38 Void
40 "_____, hath God said...?" (Gen. 3:1)
41 Tightwad
43 "_____ Pere" (Fr.)
44 Unclear
45 Soda choice
46 Gets bigger, as ego
49 He washed disciples' _____
50 Eternal home
51 Telecopy machine
52 Salt Lake City state
56 Pharisees would _____ Jesus to debate
57 Dorcas of Joppa would have one
59 Corrupt ones "take a _____" (Amos 5:12)
60 "Forever and _____"
61 "No man hath _____ God" (John 1:18)
62 Don't put candle "_____ a bushel" (Matt. 5:15)
63 French commune
64 "Ye are the _____ of the earth" (Matt. 5:13)
65 They can be good or evil

DOWN

1 Freight boat
2 Lord, "_____ mercy on us" (Matt. 9:27)
3 First murder victim
4 Gift of the Holy Spirit
5 Printing measurements
6 Ruffled tie
7 Actor Alda
8 US currency ticker symbol (abbr.)
9 Peeper
10 Be _____ of God's presence
11 Promising beginner with "up"
12 Calvary sight
13 Adversity is a _____ of faith
21 "Take, _____; this is my body" (Mark 14:22)

23 Expectancy
25 Cast
26 Roof panel, maybe
27 32 Down mother
28 Off-Broadway award
29 Asian starling
30 Fisherman disciple
32 God's Son
33 "I'm _____ your tricks!"
34 Roll
35 Plague insect
39 Chopin piece
42 Jesus cured _____
45 King (Lat.)

46 "No man can _____ two masters" (Matt. 6:24)

47 Bet

48 "Hills rejoice on _____ side" (Ps. 65:12)

49 "Pray, and not to _____" (Luke 18:1)

50 Rainbow colors

51 Combustible

53 Detergent choice

54 Not yet up

55 Belonging to a woman

58 Beverage choice

59 What Aaron's rod did

GIDEON: GOD'S MAN OF VALOR

ACROSS

1 Recedes
5 Inflexible
10 Mountain Time (abbr.)
13 Japanese dress
14 Mockery
15 Soft white cheese
16 "Upon the ___ of the rock" (Job 39:28)
17 "___ be unto thee; fear not" (Judg. 6:23)
18 Consumer
19 Sixth tribe of Israel (abbr.)
21 Gideon's job (Judg. 6:11)
23 Teaspoon (abbr.)
26 "He shall be cast into the ___ of lions" (Dan. 6:7)
28 "The ___ shall not always be forgotten" (Ps. 9:18)
29 It might fall on your head
32 These should be redeemed (Num. 3:48) (pl.)
33 Hyundai is one
34 Author of Acts (Philem. 24)(Gr.)
36 "Cast him into the ___ of ground" (2 Kings 9:26)
37 Deborah's right-hand man

38 Syllables used in songs (2 words)
42 Drop
43 "The children of Israel did ___" (Judg. 2:11)
44 Midianite prince who lost his head
46 Network
49 Trims
51 "Let all thy wants ___ upon me" (Judg. 19:20)
52 "Gideon went up by the ___ of them" (Judg. 8:11)
53 "I ___ not my heart from any joy" (Eccl. 2:10)
57 ___ Lanka
59 Reverberate
60 Bullwinkle is one
62 She follows Judg.
66 "There was no such ___ done" (Judg. 19:30)
67 Lawn tool
68 Paul's mission field ___ Minor
69 "A people that do ___ in their heart" (Ps. 95:10)
70 Sleep disorder
71 Dozes

DOWN

1 Keyboard component (abbr.)
2 It reaches from end to end (Ex. 26:28)
3 Lingerie
4 "Shew me a ___ that thou talkest with me" (Judg. 6:17)
5 Jack the ___
6 Wrath
7 "And one ___ for a sin offering" (Num. 29:38)
8 Give 'em an ___, they want a mile
9 Lydia's profession (Acts 16:14)
10 Joins together
11 Trusty horse
12 "I will ___ until thou come again" (Judg. 6:18)

15 Stuck together
20 "___ to your faith virtue" (2 Pet. 1:5)
22 "All the ___ of the world shall remember" (Ps. 22:27)
23 "Let it become a ___" (Ps. 69:22)
24 First king of Israel
25 Falafel holder
27 Mr. Ryan
30 "Israel remembered ___ the LORD their God" (Judg. 8:34)
31 Jewish holiday (Est. 9:26)
32 Tree where Gideon met the angel of the Lord (Judg. 6:11)
35 Biblical ground transportation

37 Baby essential
38 "Many are called, but ____ are chosen" (Matt. 22:14)
39 Assert
40 Italian money
41 Alcoholic (slang)
42 Interlock
44 Ps.ist's instrument
45 Gideon's was made of gold
47 Canaanite killed by Deborah
48 Samson to his father: "Get ____ for me" (Judg. 14:3)

49 Swedish citizen
50 Kinder
54 Mrs. Peel
55 Ice-skating maneuver
56 "I will break ____ this tower" (Judg. 8:9)
58 Cyrus's kingdom today (Ezra 1:1)
61 "____ there come people down by the middle of the land" (Judg. 9:37)
63 America (abbr.)
64 Part of ear to be anointed (Lev. 14:17)
65 Owns

HAMAN TRADES PLACES

ACROSS

1 Wicked fall into (Ps. 141:10)
5 Country facing judgment (Ezek. 30:5)
9 Clang
13 Give off
14 Persona non ___
15 ___ mater
16 Banquet beverage (Est. 5:6)
17 Mordecai's garment material (Est. 8:15)
18 Ball of thread
19 Nut (2 words)
21 Vashti and Esther
23 Pod vegetables
24 Pitch
25 Sway
28 Role play
31 Hebrew twelfth month (Est. 3:7)
32 "My life is ___ with grief" (Ps. 31:10)
34 A woman should "___ her nails" (Deut. 21:12)
36 Jewish days of fasting (Est. 4:16)
37 "David ___, and stood upon the Philistine" (1 Sam. 17:51)

38 "They shall ___, and not be weary" (Isa. 40:31)
39 Hook site (Job 41:2)
41 Wanderer
43 "At thy rebuke they ___" (Ps. 104:7)
44 "He appointed the moon for ___" (Ps. 104:19)
46 "Who can understand his ___?" (Ps. 19:12)
48 Mordecai's seat (Est. 2:19)
49 Removed as confirmation (Ruth 4:7)
50 Hebrew tenth month (Est. 2:16)
53 Wired for internet
57 "Thy ___ is as a flock of goats" (Song 4:1)
58 Lazy person
60 Extinct bird
61 Defunct football league
62 Month Pur was cast (Est. 3:7)
63 Leave out
64 Goliath's plan regarding Israel (1 Sam. 17:25)
65 Nerd
66 Give out a measure, as in Mark 4:24

DOWN

1 Mr. Gingrich
2 Ruler
3 Prong
4 More abrupt
5 What the Lord hears (James 5:4)
6 "He laid his ___ upon the Jews" (Est. 8:7)
7 Colorado tribe
8 Haman attended (Est. 5:5)
9 Warm-up lap (2 words)
10 French pronoun
11 Bible's last word
12 Kept in the heart (Heb. 10:16)
14 Ruth does this (Ruth 2:2)
20 "I ___ Mordecai the Jew" (Est. 5:13)
22 Large vase
24 Tattoo type

25 Adam's eldest son
26 "Bye!" (Sp.)
27 "I will ___ up a shepherd" (Zech. 11:16)
28 Cleans a hole
29 Monte ___
30 More accurate
33 Flat
35 "Salvation unto the ___ of the earth" (Acts 13:47)
40 Anxiously
41 What Est. required (Est. 2:15)
42 Take away the antlers
43 What Paul obtained (Acts 22:28)
45 Mordecai ___ at the king's gate (Est. 2:19)
47 Beryl on fourth (Ex. 28:20)
49 "___ thou unto the king" (Est. 5:14)

50 Thump

51 "At ___ and quiet" (Job 21:23)

52 Hit

53 Otherwise, as in Exodus 10:4

54 Where Jews departed from (Acts 18:2)

55 Redact

56 Be fond of

59 "Curse God, and ___" (Job 2:9)

Day 89

BOOK OF JAMES

ACROSS

1 "Grievous words ___ up anger" (Prov. 15:1)
5 Judah and Galilee, e.g.
10 "Night is far spent, the ___ is at hand" (Rom. 13:12)
13 "Faith without ___ is dead" (James 2:20)
15 Eliminate
16 Of a place (suffix)
17 "We are to God the pleasing ___ of Christ" (2 Cor. 2:15 NIV)
18 Mountain climber
19 By way of
20 Commandment number
21 "Surely there is a ___ for the silver" (Job 28:1)
23 Nulls
25 "If the ___ will, we shall live" (James 4:15)
26 Military uniform feature
28 "We count them happy which ___" (James 5:11)
31 ___ -garde
32 "Be ye ___ of the word" (James 1:22)
33 Cadence
34 Abraham, Isaac, and Jacob, e.g.
37 Heredity component
38 ___ of the ball

40 Type choice
41 NYC winter hours
42 "How great a matter a little ___ kindleth!" (James 3:5)
43 Shampoo product
44 "Is any ___? Let him sing psalms" (James 5:13)
45 Lebanese capital
46 Turin relic and others
49 God's love would ___ a troubled soul
50 One of five Jesus suffered, traditionally
51 Wheeze
52 God sought a man who would "stand in the ___" (Ezek. 22:30)
55 Shady tree
56 Loafed
59 Oust
61 Gloria in excelsis ___
62 Proclaim
63 Wanders
64 "Do not ___, my beloved brethren" (James 1:16)
65 Rendezvous
66 Born and ___

DOWN

1 Elite crime-fighter team (abbr.)
2 KJV's "rent"
3 Jerusalem's gates, e.g.
4 Yarn strength meas.
5 Rose pest
6 Many an ancient site
7 Exclamation of astonishment
8 Elizabeth conceived in her old ___
9 James's word for himself (James 1:1)
10 "Resist the ___, and he will flee" (James 4:7)
11 Stage whisper
12 Missing in unleavened bread
14 Relishes

22 "How long will it be ___ thou be quiet?" (Jer. 47:6)
24 "___ of the same mouth proceedeth blessing and cursing" (James 3:10)
25 Attract
26 "Speak not ___ one of another" (James 4:11)
27 Wan
28 Rim
29 Negatives
30 Bend
31 Pathway
34 Port city feature
35 Freedom org.

36 "No fountain both yield ___ water and fresh" (James 3:12)

38 Sparrow

39 Sins

40 Overly proper

42 Hatfield or McCoy, e.g.

43 Rock thrower

44 Weekday (abbr.)

45 Make taboo

46 Certain Scandinavian

47 Nine-___, small golf green

48 Unsubstantiated story

49 Plebe

51 Fido and Fluffy

52 Equipment

53 Tip-top

54 Wartime ailment (abbr.)

57 Rural dragster's sport (abbr.)

58 Not clerical

60 "Ye have heard of the patience of ___" (James 5:11)

BOOK OF HEBREWS

ACROSS

1 Fuel source
5 "Feet __ with...the gospel of peace" (Eph. 6:15)
9 Gossip does this
13 "Salute all them that have the __ over you" (Heb. 13:24)
14 "He will wipe every __ from their eyes" (Rev. 21:4 NIV)
15 52 Down capital
16 Eye
17 Garden tool
18 He was "fully __ in every way" (Heb. 2:17 NIV)
19 God's message "is...__ than any twoedged" 33 Across (Heb. 4:12)
21 Bible: God's __
23 Prodigal son's dwelling, for a time
24 Body art, for short
25 Saudi capital
29 "__, and ye shall receive" (John 16:24)
30 Deer
32 Debtor's note
33 See 19 Across
36 Automaton
37 Total
38 Fur
39 "By faith __,...refused to be called the son of Pharaoh's daughter" (Heb. 11:24)

40 "Holy Ghost __ is a witness to us" (Heb. 10:15)
41 Free of
42 Saunter
43 Drive a car
44 "Cast me not off in the time of old __" (Ps. 71:9)
45 Mimics
46 "The Raven" author
47 "Come boldly unto the __ of grace" (Heb. 4:16)
49 __-ray, disk choice
50 Foot part
53 "God is a consuming __" (Heb. 12:29)
55 Leaning on, as God
57 Spaghetti, e.g.
60 Like Jonah in the fish's belly
62 Courtroom figure (abbr.)
63 Hurts
64 Short times, for short
65 Horse's sound
66 "Faith is...evidence of things not __" (Heb. 11:1)
67 None but Jesus' sacrifice can __ away sins
68 "I have __ the faith" (2 Tim. 4:7)

DOWN

1 Calvary sight
2 "Holy Ghost shall teach you...what ye __ to say" (Luke 12:12)
3 Relieve
4 Stare
5 Window wipe result, at times
6 "Draw near with a true __" (Heb. 10:22)
7 Absalom hanged on one
8 Used a pencil, maybe
9 Showy
10 Point a weapon

11 Lingerie item
12 Jesus, the __ of God
15 Anointed One
20 GI ailment
22 Sandwich cookies
26 Church feature
27 Soak
28 Disposition
29 KJV "is"
30 Medicine amounts
31 He saves "all them that __ him" (Heb. 5:9)

33 Jack who could eat no fat
34 Listeners "should __ carefully what is said" (1 Cor. 14:29 NIV)
35 "Do not rebuke an __ man harshly" (1 Tim. 5:1 NIV)
36 Jesus __ on the third day
39 Sad-sack
40 Jesus __ with sinners
42 Fads
43 "Hope we have as an anchor of the __" (Heb. 6:19)
46 "Without faith it is impossible to __ him" (Heb. 11:6)

48 "As __ as ye eat this bread, and drink this cup" (1 Cor. 11:26)
49 Classic shampoo brand
50 Hebrews, Romans, or James, e.g.
51 High up (2 words)
52 15 Across nation
54 Where Magi came from
56 Talk on and on
57 Step (Fr.)
58 Get an A
59 Pronoun for Mary or Martha
61 Mediterranean, for one

A REASON TO LOVE

ACROSS

1 Philippine island
6 "Why should _____ with thee?" (2 Sam. 13:26) (2 words)
10 "Or if he _____ for a fish" (Matt. 7:10 NIV)
14 "The wind swept them away without leaving a _____" (Dan. 2:35 NIV)
15 Enthusiasm
16 Japheth's father (Gen. 6:10)
17 "Have _____ day!" (2 words)
18 Rich vein
19 "Jesus saith unto them, Come and _____" (John 21:12)
20 Start of **QUOTE** from 1 John 4:11 (4 words)
23 Actor Harrison
24 Company symbol
25 Airport abbreviation
27 "Lord, not my feet _____" (John 13:9)
30 **QUOTE**, cont'd
34 Middle-Eastern Arab group (abbr.)
35 "It was not my _____" (Num. 16:28 NIV)
36 San _____, a tiny country within Italy
37 **QUOTE**, cont'd (5 words)
40 Demons
41 "To preach the word in _____" (Acts 16:6)

42 Moon buggy (abbr.)
43 "Then _____ down upon my face" (Ezek. 11:13) (2 words)
44 Alum
45 "Shut the doors, and _____ them" (Neh. 7:3)
46 "Ye have done evil _____ doing" (Gen. 44:5) (2 words)
48 *Logue* or *center* prefix
50 End of **QUOTE** (3 words)
57 "Thou art my _____" (Ps. 71:5)
58 "Let down your _____ for a draught" (Luke 5:4)
59 "_____ him away while we slept" (Matt. 28:13)
60 "Even so, _____" (Rev. 1:7)
61 "He shall come _____ dead body" (Num. 6:6) (2 words)
62 "Who can _____ man what shall be" (Eccl. 6:12) (2 words)
63 "A _____ heart deviseth his way" (Prov. 16:9)
64 "Like fullers' _____" (Malachi 3:2)
65 "At whom do you _____ and stick out your tongue?" (Isa. 57:4 NIV)

DOWN

1 "His own parents will _____ him" (Zech. 13:3 NIV)
2 "Rule Britannia" composer
3 "He armed him with a coat of _____" (1 Sam. 17:38)
4 "They were all with one _____ in one place" (Acts 2:1)
5 He played Superman
6 "I _____ my peace, even from good" (Ps. 39:2)
7 "Jesus cried with a loud voice, saying, _____" (Mark 15:34)
8 "A _____ is coming against her from the north" (Jer. 46:20 NIV)

9 "Can _____ upon hot coals" (Prov. 6:28) (2 words)
10 "Set bars _____" (Job 38:10) (2 words)
11 "_____ good news from a far country" (Prov. 25:25) (2 words)
12 Nigerian industrial city
13 "_____ saith unto him" (John 11:27)
21 Book after Gen.
22 South Dakota native
25 Bordon's ad bovine
26 "Took a _____" (John 13:4)
28 Opposite of *positive* (abbr.)
29 Volcanic mudflow

31 One of the string instruments

32 "_____ into his gates with thanksgiving" (Ps. 100:4)

33 "In one hour your _____ has come!" (Rev. 18:10 NIV)

34 Huff's partner

35 Old-time antiseptic

36 "The _____ pleased him" (Est. 2:9)

38 Peps up

39 IRA relative (abbr.)

44 "Was _____ Padanaram" (Gen. 28:7) (2 words)

45 "If a serpent had _____ any man" (Num. 21:9)

47 "My _____ for me" (1 Chron. 22:7) (2 words)

49 "Write them upon the _____ of thy house" (Deut. 6:9)

50 Juan's hill

51 "To _____ the blind eyes" (Isa. 42:7)

52 Sicilian volcano

53 "To whom I shall give _____" (John 13:26) (2 words)

54 "Behold a _____ in the wall" (Ezek. 8:7)

55 Fashion magazine

56 "Wilt thou _____ it up in three days?" (John 2:20)

57 Father of Canaan (Gen. 9:18)

HAPPY MOTHER'S DAY

ACROSS

1 Start of **VERSE** appropriate to the theme day (Prov. 31:10)
4 "_____ vanity" (Eccl. 1:2) (2 words)
9 "Arise, and go into the _____ which is called Straight" (Acts 9:11)
15 "That no _____ can come between them" (Job 41:16)
16 Is like a broken _____" (Prov. 25:19)
17 It is time for you _____ LORD" (Ps. 119:126 NIV) (3 words)
18 "Looked out _____ window" (2 Kings 9:30) (2 words)
19 A whip for the _____" (Prov. 26:3)
20 Ciphers
21 **VERSE**, cont'd (4 words)
24 "The foal of an _____" (Matt. 21:5)
25 "Their murders, their magic _____" (Rev. 9:21 NIV)
26 "Ye are the _____ of the earth" (Matt. 5:13)
29 "Judah _____ wife for Er, his firstborn" (Gen. 38:6 NIV) (2 words)
31 "_____ him all ye people" (Rom. 15:11)
35 Third son of Jether (1 Chron. 7:38)
36 "Which is the king's _____" (Gen. 14:17)

38 Taos, for example
40 **VERSE**, cont'd (4 words)
44 "On _____ the time I punish him" (Jer. 49:8 NIV) (2 words)
45 Sandwich cookie
46 Derivative (abbr.)
47 Newspaper department
48 "Took _____ of him" (Luke 10:34)
50 "They were not _____" (Job 39:16)
51 "God saw _____ it was good" (Gen. 1:10)
53 Fort Worth school (abbr.)
55 End of **VERSE** (4 words)
64 On ice
65 Presidential candidate Ralph
66 Cry of surprise
67 State #49
68 "Of Zebulun; _____ the son of Helon" (Num. 1:9)
69 "_____ the sacrifices of the dead" (Ps. 106:28)
70 "There shall be _____ of any man's life among you" (Acts 27:22) (2 words)
71 "Their _____ were evil" (John 3:19)
72 "His eyes were _____" (1 Sam. 4:15)

DOWN

1 Women's corps in WWII (abbr.)
2 "Fighting _____ pregnant woman" (Ex.21:22 NIV) (2 words)
3 "But though we, _____ angel from heaven" (Gal. 1:8) (2 words)
4 "A woman lay _____ feet" (Ruth 3:8) (2 words)
5 Mournful water fowl
6 "The _____ is King for ever and ever" (Ps. 10:16)
7 "_____ ghost" (Matt. 14:26 NIV) (2 words)
8 Fifth Jewish month
9 "Let us _____ rebuilding" (Neh. 2:18 NIV)
10 Eagerly promotes
11 Pasta sauce brand

12 "The woodwork will _____ it" (Hab. 2:11 NIV)
13 Part of Caesar's last words (2 words)
14 "_____ thee like a ball" (Isa. 22:18)
22 "First seven _____ kine" (Gen. 41:20)
23 "_____ the Ithrite" (1 Chron. 11:40)
26 "They were _____ in two" (Heb. 11:37 NIV)
27 "I _____ in the night" (Neh. 2:12)
28 Tibetan priests
29 Day-_____ dyes
30 "_____ the land of the free"
31 Follows *jugg* or *but*
32 "Her feet _____ not in her house" (Prov. 7:11)
33 Stress result

34 "Be ye _____ of the word" (James 1:22)
36 Genetic stuff (abbr.)
37 Sternward
38 It means "before" (prefix)
39 "Spring _____ well" (Num. 21:17)
41 Arctic diver
42 "Came unto mount _____" (Num. 20:22)
43 "_____ the messenger came to him" (2 Kings 6:32)
48 "The fourth part of a _____" (2 Kings 6:25)
49 "Your sin _____ for" (Isa. 6:7 NIV)
50 Wheel center
51 Arduous journeys
52 "They _____ king over them" (Rev. 9:11 NIV) (2 words)
53 "_____ their winepresses, and suffer thirst" (Job 24:11)

54 Edges of streets
55 "_____ of mine own self do nothing" (John 5:30) (2 words)
56 Sing or fly alone
57 "A colt the _____ of an ass" (Matt. 21:5)
58 "The soldiers _____ mocked him" (Luke 23:36)
59 "The _____ of Siddim was full" (Gen. 14:10)
60 Film star Adams, Ernie Kovacs' wife
61 "Oh that _____ wings like a dove!" (Ps. 55:6) (2 words)
62 "Nothing to _____ was thirsty" (Matt. 25:42 NIV) (2 words)
63 "He shall dwell in the tents of _____" (Gen. 9:27)

FAVORITE HYMNS

ACROSS

1 Steeple bell sound
5 Paul's mission field
9 "_____, Father"
13 Gospel/country singer Cristy
14 Sharp taste
15 "In the _____ By and By"
16 Don't put them all in one basket
17 Hymn melody
18 Joint
19 "_____ Assurance"
21 Lilies "toil not, they _____ not" (Luke 12:27)
23 Conger
24 Tire reading
25 Sea Paul crossed many times
29 "Take, _____; this is my body" (Matt. 26:26)
30 Epistle (abbr.)
32 Flightless bird
33 Potter's needs
36 Scandinavian coastal inlet
37 Aaron's budded
38 "Take My _____ and Let It Be"
39 What Jesus' rode into Jerusalem, and others

40 "Child of the _____"
41 Reformation Day month (abbr.)
42 Groan-worthy
43 Loyal subject to a monarch
44 "Blest Be the _____ That Binds"
45 Choir section
46 Touch affectionately
47 Length of hair
49 "Thou hast a mighty _____" (Ps. 89:13)
50 Tax helper (abbr.)
53 Male chorister, perhaps
55 Spoke foolishly
57 Take advantage of
60 Needle need for Dorcas
62 Burden, as sorrow in the heart
63 "He's Got the Whole World in His _____"
64 Irish girl
65 "_____ in David's Royal City"
66 Wager
67 "Uphold me with thy _____ spirit" (Ps. 51:12)
68 KJV "tare"

DOWN

1 Cadet
2 Fly "as an _____ toward heaven" (Prov. 23:5)
3 Heavenly chorus member
4 James the _____, Calvary onlooker
5 Resurrection would _____ to Jesus' claims
6 Arabia dweller
7 No room for them in the _____
8 "Rock of _____"
9 Inspire with awe
10 Israel's youngest son, for short
11 "To _____ I am ashamed" (Luke 16:3)
12 Jesus often _____ with sinners
15 Take "the _____ of faith" (Eph. 6:16)
20 Salt baths

22 Animals entered the ark in _____
26 Strange
27 "Jesus, Stand _____ Us"
28 The Holy Spirit will _____ heart to faith
29 "His _____ Is on the Sparrow"
30 Choir accompaniment, often
31 "O _____ Night"
33 Coagulates
34 Lawful
35 "Hunger and thirst _____ righteousness" (Matt. 5:6)
36 Early Jerusalem was one
39 Groups of sheep
40 Caboodle go-with
42 Narrow waterways

43 "I Am Jesus' Little _____"

46 "I will sing _____ to thy name" (Ps. 9:2)

48 "_____ with Me"

49 Soldiers would _____ Jesus

50 Make a copy

51 "When _____ Like a River"

52 All "shall be _____ unto you" (Luke 12:31)

54 Ego

56 "Causeth his wind to _____" (Ps. 147:18)

57 "Found it!"

58 Truck

59 Hard worker in Prov.

61 Street sealant

Day 94

RULERS

ACROSS

1 Lengthy narrative poems, as of kings
6 Short note
10 Cooking spray
13 List of errors
15 El _____, Texas
16 Nineveh to Babylon direction
17 Rulers who are not victorious
18 Land of Gilead city
19 "You're busted!"
20 Throne
22 King Nebuchadnezzar's city
24 Cabbage salad
26 Kings' alliance, e.g.
28 Wicked king of Israel
29 "Grievous words _____ up anger" (Prov. 15:1)
30 "He shall _____ like a lion" (Hos. 11:10)
31 Colored warning flare
32 Tribes under 28 Across
33 Asian percussion instrument
34 Feline
35 Like God's wonders
37 "World _____ end"
41 OT priestly anointing digit
42 "With what measure ye _____" (Matt. 7:2)
43 Speed in Europe (abbr.)
44 Elevated, as to kingly status
47 Speak with God
48 King Priam's city in Iliad
49 First Israel king
50 OT idol
51 University figure
52 "Esther put on her royal _____" (Est. 5:1)
54 Jesus, "_____ of Jesse" (Isa. 11:1)
56 Con
57 Winglike
59 Spirit will _____ His gifts to you
63 How long "_____ they believe me?" (Num. 14:11)
64 Type choice
65 What manna would do if stored
66 What to do on a throne
67 Royal _____, king's son
68 "Deliver the poor and _____" (Ps. 82:4)

DOWN

1 Slippery fish
2 Expert
3 Tax org.
4 Augustus, for one
5 Scatter
6 3 Down employee
7 Ship's haven
8 Abraham's son
9 Jesus laid in one
10 King David's songs
11 Not at sea
12 28 Across descriptor
14 Judah king
21 Steak
23 David fought Goliath in his _____
24 What Jacob fed famished Esau
25 Jesus was from the royal _____ of David
27 Fall behind
29 Depot (abbr.)
30 4 Down throne site
31 Unbeliever's impersonal force
33 Some kings are _____; others evil
34 30 Down is one
36 Stone inscribed with king's feats
37 Marks raised by flogging
38 Southern veggie
39 He shall "rule _____ his throne" (Zech. 6:13)
40 KJV possessive

42 Medical diagnostic test (abbr.)
44 Accepted practices
45 Pharaoh's papers
46 One who acts for king, maybe
47 King's abode
48 Jerusalem worship site
50 Negate
51 Jesus cast out a _____

53 Knocks lightly
55 Epistle, for short (abbr.)
58 "Far out!"
60 Citrus cooler
61 Bright color
62 "_____ me, and know my thoughts" (Ps. 139:23)

HANNAH'S CHILD OF PROMISE

ACROSS

1 Trades
6 It may be gray
10 Carmel to Joppa (dir.)
14 Assistants
15 The ___ should bury their dead (Matt. 8:22)
16 "_____ and female created he them" (Gen. 1:27)
17 Stupid
18 "There be now an ___ betwixt us" (Gen. 26:28)
19 Modern-day Persia
20 Actress Moore
21 Large computer co.
22 "Why ___ thou not?" (1 Sam. 1:8)
24 Defensive alliance (abbr.)
26 "Eli the ___ sat" (1 Sam. 1:9)
27 CSI data
30 "From thence they went to ___" (Num. 21:16)
31 Not urban
32 "We are thy bone and thy ___" (2 Sam. 5:1)
33 "___ with the dew of heaven" (Dan. 4:33)
36 Island greeting
37 "He that hath an ___" (Rev. 2:7)
38 Dry measure (1 Sam. 1:24)

40 Crave
41 "Christ must ___ have suffered" (Acts 17:3)
43 "Samuel ___ and went to Eli" (1 Sam. 3:6)
44 "As a ___ that is told" (Ps. 90:9)
45 To think
46 Is appropriate
49 "Hannah ___ up after they had eaten" (1 Sam. 1:9)
50 Roman stoic
51 Yang's partner
52 Rocket builders
56 Alabama's Crimson
57 "Their ___ shall be broken" (Ps. 37:15)
59 Aka buffalo
60 "Barzillai was a very ___ man" (2 Sam. 19:32)
61 "He that gathered little had no ___" (Ex. 16:18)
62 The pride of Vidalia, GA
63 Made of gold and silver (Est. 1:6)
64 Epochs
65 Stone on Aaron's ephod (Ex. 28:19)

DOWN

1 "He is risen, as he ___" (Matt. 28:6)
2 Hannah abstained from this (1 Sam. 1:15)
3 The first man
4 Elkanah's other wife (1 Sam. 1:2)
5 Nazareth to Jerusalem (dir.)
6 Seasoning (Sp.)
7 Enlarge
8 "She wept, and did not ___" (1 Sam. 1:7)
9 Cleaves
10 "Saul sought to ___ David" (1 Sam. 19:10)
11 "Gather up thy ___" (Jer. 10:17)
12 "By the ___ of God they perish" (Job 4:9)
13 "But Hannah ___ not up" (1 Sam. 1:22)

21 "That which groweth of ___ own accord" (Lev. 25:5)
23 Frivolous, silly people
25 Second-largest ocean
26 Equals
27 What Hannah does at Shiloh (1 Sam. 1:9–10)
28 "The greater light to ___ the day" (Gen. 1:16)
29 Canaanite chariot material (Josh. 17:16)
30 First sign of growth (Mark 4:28)
32 Senses
33 "Stop!"
34 This wind brought the locusts (Ex. 10:13)
35 Formal "you" in KJV

39 Cleaning feathers

42 Edible

45 Charged particle

46 Neutral color

47 "The days of thy mourning shall be ___" (Isa. 60:20)

48 The raven ___ Elijah (1 Kings 17:6)

49 Chances

50 Wound that killed Eglon (Judg. 3:21)

51 YMCA counterpart

53 Paul forbidden to preach here (Acts 16:6)

54 Chimney dirt

55 Green Gables dweller

58 Bashan's were made of oak (Ezek. 27:6)

59 It may be feathery or scaly

BIBLE KISSES

ACROSS

1 "Righteousness and _____ have kissed" (Ps 85:10)
6 Why see the _____ in another's eye? (Matt. 7:3)
10 Belonging to (suffix)
13 African antelope
15 Prickly seed
16 Forbid
17 "Our heart is not _____ back" (Ps. 44:18)
18 Needler's need
19 Compassionate letters
20 Luke's book
22 Jacob's kiss would _____ Isaac (Gen. 27:26–27)
24 "_____ it might be fulfilled" (Matt. 2:15)
26 Christ, "_____ of all things" (Heb. 1:2)
28 White House dweller, for short
29 Firmament member
30 Jacob _____ to Isaac about his identify
31 Layers
32 Nile snake
33 _____ of Solomon
34 Noel mo.

35 "Rotten to _____" (2 words)
37 Nero descriptor
41 "Thy _____ and thy staff...comfort" (Ps. 23:4)
42 Joseph's brothers kissed him and _____
43 America
44 Betray (2 words)
47 "They were _____ afraid" (Luke 2:9)
48 Cereal choice
49 Over again, once more
50 Live in _____ with God's will
51 Meat alternative
52 Mob determined to _____ Jesus to death
54 Three feet
56 "He hath said in _____ heart" (Ps. 10:6)
57 Temple Mount or Lazarus' tomb, e.g.
59 "Woe unto...ye blind _____" (Matt. 23:16)
63 Chemistry suffix
64 School groups (abbr.)
65 Soldiers would _____ Paul to Rome
66 British bus. ending
67 Boaz "our _____ kinsmen" (Ruth 2:20)
68 Like a mustard seed

DOWN

1 Abyss
2 Flightless bird
3 Easter month, often (abbr.)
4 Promised Land
5 Believers
6 Business primarily controlled by disadvantaged
7 Excelled
8 More factual
9 Little Mermaid's love
10 "Be perfect and _____" (James 1:4)
11 Judas' reward for kiss
12 Moderation, not _____, is godly
14 Home security company

21 "Let your light so _____" (Matt. 5:16)
23 Paul's journeys, e.g.
24 Foolish nonsense (Brit.)
25 "My _____ is in thee" (Ps. 39:7)
27 Medical diagnostic test (abbr.)
29 Lame would lie on one
30 Judas betrayed his _____ with a kiss
31 Sinai tabernacle, for one
33 He will come again _____
34 Idiot
36 One often followed Jesus
37 "Have _____ on me!"
38 Sod
39 He kissed Jacob in reunion

40 "Swine _____...down a steep place" (Matt. 8:32)

42 Jesus has _____ the battle with evil

44 Jacob's beloved wife

45 Samuel would _____ Saul and kiss him (1 Sam. 10:1)

46 Became anxious

47 Grammar rule study

48 Dress top

50 "Sun shall not _____ thee by day" (Ps. 121:6)

51 "In thee do I put my _____" (Ps. 7:1)

53 Sports channel

55 Elisabeth bore John at advanced _____

58 KJV verb ending

60 Deer

61 Sea eagle

62 Prodigal son's dwelling

BOOK OF ACTS

ACROSS

1 Experimenter's place, for short
4 Orange gem
9 Financial products (abbr.)
12 Filler for 28 Across (Sp.)
14 Insect stage
15 Fire need
16 "Hand of the __ was with them" (Acts 11:21)
17 Attempts
18 __ mater
19 Explain Bible verse, e.g.
21 He brought Ethiopian to faith (Acts 8)
23 Droll
24 Beggar "__ for alms at the Beautiful gate" (Acts 3:10)
25 Indian garment
28 Nile, e.g. (Sp.)
31 "In every nation he __ feareth him...is accepted" (Acts 10:35)
34 City of 69 Across
36 Paul and Silas, e.g.
38 Take to court
40 Ukrainian capital
41 Improvise (2 words)
43 Bruins' home (abbr.)
44 Chicken __ king (2 words)
45 "__ unto thee, Chorazin!" (Matt. 11:21)
46 Rhoda would __ she heard Pet.'s voice (Acts 12:15)
48 Change
51 Sin
53 Site of many early churches
54 Garment for 24 Across
56 Tidal flow
58 What Paul did at 69 Across
61 Bible book: Acts of the __
66 Some listeners gave Paul __ attention
67 Wooden
69 Mars' __, Paul's sermon site
70 Pennsylvania city
71 Prodigal yearned to eat food he fed to __
72 Harvard's rival
73 Time measurement, for short
74 What Paul made for a living
75 Moses parted the __ Sea

DOWN

1 Melodic *tra* followers (2 words)
2 Competition at Greek games
3 "Did not our heart __ within us?" (Luke 24:32)
4 Paul found one to "Unknown God"
5 Deacon Stephen, e.g.
6 Cheese choice
7 First lady
8 Talks hoarsely
9 Discard
10 Half (prefix)
11 Strike
13 Disturbance
15 "So were the churches established in the __" (Acts 16:5)
20 Jacob to Esau
22 Bishop's mitre
25 Fence passage
26 I am "straining toward what is __" (Phil. 3:13 NIV)
27 Pulpit figure, for short
29 Couch potato, maybe
30 Affirmative (Fr.)
32 Computer code (abbr.)
33 Oilers' home
34 Wanted poster letters
35 Pet. "__ heaven opened" (Acts 10:11)
37 Kimono sash
39 Believers "did __ their meat with gladness" (Acts 2:46)
42 Buck's mate
43 Ship's letters

47 Captures

49 Some of Paul's listeners

50 Tic ___, mint choice

52 "___, and be baptized" (Acts 2:38)

55 Holy ___, Pentecost figure

57 Jesus' were not broken on Calvary

58 White House figure, for short

59 Unusual

60 Acts, for one

61 Like

62 KJV's "your"

63 Truth is not in one

64 Women's magazine

65 Winter rider

68 "Everyone was filled with ___ at the many... signs" (Acts 2:43 NIV)

Day 98
REJOICE!

ACROSS

1 High point
5 Web page
9 Church feature
13 If he takes your shirt, "hand over your __ as well" (Matt. 5:40 NIV)
14 Gesture of disdain
15 Microwave, informally
16 He came to save the __
17 Staring
18 Advanced math class, for short
19 Look "not on what is seen, but on what is __" (2 Cor. 4:18 NIV)
21 He calls all __ to repentance
23 Stumble
25 He brings peace to your __
26 Not (Fr.)
29 He was __ on earth
31 Garden ornament
34 He bids us __ according to His will
35 Cookie aisle product
37 NYC station, for short
39 People __ their cloaks over Jesus' colt
41 Former flyer (abbr.)

42 Succinct
43 He came to __ our wounds
44 Use a sewing machine
46 People __ palm branches and laid them down
47 Caleb and eleven others
50 Academic dwelling
51 "All you need to say is...__ or No" (Matt. 5:37 NIV)
52 49 Down ingredient, maybe
54 Abraham, Isaac, and Jacob, familiarly
56 Wind farm turbine
59 He teaches us to love __
63 He was called a __ of Jesse
64 Panic
66 Bread spread
67 What Judas may have used
68 Netherland sights
69 Org.
70 Winter slider
71 Appear
72 "__ have a feast and celebrate" (Luke 15:23 NIV)

DOWN

1 Freedom org.
2 Masked mammal, for short
3 Roman Catholic worship service
4 Diminutive suffix
5 Modest
6 Eye part
7 North African capital
8 Christmas beverage
9 KJV's "wild bull"
10 Cat's rumble
11 Winter lodge sights
12 Brain wave test (abbr.)
14 Elder
20 Funny bone locale
22 Cloistered one

24 "I __ toward the mark for the prize" (Phil. 3:14)
26 He came to light our __
27 He came to soothe our hearts' __
28 Sandal thong
30 Smelled
32 He came to have __ on us
33 Result
36 Razor sharpener
38 Pet. and James's fishing needs
40 Prompted
42 "Thou shalt not __ the Lord" (Luke 4:12)
45 Trains for
48 Sin
49 Menu choices

53 Disprove
55 Sandbar
56 Sheep's clothing
57 He came to bring ___ to the despairing
58 Eden need, maybe

60 Otherwise
61 He came to bring ___ to the weary
62 He came to make us ___ of God
63 Some Monopoly properties (abbr.)
65 Sleep stage (abbr.)

EPISTLES

ACROSS

1 Workplace regulatory agency (abbr.)
5 Ziti
10 Kansas City winter hour (abbr.)
13 "_____fast in the faith" (1 Cor. 16:13)
15 Speak off the cuff (2 words)
16 Expert
17 Bakery treat
18 63 Across giver
19 Josh.'s dad
20 Twenty-third Psalm concern
21 "Draw _____with a true heart" (Heb. 10:22)
23 Philippine dish
25 Window part
26 Many NT churches (Gr.)
28 Epistle topic
31 Adornment
32 Egg descriptor
33 Paper stock, quantity
34 Noah's son
37 Wear truth as one, per Eph.
38 Ornate

40 Ali _____
41 God's feeling toward sin
42 Widow's mite
43 To God be "dominion and _____" (Jude 25)
44 Jesus endured the _____
45 "See through a glass, _____" (1 Cor. 13:12)
46 OT sacrificial birds
49 Foremost
50 Jonathan shot one as sign for David
51 Three-epistle writer
52 Horse's mouth held with _____, bridle (Ps. 32:9)
55 Spanish aunt
56 Thoughts
59 "By faith _____was translated" (Heb. 11:5)
61 Computer key (abbr.)
62 "Le _____Pere," Paris prayer
63 18 Across recipient
64 36 Down pronoun
65 "All flesh is as _____" (1 Pet. 1:24)
66 Stun, for short

DOWN

1 Bone (comb. form)
2 Store
3 OT unclean leporid
4 Prov.' industrious insect
5 Vatican epistle descriptor
6 Purim month
7 Jesus' description of Herod
8 "_____them about thy neck" (Prov. 6:21)
9 "Faith of our father _____" (Rom. 4:12)
10 Long boat
11 Aqualung
12 Tooth filling
14 Peter _____Jesus thrice
22 Church add-on, maybe
24 "_____is at hand" (Rom. 13:12)
25 Soldiers _____in Jesus' face

26 Spirit makes each heart _____
27 God is potter, we are _____
28 Asia desert
29 Sin has no "dominion _____you" (Rom. 6:14)
30 Soul homophone
31 Pressers
34 "Doth the _____fly by thy wisdom?" (Job 39:26)
35 "By faith _____offered" better sacrifice (Heb. 11:4)
36 Jesus' mom
38 "Be not _____shaken in mind" (2 Thess. 2:2)
39 Eden serpent sound
40 "Bondwoman was _____after the flesh" (Gal. 4:23)

42 What cock was doing at 14 Down
43 "My heart is sore _____" (Ps. 55:4)
44 Corner-office occupant (abbr.)
45 Telegraphic signal
46 Meat spreads
47 St. Patrick's converts
48 "_____ be unto you" (1 Cor. 1:3)
49 "Death reigned from Adam to _____" (Rom. 5:14)

51 Filled with water at Cana
52 _____ fide
53 Chills down tea
54 KJV "you"
57 Tax agency (abbr.)
58 Airport information (abbr.)
60 Commandment imperative "Thou shalt _____"

THE EXODUS

ACROSS

1 Remove your hat
5 Adore, with "on"
9 Bird chirp
13 OT book
14 Exodus
15 Gulf nation
16 What Achan hid (Josh. 7:21)
17 Ten Commandments, e.g.
18 Single element or component
19 "They _____ him...at...waters of strife" (Ps. 106:32)
21 Not yet up
23 KJV's "yea"
24 North American Indian
25 Pharaoh _____ that God has all power
29 Sarah bore Isaac at advanced _____
30 Zeal
32 God's name in Exodus (2 words)
33 Aaron would speak Moses' _____
36 Dan.'s lion place, and others
37 Roman seven
38 Eager
39 Egyptians made Israelites _____ them
40 Hanukkah coins

41 _____ Sea
42 Dickens' "_____ of Two Cities" (2 words)
43 With 35 Down, it drowned in waters
44 Babies "delivered _____ the midwives come" (Ex. 1:19)
45 Polish city
46 Judas descriptor
47 Layer
49 Ancient Asian language
50 Moses raised as Pharaoh's daughter's _____
53 With 26 Down, where Moses was found
55 Moses feared people would not _____ him
57 Grows weary, as Israelites in Sinai
60 Aaron and Moses, for short
62 Church organ piece
63 Do not "_____ thy neighbor's house" (Ex. 20:17)
64 _____ fide
65 Mr. Disney
66 First murder victim
67 OT Samuel, for one
68 Beverages

DOWN

1 Pharaoh planned to _____ release of the Israelites
2 Pungent gas
3 Plague amphibians
4 Impersonal force
5 Erase
6 Mineral class
7 "Night Before Christmas" starter
8 R&B singer James
9 Bamboo-loving bear
10 Airport information (abbr.)
11 "Give _____ to his commandments" (Ex. 15:26)
12 Open forcefully

15 Vashti and Est.
20 Tent floorings
22 Harsh loud noise
26 See 53 Across
27 Crucifixion tools
28 "I will..._____ Egypt" (Ex. 3:20)
29 "They may _____ sin to sin" (Isa. 30:1)
30 Go to Pharaoh "_____ in the morning" (Ex. 9:13)
31 Israelites' firstborns would _____
33 Goods
34 Obvious
35 See 43 Across
36 Moses called to _____ His people

39 "Thou shalt not _____" (Ex. 20:15)
40 He spoke to Moses
42 40 Down, "Master _____"
43 Plague weather event
46 "Render...unto _____..." (Matt. 22:21)
48 _____ of the Lord in burning bush
49 Steakhouse order
50 Calyx element

51 Seed plant element
52 Birds have them
54 Flows partner
56 Hawkeye state
57 Religious sports ministry (abbr.)
58 Throw
59 "_____ Maria"
61 KJV "deer"

HEROD: THE TETRARCH

ACROSS

1 Kingdom or state treasury (abbr.)
5 Child protection agency (abbr.)
8 "He maketh ___ to cease" (Ps. 46:9)
12 Against
13 Lures
15 Weapons of iron (2 Sam. 12:31)
16 Type of jazz vocals
17 Buick model
18 What Herod did to children in Bethlehem (Matt. 2:16)
19 Fortification
21 She wept for the children (Matt. 2:18)
23 How God spoke to Joseph (Matt. 2:12)
25 Con's opposite
26 Flare
29 Took Isaac's place (Gen. 22:13)
31 Desert plant
35 Designer Laura
37 Scientist playground, for short
39 "And ___ shall be a sign unto you" (Luke 2:12)
40 "If any man will ___ thee" (Matt. 5:40)
41 Fiendish
44 "___, and it shall be given you" (Matt. 7:7)
45 Streetcar
47 Average work performance
48 Dress top
50 It's cut with a pruning hook (Isa. 18:5)
52 Roman number of Herods in the Bible
54 Tetrarch of Galilee (Luke 3:1)
55 Hind's mate (Song 2:9)
57 Heavenly messenger
59 Neckwear (17th cent.)
62 Waterways
65 Newsman Sevareid
66 Animals that heard the Good News first
68 Ivy League school
70 Given to Jesus to drink (Matt. 27:34)
71 It may be past or present
72 Send forth
73 Leer
74 "My time is not ___ come" (John 7:6)
75 "In ___ was there a voice heard" (Matt. 2:18)

DOWN

1 Musical syllables
2 Andes inhabitant
3 Wound in Jesus' side
4 Strong tower of Psalm 61:3
5 He ordered a census (Luke 2:1)
6 One who is slovenly, greedy, or gluttonous
7 Herod tracked it (Matt. 2:7)
8 Failure
9 Shaft
10 The earth will do this one day (Isa. 24:20)
11 Jerusalem to Bethlehem (dir.)
13 French province
14 Smack
20 In Isa. they clap their hands (Isa. 55:12)
22 What stones might do (Luke 19:40)
24 Infectious disease
26 Times of denial
27 Women should not "___ authority" (1 Tim. 2:12)
28 "Nabal did ___ his sheep" (1 Sam. 25:4)
30 Jesus, the Son of ___
32 Seat
33 IT leader
34 "Saul ___ counsel of God" (1 Sam. 14:37)
36 Yelp
38 Apron top
42 ___ chi
43 Singer Leonard
46 "This is again the second ___" (John 4:54)
49 Impediment

51 Joseph's role in Egypt (Gen. 42:6) (abbr.)

53 Herod Antipas' sin (Matt. 14:4)

56 Magi's origin

58 Open-mouthed stare

59 Where the eagle dwells (Job 39:28)

60 Rivulet

61 "___ rejoiced with exceeding great joy" (Matt. 2:10)

63 "Eli, Eli, ___ sabachthani?" (Matt. 27:46)

64 Western actor Pickens

65 Id's companion

67 Bethlehem to Jerusalem (dir.)

69 Seventh Greek letter

HEZEKIAH: JEHOVAH FOLLOWER

ACROSS

1 "Is there no ____ in Gilead?" (Jer. 8:22)
5 Tides
9 China island: ____ Kong
13 Off-Broadway award
14 Saw logs
15 Nighttime (Gen. 19:1)
16 Samuel's role (1 Sam. 9:19)
17 Particle
18 Asian humped ox
19 Plasterwork
21 Hezekiah's water holder (2 Kings 18:31)
23 "My ____ is easy" (Matt. 11:30)
25 Egyptian delicacy (Num. 11:5) (sing.)
26 Christian org. for young athletes
29 "The LORD will ____ me" (2 Kings 20:8)
31 "Salute every ____ in Christ Jesus" (Phil. 4:21)
34 Coffee holder
35 Inches forward
37 Air (prefix)
39 "We shall also ____ with him" (2 Tim. 2:12)

41 "Lot is cast into the ____" (Prov. 16:33)
42 Turkish ruler
43 "They shall ____ as lions' whelps" (Jer. 51:38)
44 Cain's eldest son (Gen. 4:17)
46 Danish krone (abbr.)
47 Material of Heavenly gate (Rev. 21:21)
50 Remain
51 Yes, as in John 11:27
52 Gloomy
54 "A rod out of the ____ of Jesse" (Isa. 11:1)
56 Cleaner brand
59 Tombs
63 The king "____ his garments" (2 Sam. 13:31)
64 Disconcert
66 Shipshape
67 Word of sorrow (Amos. 5:16)
68 Tightly twisted
69 Attacked Hezekiah (Isa. 36:2)
70 Hiding places (Rev. 6:15)
71 Disciple nickname
72 "Rejoicing in ____" (Rom. 12:12)

DOWN

1 Springsteen nickname
2 Aid
3 Instead: "In ____ of"
4 Seat of gold (Ex. 25:17)
5 Bethel to Shiloh (dir.)
6 Pear type
7 Cooking technique from Luke 24:42
8 Senses
9 King who saw a shadow (2 Kings 20:10)
10 "I will pass ____ you"(Ex. 12:13)
11 Gaza to Joppa (dir.)
12 African antelope
14 Food cured
20 Musician Leonard
22 Four o'clock beverage
24 "Fly away as an ____" (Prov. 23:5)

26 God's anger (Isa. 42:25)
27 How beasts move (Ps. 104:20)
28 Senile
30 Rests against
32 The Lord hears them (Isa. 41:17)
33 Three-wheeler
36 What the leopard can't change (Jer. 13:23)
38 Gumbo ingredient
40 "They sang praises with ____" (2 Chron. 29:30)
42 More timid
45 Attention-getting
48 Hind's partner (Prov. 5:19)
49 Zambia capital
53 Batman's partner
55 Asian bird

56 Appearance of death horse (Rev. 6:8)
57 Persia today
58 "God called the dry ___ Earth" (Gen. 1:10)
60 Coffee alternative brand
61 Tap in lightly

62 Eye infection
63 A little bit
65 "So many as the stars of the ___" (Heb. 11:12)

IN JESUS' TIME

ACROSS

1 Average (abbr.)
4 His time, a beast of burden
9 Relaxing place
12 49 Down solo
14 He "was dead, and is __ again" (Luke 15:24)
15 Breakfast cereal choice
16 Temple decorators' embellishments
17 Icy rain
18 Pasta option
19 Boney guy
21 61 Across harvest
23 Garment maker would do this
24 __ Father
25 Halt
28 Bethany to Bethlehem (dir.)
31 Observe
34 Squirrels' stash
36 Cart, perhaps, in Jesus' time
38 Game caller, for short
40 In His time, bread-makers' to-do
41 Most tried to __ Roman soldiers

43 Marketplace barter agreement
44 "We __, Abba, Father" (Rom. 8:15)
45 Suffer
46 Lawnlike
48 By __, Jesus' travel option
51 Excitement in marketplace, e.g.
53 Org.
54 Bottomless __, hell
56 He had five loaves and two fish
58 Plan
61 21 Across concern
66 Many people in His time
67 49 Down approval
69 Jacob's brother
70 Repeated 3 times, WWII movie
71 Anointed
72 Beget
73 Jamaican music genre
74 Extremely heavy
75 Believers are to __ an example

DOWN

1 Droops
2 Laborious journey
3 Coin
4 Social level in His time
5 Permits
6 Appearance
7 Eden gal
8 "You have __ of the commands of God" (Mark 7:8 NIV) (2 words)
9 Seafarer's vessel in His time
10 Fisherman disciple, for short
11 Center of rotation
13 Visual communication (abbr.)
15 Former Russian rulers
20 Sports channel

22 In His time, herb sometimes tithed
25 In His time, head wrap against sun
26 Japanese capital
27 Mine find
29 Hot liquid burn
30 Bundle
32 Orchard sight in His time
33 40 Across need
34 Network TV channel
35 9 Down milieu
37 In His time, many widows did this
39 Angel's travel option
42 By way of
43 Israelite tribe
47 In His time, donkey owner might do this

49 Musical production
50 Paul's son in faith, for short
52 32 Down fillers
55 Bible "thou shalt not"
57 Current receptor
58 Automotive oil brands
59 Most women did this in His time
60 Israeli circle dance

61 Gorge
62 Affirmative
63 Sale tag info (2 words)
64 Unusual
65 49 Down feature
68 7 Down formed from Adam's

LETTERS TO THE CORINTHIANS

ACROSS

1 One shined in the east
5 Wise man's house foundation, per parable
9 "Violent dealing shall come down upon his own __" (Ps. 7:16)
13 Folk singer Guthrie
14 Symphony reed
15 Expedition
16 Moon valley
17 Surrender
18 "Are you not __ of what the law says?" (Gal. 4:21 NIV)
19 In Corinth, preacher with Paul
21 Those who "preach the gospel should __ of the gospel" (1 Cor. 9:14)
23 If in Christ, "he is a __ creature" (2 Cor. 5:17)
24 Summer addition to 37 Across
25 Sluggish
29 E.T.'s ride
30 Pitcher
32 Corinth to Troas (dir.)
33 Conductor Previn
36 Swedish city
37 Four o'clock cuppa
38 Do "not muzzle...the ox that treadeth out the __" (1 Cor. 9:9)

39 Paul preached the __ of Christ
40 "Jesus __," shortest Bible verse
41 Card game
42 Bug spray brands
43 "The __ is the Lord's" (1 Cor. 10:26)
44 Also
45 Teen trouble
46 "Eye hath not seen, nor __ heard" (1 Cor. 2:9)
47 Liveliness
49 One about to graduate (abbr.)
50 __ Vegas, NV
53 Area of early church expansion
55 Most extended
57 "__ be unto you" (1 Cor. 1:3)
60 __ Span, cleaning brand
62 Galilee or Gennesaret
63 Greased
64 "__ of you has your own gift" (1 Cor. 7:7 NIV)
65 Concluded
66 Not just hearer, but a __
67 Cooler choices
68 Swiss capital

DOWN

1 Wrap brand
2 Cow's belly
3 Permit
4 Jelly or dinner go-with
5 Decorative art style
6 Extremely heavy
7 Fisherman's catch
8 Overturn
9 "Not in word, but in __" (1 Cor. 4:20)
10 Southern constellation
11 Coating for baby Moses' basket
12 "If the whole body were an __" (1 Cor. 12:17)

15 Party treats
20 "Spirit giveth __" (2 Cor. 3:6)
22 Objects
26 Biblical fisherman
27 Useless
28 "O __, where is thy sting?" (1 Cor. 15:55)
29 One of many filled with water at Cana
30 Wash away
31 Weakling
33 Critical
34 "Thou shalt nots"
35 Slump

36 Smile

39 Succulents

40 Armageddon, e.g.

42 Christ was __ from death

43 Work for

46 One who "walked with" 57 Down, and namesakes

48 Competitive runner

49 Dice partner

50 God will never __ you

51 Pray-er, perhaps

52 Strict

54 On 62 Across

56 Lump

57 "Thanks be unto __ for his. . .gift" (2 Cor. 9:15)

58 Jordan, e.g. (Sp.)

59 Brew

61 Beatnik's lodgings

OLD TESTAMENT MIRACLES

ACROSS

1 Napoleon's exile isle
5 "_____ in tears...reap in joy" (Ps. 126:5)
8 Ten Commandments
12 23 Across sight
13 Isaac's elderly mom
15 Investment choices (abbr.)
16 Goliath descriptor
17 Planet's shadow
18 It turned to blood
19 Fiery furnace sights
21 Relating to money
23 Wicked city destroyed
25 Restroom for the English
26 Plague pests
29 Job's wife descriptor
31 Scrapbook, e.g.
35 Parted waterway (2 words)
37 Today's chariot
39 One of Columbus' ships
40 Eden occupant
41 Knee boo-boos
44 Med. worker

45 Scorch
47 Mild fish
48 She bore Jesus as one
50 Serf
52 Israel tribe
54 Bullring passes
55 To be unwell
57 Many (prefix)
59 Fifth day creation
62 World in Orlando
65 God _____ the world
66 Magicians tried to _____ plagues
68 Men's toiletry brand
70 Fourth day creation
71 Chatter
72 Priestly anointing fluids
73 Prov. 31 woman descriptors
74 Eden serpent slyer than _____ beast (Gen. 3:1)
75 David would _____ over his sins

DOWN

1 KJV verb ending
2 One of five that fed 5000
3 Cotton seed pod
4 Collections of Bible maps
5 Miraculous-strength man
6 Sun or moon
7 Caesarea harbor sight
8 16th US president
9 Church soloist's song
10 Where Belshazzar saw writing
11 Israelites' wandering direction
13 Took to court
14 Plague icicles
20 35 Across partner
22 Latest technical device descriptor (abbr.)

24 Street surface made of broken stone
26 Leper's skin was made _____
27 Netherlands sight
28 Eden descriptor
30 Who will "stand in the _____?" (Ezek. 22:30)
32 Ship's bottom section
33 Detach, in a way
34 Israelite desert food
36 Sports organization (abbr.)
38 Sunday sermonizer, for short
42 OT miraculous budder
43 What a sieve does
46 Like Israelites for forty years
49 God's sign to Noah
51 NT epistle (abbr.)

53 Sin made Eden dwellers ashamed of it

56 "Thou art my _____, O Lᴏʀᴅ" (2 Sam. 22:29)

58 Plague itchers

59 40 Across for 60 Down

60 See 59 Down

61 Pre-Euro cash

63 Canal

64 Christmas

65 Flavor enhancer (abbr.)

67 "God created _____ in his . . .image" (Gen. 1:27)

69 Recipe measure (abbr.)

ALL CREATION

ACROSS

1 "Time to _____ . . .to laugh" (Eccl. 3:4)
5 Chats
9 Ratios of comparison
14 Angel's topper
15 Like wispy clouds
16 Sky layer
17 Selves
18 1857 _____ Scott Decision
19 "Blue _____ Shoes," Elvis hit
20 "I am _____ and Omega" (Rev. 1:8)
22 "His _____ over me was love" (Song 2:4)
24 Casual shirt
25 78 Across descriptor
27 Common currency
31 Des Moines state
32 KJV "yes"
34 Jerusalem's _____ Dolorosa
35 Jesus, _____ of Jesse
38 Make do, with "out"
40 Medicines
42 They were brought to Jesus' tomb
44 Church extension

46 India city
47 Whatchamacallit
48 Holy Land fruit
50 Enjoys food
51 See 78 Across
52 Sports org.
55 He will "_____ his flock" (Isa. 40:11)
57 Sunset colors
59 Sinai desert travelers
61 Herbal drink
64 Note brand (hyph.)
66 Liturgical song
68 Sweet, fleshy members of the gourd family
71 Israelites made one through Sinai
73 Cold War foe (abbr.)
74 78 Across forbidden _____
75 Slogan (Sp.)
76 Dorcas' needle need
77 _____-Saxon
78 51 Across home
79 Like Flood waters

DOWN

1 "Filleth thee with... finest..._____" (Ps. 147:14)
2 "He shall fly as an _____" (Jer. 48:40)
3 Marry secretly
4 Ritzy
5 Israelite tribe
6 Hydraulic speed reducer (2 words)
7 Manna
8 Down Under city
9 "I am the _____ of Sharon" (Song 2:1)
10 Firmament color
11 OT anointed digit
12 "World without _____"
13 "_____ the goodness of the LORD" (Ps. 27:13)
21 Back in time

23 Gaza to Nazareth (dir.)
26 "Stand in _____ of him" (Ps. 33:8)
28 Palate projection
29 "At thy _____ hand...are pleasures" (Ps. 16:11)
30 Desert sight
31 Object
33 "_____ to your faith virtue" (2 Pet. 1:5)
35 Angry screamer
36 Holy Land orchard tree
37 Seeped out
39 Santa's helper
41 "Bruised _____ shall he not break" (Isa. 42:3)
43 Seeders do this
45 God's care lasts a _____

49 Set

53 Medical research org.

54 Grass grows for them (Ps. 104:14)

56 Keyboard key (abbr.)

58 Stored manna would do this

60 Engulfed, as in sin

61 Words sweet "unto my _____" (Ps. 119:103)

62 "Seek peace, and _____ it" (1 Pet. 3:11)

63 Sinai wandering was one (2 words)

65 Aware of

67 Like a sunrise

68 Graduate degree (abbr.)

69 Sea bird

70 Drag

72 Baker's need

HOSEA: THE LONG-SUFFERING SPOUSE

ACROSS

1 Caribbean dance
6 Jewish calendar month
10 Chimney
14 Jacob's father (Gen. 25:26)
15 "___ not ye unto Gilgal" (Hos. 4:15)
16 Speech defect
17 Playfully romantic
18 "Not an ___ be left behind" (Ex. 10:26)
19 Beehive State
20 "Go quickly, and ___ his disciples" (Matt. 28:7)
21 Exacerbate
23 Self
24 Native ruler in Africa
26 "Moses ___ up the tabernacle" (Ex. 40:18)
28 Citizen of Libya
31 Bible teacher Moore
32 Epoch
33 They are bent to backsliding (Hos. 11:7)
36 "For as in ___ all die" (1 Cor. 15:22)
40 "God waited in the days of ___" (1 Pet. 3:20)
42 Charm

43 Tubular pasta
44 "Man doth not live by bread ___" (Deut. 8:3)
45 What Esther wrote regarding Purim (Est. 9:29)
48 An age
49 "The ___ was fair and beautiful" (Est. 2:7)
51 Hosea's son (Hos. 1:9)
53 "Raw" color
56 May be a good or bad sign
57 Body sys. consisting of brain and spinal cord
58 Iraq river
61 Festive party
65 "Go, take ___ thee a wife" (Hos. 1:2)
67 Paul before Damascus Road
68 Absurd
69 "Surely he shall not ___ quietness" (Job 20:20)
70 Gape
71 Male honeybee
72 Flintstone or Astaire
73 "To abound and to suffer ___" (Phil. 4:12)
74 "He reproved kings for their ___" (Ps. 105:14)

DOWN

1 "I will ___ up mine eyes" (Ps. 121:1)
2 John's prison, ___ of Patmos
3 Goliath's coat (1 Sam. 17:5)
4 Hosea's payment for Gomer (Hos. 3:2)
5 Fall mo.
6 Where Achan was destroyed (Josh. 7:24)
7 Achor was a "___ of hope" (Hos. 2:15)
8 OT prophet
9 Umpire
10 Winter malady
11 Liquid measure
12 Utilization
13 Israel didn't have one (Hos. 3:4)

21 "They shall not offer ___ offerings" (Hos. 9:4)
22 Part of the altar (Ex. 27:5)
25 Traveler's aid
27 Son of Jotham (Hos. 1:1)
28 Comedian Jay
29 Og's bedstead material (Deut. 3:11)
30 Israel served ___ (2 Kings 17:16)
31 "___ out all mine iniquities" (Ps. 51:9)
34 "The one ___ five hundred pence" (Luke 7:41)
35 "The fining ___ is for silver" (Prov. 17:3)
37 Carpe ___

38 Particle
39 Short, for short
41 Prelude to Gethsemane (Mark 14:26)
45 Intermediary
46 Trees of sacrifice (Hos. 4:13)
47 "My beloved is like a ___" (Song 2:9)
50 "Go to the ___, thou sluggard" (Prov. 6:6)
52 Goat or rabbit hair
53 Scratch
54 "The cloud filled the ___ court" (Ezek. 10:3)

55 Perfume maven Lauder
56 Bread sacrifice type (Lev. 8:26)
59 Challenge to combat
60 "The sun to ___ by day" (Ps. 136:8)
62 Priest of Jeshua (Neh. 12:7)
63 Rahab "bound a scarlet ___" (Josh. 2:21)
64 Experts
66 "Honour the face of the ___ man" (Lev. 19:32)
68 Savings accts.

ISAIAH: THE FAITHFUL PROPHET

ACROSS

1 Wilderness tree (Isa. 41:19)
6 Fashionable
10 Connect
14 "The LORD ___ shall be exalted" (Isa. 2:11)
15 Crazy (Sp.)
16 Taboo
17 "Your hands are full of ___" (Isa. 1:15)
18 Prayer ending
19 Jainism believer
20 Half
21 "My heart standeth in ___ of thy word" (Ps. 119:161)
22 Phantoms
24 G-man Eliot
26 " ___ for ashes" (Isa. 61:3)
27 Hog side
30 "This people draw ___" (Isa. 29:13)
31 Painting prop
32 Jacob had ten (Gen. 32:15)
33 Noah's building project
36 Diacritic mark
37 Shortened (abbr.)
38 Netherlands' capital

40 "Come down ___ my child die" (John 4:49)
41 "Unto us a ___ is born" (Isa. 9:6)
43 Musical composition
44 Adjust
45 "Holy One of ___" (Isa. 1:4)
46 His birth foretold in Isa. (Isa. 9:6)
49 "___ us a son is given" (Isa. 9:6)
50 "___ good tidings unto the meek" (Isa. 61:1)
51 Licensed caregiver (abbr.)
52 Seraphims held (Isa. 6:6)
56 Rejoicing, "The earth ___ again" (1 Sam. 4:5)
57 Bearded or Japanese
59 Transitional state
60 "God hath spoken ___" (Ps. 62:11)
61 "Call his ___ Immanuel" (Isa. 7:14)
62 Askew
63 "He shall ___ his flock" (Isa. 40:11)
64 "Strain at a ___, and swallow a camel" (Matt. 23:24)
65 Sound or mega

DOWN

1 Taxis
2 Women's magazine
3 Gloom and ___
4 "The LORD hath ___ me" (Isa. 61:1)
5 "___ like crimson" (Isa. 1:18)
6 "Nails like birds' ___" (Dan. 4:33)
7 Groom's first-year location (Deut. 24:5)
8 "Out of whose womb came the ___?" (Job 38:29)
9 Coagulate
10 Green-skinned pear
11 "Shall the axe ___ itself?" (Isa. 10:15)
12 "Keep the ___ of the Spirit" (Eph. 4:3)
13 Thousands of pounds
21 Tree the carpenter planted (Isa. 44:14)

23 Most unpleasant
25 Diverse
26 Razor consumes this (Isa. 7:20)
27 Lavish party
28 Hideout
29 "Howl, ye inhabitants of the ___" (Isa. 23:6)
30 "Not many ___, are called" (1 Cor. 1:26)
32 "They shall walk, and not ___" (Isa. 40:31)
33 Water (Sp.)
34 Describes Paul's speech (2 Cor. 11:6)
35 Musical actor Howard
39 Cruelty
42 Muting
45 No room here

46 Chattering bird (Isa. 38:14)

47 Command the idol, "Get thee ___"
(Isa. 30:22)

48 "The heathen ___" (Ps. 46:6)

49 Toppled

50 University instructor (abbr.)

51 Peru capital

53 Leave out

54 " Believe ye that I am ___?" (Matt. 9:28)

55 These were cast for Jesus' clothes
(John 19:24)

58 "David ___, and stood upon the Philistine"
(1 Sam. 17:51)

59 Canine retriever (abbr.)

GENESIS

ACROSS

1 Honey homes
6 Military school (abbr.)
10 "We cry '___, Father'"(Rom. 8:15)
14 Ephesus marketplace
15 "Ali ___ and the Forty Thieves"
16 Derogatory remark, as in Psalm 15:3 NIV
17 "Thy brother's ___ crieth unto me" (Gen. 4:10)
18 Abraham, financially
19 Lotion brand
20 "The Lord God ___ him out of...Eden" (Gen. 3:23 NKJV)
21 Created on Day 6
22 Texas or Ukraine city
24 A mark kept Cain from this
26 In the middle
27 Postpones
30 "I led them with... ___of love" (Hos. 11:4 NIV)
31 Woman will not "___ authority" over man (1 Tim. 2:12)
32 Ephod stone
33 Adam, Enos, e.g.
36 Parsonage
37 Downwind, as in Acts 27:4 NIV
38 Egg-shaped
40 Unopened flower
41 Magnificent
43 Tabernacle curtain components
44 Juicy Fruit and Dentyne
45 Arctic outerwear
46 It drove Abram to Egypt
49 West African nation
50 "I will make of thee a great ___" (Gen. 12:2)
51 Amount, as in Numbers 1:2
52 "___ is mount Sinai in Arabia" (Gal. 4:25)
56 Aaron's expression of woe (Num. 12:11)
57 Egyptian wader
59 Travelocity spokesman
60 Patmos or Malta (poet.)
61 Faithful ark builder
62 Bitter
63 Stare
64 Musky
65 Moses did mighty ones (Acts. 7:22)

DOWN

1 Taxis
2 Gawk
3 Night light
4 Joseph's betrayed him
5 Nehemiah's countenance
6 Father of nations
7 Abel's slayer
8 TV network
9 Former name for Benin
10 "Jesus ___, 'Who do you say that I am?'"
11 God promises to ___ Abram (Gen. 12:2)
12 "___ into song, you mountains" (Isa. 49:13 NIV)
13 Opera solo
21 Sarah to Abraham (abbr.)
23 Unfaithful, as Psalm 78:57 NIV
25 Chord type
26 Voiced
27 Jesus "maketh. . .the ___ to speak" (Mark 7:37)
28 Jacob's twin
29 Finance
30 Shadrach and Daniel age range
32 "We should be holy and without ___" (Eph. 4:4)
33 Third Gospel
34 Italy volcano
35 G-man Eliot
39 A work of the flesh (Gal. 5:20)
42 Ceremonial water (Lev. 14:5)
45 Brand of non-stick spray
46 "Thou shalt not bear ___ witness" (Ex. 20:16)
47 Our years are "___ that is told" (2 words) (Ps. 90:9)

48 "Do not eat the bread of a __" (Prov. 23:6 NKJV)

49 Soft

50 Jael's weapon (Judg. 4:22)

51 *The King and I* locale

53 Ox or bull might do this

54 "God has ascended __ shouts of joy" (Ps. 47:5 NIV)

55 Cincinnati baseball team

58 Snake

59 Son of Jacob and Leah

ANIMALS

ACROSS

1 Dismay (var.)
6 Dog food brand
10 "Will the unicorn be willing to... abide by thy __?" (Job 39:9)
14 Water bird
15 In __ of (instead)
16 Parable guests found here (sing.)
17 Slogan
18 Annoying insect
19 Meshach destination
20 Eden angel held one (Fr.)
21 "Appointed unto men once to __" (Heb. 9:27)
22 Distract
24 "__ me in thy truth" (Ps. 25:5)
26 Mouse, e.g.
27 Nebuchadnezzar's temporary fate
30 Moses removed one at Sinai
31 Speaks with a hoarse voice
32 *Phantom of the __*
33 LP meas.
36 Tiny island
37 Flying 26 Across

38 Queen of Sheba headwear, perhaps
40 Pronoun for Eve
41 Deflect
43 Block of metal
44 Elephant's "tooth"
45 Insect of Egypt
46 "Come ye...and rest __" (Mark 16:31) (2 words)
49 Computer drop-down
50 "He shall __ thy paths" (Prov. 3:6)
51 See 26 Across
52 Ursa of Isaiah 11:7
56 Dead flies cause (Eccl. 10:1)
57 Benjamin and Abner became one (2 Sam. 2:25)
59 Brazilian dance
60 Oppose
61 Memorization technique
62 Pisa tower position
63 First animal site
64 Rebekah filled at the well
65 Roman goddess

DOWN

1 Zenith
2 Support
3 Elisha's was bald
4 Clean animal of Deuteronomy 14:6
5 King of beasts (Lat.)
6 Chilly
7 Rahab's was scarlet
8 Green soup
9 "Put your __ work in order" (Prov. 24:27 NIV)
10 Garlic part
11 Elijah's feeder, once
12 Inactive
13 Prepped a bow
21 Animals created on fifth __

23 Imagination
25 Joyful
26 Scarlett's husband
27 Part of the eye
28 Destroy, as Psalm 2:9
29 John's home, __ of Patmos
30 James 3 fire starter (NIV)
32 Eglon descriptor (Judg. 3:17)
33 Meat-based sauce
34 Cons opposite
35 Disciple's nickname
39 Hen birthing process
42 Carcass eater
45 "__ me not be ashamed" (Ps. 25:2)

46 Helped

47 "Moses ___ all the words of the Lord" (Ex. 24:4)

48 Long-legged bird

49 Mary to Jesus (Lat.)

50 Ark flyer

51 Passover, e.g.

53 Eastern ruler

54 Jesus is ___ to save us

55 Philistine destroyers (1 Sam. 6:4 NIV)

58 "This is ___ bone of my bones" (Gen. 2:23)

59 Pocket

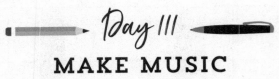

MAKE MUSIC

ACROSS

1 Egypt to Mt. Sinai (dir.)
4 "_____ the music!"
9 Bounce up and down
12 Volcano spew
14 French physicist Marie
15 "_____ scriptura"
16 Chilled
17 David ruled twelve tribes as a _____
18 Praise to "_____ of the earth" (Ps. 48:10)
19 Pulsated
21 Jezebel descriptor
23 "Give _____ unto my prayer" (Ps. 17:1)
24 Pastor, for short
25 Abba
28 God forgives it
31 Nobel Prize winner Walesa
34 Sacred music piece, maybe
36 Rover's doc
38 Prodigal son's charge
40 Sing praise to God most _____
41 God _____ His love for us
43 Eastern queen

44 Hydrocarbon suffix
45 Course average
46 Repentant one makes them
48 "Be _____ in the LORD" (Ps. 32:11)
51 Body builder's place
53 Choir section
54 "Sing unto _____, sing praises" (Ps. 68:4)
56 Slippery swimmer
58 Pizza-makings brand
61 54 Across descriptor
66 Purim month
67 Servant who became wealthy through corruption
69 Franc alternative
70 Choir solo
71 David would _____ Saul's sword
72 Sad song may make you _____ up
73 "_____ them sing praises" (Ps. 149:3)
74 Forest nymph
75 Lydia's need

DOWN

1 Open, as with a knife
2 Sacred music composer J.S.
3 "Eyes are _____ toward the LORD" (Ps. 25:15)
4 Underwater breathing gear
5 Piano fixers
6 Like Sinai Desert
7 Jordan (Sp.)
8 Male chorister, maybe
9 "_____ of him. . .not be broken" (John 19:36)
10 General Motors car, for short
11 SATB hymn part
13 "Why make ye this _____?" (Mark 5:39)
15 "All nations shall _____ him" (Ps. 72:11)
20 Rhythm

22 Hair product
25 "This is the LORD'S _____" (Ps. 118:23)
26 Heavenly choir member
27 Morse code code
29 Ahab's palace (1 Kings 22:39)
30 "Sing unto him a _____ song" (Ps. 33:3)
32 Liturgical song
33 Texas town
34 _____ Na Na, rock group
35 Nile slitherer
37 JFK screeners
39 Vets, for short
42 Crone
43 Faith category, for short
47 Timbuktu nation

49 Ancient Greek marketplace
50 Jobs org.
52 Soprano part, usually
55 Has dinner
57 Sodom remain
58 False god
59 Wineskin (Sp.)

60 Lure, as to temptation
61 Border
62 "Therefore _____ wisdom" (Prov. 4:7)
63 Like Joseph's coat
64 Butler's need
65 Days of _____
68 Menu words

OCCUPATIONS

ACROSS

1 Priestly job site
6 They "lie upon _____ of ivory" (Amos 6:4)
10 "My flesh...shall _____ in hope" (Ps. 16:9)
14 In "resurrection they neither _____"
   (Matt. 22:30)
15 First gardener
16 "Follow _____ know the Lᴏʀᴅ" (Hos. 6:3)
   (2 words)
17 Teardrop shaped
18 Airborne toy; hawk
19 Bible weapon material, often
20 Big truck
21 19 Across, and others
23 Three Persons, _____ God
24 European river
26 King and centurion, e.g.
28 Meager
31 Singing cowboy Autry
32 Card game
33 Hard roll
36 Solomon's exotic creatures
40 Isn't "life _____ than meat?" (Matt. 6:25)
42 Hoover, e.g.
43 Brood

44 71 Across bro
45 Detector
48 "Blind shall _____" (Isa. 29:18)
49 Sicilian rumbler
51 He or she handles others feet
53 Dorcas' job need
56 "Enter _____ the kingdom of God"
57 Who "can _____ one cubit" of height?
   (Matt. 6:27)
58 Sinai desert travelers
61 Bible potter's need
65 "Rock of _____," Sunday song
67 Lotion brand
68 Modern-day chariot choice
69 Soldier's dwelling
70 Austen novel
71 Fisherman disciple
72 "Unto thee will I _____" (Ps. 5:2)
73 Bible bricklayer's job site
74 He will "_____ down our enemies"
   (Ps. 60:12)

DOWN

1 Shepherd prophet
2 Wash
3 Shuttle bus
4 Temple decorator, e.g.
5 Bread choice
6 Joseph's jail mate
7 Forbidden to _____ scripture (Rev. 22:18)
8 Information
9 19 Across worker
10 French king
11 Recruit
12 Temple builder's need
13 Organ sounds
21 Central American civilization

22 Devil's work
25 Noah's building project
27 Needed to plow a field
28 Mountain lion
29 Some "_____ with joy" believe (Matt. 13:20)
30 Bible sovereign
31 4 Down supplies
34 Thought
35 Spanish holy man
37 46 Down dwelling descriptor, e.g.
38 Fencer's weapon
39 Samuel's calling
41 Looked at
45 Athlete's shoe

46 Parable rich man _____ much
47 Rodent
50 Jesus gave it (abbr.)
52 Field sport
53 Civil rights org.
54 Author Poe
55 Swelling
56 Homeric epic

59 Note
60 Writer Bombeck
62 Musician's strings
63 Galilee or Judea
64 Gardener's space
66 Caleb, e.g.
68 Bishop "must be..._____ to teach"
(1 Tim. 3:2)

JACOB: THE USURPER

ACROSS

1 Western state
5 Wise king (abbr.)
8 Musical symbol
12 "I sink in deep ___" (Ps. 69:2)
13 Brief witty speech
15 Jacob held Esau's ___ (Gen. 25:26)
16 Urgent request
17 Learner
18 "Fear not: believe ___" (Luke 8:50)
19 Baltic state
21 Brains (slang)
23 Rental car company
25 "The LORD shall ___ to me another son" (Gen. 30:24)
26 Part of the offering in Leviticus 8:26
29 How the rich ruler felt (Mark 10:22)
31 Lettuce and toppings
35 Color between red and yellow
37 Ballet steps
39 Jacob's priestly son (Gen. 34:25)
40 Unrefined metal
41 Country bordering Latvia

44 Convert into leather
45 "Thou hast now ___ foolishly" (Gen. 31:28)
47 Isaac did before blessing his son (Gen. 27:4)
48 Cat food brand
50 Actress Hilary
52 Bookstore section (abbr.)
54 "I will surely give the ___ unto thee" (Gen. 28:22)
55 NT author, for short
57 Imitation chocolate
59 Jacob's new name (Gen. 32:28)
62 Jacob's favored son (Gen. 37:3)
65 "The truth shall make you ___" (John 8:32)
66 Legitimate
68 To maintain, as in Genesis 17:9
70 "Eli, Eli, ___ sabachthani?" (Matt. 27:46)
71 Jacob dwelt in these (Gen. 25:27)
72 Paul was forbidden to preach here (Acts 16:6)
73 Troop
74 Springsteen's "Born in the ___"
75 Shofar, as in Joshua 6:5

DOWN

1 Referee (abbr.)
2 Plow, as in Genesis 2:5
3 Region
4 "Among the ___, and I will sing praises" (2 Sam. 22:50)
5 Weightlifting exercise
6 "Get thee ___ of thy country" (Gen. 12:1)
7 "A false witness that speaketh ___" (Prov. 6:19)
8 Harmonic
9 "I have ___ him to the LORD" (1 Sam. 1:28)
10 Morays
11 "He shall ___ away as a dream" (Job 20:8)
13 "Grievous words ___ up anger" (Prov. 15:1)
14 Judgment seat (Gr.)
20 Brink

22 Spots
24 Southern Mexican Indian
26 Where God's people will sleep (Ezek. 34:25)
27 "Their tongue is as an ___" (Jer. 9:8)
28 Matador's passes at bull
30 Jacob's fifth son (Gen. 29:32—30:6)
32 Induct (2 words)
33 ___-garde
34 Jacob's daughter (Gen. 34:1)
36 Shiloh to Jericho (dir.)
38 Drink slowly
42 Sticky black substance
43 Vehicles
46 "I will cause the enemy to ___ thee" (Jer. 15:11)
49 Isaac's wife (Gen. 24:67)

51 Soldier killed while in active service (abbr.)
53 Tortilla rollup
56 "Our hearts did ___" (Josh. 2:11)
58 Decays
59 Cyrus's kingdom today (2 Chron. 36:22)
60 Very large truck

61 Instead, "in ___ of"
63 Mexican money
64 Jesus, "___ of all things" (Heb. 1:2)
65 Winter malady
67 Body sys. consisting of brain and spinal cord
69 "A meat offering baken in a ___" (Lev. 2:5)

JAMES: THE DISCIPLE

ACROSS

1 "___ that great city Babylon" (Rev. 18:10)
5 Ancient Greek marketplace
10 "Ye ___. . .by works a man is justified" (James 2:24)
13 "Resist the ___, and he will flee" (James 4:7)
15 Small appliance maker
16 Cable network
17 Burning, as in Exodus 3:2
18 Type of offering
19 Sackcloth partner
20 Cable music network
21 Stuck-up person
23 Offspring (Matt. 22:25)
25 "Every good ___. . .is from above" (James 1:17)
26 James to Jesus (Mark 6:3)
28 Tyrannus led one (Acts 19:9)
31 Insolent
32 Constellation (Job 9:9)
33 "Receive ___ meekness the engrafted word" (James 1:21)
34 Unruly crowd
37 Crossing place in Genesis 32:22
38 "Weeping and gnashing of ___" (Matt. 25:30)

40 Musical instrument (Isa. 5:12)
41 Peacock partner (2 Chron. 9:21)
42 Vulture gathers with (Isa. 34:15)
43 Keyed
44 ___ of Olives
45 "A time ___, and a time to heal" (Eccl. 3:3) (2 words)
46 Home of the Braves
49 Emaciated
50 "And if children, then ___" (Rom. 8:17)
51 Horsefly
52 Greek letter
55 Suffix meaning direction
56 Shewbread sat upon this (Ex. 25:30)
59 Turn over
61 Is (pl.)
62 Seen at transfiguration (Luke 9:30)
63 Uncanny
64 Father, familiarly
65 Tear, as in John 19:24 (sing.)
66 Unhatched insect

DOWN

1 Eve's husband
2 Goat side (Matt. 25:33)
3 Tel ___ (Israel's capital)
4 What John called the elder (Rev. 7:14)
5 Monastery superior
6 Dig
7 Mariner's tool (Ezek. 27:29)
8 "Eyes of the LORD ___ to and fro" (2 Chron. 16:9)
9 Early Church site (Acts 15:35)
10 Hide away
11 Pursue, as in 1 Pet. 3:11
12 Anesthetic (arch.)

14 Leprosy scab
22 Football assoc.
24 Pig's home
25 Gift from above (see 25 Across)
26 Lure
27 Wife of Boaz (Ruth 4:13)
28 Divan
29 Prune, as in Leviticus 25:3
30 "Labourer is worthy of his ___" (Luke 10:7)
31 Bitter's opposite (James 3:11)
34 Short
35 Australian gemstone
36 Hangs on priest's garment (Ex. 28:34)

38 Tight

39 Volcano

40 Dawdling

42 Creature of Lamentations 4:3 (sing.)

43 This is hard to tame (James 3:8)

44 Endanger, as in Ruth 4:6

45 Anointing spot (Lev. 14:28)

46 In the lead

47 ___ firma

48 Covered

49 "___ them which persecute you" (Rom. 12:14)

51 Dressed

52 South American nation

53 Trim

54 Notion

57 Lager

58 Container

60 Vigor

THE GARDEN OF EDEN

ACROSS

1 Moses wrote just one
6 Plants were Adam and Eve's
10 Eye infection
14 Forbidden (var.)
15 Paul describes his speech as (2 Cor. 11:6)
16 Sailor "Hi" to Jonah, maybe
17 Eve created while Adam did this
18 "The law is good if one __ it lawfully" (1 Tim. 1:8 NKJV)
19 __ of fire
20 PC key
21 Take away
23 Where Israelites dwelt
25 Sausage
26 First woman
27 Be next to
30 Chihuahua (2 words)
34 Daniel and Mary age range
35 A __ wind blew away locusts (Ex. 10:19)
36 "Will a man __ God?" (Mal. 3:8)
38 Group of eight
39 Lyricist David

40 Musical composition
42 Sleeping rug
43 What Esau hunted
44 Accepted practice
45 Luke's study sites, perhaps
48 Tools for Jesus, perhaps
49 Iron is one
50 Sheep attacker
51 Grew in Eden post-Fall
54 Mite or penny
55 Gas mileage grp.
58 German mister
59 France and Germany river
61 What locusts do to crops (2 words)
63 Allotted portion
64 Tree of knowledge of good and __
65 Encourages, __ on
66 Adam used to till garden
67 "He shall __ his angel before thee" (Gen. 24:7)
68 Steps for crossing a fence

DOWN

1 Battle-related illness (abbr.)
2 Abraham/Hittites transaction
3 Adam's son
4 Chop
5 Driver
6 Plentiful in Eden
7 Expel, like Adam and Eve
8 "__ on a Grecian Urn"
9 Lineage
10 Seasoned, as in Mark 9:49
11 Pad __
12 Jesus, "My __ is easy" (Matt. 11:30)
13 Adam and Eve's were opened
22 Made in God's image
24 __ League school

25 "This is now __ of my bones" (Gen. 2:23)
27 Molecule
28 Decorative sticker
29 Jonah's departure point
30 Oxen pairs
31 Patmos or Cyprus
32 Psalmist's instrument, as in Genesis 4:21
33 See 48 Across (sing.)
35 Smack
37 Buzzers Samson found
40 "In Your presence is __ of joy" (Ps. 16:11 NKJV)
41 Flying military branch (abbr.)
43 Samson riddle responses
46 David's horse's home
47 Suffix indicating direction

48 Taro dish

50 "For God so loved the __" (John 3:16)

51 "It is not good __ man should be alone" (Gen. 2:18)

52 Goliath to Philistines

53 Favorite dipping cookie

54 See 3 Down

55 Decorative needle case

56 Knitting stitch

57 Church niche

60 Hail (Lat.)

62 Bishop should be "__ to teach" (1 Tim. 3:2)

ISAAC: SON OF PROMISE

ACROSS

1 Sun and moon (poet.)
5 Toothbrush brand
10 Utah or Maine site (abbr.)
13 Seasoned rice
15 Happen again
16 Second day of week (abbr.)
17 Swelling
18 San __, CA
19 Tap
20 __ Testament
21 Daniel's age group
23 Curt
25 Gomorrah fire result
26 Isaac's half-brother
28 Sarah to Isaac
31 Parisian goodbye
32 Jacob felt for Rachel (Fr.)
33 Eden tree, perhaps
34 Shake head
37 Offering animal
38 Isaac's father

40 "Fear not __ down into Egypt" (Gen. 46:3) (2 words)
41 Mamre to Moriah (dir.)
42 Coffee alternative
43 South Korea capital
44 Wading bird
45 How camels travel
46 Asian citrus fruits
49 Hagar resting spot
50 Holy, set __
51 Abraham's became many nations
52 Eliezer was __ to Rebekah
55 Esau's coloring
56 Wrathful
59 Take off
61 Baseball stat
62 Adam & Eve early state
63 Saul saw David as one
64 Offering in Isaac's place
65 Mouse mastications
66 Hawaiian island

DOWN

1 "I have set before thee an __ door" (Rev. 3:8)
2 Isaac's horse purpose
3 Walls fell when trumpets __
4 Prophet's nickname
5 "Let all things be done. . .in __" (1 Cor. 14:40)
6 Isaac's horse control
7 Genius
8 Tote
9 Abel to Cain
10 Planet's shadow
11 To marinade
12 Heavenly messenger
14 Abraham to Isaac
22 To listen, give __
24 Ark's flightless bird

25 Israel's enemy (Ezek. 30:5)
26 Athenians loved a new one (Acts 17:20 NIV)
27 Thailand, once
28 Isaac, Adam, e.g.
29 Saudi Arabia neighbor
30 Volume, as in Psalm 40:7
31 Adam's response to 62 Across (Gen. 3:7)
34 Used for Isaac sacrifice
35 Flu
36 Given to Rebekah
38 Air (prefix)
39 Esau and Jacob (abbr.)
40 Joseph's coat color, perhaps
42 Attacking
43 Braze
44 Pronoun for Sarah

45 Confederate general
46 Small knife
47 Musical production
48 Woman
49 Burnt grass (Matt. 13:30 NIV)
51 Meal for Isaac
52 Found atop Sinai, perhaps

53 Jacob's twin
54 Sandwich spot (abbr.)
57 Esau ___ to meet Jacob
58 Saul, ___ Paul
60 Edge

OLD TESTAMENT PARABLES

ACROSS

1 Sheriff's searchers
6 Type of pear
10 Jesus embraced them
14 "Perform unto the Lord thine _____" (Matt. 5:33)
15 Eastern ruler
16 OT scribe
17 4 Down Israelites
18 Parable: _____ plucked up (Ezek. 19:10–14)
19 Christmas
20 Camel feature
21 "You _____!"
22 Parable: _____ under the throne (Jer. 43:8–13)
24 Outer shell
26 Jesus' sacrifice _____ for sins
27 God's path is the _____
30 Fencing weapon
31 God "had _____ prepared unto glory" (Rom. 9:23)
32 I've "broken the _____ of your yoke" (Lev. 26:13)
33 Parable: _____ harlot sisters (Ezek. 23:1–49)

36 Worshiper _____ and praises God
37 Adam and Eve _____ forbidden fruit
38 Orange yellow
40 They "_____ that devise evil" (Prov. 14:22)
41 Paul traveling, often
43 European river
44 Face feature
45 Parable: _____ from ocean (Dan. 7)
46 Angry mob would _____ Paul
49 Chest
50 Parable: _____ flowing from door (Ezek. 47:1–12)
51 Parable: Almond tree _____ (Jer. 1:11–19)
52 Making bricks was Israelites' daily _____
56 Bible's Persia
57 Man "little lower _____...angels" (Ps. 8:5)
59 Teacher or rabbi, for example
60 Doting, with "of"
61 Delight in "law of the _____" (Ps. 1:2)
62 Moses went _____ Mt. Sinai (2 words)
63 Praise to the "_____ of the earth" (Ps. 48:10)
64 "Mine _____ are" toward God (Ps. 25:15)
65 52 Across site

DOWN

1 Like Ahab's palace
2 Hawaii island
3 Jesus, "_____ of Jesse" (Isa. 11:1)
4 Parable: An unfaithful _____ (Ezek. 34)
5 Seer's gift
6 To slant the edge of wood or glass
7 Leave out
8 "Cleanse me from my _____" (Ps. 51:2)
9 Crowned
10 Part of a joint used to join wood pieces
11 Air layer
12 Parable myrtles (Zech. 1:8–17)
13 "My gal" of song, and others
21 Sandwich choice

23 Walker's bruises (2 words)
25 Drives (3 words)
26 Sleep disorder
27 Merchant's goal
28 Abraham "saw the place _____ off" (Gen. 22:4)
29 45 Across number
30 Parable: Scroll is _____ (Ezek. 3:1–2)
32 Herb
33 "Give us _____ day"
34 "A river _____ out of Eden" (Gen. 2:10)
35 Mined metals
39 Church basement goings-on
42 Parable: Cedar, _____ of Lebanon (2 Kings 14:9)

45 "Israel shall blossom and _____" (Isa. 27:6)

46 Moses' brother

47 "Who may _____ in thy sight?" (Ps. 76:7)

48 Jesus _____ disciples out into world

49 Parable: Wear _____ and yokes (Jer. 27:2)

50 Gomer to Hos.

51 Unusual

53 Court figure (abbr.)

54 Spill

55 "Moses _____ the flock of Jethro" (Ex. 3:1)

58 "Come here!"

59 OT anointed digit

NEW TESTAMENT PARABLES

ACROSS

1 "_____your hands, all ye people" (Ps. 47:1)
5 Widow's mite
9 KJV pronoun
13 "Now abideth faith, _____, charity" (1 Cor. 13:13)
14 Goliath descriptor
15 Martyrdom site
16 KJV "Mount Sinai"
17 "God; there is none _____" (Deut. 4:35)
18 Parable seed scatterer
19 Parable: _____others from your heart (Matt. 18:35)
21 Word reference book (abbr.)
23 US purchase price add-on
24 Parable: Goats' condition (Matt. 25:32)
25 Nero, e.g.
29 Suffer
30 Thin pancake
32 NT or OT period, for example
33 Like Pharisees vis-à-vis Jesus
36 "Hen doth gather her _____" (Luke 13:34)
37 Street paving materials
38 Parable: _____horsemen (Rev. 6:1–8)

39 "What the ark did
40 'With what measure ye _____" (Mark 4:24)
41 Anointing fluid
42 Pharisees asked Christ for _____
43 "He _____for you"
44 Navy ship initials
45 Samson tress, for example
46 "Shout for _____" (Ps. 32:11)
47 Passover bread had none
49 Phone book (abbr.)
50 Broken spirit would do this
53 One _____bread at Communion
55 Creates a flame
57 Parables give _____to heavenly truths
60 Tekoa prophet
62 "Why do the heathen _____?" (Ps. 2:1)
63 _____diem
64 Nothing
65 Choir solo
66 Parable: Rich man _____much (Luke 16:19)
67 Parables _____picture of spiritual reality
68 Swallow has one in Ps. 84

DOWN

1 "What is the _____to the wheat?" (Jer. 23:28)
2 The Word (Greek)
3 Lord sets _____godly for Himself (Ps. 4:3)
4 Austria city
5 Being of the same age, date, or duration
6 David _____Bathsheba on roof
7 Govt. bureau
8 God knows everything you _____(Matt. 6:8)
9 Moves horselike
10 Parable: _____down fruitless tree (Luke 13:9)
11 Egypt to Canaan (dir.)
12 "Give _____unto my prayer" (Ps. 17:1)

15 Jesus would _____into heaven
20 Water bird
22 Dummy
26 Jesus' disciple
27 What Paul did on Mars Hill
28 Parable: What Satan sows (Matt. 13:25)
29 Parable: Birds of _____ate sown seed (Mark 4:4)
30 Kidron or Cherith
31 Last Supper staple
33 Wrongdoers run _____of God's law
34 "Make a joyful _____" (Ps. 66:1)
35 Oklahoma city

36 Voting group

39 Uriah placed at _____ of army (2 Sam. 11:15)

40 "Thine alms _____ be in secret" (Matt. 6:4)

42 "If it _____ the king..." (Est. 9:13)

43 Disciples picked _____ on Sabbath (Mark 2:23)

46 Puzzle choice

48 Washington execs

49 Semiconductor device

50 Gaze, as at God's wonders

51 Breastplate, as of faith

52 Herod the _____

54 Abraham's offspring numerous as _____ (Gen. 32:12)

56 Cyrus' kingdom today

57 Org. development executive

58 Ten Commandments, e.g.

59 Cana water container

61 What sin would do to Eden

JEHOVAH: THE GREAT AND MIGHTY ONE

ACROSS

1 Will come out of Jacob (Num. 24:17)
5 Try
9 Hungry
14 Coca-___
15 Scent
16 Sifter (Amos 9:9)
17 "Cast me not ___" (Ps. 51:11)
18 Judgment seat (Gr.)
19 Ms. Lauder
20 Deep sleep
21 Bahrain capital
23 "Behold, I ___ an Angel" (Ex. 23:20)
24 Romp around
26 Après ___
28 Business name ending (abbr.)
29 Pine
31 Cooking measurement (abbr.)
34 Pizza brand
37 Noah found this in the eyes of the Lord (Gen. 6:8)
39 Snack
40 "Even to your old ___ I am he" (Isa. 46:4)

41 Arab Peninsula country
42 Closes, as in 2 Samuel 13:17
44 "For their ___ is mighty" (Prov. 23:11)
47 Until, as in Job 18:2
48 Exploiter
50 Gov. agency responsible for food and drug regulations
51 Grown in a pod (sing.)
52 Best, as in Psalm 81:16
56 Ali, with 40 thieves
59 Absolute ruler
63 Fasted's opposite
64 What the trumpets sound (Joel 2:1)
66 Raise, as in John 2:20
67 PC Security card (abbr.)
68 Types, as in Psalm 78:45
69 Ship part (Isa. 33:23)
70 Gas burner used in laboratories
71 "Thou God ___ me" (Gen. 16:13)
72 Prophet of Tekoa (Amos 1:1)
73 Not now

DOWN

1 Kerchief
2 The Lord is a strong one (Ps. 61:3)
3 Crockett battle site
4 R&B singer Charles
5 Southern crop
6 Eve's garden
7 Core
8 Trolley
9 Employ
10 Ending for Jehovah, meaning "Lord our banner" (Ex. 17:15)
11 Lavish party
12 Evening, as in Genesis 19:1
13 "A prophet mighty in __" (Luke 24:19)

21 Cooper automobile
22 Tree of Isaiah 44:14
25 "I will make darkness ___" (Isa. 42:16)
27 Cask
29 "His ___ is not turned away" (Isa. 9:12)
30 Dorm dweller
31 "The tongue can no man ___" (James 3:8)
32 Former wound
33 Writing tool in Isaiah 8:1
34 What Maaseiah kept (Jer. 35:4)
35 Patmos is one
36 Unusual (Dan. 2:11)
38 Cannot be scourged (Acts 22:25)
39 Jerusalem to Salim (dir.)

43 Take to court, as in Matthew 5:40

45 Exertions

46 Condense

49 Hypocrites' look (Matt. 6:16)

51 "Thou shalt see my back ___" (Ex. 33:23)

53 "God created the heaven and the ___" (Gen. 1:1)

54 "A precious corner ___" (Isa. 28:16)

55 Dallas dweller

56 Deep voice

57 Sweet-smelling herb from Psalm 45:8 (sing.)

58 Gave birth, as in Genesis 4:2

60 Writer Bombeck

61 Jesus' coat was without this (John 19:23)

62 El ___, TX

65 Montana time zone (abbr.)

67 Stroke an animal

JEREMIAH: THE GREAT PROPHET

ACROSS

1 Agricultural org.
4 "Believe ye that I am ___?" (Matt. 9:28)
8 Eight ounces
14 He had loaves (John 6:9)
15 Entice
16 Discomfort
17 Israel did this (Jer. 23:13)
18 Volcano
19 Frightened
20 Terrier
22 Pouch
23 What the Ammonites did not have (Jer. 49:1)
24 "Before I formed thee. . .I ___ thee" (Jer. 1:5)
27 Bird's seat
31 Shut, as in Psalm 107:42
33 "___, though I walk through the valley" (Ps. 23:4)
35 French affirmative
36 Made in the ___
38 Word receiver in Jeremiah 9:20
39 Pixies
40 Unsurpassed to the present (2 words)

44 Uncooked nature
46 "The prophets prophesy ___" (Jer. 14:14)
47 Adam's wife
49 Nocturnal flyer (Lev. 11:19)
50 Hovercraft (abbr.)
51 Cut
52 "He maketh the storm a ___" (Ps. 107:29)
55 Earthquake
58 The Lord gives a pleasant one (Jer. 3:19)
61 This was embroidered for a priest (Ex. 28:39)
63 Pod vegetable
65 Small chapel
67 What a woman buys in Proverbs 31:16 (2 words)
70 What Publius's father has in Acts 28:8
71 Part to dip (Luke 16:24)
72 What Simon did at night (Luke 5:5)
73 Curse
74 Israel to Babylon (dir.)
75 What Israelites were in Babylon
76 Used to write with (Jer. 36:18) (pl.)
77 Heb. crossed the ___ Sea

DOWN

1 "The LORD, the God of all ___" (Jer. 32:27)
2 Comedies
3 Adept
4 A wager (2 words)
5 Hand-dyed fabric
6 Jer.'s girdle material (Jer. 13:1)
7 Arrival time info.
8 Curse
9 Take off the lid
10 "Thoughts of ___, and not of evil" (Jer. 29:11)
11 Where watchers come from (Jer. 4:16)
12 "___ not vain repetitions" (Matt. 6:7)

13 "Thou hast ___ captivity captive" (Ps. 68:18)
21 Rainbow fish (pl.)
25 "Lift up thine ___" (Jer. 3:2) (sing.)
26 "Waters ___ the stones" (Job 14:19)
28 Paul's destination in Acts 28:14
29 Used to drink in Jeremiah 52:19
30 Snake speech
32 Greek letter
34 City of Joshua in Joshua 15:52
37 A woman's affirmation (Num. 5:22)
39 Inviolate
40 "___! for that day is great" (Jer. 30:7)
41 Fourth plague (Ex. 8:16)
42 Leah's son (Gen. 29:34)

43 This comes from the north in Jeremiah 4:6
45 Corps of women serving in the armed forces
48 Gov. agency for environmental regulations
53 Raider
54 Military branch member
56 Short period
57 Disturbance
59 Mr. Ryan
60 Princes' state (Jer. 51:57)

62 Used a keyboard
64 Totals
66 Chopping tools (Jer. 46:22)
67 Dan. "___ no pleasant bread" (Dan. 10:3)
68 Herod's nickname in Luke 13:32
69 Roman number of doorkeepers in Jeremiah 52:24
70 Gov. agency housed in the US Dept. of Justice

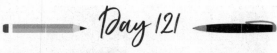

THE TWELVE TRIBES

ACROSS

1 French "not"
4 Father of Dan, Gad, e.g.
9 Dan., to Rom.
14 Naphtali to Dan (dir.)
15 Give off
16 Smelly vegetable
17 Strange
18 Crop-destroying weather
19 Eyed
20 "He is thy __, and he is thy God" (Deut. 10:21)
22 Canaan: Israel's new __
24 Pharaoh __ the people go
25 Thieves' hideout (2 words)
27 Trick, as Josh. 9:4 NIV
31 Water pitcher
32 Quick-witted
33 Last Bible book (abbr.)
34 Quaking tree
36 Judgment comes "as swift as the __" (Deut. 28:49)

38 Candies
40 Elijah's victory site
42 Violin's cousin
43 British county
44 "Let __ the earth fear the LORD" (Ps. 33: 8)
45 Describes road to destruction
47 Mother of six tribes
51 Meat alternative
53 Hannah __ Samuel to God
54 Andean empire
55 Pocket bread
57 Respite
59 Speed
62 Unclean animal (Fr.)
65 Unclean rodent
66 Resource
67 Offering type
68 Israelites __ manna
69 Small bright fish
70 Distance measurements
71 Writer's tool

DOWN

1 Israel, God's chosen __
2 Philip's brother
3 Staid
4 David's dad, for short
5 Cart part
6 Remind
7 Poem
8 Jacob dream site
9 Judgment, as Job 21:30 NKJV
10 Simeon and Levi condemned for (Gen. 49:7)
11 Goose egg
12 Anointed part
13 "I am...the beginning and the __" (Rev. 1:8 NKJV)
21 Twelve tribes of __
23 The Lord our God is __

25 Gets older
26 Cacophony, as in Jeremiah 51:55 NIV
28 Exhort
29 Transact business
30 Adam's wife
32 Able
35 Red __
36 Stray, as in Psalm 95:10
37 Pilot Earhart
38 Granary
39 Animal describing Benjamin (Gen. 49:27)
40 Gab
41 Assist
42 Wine holder
43 Issachar to Jacob
45 Deli order (abbr.)

46 Property
48 Snare
49 Pointed
50 "Hurry," KJV-style
52 The ___ Room
56 Small particle
57 Roe's mate

58 Used to make 59 Down
59 Body art, for short
60 Naphtali to Manasseh (dir.)
61 Santa Fe time zone (abbr.)
63 Mocker's exclamation
64 Golf score

THE TABERNACLE

ACROSS

1 Bethel to Mizpah (dir.)
4 Ascend
9 Upset
14 Downwind
15 Relating to the moon
16 Vice __
17 "Take, __: this is my body" (1 Cor. 11:24)
18 West African capital
19 Vexed
20 Cluttered
22 Solomon's sailed Red Sea
24 "I led them...with __ of love" (Hos. 11:4 NIV)
25 Bridge support
27 Passover sacrifice
31 Sir (Ger.)
32 Nebraska city
33 Hair styler
34 Moses' brother
36 Cursed in Malachi 1:14 NIV
38 *The Matrix* actor Keanu

40 Tabernacle overseer
42 It held shewbread
43 "It is mine to avenge; I will __" (Deut. 32:35 NIV)
44 Planet Earth (poet.)
45 Gulf
47 Palm fruit
51 42 Across (Sp.)
53 Real estate document (abbr.)
54 Sanctuary or courtyard
55 11 Down covering
57 Forbidden temple activity
59 Sacrifice place
62 Fights
65 It stood still for Joshua (Lat.)
66 Position
67 Pursue, as 1 Pet. 3:11
68 "Before", KJV-style
69 Kinds
70 Written down
71 Concorde, e.g. (abbr.)

DOWN

1 Caleb was one
2 Tiny hat
3 More damp
4 Dressed
5 Charlie Brown's nemesis
6 Business abbreviation
7 Damage
8 Lampstand part
9 Tel __
10 Ephod gem
11 __ of the covenant
12 Syria to Israel (dir.)
13 Owned
21 God's chosen people
23 Expression of surprise
25 OT prophet

26 How Elijah got to Jezreel
28 Gets older
29 Burnt offering
30 Deli sandwich, for short
32 It's refined by fire
35 Fifth or Madison (abbr.)
36 US spy grp.
37 Successful period
38 29 Down cooking style
39 Flows' opposite
40 Picnic ant, perhaps
41 LP speed
42 Actor Hanks
43 Really cool
45 Baseball's Ripken
46 "I have __ your word in my heart" (Ps. 119:11)

48 Comes up, as in Job 30:12 NKJV
49 Psalm-singing voices
50 Isa. 40:31 offspring
52 See 10 Down
56 Silver and gold, e.g.
57 Priest's garment color
58 Secondhand

59 Play a role
60 "__ up for yourselves treasures in heaven" (Matt. 6:20)
61 Cooking meas.
63 Spanish "one"
64 NYC time zone

PLOTS AND PLOTTERS

ACROSS

1 Martin Luther's wife, informally
5 KJV "walked"
9 Court figure Steffi
13 Censer producer
14 Third person of the Trinity; _____ Spirit
15 Recipe word
16 Israelites would _____ in desert
17 Jesus _____ a donkey into Jerusalem
18 Prepared a guitar, e.g.
19 David's plotter son
21 Air pollution
23 Excited, with "up"
24 "If _____ would not work" (2 Thess. 3:10)
25 Lack of iron
29 "_____ not vain repetitions" (Matt. 6:7)
30 Plotters: the _____ of one's existence
32 Cana miracle need
33 Satan plotted to shake Job's _____
36 End Times indicators
37 Shirt neck dangler
38 _____ of Sharon
39 Plot to kill Paul city (Acts 17:13)
40 Fisherman disciple, for short

41 New Testament is one
42 Sheathes
43 Alpine sound
44 Depot infor.
45 Decorated in Ex.39:24
46 "Stand in _____ of him" (Ps. 33:8)
47 Prize seekers (1 Cor. 9:24)
49 Rainbow shape
50 To a _____
53 Essence
55 Temple _____ plotted against Jesus
57 Electronics brand, and others
60 Moon crater name
62 Sins
63 God will _____ believers as His own
64 Pre-Euro currency
65 Judea or Galilee, for example
66 "I forgave thee all that _____" (Matt. 18:32)
67 "_____ of the kingdom of heaven" (Matt. 16:19)
68 "Elect _____," 2 John addressee

DOWN

1 He plotted against Moses
2 Israelites forced to produce it
3 Breakfast choice
4 Writer Bombeck
5 What 19 Across plotted to get
6 Like king's palace, for example
7 "God is my King of _____" (Ps. 74:12)
8 Lydia's fabric needs _____
9 Estimate
10 "Their feet _____ to evil" (Isa. 59:7)
11 "I _____ no pleasant bread" (Dan. 10:3)
12 Jesus _____ 5,000
15 "Time to cast away _____" (Eccl. 3:5)
20 Used at Jesus' trial

22 Sinai food
26 Music in the background was _____
27 55 Across _____ at Jesus' teachings
28 Gabriel or Michael
29 Southwest Indian
30 "Singing of _____ is come" (Song 2:12)
31 "Rock of _____," hymn
33 Moses was this to enslaved Israelites
34 Main artery
35 Jacob plotted to deceive him
36 Dorcas' expertise
39 "God shall _____ us" (Ps. 67:7)
40 "Raven" author
42 Messiah

43 Community org.

46 Christian martyr sites

48 Israelite bondage land

49 Wing shaped

50 Red Sea crossed on _____ firma

51 "I _____ not from thy precepts" (Ps. 119:110)

52 Epistle

54 "I will _____ of thy doings" (Ps. 77:12)

56 Judas made a _____ with plotters

57 Mourner's appearance

58 Ps.

59 OT city near Jerusalem

61 Plotter's story

ALL ABOUT PRAYER

ACROSS

1 Abba, Father
5 Charmed snake
10 KJV "are"
13 Expenditure
15 "Wing it!" (2 words)
16 Stock market indicator
17 Gen.
18 Mechanical turner
19 _____Wan Kenobi
20 Org. ending
21 "LORD will _____when I call" (Ps. 4:3)
23 Moses prayed on his behalf
25 Gomer descriptor, perhaps
26 Prize receiver (1 Cor. 9:24)
28 Repentance will _____sinner to God
31 Longitudinal
32 Computer consumers
33 Spirit plants _____of faith in heart
34 Seeds are sown in a _____
37 Horse hair
38 Prayer inhibitor

40 Many a Bible story
41 "_____your trust in the LORD" (Ps. 4:5)
42 He prayed about thorn in flesh
43 Hannah prayed for one
44 Chili con _____
45 Cells
46 Witty retort
49 Heavy shoe
50 Israelite bondage land
51 9 Down prayed for one
52 Mary or Martha, informally
55 Church addition, e.g.
56 Badger relative
59 Texas battle site
61 John, but not Paul, George, Ringo
62 Kingdom of heaven, for one
63 Prayer for clean skin
64 Jesus, _____of God
65 Trims
66 Adam would _____Eden

DOWN

1 "Wash in the _____of Siloam" (John 9:7)
2 Forbidden relative in Lev. 18:14
3 GI disorder
4 Sarah conceived in her old _____
5 Diamond weight unit
6 Incense result
7 Sandwich choice (abbr.)
8 Jordan (Sp.)
9 See 51 Across
10 Worship
11 R2D2, for one
12 Strong cord
14 Pray for self and _____
22 Sea bird
24 Pray for _____people
25 Lord's words "are _____words" (Ps. 12:6)

26 Unfruitful trees are _____
27 God will not _____of your prayers
28 Hind end
29 Jacob's twin brother
30 Tabernacle
31 Nimble
34 Elijah prayed for it to fall
35 Stare
36 Fistfuls
38 Moses prayed to _____the Red Sea
39 Old Norse letter
40 "He _____out lightnings" (Ps. 18:14)
42 Pulpit fillers
43 Church musical piece, perhaps
44 Trooper
45 Luau dish

46 Fishing needs
47 Ice house
48 Temple structural feature
49 Garden mounds
51 "Haste thee to _____ me" (Ps. 22:19)
52 Stand open-mouthed

53 Prayer ending
54 Prayer addressee
57 Commandment number
58 Ivory Coast town
60 "_____ them ever shout for joy" (Ps. 5:11)

JEZEBEL: THE EVIL QUEEN

ACROSS

1 Won't remove iniquity (Jer. 2:22)
5 Bobcat
9 Paul's fleshly messenger (2 Cor. 12:7)
14 Motor vehicle
15 Track
16 Cotton fabric
17 "Praise him for his mighty ___" (Ps. 150:2)
18 "World without end. ___" (Eph. 3:21)
19 "Let us lay ___ every weight" (Heb. 12:1)
20 Patterns
22 Pharisees did this to the weightier matters of the law (Matt. 23:23)
24 Pod vegetable (sing.)
25 The Lord will "___ his people" (Joel 2:18)
26 Ahab and Jezebel worshipped these
28 "___ painted her face" (2 Kings 9:30)
29 New Jersey neighbor (abbr.)
32 He bee
33 Jacob's pillow (Gen. 28:18)
35 Samaria to Jerusalem (dir.)
36 "Bread ___ in secret is pleasant" (Prov. 9:17)
37 Arrest
38 Offered with meat (Lev. 2:13) (pl.)

40 "I ___ no pleasant bread" (Dan. 10:3)
41 "___ the harvest, when the bud is perfect" (Isa. 18:5)
43 The Lord hears these (James 5:4)
44 Esau's color (Gen. 25:25)
45 All the poor man had (2 Sam. 12:3)
46 "Thou shalt not ___ the deaf" (Lev. 19:14)
47 "Immediately the cock ___" (Matt. 26:74)
49 "Why make ye this ___?" (Mark 5:39)
50 Elijah's resting place (1 Kings 17:3)
53 Choked
57 Halos
58 Manasseh put this in the house of the Lord (2 Chron. 33:7)
60 Air (prefix)
61 Tier
62 "The tongue can no man ___" (James 3:8)
63 Jael's weapon (Judg. 4:21)
64 Comforts
65 "Saul ___ David from that day" (1 Sam. 18:9)
66 Elijah rested under this in 1 Kings 19:4

DOWN

1 France and Germany river
2 "That hurts!"
3 Attorney (abbr.)
4 Defer
5 Alpaca cousins
6 Sweet potatoes
7 Samaria to Galilee (dir.)
8 One scared of foreigners
9 Characteristic
10 "Be not ___ in thy spirit" (Eccl. 7:9)
11 Leave out
12 "In thy majesty ___ prosperously" (Ps. 45:4)
13 "I have ___ to be baptized of thee" (Matt. 3:14)

21 Montana capital
23 Appearance
26 Angry
27 "She ___ upon the Assyrians" (Ezek. 23:12)
28 "They look and ___ upon me" (Ps. 22:17)
29 Cafés
30 ___ Lauder cosmetics
31 "Some more, some ___" (Ex. 16:17)
32 "Followers of God, as ___ children" (Eph. 5:1)
33 1937 Disney classic (2 words)
34 Spanish gold
39 Cocky
42 "He will keep the ___ of his saints" (1 Sam. 2:9)

46 "Jesus ___ a little child" (Matt. 18:2)
47 Bird of Isa. 38:14
48 The sun does this each day
50 Point
51 Island dance
52 Epochs

53 "Let fire ___ down from heaven"
(2 Kings 1:12)
54 May be in first or park
55 Canal
56 Portion
59 "God called the light ___" (Gen. 1:5)

JOB: PUT TO THE TEST

ACROSS

1 "His ___ abhorreth bread" (Job 33:20)
5 One-celled creature
10 Jerusalem to Bethlehem (dir.)
13 Beautiful Japanese city
15 "Can that which is unsavory be ___?" (Job 6:6)
16 Boxer Muhammad
17 "Count me for a stranger: I am an ___" (Job 19:15)
18 Canned chili brand
19 Number of Job's children (Job 1:2)
20 First state in US (abbr.)
21 "Lift up thy face without ___" (Job 11:15)
23 "Not ___ your liberty" (1 Pet. 2:16)
25 Trade possessions
26 "My ___ scorn me" (Job 16:20)
28 Place of lodging
31 Soak
32 Contract
33 "He maketh peace in his ___ places" (Job 25:2)
34 TB vaccine
37 *American Idol* host Seacrest
38 "Upon the ___ of my feet" (Job 13:27)
40 Sore that afflicted Job (Job 2:7)

41 Extension (abbr.)
42 Brand of coffee alternative
43 Main artery
44 "Gat our bread with the ___ of our lives" (Lam. 5:9)
45 Hummed
46 Pre-Columbian civilization
49 "In his ___ remaineth strength" (Job 41:22)
50 Make joyful
51 "He shall not be ___" (Job 15:29)
52 Coloring substance
55 Pig's abode
56 "Who provideth for the ___ his food?" (Job 38:41)
59 "Let mine ___ be as the wicked" (Job 27:7)
61 Twentieth English letter
62 To be
63 "And their children ___" (Job 21:11)
64 "Times ___ not hidden" (Job 24:1)
65 "There is no darkness, nor shadow of ___" (Job 34:22)
66 Parent/teacher groups (abbr.)

DOWN

1 Put ammunition in
2 "Howl, ye inhabitants of the ___" (Isa. 23:6)
3 "But the eyes of the wicked shall ___" (Job 11:20)
4 Stretch to make do
5 Fable writer
6 First Gospel writer, familiarly
7 Airport flight arrival info.
8 "To ___ I am ashamed" (Luke 16:3)
9 "I will speak in the ___ of my spirit" (Job 7:11)
10 Soft, shiny fabric
11 Starbucks' daily
12 "Gavest thou the goodly ___ unto the peacocks?" (Job 39:13)

14 "How much less shall I ___ him?" (Job 9:14)
22 VHS alternative
24 "The righteous ___ it" (Job 22:19)
25 *Star Trek* phaser setting
26 Small fencing sword
27 Toupees (slang)
28 "Thou shalt give him his ___" (Deut. 24:15)
29 Gold and "precious ___" (Job 28:16)
30 Type of jazz vocals
31 Hebrew term for "hell"
34 "Let the day perish wherein I was ___" (Job 3:3)
35 State your source
36 "The righteous see it, and are ___" (Job 22:19)

38 "Gray hairs are ___ and there" (Hos. 7:9)

39 Newsman Sevareid

40 "Oh that they were printed in a ___!" (Job 19:23)

42 Tired: ___ out

43 Curved

44 "He maketh the deep to boil like a ___" (Job 41:31)

45 Wintry mo.

46 Saltine cracker brand

47 "He shall not ___ it, nor change it" (Lev. 27:10)

48 One to whom money is due

49 From the sixth to the ___ hour there was darkness (Matt. 27:45)

51 "My sinews take no ___" (Job 30:17)

52 Make an impression

53 YWCA companion

54 "I made a covenant with mine ___" (Job 31:1)

57 "Abimelech took an ___ in his hand" (Judg. 9:48)

58 Road to the cross: ___ Dolorosa

60 Quick sleep

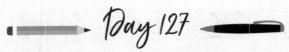

THE TEN COMMANDMENTS

ACROSS

1 Ten Commandments: __ law
5 Summary
10 Notes that follow *mi*
13 Filipino dish
15 God's highest "law" (Fr.)
16 "__ my people go" (Ex. 5:1)
17 Commandment receiver
18 Mushrooms
19 Copper made from this
20 Before, as in Ex.1:19
21 Domestic friends
23 Teacher's role (Eph. 4:12 NIV)
25 Epochs
26 Covers
28 Country separator
31 Greek philosopher
32 Lamenting poetry
33 Charity
34 Typing speed (abbr.)
37 Actor Hackman
38 Do not bear __ witness

40 Roman church "Goodbye"
41 Boiled, as in 2 Chronicles 35:13
42 Surrender
43 Book of Numbers purpose
44 Offering site
45 "I bore you on __ wings" (Ex. 19:4 NKJV)
46 More terrifying
49 Keep the Sabbath day __
50 Same, as Deut. 1:17 NIV
51 Fallen
52 Average work performance
55 Land east of Eden
56 Doves' homes
59 Make no graven __
61 Day after Mon.
62 Kinds
63 Comforts
64 " __ to your faith virtue" (2 Pet. 1:5 NKJV)
65 Sordid
66 Blood placed on a door __

DOWN

1 Esau hunted this
2 Aroma
3 Medicine amount
4 Marah to Elim (dir.)
5 Nile floaters
6 Australian birds
7 Prisoner (slang)
8 Mo. before Sept.
9 God's people: a kingdom of __
10 Unleavened bread ingredient
11 45 Across home (var.)
12 "A man's __ are of the Lord" (Prov. 20:24 NKJV)
14 Hawk
22 Listen, give __
24 Status __

25 Heb. camped on __ of the wilderness
26 Evils
27 Don't take the Lord's __ in vain
28 Pleads
29 Fake butter
30 "A time to __, and a time to sew" (Eccl. 3:7)
31 Whiter
34 You shall not __
35 Revelation horse named Death
36 Heavy barges
38 Esther's banquet (Fr.)
39 Sixth month (Jewish calendar)
40 Wary
42 Customers
43 Walkie-__
44 __ of the Covenant

45 Long time
46 Christmas man
47 Hebrews led by this
48 Helped
49 Saucy girl
51 Lampstand part
52 El __, TX

53 Gets older
54 Sabbath activity
57 Keep the law "as the apple of thine __"
(Prov. 7:2)
58 Resort hotel
60 Joshua's men made one

Day 128

JUDGES

ACROSS

1 Jael, __ of 48 Down
5 Caught with a lasso
10 Leah was Rachel's, for short
13 Burst out
15 Wedding walkway
16 Dynamite (abbr.)
17 Canaanite city
18 How vines grow
19 "Long, long __"
20 Tyre to Sidon (dir.)
21 "The Israelites did evil in the __ of the Lord" (Judg. 2:11 NIV)
23 Fire appeared __ of Mount Sinai (2 words)
25 Prod
26 Lunges
28 Israel would do to enemies
31 Psalm
32 Humor
33 Boaz's kin
34 The anger of the Lord was __ against Israel
37 __ of Solomon
38 "Said," KJV-style

40 Tropical edible root
41 Sensory info conductor (abbr.)
42 "He shall __ his people from their sins" (Matt. 1:21)
43 OT measurement
44 Protection
45 Mr. Mandela
46 First judge
49 Aramaic Father
50 Stalks
51 Left by boil or burn
52 Israel's enemy, in general
55 Eve's beginning
56 He hid idols (Judg. 17:5)
59 "The Lord __ the eyes of the blind" (Ps. 146:8 NKJV)
61 Samson __ honey
62 Wroth
63 African-American grp.
64 Pronoun for Deborah
65 Roman goddess
66 Tiny ark flyer

DOWN

1 Gaal saw shadows, "as if they __ men" (Judg. 9:36)
2 Modern name for Xerxes's land
3 Be angry
4 Nature conservation grp.
5 Had a speed contest
6 Anointing liquids
7 Greek twenty-third letter
8 Shade tree
9 Fourth judge
10 RBI, ERA, e.g.
11 Block of metal
12 Ceases, as in Job 18:5 NIV
14 Athens debate topic
22 Sweet potato
24 Joshua's father

25 Group of criminals
26 Like a bow string
27 Hebrew eighth letter
28 Record
29 Chariot metal
30 Anak had three (Judg. 1:20)
31 Uses a lever
34 Belonging to Noah's son
35 Brand of sandwich cookie
36 Unclean items must be __ out
38 Cooking herb
39 Antihistamine
40 Issachar son
42 Caused by earthquake
43 Land given to Caleb

44 Whichever
45 Pro sports grp.
46 Ms. Winfrey
47 Corny
48 His wife killed Sisera
49 Heart sometimes does this
51 Fill

52 Israel's God inspired this
53 __ upon a time
54 Sports channel
57 God's wrath
58 Wheeled vehicle
60 Lion's foot

SPOKEN WORD

ACROSS

1 Government bureau (abbr.)
4 Apexes
9 Pertaining to North or South Pole
14 Repeated, laughter
15 Sinai today
16 Believers will "not _____ in darkness" (John 12:46)
17 "_____ Maria"
18 First Pentecost preacher
19 "He is _____!"
20 "_____ ye the word" of God (Jer. 21:11)
22 Roman orator of Jesus' time
24 Tunnel blaster (abbr.)
25 Leipzig grandma
27 Vane direction (abbr.)
29 Church leaders
32 Spain cathedral city
35 Jesus _____ Last Supper with disciples
36 "_____ a right spirit within me" (Ps. 51:10)
38 Word sent throughout the _____
40 Brimstone would do this
42 Gospel now _____ globally

44 Tax collector Levi established his own tax _____
45 Sermon feature
47 Missionaries often in _____
49 Sermon-listener's seat
50 Curly was one
52 "Our Father," e.g.
54 Commandment number
55 23rd Psalm subject
56 Mary to Martha, for short
59 Canadian province
63 "I _____ you the truth" (John 16:7)
67 "Ta-ta"
69 66, for one
71 22 Across seven
72 African nation
73 He spoke for Moses
74 Santa helper
75 Artist's need
76 Israelites could not _____ manna
77 Deli bread

DOWN

1 Iran's former head
2 Jesus came to _____ the lost
3 Galilee or Samaria, e.g.
4 Nile nester
5 18 Across sent to preach there
6 Like Zacharias, temporarily
7 First garden
8 Beget
9 Jesus' sermon feature
10 Tokyo tie
11 Jesus' genealogy, e.g.
12 Arabian gulf
13 KJV "tore"
21 Moses would do signs and wonders with it

23 Term of sale (abbr.)
26 Mediterranean is one (Fr.)
28 "Kingdom of heaven is _____"
29 Imparted in a sermon
30 Healed lame man _____ for joy
31 Long-billed bird
32 David to Goliath, initially
33 Shroud would _____ over Jesus' body
34 Weasel relative
35 Deed
37 How long "_____ they believe?" (Num. 14:11)
39 Prune, as unfruitful branch
41 Paul's sermon caused one (Acts 22)
43 Choir facilitator

46 Father, Son, Spirit are _____

48 "_____ of the LORD is perfect" (Ps. 19:7)

51 African antelope

53 "I shall _____ praise him" (Ps. 42:5)

56 "For thy name's _____" (Ps. 25:11)

57 Sermon inspiration, maybe

58 Christ died for our _____

60 Long time periods

61 Jesus preached from one

62 Vacation cash, maybe

64 "Forever and _____. Amen"

65 "I am..._____ of the valleys" (Song 2:1)

66 Jesus brings eternal _____

68 "_____ hath not seen" (1 Cor. 2:9)

70 Hydrocarbon suffix

SHEEP AND SHEPHERDS

ACROSS

1 Jesus, _____ Shepherd
6 Bloom bringers
10 Health food choice
14 Like sheep's pasture area
15 Choir offering
16 Shepherd prophet
17 Place for Paul in Athens
18 Sheep hear God's _____
19 Samuel said, "_____ am I" (1 Sam. 3:4)
20 Jesus _____ battle against sin
21 The shepherd "I shall not _____" (Ps. 23)
23 A sheep _____ from still waters
25 Swiss peaks
26 Sodom fleer
27 Groove, usually in wood
30 Jesus, lamb without _____
34 Pasture measurements
35 Jesus, "_____ of the sheep" (John 10:7)
36 Beatnik's digs
38 Heaven's gate never ____ (Rev. 21:25)
39 Sin
40 God _____ Commandments on stone
42 Sheep enclosure

43 Jesus to Peter: "_____ my sheep" (John 21:17)
44 Some old buckets
45 "He brought _____" from rock (Ps. 78:16)
48 Mischievous or cranky
49 "I am like an _____ of the desert" (Ps. 102:6)
50 OT sheep's product
51 God's sheep, figuratively
54 Shepherd's concern
55 Little bit
58 Dairy sounds
59 Jesus would not _____ his mouth
61 Goodness partner in Psalm 23
63 Small ground plot
64 Miracle
65 Wonderland name
66 Lawns
67 "_____ye well" (Acts 15:29)
68 Judas' plans, and others

DOWN

1 Sheep stomach
2 Author Victor
3 Sharpening metal in Proverbs 27
4 Praying sheep has Shepherd's _____
5 30 Across descriptor
6 Deer's little dears
7 Sheep's gait
8 Course or path (abbr.)
9 Ranch hand, maybe
10 Society Islands island
11 OT seer sight
12 It could be in the road
13 "Good works for necessary _____" (Titus 3:14)

22 "Bishop... _____ to teach" (1 Tim. 3:2)
24 CD-_____
25 Aid
27 Grating sound
28 Pains partner
29 Impact
30 Tires
31 Shepherd in Psalm 23
32 Aaron _____ for Moses
33 Pharisee, often
35 View as
37 Peter would _____ Jesus
40 Holy Land is on one (2 words)
41 Stored manna condition

43 Swine would _____ cliff (2 words)
46 OT lamb offerings
47 Ram's dame
48 Shepherd ointment in Ps. 23
50 _____ Carlo
51 Pixies
52 Song by a lone singer
53 Good Shepherd leads on right _____

54 Angel's greeting: "_____ not!"
55 Small-group choir
56 CPA concern
57 Lydia's needs
60 Pod partner
62 Church add-on, maybe

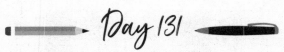

JOHN: THE BELOVED DISCIPLE

ACROSS

1 In ___ (together)
5 Oregon time zone (abbr.)
8 He walked with God (Gen. 6:9)
12 Char
13 Partly frozen rain
15 Ms. Aragon or Cleves (var.)
16 Restrain
17 Egg's fate (Isa. 34:15)
18 Idol
19 "Let us ___ together" (Isa. 1:18)
21 Trinity's home (1 John 5:7)
23 Wave offering (Lev. 23:12)
25 Jordan River to Jerusalem (dir.)
26 Last Supper room (Luke 22:12)
29 Hunted animal (Prov. 6:5)
31 Suffix meaning "material-forming"
35 Shred (2 words)
37 Sphere
39 Family-oriented health ctr.
40 Mad at John and James (Matt. 20:24)
41 Chewy candy
44 Disciples urged Jesus to do this (John 4:31)

45 Nighttime (John 6:16)
47 The Lord delivered David from this
   (1 Sam. 17:37)
48 Teeter
50 Tree product
52 MGM mascot
54 A pillar of cloud ___ the way (Ex. 13:21)
55 John doesn't write with this
   (3 John 13)
57 Cooking style in Luke 24:42
59 Type of sewer system
62 Mathematical conclusions
65 Crown of glory will not (1 Pet. 5:4)
66 Woodworker's tool
68 Stringed instrument (Amos 6:5)
70 "Will of God abideth for ___" (1 John 2:17)
71 He will restore all things (Matt. 17:11)
72 Gospel singer Franklin
73 Beastly homes (Job 37:8)
74 "I write unto you, young ___" (1 John 2:13)
75 "He that was ___ came forth" (John 11:44)

DOWN

1 Super speedy transport (abbr.)
2 "Proclaim the acceptable ___ of the LORD"
   (Isa. 61:2)
3 "How excellent is thy___" (Ps. 8:1)
4 Folder
5 Two-dimensional
6 "For the joy that was ___ before him"
   (Heb. 12:2)
7 Virginia ___ University
8 Innocently
9 "Appointed unto men ___ to die"
   (Heb. 9:27)
10 Immediately, as in Matthew 13:20
11 "As a ___ gathereth her chickens"
   (Matt. 23:37)
13 Removed this in holy place (Josh. 5:15)

14 "Neither do I condemn ___" (John 8:11)
20 Express indifference
22 Poisonous snake (Rom. 3:13)
24 Ecological food chain (2 words)
26 Speak (Lev. 5:1)
27 Annoyance
28 Enclosed sections of windows
30 Sin, as in Psalm 95:10
32 One-celled water creature
33 Hot liquid burn
34 Spouses
36 Baby dog
38 Covenant sign (Gen. 9:13)
42 Last OT book (abbr.)
43 Salk's vaccine

46 Pliers

49 "___, let us love one another" (1 John 4:7)

51 Fish holder (John 21:11)

53 Kin to fatherless (Lam. 5:3) (sing.)

56 Pharaoh's river

58 Mined metals

59 Jesus came "to ___ the world" (John 12:47)

60 Nod is east of (Gen. 4:16)

61 Sea after rebuke (Luke 8:24)

63 "It rained ___ and brimstone" (Luke 17:29)

64 Body

65 Nourished

67 "___them about thy neck" (Prov. 6:21)

69 One with loaves and fishes (John 6:9)

JOHN THE BAPTIST:
FORERUNNER OF THE LORD

ACROSS

1 Nazareth to Jordan River (dir.)
4 "___ them upon the door posts" (Deut. 11:20)
9 Resort
12 Frilly
14 He arrested John (Matt. 14:3)
15 "___ the sick, cleanse the lepers" (Matt. 10:8)
16 Woodwind instrument
17 Impersonating
18 Leave out
19 They trust in Jesus (Matt. 12:21)
21 Pacific current (2 words)
23 Joseph's brother, for short (Gen. 35:24)
24 Tyre to Jerusalem (dir.)
25 Mongolian desert
28 Disciple nickname (Matt. 10:3)
31 Tinter
34 "Thou art ___ the Son of God" (Luke 4:41)
36 "Give us this ___ our daily bread" (Matt. 6:11)
38 Fair weather color (Matt. 16:2)

40 Jonah did this with the fare (Jon. 1:3)
41 ". . .shall not live by bread ___" (Matt. 4:4)
43 Lion's voice (Ps. 104:21)
44 One (Sp.)
45 Baby essential
46 Trashy
48 Photographer Geddes
51 Animal home
53 "Winds and the sea ___ him" (Matt. 8:27)
54 Snake (Isa. 11:8)
56 Gov. agency for US workforce
58 Afternoon nap (Sp.)
61 Keying in again
66 Hannah made for Samuel (1 Sam. 2:19)
67 Debris
69 "Am I ___, or a whale?" (Job. 7:12) (2 words)
70 Askew
71 Mordecai rode (Est. 6:11)
72 Stave
73 Light brown
74 Pledge (Heb. 6:13)
75 Lest, as in John 4:49

DOWN

1 Plod
2 "The ___ leaped in her womb" (Luke 1:41)
3 Economics (abbr.)
4 Large ocean mammal in Ezekiel 32:2
5 John's message (Matt. 3:2)
6 Rainbow goddess
7 2,000 pounds
8 Sword has two (Rev. 2:12)
9 Prefix meaning half
10 Creation feels this (Rom. 8:22)
11 Singing voice
13 "___ in my flesh shall I see God" (Job 19:26)
15 John ate this in Mark 1:6

20 Wading bird
22 Psychedelic drug (abbr.)
25 African nation
26 Constellation (Job 9:9)
27 "___ me come unto thee" (Matt. 14:28)
29 Seasoning (Sp.)
30 Tribe of Israel (Gen. 49:16)
32 Wear away
33 "Be ye therefore ___ also" (Luke 12:40)
34 Computer part (abbr.)
35 Charges
37 "Affirmative," as in Mark 7:28
39 Not wet (Gen. 8:13)

42 John's mother, to friends (Luke 1:57)
43 "Will a man ____ God?" (Mal. 3:8)
47 Jesus baptized with the ____ Ghost
49 Mean-spirited
50 New York time zone
52 West Texas city
55 "Make his ____ straight" (Mark 1:3)
57 Additional, as in Matt. 5:9
58 "Scram!"

59 Hawkeye State
60 Make money
61 Highly unusual, as in Daniel 2:11
62 French "not"
63 The inhabitant of this can't escape (Isa. 20:6)
64 "Draw ____ with a true heart" (Heb. 10:22)
65 "Enter in at the strait ____" (Luke 13:24)
68 Fourth contained beryl (Ex. 28:20)

Day 133

OLD TESTAMENT KINGS

ACROSS

1 Chinese seasoning (abbr.)
4 Mansion
9 Offering residue
14 US Gulf state (abbr.)
15 Software
16 Laugher on the ark
17 Taste and __ that the Lord is good
18 Man after God's own heart
19 State of king's military
20 King's assistant
22 Mongolian desert
24 27 Across, this type of king
25 Always
27 Son of Manasseh
31 Ten (prefix)
32 Mortar, as in Gen. 11:3
33 Org. concerned with energy
34 Not expensive, like sparrows
36 Arose (2 words)
38 Rift

40 Roe and hind playgrounds
42 Visitor
43 Pressed oil
44 Good king of Judah
45 Son of Jeroboam
47 Caesar was king here
51 Defunct monetary unit
53 Israel refused this command
54 Prophet during Uzziah's reign
55 Commander and king
57 Saul pursued David here
59 Bitty
62 Son of 9 Down
65 Jeans maker
66 "We eagerly __ a Savior" (Phil. 3:20 NIV)
67 Trumpet sound
68 Hebron to Masada (dir.)
69 Bird's seat
70 Vineyard blossoms (Song 1:14 NIV)
71 Doubting disciple, to friends

DOWN

1 Sixties dance, __ Potato
2 King's robe part
3 Celtic language
4 Fixed
5 Sixth Jewish calendar month
6 Veterans Day mo.
7 __-Wan Kenobi
8 Describes ruby (2 words)
9 Jezebel's husband
10 Israel's adversary
11 Jesus' healed (Matt. 9:20)
12 Judah to Aram (dir.)
13 Neh. emotion
21 Sacrifice sites: high __
23 Unrefined metal
25 David vs. Goliath site
26 King descriptor (abbr.)

28 Dole out
29 Musical composition
30 Snooze
32 NYSE oversight grp.
35 Beret
36 Joseph role (abbr.)
37 Some 29 Down
38 Occupied
39 Valid
40 Kill
41 __ of Congress (abbr.)
42 Helium or radon
43 Poem
45 Neither's partner
46 Wicked king of Judah
48 Breakfast egg
49 Overly (2 words)

50 "Let each __ others better than themselves" (Phil. 2:3)
52 Doric alternative
56 Skeptic's opinion of Flood
57 Repair socks
58 Jane Austen heroine

59 Type of dance
60 Ram's mate
61 Serving of corn
63 Bullfight exclamation
64 How deserters fled

MAJOR PROPHETS

ACROSS

1 Manasseh's tribe size
5 "Make __ to help me, O Lord" (Ps. 38:22)
10 Flight control (abbr.)
13 Elude
15 Abraham's son
16 Neither's partner
17 Island nation
18 Kislev month number
19 __ of the Lord
20 Ram's mate
21 Nothing
23 Makes money
25 Satan, father of these (slang)
26 Goliath, compared to others
28 Assents to
31 36 Down's home
32 Porridge
33 Elijah's prayer-brought liquid
34 Resort hotel
37 Throw out
38 Boat's back end
40 Dregs, as in Ezek. 24:11

41 Samaria to Damascus (dir.)
42 Belonging to Miriam
43 Car rental firm
44 Those of Ezek.'s prophecy were dry
45 Fauna's kin
46 Clash
49 Cain __ Abel
50 Gives off
51 "I will __ out my wrath on you" (Ezek. 21:31 NIV)
52 "Every knee shall __, every tongue shall swear" (Isa. 45:23)
55 14 Down cell
56 Lukewarm
59 Typographic character
61 "Even to your old __ I am he" (Isa. 46:4)
62 Mrs. Peron
63 Winter vehicles
64 Awesome, for short
65 Doesn't own
66 Craving

DOWN

1 "__ the evil, and love the good" (Amos 5:15)
2 Promise
3 The __ Ranger
4 Bible land tree
5 "He will make my feet like __ feet" (Hab. 3:19)
6 Babylon's continent
7 __ Francisco
8 Make lace
9 Level
10 Pet.'s brother (Fr.)
11 Financial transactions
12 David and Bathsheba event
14 55 Across prophet
22 Core muscles, for short

24 Tuscaloosa state (abbr.)
25 Beautiful appendages (Isa. 52:7)
26 "A time to __ down...a time to build" (Eccl. 3:3 NIV)
27 Like
28 Conflict
29 Cadge
30 Gibeonites' tactic
31 Lock of Samson's hair
34 Wound result
35 Isa. 11:6 kin
36 Fig-growing prophet
38 "Here am I; __ me" (Isa. 6:8)
39 Fig, olive, or almond, e.g.
40 "The Lord is __ to anger" (Nah. 1:3)

42 Lifting machine
43 Prophecies, perhaps
44 Deli sandwich (abbr.)
45 Ague-like illness
46 Lebanon wood source
47 "I am the Alpha and __" (Rev. 1:8, 11)
48 Temple walls __ with cedar
49 Carbonated drinks

51 Brad ___, actor
52 Sky color (Fr.)
53 Chances of winning
54 Horizon direction
57 First woman
58 Attach
60 Jesus healed the __

BIBLE PRAYERS

ACROSS

1 Lockups
6 International clock starter (abbr.)
9 "I will _____" Israel among nations (Amos 9:9)
13 Fishing for Peter, for example
14 "Give ear. . .to my _____" (Ps. 78:1)
15 He prayed in fish's belly
16 Eight singers
17 Paris affirmative
18 John unworthy to _____Jesus' sandals
19 Boat (Ger.)
20 Paul and Silas prayed in one (Acts 16)
22 Miner's goal
23 Chemistry suffix
24 "Make thy _____straight" (Ps. 5:8)
25 *Swan Lake* wear
27 See 67 Across
29 Type choice
33 "who _____in heaven"
34 Computer program releases (abbr.)
35 "Lord, deliver my _____" (Ps. 6:4)
36 Believers, "_____of Abraham" (Acts 13:26)
39 Oil platform
40 How to show yourself approved (2 Tim. 2:15)

41 Expensive wood
42 _____of Galilee
43 Satan is our _____
44 Upset (2 words)
46 "_____Prayer"
49 Smear
50 Number of lepers healed
51 "Purge away _____sins" (Ps. 79:9)
53 "That's it!"
56 Happy and carefree
58 Fido's food
59 Relating to point of origin
61 Jordan (Sp.)
62 Venerated object
63 "_____adorneth herself with. . .jewels" (Isa. 61:10)
64 Nutritionist's credentials (abbr.)
65 Stunt
66 "Have ye not _____this scripture?" (Mark 12:10)
67 David prayed forgiveness for one
68 Ethics

DOWN

1 Fuel a fire
2 Like many Pharisaic laws
3 "Our _____"
4 First garden
5 "I _____my king upon...Zion" (Ps. 2:6)
6 "Who is this King of _____?" (Ps. 24:8)
7 Pacific vacation spot
8 Coiling
9 Hannah prayed for one
10 "Pray, lest ye enter _____temptation" (Mark 14:38)
11 "My love, my _____one" (Song 2:10)
12 KJV "you"
15 Governing group

20 Moses prayed to _____Red Sea
21 Ins opposite
24 "I must _____the works" of God (John 9:4)
26 Northern Ireland
28 Tormented, as by guilt
30 Debtor's note (abbr.)
31 What 54 Down chews
32 Judas descriptor
34 "_____Dolorosa"
36 Dementia failing (abbr.)
37 Downton Abbey cuppa
38 Bible land tree
39 Cardinals (2 words)

40 "They shall _____ be cut down" (Ps. 37:2)
42 David prayed for safety from him
43 "Devil. . .will _____ from you" (James 4:7)
45 Fur
47 Bill
48 Prostrate, as in prayer
50 Paul prayed for its removal
52 Wise man's building materials

53 Shorten, for short
54 Unclean critter in Lev.
55 Paul's mission field
57 South American monkey
58 Airy prefix
60 "_____ to your faith virtue" (2 Pet. 1:5)
62 78 or 33, (abbr.)

WORDS OF COMFORT

ACROSS

1 "My blood..._____ for many" (Mark 14:24)
5 "_____ not" because of evil (Ps. 37:1)
9 Lass
13 "_____ unto me" for rest (Matt. 11:28)
14 Mechanic's task
15 Holey treat
16 Masculine Arab name
17 "We cry, _____, Father" (Rom. 8:15)
18 Irritated
19 "Be not afraid, only _____" (Mark 5:36)
21 Volcano spew
23 Egypt to Sinai (dir.)
24 "Deck the Halls" word
25 They neither toil nor spin (Matt. 6:28)
29 "Birds of the _____ have nests" (Matt. 8:20)
30 Kine and corn in Pharaoh's dream
32 Denver winter hour (abbr.)
33 "Whither thou _____..." (Ruth 1:16)
36 "Make his face _____ upon thee" (Num. 6:25)
37 School organization (abbr.)
38 Skating site

39 Quench
40 Like sword of Prov. 5:4
41 Brew
42 "God will wipe away _____" (Isa. 25:8)
43 See 40 Across
44 9 Across (abbr.)
45 Oar woods of Ezek. 27:6
46 _____ of Galilee
47 Qualifying round
49 Drunkard
50 "That your _____ may be full" (John 16:24)
53 Pain, as of guilt
55 "I..._____ a place for you" (John 14:3)
57 Model wood
60 "Draw _____ to God" (Ps. 73:28)
62 First gardener
63 God will "bring me up _____" (Ps. 71:20)
64 Guinea town
65 Disciple Andrew's brother, for short
66 Lots
67 Esau's birthright trade
68 Red Sea entrance port

DOWN

1 Wound caps
2 Iron _____ iron in Prov. 27:17
3 Author Zola
4 He loved Lucy
5 Good fruit has it
6 Gospel singer Studdard
7 46 Across movement
8 Greenish-blue
9 God-fearing
10 Scribe's need
11 "If any man will _____ thee..." (Matt. 5:40)
12 Typical (abbr.)
15 "Partakers of the _____ nature" (2 Pet. 1:4)
20 Book no-no in Rev. 22:18
22 Dress style (hyph.)

26 God will _____ no one toward evil
27 First name in cosmetics
28 "Feet shall _____ within thy gates" (Ps. 122:2)
29 "_____, and ye shall receive" (John 16:24)
30 Weekday (abbr.)
31 Satan sound
33 Splice
34 Houston team member, formerly
35 "He delivered me from my..._____" (Ps. 18:17)
36 Enjoy a bath, e.g.
39 He "delivered my soul from _____" (Ps. 56:13)
40 SUV choice
42 Rainforest flier

43 Jubilee

46 "Godly _____ worketh repentance" (2 Cor. 7:10)

48 Welcome Sinai sight

49 God did not _____ His Son

50 Cynical

51 What Paul did in Athens

52 68 Across nation

54 "Salvation unto the _____" of earth (Acts. 13:47)

56 English Abba

57 Judas' fund holder

58 Like Bible times

59 Popular pooch breed

61 "_____ bread in" God's kingdom (Luke 14:15)

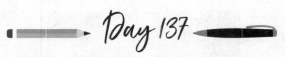
JONAH: IN THE BELLY OF THE WHALE

ACROSS

1 Times
5 Moses' brother (Ex. 4:14)
10 Farming org.
13 Exotic bird
15 ___ Arabia
16 This should be made bare (Isa. 47:2)
17 Florida metropolis
18 Clean feathers
19 "___ Father which art in heaven" (Matt. 6:9)
20 Don't do this unto the law (Deut. 4:2)
21 Jonah's ride (Jon. 1:3)
23 Music used as practice
25 Fashionable
26 Counterpart
28 Jonah was this during the storm (Jon. 1:5)
31 Visitor from Sheba (1 Kings 10:1)
32 Pass time, as in Psalm 90:9
33 Beehive State
34 Ministry org. for young athletes
37 Side where Jonah sat (Jon. 4:5)
38 Called to fast in Nineveh (Jon. 3:7)
40 Stubborn Israel's made of brass (Isa. 48:4)
41 "Go to the ___, thou sluggard" (Prov. 6:6)

42 "Light of the ___ is the eye" (Matt. 6:22)
43 Test, as in Exodus 20:20
44 Crimps
45 Appeared, as in Acts 15:25
46 In abundance
49 "The Lord sent out a great ___ into the sea" (Jon. 1:4)
50 What the gourd delivered Jonah from (Jon. 4:6)
51 This ate Jonah's gourd (Jon. 4:7)
52 Morse code "T"
55 Confederate Gen. Robert E.
56 Famous potatoes
59 "___, go to Nineveh" (Jon. 1:2)
61 Found in a nest (Isa. 10:14)
62 Unyielding
63 Lowest point
64 Anointed part (Lev. 8:23)
65 A friend of the world is one (James 4:4)
66 Shamgar's weapon (Judg. 3:31)

DOWN

1 Poetess Lazarus
2 Insect killer
3 Learning institution (abbr.)
4 OT prophet to his friends
5 Savory jelly
6 Senior org.
7 Herbal tithe (Luke 11:42)
8 Keats' specialty
9 Wicked city turned good (Jon. 3:5)
10 Cake ingredient (Ex. 29:2)
11 Violent quarrels
12 "___ with thine adversary quickly" (Matt. 5:25)

14 Desired, as in Jonah 4:8
22 Philistines' injury (Judg. 15:8)
24 Lepers cleansed (Luke 17:17)
25 Penny
26 Not ins
27 "Sun ___ upon" Jonah's head (Jon. 4:8)
28 Before God's throne (Rev. 15:2) (2 words)
29 Length of measure (Ex. 28:16)
30 For fear that, as in Mark 13:5
31 Wharfs
34 Jonah "fled ___ the presence of the Lord" (Jon. 1:10)
35 Sheltered inlet

36 Reverent
38 Lock, as in 2 Samuel 13:17
39 Baritone Nelson
40 Manna "___" worms the next day (Ex. 16:20)
42 Campsite warmer
43 Scribe
44 Fixed charge
45 Man's title, as in John 12:21
46 Metal tip on the end of a lance
47 Ragu's competition

48 Superior
49 *Toy Story* cowboy
51 Sudden fancy
52 Prank
53 Seven churches site (Rev. 1:4)
54 Fasted in Nineveh (Jon. 3:8)
57 Boom
58 Life, as in Job 11:17
60 Sin is filthy like this (Isa. 64:6) (sing.)

Day 138

JONATHAN: BEST FRIEND FOREVER

ACROSS

1 Loads
6 Slice
10 "There is none ___ beside him" (Deut. 4:35)
14 Moses' brother (Ex. 4:14)
15 "A thousand ___ with Jonathan" (1 Sam. 13:2)
16 Complain
17 Military groups
18 Grown in Bashan (Isa. 2:13)
19 Went with Saul to Gibeah (1 Sam. 10:26)
20 Limited (abbr.)
21 Geek
23 Practical jokes
25 Jonathan's father troubled this in 1 Samuel 14:29
26 To plow, as in 1 Samuel 8:12
27 Stick fast
30 Bedcover
34 Bird of Isaiah 38:14
35 Bird appendage
36 Edge
38 Avian homes (Luke 9:58)
39 Burnt offering (Ex. 29:18)
40 Expected, as in Luke 12:46
42 Jonathan would not do this (1 Sam. 20:34)
43 Where jewels may be (Isa. 3:21)
44 Start over
45 "What ___ thou, O sleeper?" (Jon. 1:6)
48 Hinder progress
49 Repetition (abbr.)
50 Type of jazz
51 Affection
54 Sharpen (Ps. 7:12)
55 Vigor's partner
58 Paul visited this place (Acts 19:22)
59 Afghan ruler
61 "___ my heart to fear thy name" (Ps. 86:11)
63 Tear, as in Joel 2:13
64 Walk through water
65 Gets up, as in Psalm 119:62
66 Long narrative
67 David did this to the lion (1 Sam. 17:36)
68 Inspections

DOWN

1 Jonathan's father (1 Sam. 13:16)
2 Trample, as in Amos 2:7
3 Waterless
4 Tater snack
5 Entangles
6 Jonathan gift to David (1 Sam. 18:4)
7 "___ us not into temptation" (Luke 11:4)
8 Stolen by Philistines (1 Sam. 6:18)
9 Ask in advance
10 Begin a journey
11 Elkanah was blessed because of Hannah's (1 Sam. 2:20)
12 Egyptians "___ into the bottom" (Ex. 15:5)
13 Where cherubim stood (Ex. 25:19)
22 Gilgal to Gilead (dir.)
24 "Esau ___ to meet him" (Gen. 33:4)
25 Days before Easter
27 Pimples
28 Pilate's wife suffered many things in this (Matt. 27:19)
29 Hurry, as in 1 Samuel 20:38
30 Animal, as in Genesis 8:19
31 Jonathan's son's condition (2 Sam. 4:4)
32 Rub out
33 Jezebel beautified (2 Kings 9:30)
35 Ringling ___
37 Measure (Mark 4:24)
40 Protective covering

41 David and Jonathan did this (1 Sam. 20:41)
43 Abdon had thirty (Judg. 12:14)
46 Naval fleet
47 Fishing essential for Peter and Andrew (Matt. 4:18)
48 Cast forth like morsels (Ps. 147:17)
50 Shakespeare's was tamed
51 Will hear rumors of (Mark 13:7)
52 Of glass in Revelation 4:6 (2 words)

53 Pharaoh gave this to Joseph (Gen. 41:42)
54 "Open thy mouth ____, and I will fill it" (Ps. 81:10)
55 Credit card
56 Detail
57 Benjamin had 5 times more (Gen. 43:34)
60 Minor prophet (abbr.)
62 Call off

RETURN FROM EXILE

ACROSS

1 Nehemiah's singers, Sons of __
6 Pilate's garb
10 Cousins of prodigal pals (Luke 15:16)
14 Beneficiary
15 Missing soldier's status (abbr.)
16 Neh. contemporary
17 Jerusalem sacrifice site
18 His sons provided offerings (Neh. 10:39)
19 Person, place, or thing
20 Great Barrier __
21 Aaron's rod topper
22 Walls at Ezra's arrival
24 Mined metals
26 Exile prophet
27 Sacrifice must be perfect, not this
30 Baseball player Ty
31 Calms
32 Shiny balloon material
33 Chicken __ King (2 words)
36 Disturbed, Neh. __ in the night
37 God's bow shape
38 Sin offering part (Lev. 4:11 NKJV)
40 First letter of Psalm 23
41 "Will you __ the case for God?" (Job 13:8 NIV)
43 Cabbage, to frau
44 Neh. sacrifices
45 Strange person
46 Layer of tissue
49 See 44 Across
50 Exiles' new dwellings
51 Peter __ to Jesus' tomb
52 "There is none righteous, no __" (Sp.)
56 Land unit in Jerusalem
57 "Iron sharpeneth __" (Prov. 27:17)
59 Author Rice Burroughs
60 Neh. rebuilt Fish __
61 Moses' temporary home
62 Forest clearing
63 Jesus' torment
64 Gift to rebuild Jerusalem
65 Greek sandwiches

DOWN

1 Month temple completed
2 Bottom of Ezra's foot
3 Before (prefix)
4 Large Asian pheasants
5 Pronoun for Rahab
6 Ankle bone
7 Payable
8 Joseph's title, for short
9 Arabian Nights man (2 words)
10 ___ Matisse, painter
11 Atmosphere layer
12 Porridge
13 Abraham's descendants like the __
  of the sea
21 Daniel's sleeping place
23 Condition of Jesus' bones
25 Conducted in labs
26 Offerings of Ezra 6:10 were this (Lat.)
27 How Jericho's walls fell
28 Tempt
29 Perfume plant (sing.)
30 King who helped exiles to return
32 Lava
33 Weeping "was heard __ off" (Ezra 3:13)
34 "__ Him, all you peoples!" (Ps. 117:1 NKJV)
35 Psalm-singing voice
39 "A man who has friends must himself be __"
  (Prov. 18:24 NKJV)
42 Growing
45 Defeat the foe
46 Central
47 Large artery

48 Swine ran down a "___ place" (Mark 5:13)
49 Nile tides did this
50 Joseph filled his brother's with silver
51 Darius read this (Ezra 6:2)

53 Another name for Sinai (Gal. 4:25)
54 Pedestal part
55 Worshiped in Philippi
58 Kishon is one (Sp.)
59 Child might ask for (Luke 11:12)

OLD TESTAMENT WOMEN

ACROSS

1 Garret
6 Esther's banquet
10 Boaz put Ruth "at __ by speaking kindly" (Ruth 2:13 NIV)
14 Mentor
15 Aroma
16 Ooze
17 Husband of 6 Down
18 First Gospel (abbr.)
19 Deborah's was a palm
20 Mooselike ark dweller
21 Lampstand center
23 Pakistan city
25 Arouse, as in 2 Peter 3:1
26 First woman
27 "Glorious things are __ of thee" (Ps. 87:3)
30 Attests
34 Mischievous
35 Unclean swimmers
36 20 Across Asian cousin
38 Pinches

39 To be
40 Hebrew night guide (2 words)
42 Fixed charge
43 Describes wilderness
44 Barbarian of films
45 Basketball move
48 Describes 40 Across
49 Wheeled vehicle
50 Mark 4:37 activity
51 Greek wisdom goddess
54 "How can one be __ alone?" (Eccl. 4:11)
55 Delivery service
58 Proper
59 Gray, as in Isaiah 46:4
61 Ruth's sister-in-law
63 Cracker type
64 Angels' glow
65 Used to hang Haman
66 Eve's home
67 Ladies' fur coat
68 Matchmaker

DOWN

1 Pain
2 Building implement
3 Woman's work
4 "The breath of God produces __" (Job 37:10 NIV)
5 "For whom the Lord loves He __" (Heb. 12:6 NKJV)
6 Hosea's wife
7 26 Across husband
8 His wife turned to salt
9 Dull
10 Woman "for such a time as this" (Est. 4:14)
11 Air (prefix)
12 Miriam's role (var.)
13 David's weapon (Fr.)
22 Alloy
24 Hail (Lat.)

25 Brief play
27 We must die to __
28 Delilah __ Samson for info
29 "I will __...the sacrifice of thanksgiving" (Ps. 116:17)
30 Eagle's nest
31 Sleigh
32 Fastening
33 Isaac's mother
35 English nobleman
37 35 Down home, perhaps
40 Asperity
41 Thwart, as in Ps. 33:10 NIV (sing.)
43 33 Down husband
46 He delivers 4 Down
47 Disallow

48 Prefix meaning "son of"
50 Deborah's partner
51 Niche
52 Walked
53 "__ me under the shadow of Your wings" (Ps. 17:8 NKJV)
54 Esther's task

55 Xerxes "set the royal crown __ [Esther's] head" (Est. 2:17)
56 Future's opposite
57 Queens stadium of old
60 French "yes"
62 Hind's mate

PRIESTS AND PASTORS

ACROSS

1 41 Down missionary partner
6 "Whence come _____ and fightings?" (James 4:1)
10 False preachers _____ men of God
14 Hecklers try to _____ godly speakers
15 God says, "_____ my voice" (Jer. 7:23)
16 Bethlehem star
17 Worship offering
18 Sunset hues
19 Leave out
20 Belonging to (suffix)
21 Jordan River, in places
23 26 Across milieu
25 Truth might _____ sinner to confess
26 OT priest _____
27 Reformer Luther
30 Without purpose or goal
34 "God _____ to judgment" (Ps. 76:9)
35 Staffs
36 30,000+ megahertz (abbr.)
38 Devout believer _____ the Bible
39 Sermon might _____ guilty one
40 Pole weapon with a pointed head

42 Kangaroo's pocket
43 OT preacher
44 Trained group of missionaries, e.g.
45 Iron will _____ iron, per Prov.
48 Hesitated
49 Two working together
50 Preachers warn against it
51 Jacob's wife
54 Hawkeye state
55 Behind
58 Ointment brought to Jesus' tomb
59 Pre-Easter season
61 Hypocrite's thoughts _____ his deeds
63 Sermon might _____ hearer to repent
64 "Appointed unto men _____ to die" (Heb. 9:27)
65 Jesus said, "_____ of me" (Matt. 11:29)
66 "Now abideth faith, _____, charity" (1 Cor. 13:13)
67 One of seven opened in Rev.
68 Long-necked pond wader

DOWN

1 Fill
2 Wee water wader
3 God rarely early, never _____
4 59 Across Wednesday
5 Dessert wines
6 "Go...into all the _____" (Mark 16:15)
7 First murder victim
8 _____ Sea
9 Procedures
10 Without values
11 Kingly bearing
12 "Deliver us from _____"
13 Holy Land palm
22 Charged atom

24 Church addition, maybe
25 Shock victim's ailment (abbr.)
27 _____ Hill, 41 Across sermon site
28 Israel and Judea, e.g.
29 Black bug
30 Israel's first high priest
31 Scribes' needs
32 Preachers plant _____ of faith
33 Preachers _____ the Gospel
35 Silent speaker
37 Mr. Flintstone
40 Like Mount Sinai, e.g.
41 Missionary-preacher
43 Aquila and Priscilla taught him

46 "_____ to the Word of God!"

47 Regret, as sins

48 Congregant's place

50 Bethlehem inn, today

51 "Be not _____ with thy mouth" (Eccl. 5:2)

52 Fido's feed

53 Takeover

54 South American people

55 Winged

56 Brimstone partner

57 Sinai tabernacle

60 Egypt to Canaan (dir.)

62 Medical diagnostic test (abbr.)

PRISONERS

ACROSS

1 Elijah's royal foe
5 Basics
9 Herod imprisoned him
14 Jezebel to 1 Across
15 Moses would _____ waters
16 Askew or awry in Scotland
17 Drama conflict
18 Iliad city
19 Complete round
20 Girl at door for 9 Across
22 Angel found 9 Across _____
24 KJV verb ending
25 Lower category
27 Seals a road
31 Prisoner's _____ is distinctive
32 Creation period
34 Scorners "shoot out the _____" (Ps. 22:7)
35 Rocket science organization
38 Disciples took one in Gethsemane
40 "_____ with Me," Sunday song
42 Miracles _____ watchers
44 "Forgive...my _____" (Ex. 10:17)

46 Canine skin disease
47 9 Across prison mate
48 Pull on
50 Parable sower's threw this
51 Keyboard key
52 "My _____ runneth over" (Ps. 23:5)
55 Paul's house arrest city
57 Sheep grass or pastureland
59 Zone, as of Jerusalem
61 Chatter
64 Lesotho city
66 "Garments _____ of myrrh" (Ps. 45:8)
68 Battlefield doctor
71 St. John's, for example
73 Against (prefix)
74 Small fish
75 Cana miracle need
76 Horse coat color
77 Hymns have them
78 Whirlpool
79 Convenient playground

DOWN

1 Be _____ of God's presence
2 Spiritual joys, e.g.
3 Crowds "ran _____" after Jesus (Mark 6:33)
4 Liars "_____ their tongues" like bows (Jer. 9:3)
5 Men "strong and _____ for war" (2 Kings 24:16)
6 Prisoner Pilate freed
7 Calvary sight
8 Aaron crafted and _____ a golden calf
9 Step
10 Joseph imprisoned there
11 Compassion, for short
12 Conger
13 Deli loaf
21 OT Judah king

23 JFK letters
26 See 75 Across
28 Dress design (hyph.)
29 Mount Sinai sight
30 "Bid him God _____" (2 John 10)
31 Samson's prison site
33 Sweet potato
35 Whining speech descriptor
36 Asked to go _____, go two (Matt. 5:41) (2 words)
37 Dead Sea descriptor
39 Joseph thrown in one
41 "_____ things of the world" (1 Cor. 1:28)
43 Prisoner's keyboard key, maybe (abbr.)
45 Spirit has _____ faith in hearts of believers

49 Sticky mess

53 Navy ship letters

54 Mini

56 Eve or Sarah title

58 Pleased look

60 One yelled "Crucify him!"

61 Italy seaport

62 Priest's table

63 "_____gropeth in darkness" (Deut. 28:29)

65 NT book

67 Christ's mother

68 Colorado Christmas hour (abbr.)

69 Flightless bird

70 Daniel's prison

72 "Search me..._____me" (Ps. 139:23)

JOSEPH: GOD'S MAN IN EGYPT

ACROSS

1 Did well
5 "We cry, '___, Father' " (Rom. 8:15)
9 Tool
13 Favorite (slang)
14 Squirrel's dinner
15 Truth-girded, as in Ephesians 6:14 (sing.)
16 Against
17 Infatuate
18 Run easily
19 Savor
21 Joseph's coat had many (Gen. 37:3)
23 Bowed to Joseph (Gen. 37:9)
25 Brass was used to do this (2 Chron. 24:12)
26 The trees of the Lord are full of this (Ps. 104:16)
29 Warm-up activity (abbr.)
31 "Shalt thou indeed ___ over us?" (Gen. 37:8)
34 Kimono sash
35 In worship everyone hath one of these (1 Cor. 14:26)
37 When Joseph dined (Gen. 43:16)

39 Found in sacks (Gen. 42:35)
41 Ball holder
42 Ephod stone (Ex. 39:12)
43 Eve's garden
44 Joseph's brothers "___ him" (Gen. 37:5)
46 Gideon's sign (Judg. 6:37)
47 Organic compound
50 "Midianites ___ him into Egypt" (Gen. 37:36)
51 Concorde, e.g.
52 Tubalcain worked with this (Gen. 4:22)
54 Arabian Peninsula country
56 Saloon
59 Wields
63 Dream bovine (Gen. 41:2)
64 Less restricted
66 Sign of dad's favor to Joseph (Gen. 37:3)
67 Asa destroyed this (1 Kings 15:13)
68 ___ Park, CO
69 Metric weight unit
70 "Thou shalt ___ me thrice" (Matt. 26:34)
71 Stagger, as in Psalm 107:27
72 Herod "___ all the children" (Matt. 2:16)

DOWN

1 At a distance, as in Mark 5:6
2 Bird's home (Jer. 5:27)
3 "Ye thought ___ against me" (Gen. 50:20)
4 Jeans fabric
5 Low or high card
6 Pear type
7 Housekeeper's tool
8 Branched horn
9 Referring indirectly
10 "I stand at the ___, and knock" (Rev. 3:20)
11 Fastens
12 Timnah to Gilead (dir.)
14 Hates, as in Romans 12:9 (sing.)
20 Soaked

22 "The LORD our God is ___" (Deut. 6:4)
24 Under (poet.)
26 "___ evil beast hath devoured him" (Gen. 37:20)
27 "But his bow ___ in strength" (Gen. 49:24)
28 Trees in the desert (Isa. 41:19)
30 Two in Deuteronomy 17:8
32 "Words of the wise are as ___" (Eccl. 12:11)
33 Scale components
36 Ditto (2 words)
38 Former Speaker Gingrich
40 Completely
42 Large whitish antelope
45 Gantry and Bernstein

48 Sin, as in Psalm 95:10
49 Shingler
53 Nordic
55 These were hardened (Neh. 9:16)
56 Wait
57 At once, as in Matt. 13:20

58 Measure
60 Annoy
61 Old wife tells one, as in 1 Timothy 4:7
62 Store
63 Baby goat (Lev. 4:28)
65 Slippery as an ____

Day 144

JOSEPH: FATHER OF OUR LORD

ACROSS

1 Coffee (slang)
5 Turf
10 Santa's helper
13 Bad smells
15 Netherlands' capital
16 "Raven" author
17 Lloyd Webber heroine
18 May be barbed, as in Job. 41:7
19 "___ no man any thing" (Rom. 13:8)
20 Type of partnership (abbr.)
21 "Jesus was ___ in Bethlehem" (Matt. 2:1)
23 Caesar decreed that all should be ___ (Luke 2:1)
25 Mary to Joseph
26 "With the blood of the ___ of Jesus" (Rev. 17:6)
28 Broken bone treatment
31 Long, narrow boat
32 Awakened, as in Matthew 2:14
33 Pretentiously artistic
34 Not hers
37 Gripping tool

38 "___, and take the young child" (Matt. 2:13)
40 Wise men's home (Matt. 2:1)
41 Extension (abbr.)
42 Joseph, "___ not to take unto thee Mary thy wife" (Matt. 1:20)
43 Lily type
44 Chisel
45 Resurrection Day
46 Woman's sunshade (arch.)
49 Joseph told to "___ into Egypt" (Matt. 2:13)
50 Gives off
51 Fades
52 Witch
55 Drink slowly
56 Imbecile
59 Indoor football stadium
61 "Voice of ___ crying" (Matt. 3:3)
62 Stairway post
63 To be rebuilt in Amos 9:11
64 "Joseph, thou ___ of David" (Matt. 1:20)
65 "___ to God in the highest" (Luke 2:14)
66 Wicked men set one (Jer. 5:26)

DOWN

1 OT prophet
2 Advertisement (abbr.)
3 Earth at creation (Gen. 1:2)
4 "Blessed ___ thou among women" (Luke 1:42)
5 British county
6 "___ them that are unruly" (1 Thess. 5:14)
7 Hence, as in Acts 10:30
8 "Their feet ___ to evil" (Prov. 1:16)
9 Herod's plan is to ___ "the young child" (Matt. 2:13)
10 Synthetic resin
11 Man to angels (Ps. 8:5)
12 Five loaves and 2 fishes ___ many in John 6:9

14 Texas river
22 Frequently, as in 2 Timothy 1:16
24 Daniel "___ no pleasant bread" (Dan. 10:3)
25 "There came ___ men" (Matt. 2:1)
26 Paul speech site (Acts 17:22)
27 Wager
28 Jesus "shall ___ his people" (Matt. 1:21)
29 Grand ___ race
30 "To save that which was ___" (Matt. 18:11)
31 Marker
34 Jesus healed them (John 5:3)
35 Patmos
36 Wise men's guide (Matt. 2:9)
38 Air (prefix)
39 Insult, as in 2 Chronicles 32:17

40 "His soul shall dwell at ____" (Ps. 25:13)
42 Complaining
43 He decreed all should be taxed (Luke 2:1)
44 Flying rodent of Leviticus 11:19
45 Tree of Hosea 4:13
46 Cents south of the border
47 Type of acid
48 Mature

49 "Body ____ joined together" (Eph. 4:16)
51 One who does
52 Noah, "____ of the righteousness" (Heb. 11:7)
53 NT prophetess
54 Pant
57 First state (abbr.)
58 Battle site, ____ Jima
60 Track

PSALMS

ACROSS

1 Keying error
5 Anointed finger
10 Jerusalem to Gaza (dir.)
13 "I will praise thee…with my whole __" (Ps. 9:1)
15 Artist's tool
16 Expression of surprise
17 Defense
18 Carpenter's tool
19 Moses' basket covering
20 God heals when we are __
21 The godly flourish like one
23 See 22 Down
25 Footwear
26 Hates
28 "The way of the __ leads to destruction" (Ps. 1:6 NIV)
31 Witches' group
32 "I have eaten __ like bread" (Ps. 102:9)
33 Eager
34 Deaf communication (abbr.)
37 The Lord is __ to anger
38 Prize for excellence

40 Veer
41 Spiritedness
42 Indian dress
43 Heavenly lights
44 Ruth, Est., e.g.
45 Stages
46 Sufferings
49 "I will __ no evil, for you are with me" (Ps 23:4)
50 The wrongdoer's walk, as in Psalm 12:8 NKJV
51 "At Your right __ are pleasures forevermore" (Ps. 16:11 NKJV)
52 Energy measurement (abbr.)
55 Dispensable candy
56 Jacob's father
59 Sandwich cookies brand
61 Downwind
62 Daring
63 Eagle's "arms"
64 Finis
65 Athletic contests
66 Aroma

DOWN

1 Asian cuisine
2 Holler
3 Water carrier
4 Sphere
5 Wigwam
6 Patriot Nathan
7 "Born in the __"
8 Adam, David, et. al.
9 __ be the Lord
10 He stands with wrongdoers (Ps. 109:6)
11 Arrow body
12 Piers (var.)
14 10 percent gift
22 With 23 Across, a comfort
24 Number of lyre's strings

25 Alter
26 Wander
27 "Turn from __ and do good" (Ps. 37:27)
28 Hornet
29 Malta or Cyprus
30 Cut apart
31 Log house
34 Word of woe
35 "The testimony of the Lord is __" (Ps. 19:7)
36 James's nickname, with "the" (Mark 15:40)
38 "How majestic is your __ in all the earth!" (Ps. 8:1 NIV)
39 Iron, silver, e.g.
40 Magi's guide
42 Dirtying

43 Valley of the __ of death
44 Babylon to Assyria (dir.)
45 Psalmist's writing instrument
46 "Keep me as the __ of your eye" (Ps. 17:8 NIV)
47 Psalm 23 pastures
48 Seeped out
49 Seraphim wings covered these (Isa. 6:2 NIV)
51 To __ and to hold

52 Prep a bow
53 African country
54 Cold war foe (abbr.)
57 __ of Galilee
58 "Mine __ also shall strengthen him" (Ps. 89:21)
60 Nile or Jordan (Sp.)

PSALM 119

ACROSS

1 Hertz measurement (abbr.)
4 "I have chosen the way of __" (Ps. 119:30)
9 Before, as in Luke 7:27 NIV
14 "For your laws __ good" (Ps. 119:39 NIV)
15 Moses' mountain
16 Drum
17 IBM competitor
18 Shirk
19 Pay for, as in Exodus 22:16
20 Peter in Paris
22 Patmos, for one
24 Org. with farm oversight
25 Has possession
27 Christmas
31 "The Lord looks down and __ all mankind" (Ps. 33:13 NIV)
32 Proverb
33 Buddy
34 "Your __ made me and formed me" (Ps. 119:73 NIV)
36 Frown angrily

38 Authorities, __ of wrath
40 Changes, as in Hosea 11:8 NKJV
42 The heavens declare the __ of God
43 Describes ephod's gems
44 Finger spelling (abbr.)
45 Vineyard areas
47 The Seven-Year __
51 Pig food (Luke 15:16 NIV)
53 Grand __
54 Roman emperor
55 Item for sale
57 Young swan
59 One who counts on
62 "Let him seek peace, and __ it" (1 Pet. 3:11)
65 Small amount
66 Channel
67 Ridged surface
68 Cyprus to Babylon (dir.)
69 In Christ all the fullness of the __ lives
70 Blow away, as in Isaiah 8:8 NIV
71 Color describing Esau

DOWN

1 College grounds and buildings
2 "Let me live that I may __ you" (Ps. 119:175 NIV)
3 Separate
4 Russian ruler
5 Rip
6 Jose's one
7 __ Chi
8 "Thou art my __ place and my shield" (Ps. 119:114)
9 Cain killed him
10 Bees' production
11 Alpha/Omega, Beginning/__
12 "Long __ I learned from your statutes" (Ps. 119:152 NIV)
13 __ Jones Industrial average
21 Thin slice of ham

23 Gilead to Moab (dir.)
25 Chances of winning
26 "Before I __ afflicted I went astray" (Ps. 119:67 NIV)
28 "Look thou __ me, and be merciful" (Ps. 119:132)
29 The Lord's are righteous (Ps. 119:106 NIV)
30 First letter of Lev.
32 Industrious insect
35 "Let not __ iniquity have dominion over me" (Ps. 119:133)
36 Daytime light
37 Weeping
38 "Keep your servant __ from willful sins" (Ps. 19:13 NIV)
39 God's Word more precious than (Ps. 19:10 NIV)

40 Crispy squares cereal
41 "He hath set __ love upon me" (Ps. 91:14)
42 Void
43 __ Lanka
45 Investment term (abbr.)
46 Streams
48 God's mercies are __ (Ps. 119:77)
49 Put a fold in
50 Breeding ground
52 "How __ are your words to my taste"

(Ps. 119:103 NIV)
56 Chichi
57 Naaman's desire, per 2 Kings 5
58 Dog's cry
59 "Thy word have I __ in mine heart" (Ps. 119:11)
60 Trinity: three-in-__
61 Greek letter
63 Hebron to Joppa (dir.)
64 Luke 8:3 woman, to friends

END TIMES

ACROSS

1 Cul-de-_____
4 With God, "I shall be _____" (Ps. 119:117)
8 Unused bow
14 Prompt
15 Est.'s month
16 End Times: Universal _____
17 Cana miracle need
18 End Times: Jesus will _____
19 35 Across home
20 Archaeology finds
22 "City _____ no need of...sun" (Rev. 21:23)
23 "Truth shall make you _____" (John 8:32)
24 End Times trial, for many
27 Tether
31 Via Dolorosa overpass
33 "_____ of the bottomless pit" (Rev. 9:1)
35 Samson riddle swarmer
36 "_____ Father"
38 Thanksgiving dish
39 Halo
40 Crashed together, as metal
44 Jesus' throne accessory

46 "_____ God who judgeth her" (Rev. 18:8)
47 Mythical dawn deity
49 Nile slitherer
50 Shade tree
51 E-address part
52 Makes lace
55 Showy aviation display
58 Sunday service for Catholics
61 Doggie kiss
63 "Rule...with a _____ of iron" (Rev. 2:27)
65 Choir leader
67 Wear away
70 Pocket bread
71 Water closet
72 "I saw a new _____" (Rev. 21:1)
73 End Times cry, maybe
74 Deer relative
75 Figures around God's throne
76 Unbelievers _____ God's truths
77 Judas Iscariot descriptor

DOWN

1 Scrape
2 Celestial display
3 Rev. incense holder
4 Indian garment
5 Man or woman
6 End Times: Many _____ gods
7 "Come down _____ my child die" (John 4:49)
8 Salt Lake site
9 India neighbor
10 "Spirit and the _____ say, Come" (Rev. 22:17)
11 OT or NT period, e.g.
12 "Neither sorrow, _____ crying" (Rev. 21:4)
13 "_____ the spirits whether" they're true (1 John 4:1)
21 _____ Coming

25 KJV "firmament"
26 Celestial Seasonings bags
28 Adjoin
29 Like Sinai dessert
30 "Let him _____ what" Spirit says (Rev. 2:7)
32 Greetings squeeze
34 Community org.
37 "Golden _____ to measure the city" (Rev. 21:15)
39 Shocks, as End Times omens
40 Choir music symbol
41 Lounge
42 End Times horsemen
43 End Times: Gloom and _____
45 KJV verb ending

48 Depot (abbr.)

53 King of kings, and others

54 Heaven rolled as one (Rev. 6:14)

56 Courageous

57 Alpine echo

59 KJV "cheerful countenance"

60 Dragon of Rev. 20:2

62 Quirky

64 Hiding places of Rev. 6:15

66 "Wisdom..._____to be intreated" (James 3:17)

67 "Look here!"

68 Jacob's youngest, for short

69 Filthy item of Isa. 64:6

70 Mat

WATERWAYS

ACROSS

1 Pushes gently, as a ball
6 David _____ Goliath
10 Galilee fishing need
13 Far off the track
15 "_____ am I; send me" (Isa. 6:8)
16 Sodom remain
17 Capelike sleeve
18 Palace rank
19 Score well
20 Parent school groups (abbr.)
22 His realm reached to Euphrates
24 Hay pack
26 Ogle
28 Artist Chagall
29 Parted waters would _____ Israelites
30 Sign at Jesus' Jordan baptism
31 "Inferno" author
32 _____ Lanka
33 Small epistle, maybe
34 Cheerleader cheer
35 Scorners would _____ against Jesus
37 Cold medicine brand

41 Brew
42 Anointing ointments
43 Poem
44 "_____ from thine own wisdom" (Prov. 23:4)
47 66 Across movement
48 David vs. Goliath, e.g.
49 German philosopher Arnold _____
50 Where parable rich man stored goods
51 Priests would _____ incense
52 Long-lasting (2 words)
54 Tidy
56 Commandments number
57 Tyre or Sidon, e.g.
59 Cornwall coastal town (2 words)
63 "World without _____"
64 Choir music part, maybe
65 "Tears are on her _____" (Lam. 1:2)
66 Red _____
67 KJV "in case"
68 First name in cosmetics

DOWN

1 Like an evildoer
2 Space mystery, (abbr.)
3 Zero
4 OT Jerusalem site
5 Former chalkboard surface
6 Pronoun for Mary or Martha
7 Renter
8 Bad doctrine
9 Where Jesus met Samaritan woman
10 Elisha sent him to Jordan River
11 Chaperone
12 KJV "there"
14 Genetic information carrier (abbr.)
21 One of seven deadly sins
23 Nebraska city

24 See 50 Across
25 Tel _____, Israel
27 See 39 Down
29 Federal benefit add-on (abbr.)
30 Former Venetian official
31 Abraham, Isaac, and Jacob, e.g.
33 Moses' river
34 Commandment
36 Painting prop
37 Port city
38 39 Down river number
39 27 Down home
40 Eastern state (abbr.)
42 Olive product
44 Boxes

45 _____ Onegin, Pushkin figure
46 Plan
47 39 Down river
48 God-given tasks
50 Saw logs
51 10 Down to _____ in Jordan River

53 Iridescent gem
55 Keyboard key (abbr.)
58 Make lace
60 Noah's ark need, maybe
61 Make do with
62 Megiddo to Jerusalem (dir.)

JOSHUA: THE SUCCESSOR

ACROSS

1 Come to ___: KJV for "It will happen" (Gen. 4:14)

5 Sign of despair on Joshua's head (Josh. 7:6)

9 Nonfunctioning smeller (Ps. 115:6)

13 Women's magazine

14 Dueling sword

15 At battle's end, Amalek was this (slang)

16 Joshua went ___ the mount of God (Ex. 24:13)

17 "The LORD said unto Joshua, ___ not, neither be thou dismayed" (Josh. 8:1)

18 One way to accomplish 19 Across

19 "The ___ of the LORD's host said unto Joshua, Loose thy shoe from off thy foot" (Josh. 5:15)

21 Joshua was one

23 Bard's "before"

24 Presented to the people by Moses, Joshua ___ the Israelites (Num. 27:22–23)

25 Israelites' loot from Ai (Josh. 8:26–27)

29 Joshua said, "How long are ye slack to go to possess the land, which the LORD ___ of your fathers hath given you?" (Josh. 18:3)

30 Deutsche ___, German railway

32 Sweet potato

33 Distribute

36 Southern states, popularly

37 ___ Lanka

38 Baseball glove

39 Rahab ___ the spies (Josh 2:1) (2 words)

40 Jericho was one (Josh. 6:1)

41 Swee' ___, Popeye tot

42 Joshua was minister to him (Ex. 24:13)

43 Broadway awards

44 "Is there any taste in the white of an ___?" (Job 6:6)

45 John will not use these to write (3 John 13)

46 One of the watchers of Joshua's battle with Amalek (Ex. 17:10)

47 Bean

49 Joshua's dad (Ex. 33:11)

50 "Their works are works of iniquity, and the ___ of violence is in their hands" (Isa. 59:6)

53 "The people served the ___ all the days of Joshua" (Judg. 2:7)

55 Joshua's priest (Num. 27:22)

57 Israelites' dwellings (Josh. 22:6)

60 Mount of 2 Down

62 One of the Ten Commandments, e.g.

63 Ancient Greek marketplace

64 Stringed instrument

65 "I was blind, now ___" (John 9:25) (2 words)

66 Star

67 Stravinsky's first name

68 Small amounts, as of paint

DOWN

1 The city of Gibeon "made ___ with Joshua and with the children of Israel" (Josh. 10:4)

2 What Joshua built at 60 Across (Josh. 8:30)

3 Land feature of 60 Across

4 Labor Day mo.

5 "How shall I defy, whom the LORD hath not ___?" (Num. 23:8)

6 Turn over

7 "The way. . .of the Red ___" (Ex. 13:18)

8 Period of time

9 Feature of a daring aerial escapade (2 wds.)

10 Horse nibble

11 Govt. benefits program

12 Vacation time in Versailles

15 Louisiana university

20 Bible fragrance source (Prov. 7:17)

22 Describes Achan as "all Israel stoned him with stones" (Josh. 7:25)

26 Poultry products producer

27 One of the Stooges

28 Burning incense ___ a fragrance (Gen. 8:20–21)

29 Fishing cord
30 Adder's threats to horse heels (Gen. 49:17)
31 Geometry word
33 A pillar of a cloud would ___ the Israelites to move (Ex. 13:21)
34 Reason "Jericho was straitly shut up" (Josh. 6:1–3)
35 Canned chili choice
36 Writing table
39 Hermit
40 Pro
42 White-flowered plant
43 Piper's product (Matt. 11:17)
46 Nutty tool

48 Extreme prefix
49 "Cool!"
50 Street of noted 1906 revival
51 Only he and Josh. entered the land (Num. 26:65)
52 Joshua's yuccas
54 Go-to place for a pastrami on rye
56 Sinai wilderness descriptor
57 What Simon could do (Acts 10:6)
58 Pharaoh's problem (Ex. 5:2)
59 Veteran's Day mo.
61 John the Baptist would eat one (Matt. 3:4)

JUDAS ISCARIOT: THE BETRAYER

ACROSS

1 Connery of Bond fame
5 Noah's float
8 Those who "gnash the teeth" might do this too (Lam. 2:16)
12 Tropical tubers
14 Caesar's seven
15 Clearly, Jesus was not preparing this (John 21:9)
16 Judas to Jesus (Matt. 26:25) (3 words)
17 Greek goddess of dawn
18 Judas' money, he thought (Matt. 27:3)
19 Hotel arrangement, for short
20 Aim of Simon Peter's sword (John 18:10)
22 Concorde was one
24 Bravo in Toledo
25 Vivien of Scarlett fame
27 Civil rights org.
29 "If thou hadst ___ here" (John 11:21)
31 "Judas then, having received a ___ of men" (John 18:3)
32 Peter could not do this (Matt. 14:30)
35 To avoid one, Judas identified Jesus (Matt. 26:48) (2 wds.)
37 Jesus identified the soldiers held ___ Him in Matt. 26:57
41 Novelist McEwan
42 Hiram's evergreen gift to Solomon (1 Kings 5:10)
43 "Saw we thee an hungred, and ___ thee?" (Matt. 25:37)

44 Asian starling
46 "O death, where is thy ___?" (1 Cor. 15:55)
48 Chief priests, to hear Judas's proposal (Mark 14:11)
49 Chief priests "sought to ___" Jesus (John 5:16)
51 StarKist fish
53 Very, in music
55 Señora's diacritic
58 Judas would ___ for death rather than repentance (Matt. 27:5)
59 Kansas City summer hour (abbr.)
61 Sodom and Gomorrah were reduced to this (Gen. 19:28)
62 Series ender, often
64 Judas's reaction to see Jesus condemned, maybe (Matt. 27:3)
66 "The sucking child shall play on the hole of the ___" (Isa. 11:8)
68 Jesus' answer to the soldiers (John 18:5) (3 words)
70 Daniel's den dwellers (Dan. 6:16)
71 Two in Acapulco
72 Architect Frank ___ Wright
73 Chances of winning
74 Sailed with the navy of Tarshish (2 Chron. 9:21) (sing.)
75 Paul and Barnabas's sailing destination, e.g. (Acts. 13:4)

DOWN

1 "That thou ___ up the gift of God" (2 Tim. 1:6)
2 Artist's item
3 "There shall ___ false Christs" (Matt. 24:24)
4 Modern response to a statement like: "Judas was a nice guy."
5 Jesus would ___, "Thou hast said" (Matt. 26:25)
6 River (Sp.)
7 "Judas, betrayest thou the Son of man with a ___?" (Luke 22:48)

8 Jitney
9 Org.
10 Judah: "A lion's ___" (Gen. 49:9)
11 Some ice creams
13 "Draw thee waters for the ___" (Nah. 3:14)
15 "Then entered ___ into Judas" (Luke 22:3)
21 "___, excuse me."
23 Crackle and Pop's pal
26 Computer corp.
28 There was one in the garden when Judas arrived (John 18:4–6)

30 "Cool!"
31 OT offerings, often
32 Alike (abbr.)
33 Jesus said, "I am the ___, the truth, and the life" (John 14:6)
34 "There was no room for them in the ___" (Luke 2:7)
36 One dozen, to Felix, the Roman governor (Acts. 23:24)
38 Football assoc.
39 Beverage Pharisees could have made with mint (Luke 11:42)
40 Of the twelve disciples, Judas made himself the ___ man out
45 "An ___ tied" (Matt. 21:2)
46 Jesus to Judas: "Thou hast ___" (Matt. 26:25)
47 Judas did not have the ___ to resist temptation

48 Goes with a guy
50 The Promised Land would have none of these (Deut. 8:9)
52 Nothing
53 Rose pest
54 "Judas also, which betrayed him, ___ with them"(John 18:5)
56 How-to exhibits, for short
57 Pre-1970s gas choice
58 Norwegian capital
60 Christian author Joni Eareckson
61 Church part
63 Judas would ___ his position among the disciples
65 Body coordinator
67 What Jesus gave to Judas at the Last Supper (John 13:26)
69 Last name in boxing

THE BOOK OF PROVERBS

ACROSS

1 Squabble
5 Israel was Jacob's
10 Kansas summer time zone (abbr.)
13 Left out of gear
15 Brand of card game
16 Pronoun for Proverbs 31 gal
17 Commoner
18 Poor man might do this (Prov. 30:9)
19 Roberto's bravo
20 Make clothing
21 Lotion ingredient
23 Misses
25 Very strong metal
26 Polaroids or Kodaks
28 "___thy works unto the Lord" (Prov. 16:3)
31 Noble gas
32 Unconditional love (Gr.)
33 Horse control
34 Exceed
37 Sins
38 How trumpet is played
40 Adam or Solomon, e.g.

41 Snare
42 Greek rainbow goddess
43 Grown, as in Jeremiah 5:28
44 "Put a ___ to your throat if you are given to gluttony" (Prov. 23:2 NIV)
45 Without this, the people perish (Prov. 29:18)
46 Edit
49 Jonah's boarding site
50 It goes before a fall (Prov. 16:18)
51 "Those who ___ in wisdom are kept safe" (Prov. 28:26 NIV)
52 Expression of surprise
55 Mo. before Dec.
56 Apex opposite
59 Willing, as in Proverbs 31:13 NIV
61 Lamb's mom
62 "___ in the Lord with all your heart" (Prov. 3:5 NIV)
63 Lived
64 "Go to the ___, you sluggard" (Prov. 6:6 NIV)
65 Man plans, but God directs these (Prov. 16:9)
66 Jordan's current

DOWN

1 Crests
2 This person will be hungry
3 Seraphim action (Isa. 6:6)
4 Mo. after Jan.
5 Malicious burning
6 Not early
7 God's breath produces (Job 37:10 NIV)
8 The Preacher, ___ 9 Down (abbr.)
9 Eccl. author
10 Ps. singers
11 D in Corinth
12 Lock of Samson's hair
14 Endearment
22 Abraham's nephew
24 40 Across in a group

25 Demons (var.)
26 Met Jonah at 49 Across
27 Fer's opposite (var.)
28 Adam's son
29 Stare at
30 Thick drink
31 "The sea ___ by...a great wind" (John 6:18)
34 Cab
35 Tub spread
36 NYC's ___ Station
38 Paul's cell (var.)
39 It comes from the heart (Prov. 4:23)
40 Hide
42 Forms a depression
43 Unrighteous

44 Offering animal
45 Tome (abbr.)
46 Sleep disorder
47 Cattle color
48 Metal bolt
49 Absalom killers
51 Bit of smoke
52 Grandchildren bring joy to them
(Prov. 17:6 NIV)

53 Stayed silent: __ your peace
54 Pretentious
57 "Are," KJV-style
58 "A word spoken in __ season, how good is
it!" (Prov. 15:23)
60 Felt in God's presence

PROVERBS 31

CROSS

1 Kung Pao flavoring (abbr.)
4 Peter's Pentecost preaching, to some (2 words)
9 Locust group
14 Simian ark-dweller
15 Wading bird
16 The wise maintain this (Prov. 28:2 NIV)
17 Actress Dawber
18 Greatest (Lat.)
19 Jacob's post-injury gaits
20 Costly
22 "Write them __ the table of thine heart" (Prov. 3:3)
24 Bunsen burner
25 First Gospel (abbr.)
27 "She brings him __, not harm" (Prov. 31:12 NIV)
31 Cloud product
32 Israel enemy
33 Creation days number (Rom.)
34 Thinks
36 Prov. 31 woman might do to her décor

38 Taste buds
40 See 36 Across
42 Awl
43 Prov. 31 woman is this to her husband
44 Doubting apostle, to friends
45 Expel, with "out"
47 Hoist
51 Job 9:9 constellation (Lat.)
53 55+ org.
54 Prov. 31 pronoun (Fr.)
55 Ewes' partners
57 Grant forgiveness
59 Witch of Endor power
62 Rahab's cord type of message
65 Time period
66 Breastplate protects it
67 Reduce
68 Dashed
69 "Her husband is known in the __" (Prov. 31:23)
70 "She makes __ garments" (Prov. 31:24 NIV)
71 Cold War–era plane (abbr.)

DOWN

1 Plotter
2 Ancient Greek city
3 Zodiac's twins
4 Peak
5 Ark of the Covenant carrier
6 Dawdle
7 Lodging
8 "Charm is deceptive...__ is fleeting" (Prov. 31:30 NIV)
9 Sing alone
10 Extort
11 Naval rank (abbr.)
12 Legislator (abbr.)
13 Prov. 31 woman title (abbr.)
21 "Her __ goeth not out by night" (Prov. 31:18)

23 "Harper Valley __"
25 Silent actor
26 Core muscles, for short
28 "She watches __ the affairs of her household" (Prov. 31:27 NIV)
29 Swine noise
30 "He was despised...we __ not esteem Him" (Isa. 53:3 NKJV)
32 "__ her own works praise her" (Prov. 31:31)
35 To listen: give __
36 Reverence
37 Prov. 31 woman role
38 "She stretcheth out her hand to the __" (Prov. 31:20)
39 "Her __ are strong for her tasks" (Prov. 31:17 NIV)
40 Invitation abbreviation

41 Cyprus to Babylon (dir.)

42 U.K. measurement (abbr.)

43 Birds' domain

45 Female animal

46 Scamp

48 "Her husband...sitteth among the ___" (Prov. 31:23)

49 Third day creations (var.)

50 Occupant

52 "Her children ___ up, and call her blessed" (Prov. 31:28)

56 ___ of the Apostles

57 Apostle, for short

58 Thieves' dwelling (2 words)

59 Tiny unit of mass (abbr.)

60 Expression of discovery

61 God to Abram, "___ thee out of thy country" (Gen. 12:1)

63 Kimono sash

64 One of twelve tribes

Day 153

STONES

ACROSS

1 Canaan to Egypt (dir.)
4 Swamp
9 News broadcaster
12 Black-and-white bite
14 Island greeting
15 "Stop" to horse
16 Surrealist Salvador
17 Mary, e.g. (Lat.)
18 What church bells did
19 Seminary class outline
21 KJV "houses"
23 Cain's exile land
24 Snare of Ps. 57:6
25 Miracle, e.g.
28 Noah's floater
31 Seminary section, (abbr.)
34 Assistant to greens player
36 "Birds of... _____ have nests" (Luke 9:58)
38 "Give _____ to my words" (Ps. 5:1)
40 Christ _____ for sins of world
41 Wicked "turn _____ to lies" (Ps. 40:4)
43 Gas burner

44 Recollection ability (abbr.)
45 Commandments number
46 Mucus
48 KJV verb
51 Brimstone result
53 Pod veggie
54 One stoned Stephen
56 Sports figure, for short
58 Environment
61 Jacob _____ stone at Bethel
66 Consumer
67 Ephod gold add-ons
69 Herr's wife
70 Sass
71 32 Down _____ he knew not Jesus
72 Rents out
73 Wetland or mire
74 Theater awards
75 KJV verb ending

DOWN

1 Sections of lawn
2 Donkey noise
3 Jacob removed stone at one
4 Caribbean dance
5 Skylark family
6 What stored manna does
7 Pronoun for Leah or Rachel
8 3 Down site
9 African nation
10 "There is _____ that doeth good" (Ps. 14:1)
11 What Job's wife does
13 61 Across need
15 God _____ Commandments on stones
20 Opposed
22 "Perfumed my _____ with myrrh" (Prov. 7:17)

25 "Just shall live by his _____" (Hab. 2:4)
26 Swelling
27 Who "can _____ to his stature?" (Luke 12:25)
29 Noah's weather report
30 Leopard lies with one in Isa. 11:6
32 His name means "Rock"
33 Tanzania port
34 Investment options, (abbr.)
35 "Take, _____; this is my body" (Matt. 26:26)
37 Agent, (abbr.)
39 Sacrificed in Isaac's place
42 _____ of Galilee
43 Deer cousin
47 Arizona Indian

49 Praying Pharisee's look

50 Digit

52 "Filled the _____ with good things" (Luke 1:53)

55 "_____ thy bonds in sunder" (Nah. 1:13)

57 He struck a stone for water

58 Hand warmer

59 Patmos, for one

60 Cows of Pharaoh's dream

61 KJV "soon"

62 Athletic org.

63 Knowledge of good, evil plant

64 What Eve does at 63 Down

65 Adam's origins

68 _____ Jima

SALVATION

ACROSS

1 Last word in prayer
5 What Proverbs sluggard does
10 Lord's trees full of it (Ps. 104:16)
13 Coffee choice
15 Desert plant
16 KJV "art"
17 Sweet smell of Phil. 4:18
18 Jesus died in our _____
19 Parable woman's _____ silver pieces
20 Disciples made "fishers of _____" (Matt. 4:19)
21 Brief life stories
23 Late Princess of Wales
25 Calvary
26 Jesus won _____ life
28 Breakfast bowl filler
31 Master Gardener will _____ fruitless branches
32 Birdie
33 See 51 Across
34 Czech reformer Jan
37 "_____ your heart," not garments (Joel 2:13)

38 "By _____ are ye saved" (Eph. 2:8)
40 Paris station
41 "World without _____"
42 "LORD... _____ my soul" (Ps. 41:4)
43 Smithy
44 British term for half note
45 Ran to wed
46 Tranquilized
49 Lydia _____ linen
50 The Fall or Flood, e.g.
51 Jesus _____ for 33 Across
52 First woman
55 Thanksgiving mo.
56 Characteristic mode of expression
59 Adhered
61 Snow slider
62 Stairway post
63 Lop-_____ rabbit
64 Moray
65 "_____ is great in thy salvation" (Ps. 21:5)
66 Flatbottom boat

DOWN

1 52 Across spouse
2 Scant
3 MBA class (abbr.)
4 Viet _____
5 Cleaner choice
6 Not ins
7 Genius
8 Government agricultural org.
9 Disobedience _____ God
10 First rebel
11 Early Christian martyr site
12 Pertaining to punishment
14 British Socialist organization
22 "It shall be _____ with" evildoers (Isa. 3:11)
24 Jesus' response to temple moneychangers
25 "It shall bruise thy _____" (Gen. 3:15)

26 Little Mermaid's love
27 Hymn feature
28 Jesus does _____ for you
29 "Foot standeth in an _____ place" (Ps. 26:12)
30 Citrus scrap
31 David's poem
34 Angel's strings
35 Pharisees would _____ Jesus to debate
36 Parable sower's scatter
38 DNA component
39 Philistines would _____ Israelite camps
40 Some soil for 36 Down
42 Slugging
43 Grow feathers
44 Jesus, Son of _____

45 "His _____ Is on the Sparrow,"
   spiritual song
46 Understanding
47 Conjure
48 See 10 Down
49 How Paul saw through glass (1 Cor. 13:12)
51 Not hearer, but this of James 1:25
52 Vacation bill, maybe
53 Swerve
54 Whirlpool

57 Keyboard key (abbr.)
58 _____ Jima
60 One brought loaves, fishes to Jesus

LABAN: THE TRICKSTER

ACROSS

1 "___ an alarm" (Num. 10:5)
5 "Abraham. . .saw the place ___ off" (Gen. 22:4)
9 Cabbage dish
13 Flot preceder
14 Biblical accounts of the patriarchs, e.g.
15 Sour cream addition, perhaps (sing.)
16 The kingdom of God should be the ___ thing (Matt. 6:33)
17 Paul's physician (Col. 4:14)
18 Lazarus's sores undoubtedly did this in Luke 16:20
19 Laban to Rebekah (Gen. 24:29)
21 Jesus' disciples did not do this (Matt. 9:14)
23 There was no room here for Mary and Joseph (Luke 2:7)
24 Response to Laban's trickery in Genesis 29:25, perhaps
25 After three days, Jacob was ___ by Laban (Gen. 31:22)
29 Brooks are "blackish by reason of the ___" (Job 6:16)
30 Smile
32 Pronoun for Leah or Rachel
33 God to Laban: " ___ not to Jacob either good or bad" (Gen. 31:24)
36 Laban "brought [Jacob] to his ___" (Gen. 29:13)
37 "Give me my wife, for my days ___ fulfilled" (Gen. 29:21)
38 Big ships are "turned about with a very small ___" (James 3:4)
39 Taking the gates of Gaza was one of Samson's (Judg. 16:3)

40 Samoan capital
41 LAX info
42 Isaac to Esau: "I am old, I know not the day of my ___" (Gen. 27:2)
43 Basketball player Olajuwon
44 What Laban and Jacob do at the feast in Genesis 29:22
45 God to Moses: "Rehearse it in the ___ of Joshua" (Ex. 17:14)
46 Basketball assoc.
47 A modest woman's hair should not sport these (1 Pet. 3:3)
49 "Lift up now thine eyes, and ___. . .I have seen all that Laban doeth unto thee" (Gen. 31:12)
50 Jacob to Isaac: " ___ and eat of my venison" (Gen. 27:19)
53 Racetrack activities
55 Oval shape
57 Describes the mob outside Pilate's palace (John 19:12)
60 A sinner does this
62 "Soldiers cut off the ropes of the ___" (Acts 27:32)
63 A craftsman ___ the doors of the temple in 1 Kings 7:50
64 De ___ : anew
65 "The waters thereof ___ and be troubled" (Ps. 46:3)
66 Laban tricked Jacob more than ___
67 Leah when she married Jacob, probably
68 Indian of South America

DOWN

1 Disney deer
2 Laban would ___ (Gen. 30:27)
3 God to Job: "Canst thou. . .loose the bands of ___?" (Job 38:31)
4 Balaam's donkey after abuse: "Was I ever ___ to do so unto thee?" (Num. 22:30)
5 Laban would ___ that Jacob had kidnapped his daughters (Gen. 31:26)
6 Rural club, the long way (2 words)
7 Noah's vessel

8 Shallow area
9 The archers' actions (Gen. 49:23)
10 Mary's cuz (Luke 1:36)
11 "___ Maria"
12 Jacob proposed to ___ Laban's daughter, Rachel (Gen. 29:18)
15 Trigonometry term
20 Twain boy
22 12 Down went badly ___ for Jacob (Gen. 29:25)

26 "Descended in a bodily ___ like a dove" (Luke 3:22)

27 Scary

28 "God came to Laban the Syrian in a ___ by night" (Gen. 31:24)

29 "___ hath sent me" (Ex. 3:14) (2 words)

30 Jacob chose "the spotted and speckled among the ___" (Gen. 30:32)

31 Judges follower

33 Jacob watered these of Laban (Gen. 29:10)

34 A decorative flower in Exodus 25:33 would have had one

35 Rachel would ___ Jacob when he saw her (Gen. 29:10)

36 He who has 45 Across, "let him ___" (Mark 4:9)

39 Laban gathered all the men "and made a ___" (Gen. 29:22)

40 Modern ID: Esau ___ Edom (Gen. 25:30)

42 Jacob and Laban's deceit ___ trust in either one

43 First murder victim (Gen. 4:8)

46 Mandella

48 Laban's invitation to Jacob: "___ with me" (Gen. 29:19)

49 Jacob to Laban: "Did not I ___ with thee?" (Gen. 29:25)

50 Shekel measure (Num. 7:14)

51 Laban's brother-in-law (Gen. 28:5)

52 Tank dweller

54 "Jacob ___ and called Rachel and Leah to the field" (Gen. 31:4)

56 Son of Merari (1 Chron. 24:27)

57 Laban lived long ___

58 Jacob to Laban: "What is my ___, that thou hast so hotly pursued after me?" (Gen. 31:36)

59 Laban and Jacob did not treat each other with this

61 "Asahel was as light of foot as a wild ___" (2 Sam. 2:18)

LAZARUS: A NEW
LEASE ON LIFE

ACROSS

1 Paul's interrogator (Acts 22:27) (abbr.)
5 Shelter for the prodigal son, perhaps (Luke 15:15)
8 Mussolini title
12 Island greeting
14 ___ Jima
15 With 29 Across, shortest verse of the Bible (John 11:35)
16 Not a consonant
17 Wheel tooth
18 Martha hoped for ___ for Lazarus (John 11:21–22) (2 words)
19 Bethany to Jericho (dir.)
20 Jesus' sayings would ___ the Pharisees, as in Matthew 15:12
22 "The hole of the ___" (Isa. 11:8)
24 Lazarus does this in John 11:1
25 Jesus went to Lazarus's (John 11:38)
27 Place at which Lazarus sat with Jesus (John 12:2)
29 See 15 Across
31 Mustard seed (Mark 4:31)
32 "Love the Lord thy God. . .with all thy ___" (Matt. 22:37)
35 Sweetener, like the honey Jesus ate in Luke 24:42
37 Ps. valley (Ps. 84:6)
41 Samson's were strong (Judg. 16:29–30) (abbr.)

42 The Lord is not ___ with those He loves, Proverbs 3:12, e.g.
43 Business ending, often (abbr.)
44 Roman "bye-bye"
46 Winds from the north (Job 37:9)
48 Graduate of 39 Down (abbr.)
49 With 68 Across, Jesus' words to Lazarus (John 11:43)
51 Martha served one (John 12:2)
53 Subway
55 Having wings
58 Disciples wanted to ___ Jesus' plan to go to Bethany (John 11:8)
59 Jerusalem to Bethany (dir.)
61 At the sisters' house, there would have been much (John 11:19)
62 Equine nibble
64 Sun Valley resort locale
66 "God shall ___ unto him the plagues" (Rev. 22:18)
68 See 49 Across
70 "Rejoice, because your ___ are written in heaven" (Luke 10:20)
71 Spy guys and gals org.
72 Apollos was one (Acts 18:24–26)
73 Group (abbr.)
74 Pronoun referring to Mary or Martha
75 Condition

DOWN

1 Lazarus lay in one (John 11:38)
2 Mary "rose up hastily" and others went ___ (John 11:31)
3 Jesus displayed this in John 11:43
4 Martha to Jesus: "Thou art ___ Christ" (John 11:27)
5 "A certain man was ___, named Lazarus" (John 11:1)
6 Number of Lazarus's sisters (John 11:1)
7 Exercise
8 Christmas mo.
9 Business as ___

10 Marie ___, chemist
11 JavaScript word
13 Jesus made it clear Lazarus wasn't this (John 11:14)
15 Osaka site
21 We're these for Christ (2 Cor. 5:20) (abbr.)
23 Maybe Martha wanted Mary to do this in the kitchen (Luke 10:40)
26 Tanner's tool, perhaps (Acts 9:43)
28 Baby Jesus' need, perhaps
30 Sheer fabric

31 Proverbs 10:23, e.g.

32 Joey sits in mama's

33 You may see one in 15 Down

34 Red, white, and blue nation

36 A fool might pull one (Prov. 10:23)

38 Jesus came so "___ men through him might believe" (John 1:7)

39 Chicago seminary

40 Naval figure (abbr.)

45 Halloween mo.

46 Book after Joel

47 People came to "see Lazarus also, whom he had raised from the ___" (John 12:9)

48 ___ carte, menu choice (2 words)

50 You can fiddle with their middles

52 Moses held the brass serpent this way (Num. 21:9)

53 He who is "greedy of gain" (Prov. 1:19) might be called one

54 Tests

56 Light cake

57 Drunkard's companion (Prov. 23:21)

58 Girl (Sp.)

60 Jesus loves ___ of us

61 Twelfth month (Est. 3:7)

63 "Jesus saith unto ___, Loose him" (John 11:44)

65 "As a ___ gathereth her chickens" (Matt. 23:37)

67 Jesus knew "what death he should ___" (John 18:32)

69 Jesus "called Lazarus ___" of the tomb (John 12:17)

ECCLESIASTES

ACROSS

1 Wall St. org.
4 Designer Lauren
9 Daniel in lions' __
12 1/5 given to Pharaoh
14 Paul's Athens speech site
15 Shaveh, aka king's __ (Gen. 14:17)
16 Put on __, as in 2 Corinthians 11:20 NIV
17 Train station
18 Winged
19 A merry heart is like this
21 Pacific weather system (2 words)
23 Archer's result
24 Twelfth mo.
25 "Time to __ ...time to hate" (Eccl. 3:8)
28 "I __ vanity under the sun"
31 Fleece in the morning
34 Rahab gave spies one (2 words)
36 Body art (slang)
38 "What profit __ a man from all his labor?" (Eccl. 1:3 NKJV)
40 Elijah purified (2 Kings 4:40)
41 To worship
43 Actress Russell
44 Eccl. writer's tool
45 Used to anoint
46 Many Bible-land people
48 Luke 14 invitation response
51 Shade tree
53 Feed for Solomon's horse
54 Time period
56 Radio frequency (abbr.)
58 Abednego's friend
61 Eccl. author
66 Jesus, "My flesh is __ food" (John 6:55 NIV)
67 Alpha and __
69 Insect nursery
70 Makes strong, as in Genesis 49:24
71 Fertilizer component
72 "Time to __, and a time to lose" (Eccl. 3:6 ESV)
73 "__ to him who is alone when he falls" (Eccl. 4:10)
74 To exercise
75 Solomon's desire (Eccl. 2:3)

DOWN

1 Fraud
2 Pennsylvania city
3 "Threefold __ is not quickly broken" (Eccl. 4:12)
4 Circle measurements
5 Egypt's representatives
6 Rachel's easygoing gait, perhaps
7 For (prefix)
8 "Therefore I __ life" (Eccl. 2:17)
9 Surrealist painter
10 Zeal
11 Emperor in Paul's time
13 Greek letter
15 "Time to mourn. . .time to __" (Eccl. 3:4)
20 Jacob's role for Esau
22 God did by cloud and fire
25 Liquid measurement
26 "What he __ no one can shut" (Isa. 22:22 NIV)
27 When made, must be fulfilled (Eccl. 5:4)
29 Coral reef
30 "Time of __. . .time of peace" (Eccl. 3:8)
32 Gideon threshed it
33 Used for tabernacle curtains
34 Smaller than tbs.
35 __ Schwartz
37 4 o'clock beverage
39 Miriam to Aaron (abbr.)
42 "Time to be born...time to __" (Eccl. 3:2)
43 Compact car
47 Job resting place (Job 7:13) (syn.)
49 Leah and Rachel head coverings

50 Before (prefix)
52 Business venture
55 Not good for Adam to be this way
57 It is deceptively wicked
58 "__ near to God" (Ps. 73:28)
59 Chocolate biscuit
60 A good one is better than riches (Prov. 22:1)

61 An apostle, for short
62 Anti-abuse agency (abbr.)
63 Joseph's coat had many
64 Goliath weapon (Fr.)
65 Eden tool, perhaps
68 Israel warned not to do with other nations

Day 158

MINOR PROPHETS

ACROSS

1 Investment term (abbr.)
4 Path
9 Keen, as in Zephaniah 3:7 NIV
14 "Diviners see visions that ___" (Zech. 10:2 NIV)
15 Amos's home
16 Explorer Francis
17 Poisonous snake
18 Great ape
19 Bread type (Ex. 29:23)
20 Asian grassland
22 Ephod adornments
24 "Cow"-style, KJV
25 Sixth month on Jewish calendar
27 Obadiah prophesies against
31 Psalm-singing voice
32 Vigorously (arch.)
33 Torso muscles (abbr.)
34 Philanthropist H. Ross
36 Honey holders
38 Angelic auras

40 Slide fastener
42 Water dispensers
43 Wash cycle
44 Jerusalem to Damascus (dir.)
45 White vegetable
47 Offerings of Micah 6:7
51 Last Supper, e.g.
53 Big cat of Nahum 2:11
54 Eve's son
55 Chances of winning
57 "He leads me ___ quiet waters" (Ps. 23:2 NIV)
59 Internal flap
62 Calf home, as in Amos 6:4
65 "Where is the honor ___ me?" (Mal. 1:6 NIV)
66 Stranger
67 Terrible
68 Clairvoyance (abbr.)
69 Twenty-sixth president, to friends
70 Trinity pronoun (Fr.)
71 ___ of judgment

DOWN

1 Mount McKinley state
2 Flower part
3 Turn from sin
4 Cease
5 Be, past tense, plural
6 Jacob, ___ Israel
7 Measurement of weight
8 Zerubbabel's prophet
9 Joel prophesied against
10 "___, go to Nineveh, that great city" (Jon. 1:2)
11 Sarah, e.g., slang
12 Stretch to make do
13 Horse of Zech.'s vision
21 Lo-Ammi means "not my ___"
23 Sea eagle
25 15 Across inhabitant

26 Music storage format (abbr.)
28 Jesus Christ is the ___ yesterday and today
29 To shorten (abbr.)
30 Ship initials
32 "For ye ___ not my people" (Hos. 1:9)
35 Corinthian goddess
36 Hertz (arch.)
37 Puccini compositions
38 Sharpen
39 Galilee is one (2 words)
40 God's holy mountain
41 Lodging
42 Garment's edge
43 ___ de Janeiro
45 ___ Testament
46 Car maker
48 Remained

49 Snake-haired woman
50 Peter in Gethsemane (Luke 9:32 NIV)
52 Lo-Ruhamah means "not __"
56 Peter would __ Christ three times
57 Make unclear
58 Women's magazine

59 Wine holder
60 Lager
61 Chest top
63 "Can __ walk together, except they be agreed?" (Amos 3:3)
64 Ship's back

BIBLE FACTS

ACROSS

1 *Little _____ Coupe*, Beach Boys LP
6 Choir warm-up syllables, maybe
10 "How long. . . _____ thou be quiet?" (Jer. 47:6)
13 Prodigal son descriptor
15 Writing appeared there
16 "Now I _____ me down to sleep"
17 Big gun
18 Greek architectural pier
19 "_____ Maria"
20 NT book
22 Zacharias' messenger-angel
24 Flood man
26 Temple patio
28 Mary's mom, traditionally
29 Long, long time
30 One who saw Pet. with Jesus
31 "Every day they _____ my words" (Ps. 56:5)
32 Number of disciples, (abbr.)
33 Former 1 Across player
34 "_____ down in green pastures" (Ps. 23:2)
35 Me
37 Spirit will _____ the weary soul

41 Moose relative
42 "I am the true _____" (John 15:1)
43 Pod partner
44 Rich man "_____ sumptuously" daily (Luke 16:19)
47 God sent manna for _____
48 Compost
49 Purim month
50 Lot's wife became pillar of _____
51 Greek Mars
52 Cake of _____, common Bible food
54 Bible narrative descriptor
56 Silver symbols
57 Mexican sandwich
59 Philistines _____ Israelite camps
63 Near-failing grade
64 Little Mermaid's love
65 Lips
66 Service registry org.
67 After Flood, people ate _____
68 Strange gods "came _____ up" (Deut. 32:17)

DOWN

1 Noel mo.
2 Early Church period, e.g.
3 Cana miracle need
4 Promised Land
5 OT prophesier
6 Former flyer org.
7 Wandered
8 Church feature
9 Pad, as of concrete
10 Lancelot's mom
11 God sent them to feed Elijah
12 Fancy lace
14 Explosive letters (abbr.)
21 Aaron's blossomed

23 Less common
24 Garish sign
25 Slime
27 Caesar's trinity
29 Disturbance
30 4 Down plenty
31 Hosea's was adulterous
33 "My foot hath _____ his steps" (Job 23:11)
34 Do "not _____ upon usury" (Deut. 23:19)
36 Eli and Samuel
37 Paul's sermons caused them
38 Fencing sword
39 Mediterranean and Red
40 Angel halo, maybe

42 Bible commentary section (abbr.)
44 Electrical measurements
45 Proverbs in Prov.
46 Jesus _____ Lazarus from death
47 Board band, as on a house
48 "I will _____ the LORD" (Ps. 7:17)
50 Evildoer's trap

51 Jesus will come _____
53 Individual unit
55 _____ of the Covenant
58 Reformation Day mo.
60 Community care professional's degree (abbr.)
61 Moray
62 Valley of _____ bones

BEATITUDES

ACROSS

1 Deep pit, as hell
6 Creative thought
10 Westminster show letters
13 Multitude fed with loaves, _____
15 Jesus' burial chamber
16 Genetic information carrier (abbr.)
17 Believers _____ to God's laws
18 Paul would _____ to Asian ports
19 Daniel and lion's quarters
20 Passes, as a test
22 Beatitudes word
24 Lame man after healing
26 Third part of the Trinity: _____ Spirit
28 Boat part
29 Thailand neighbor
30 Adam tried to _____ from God
31 Backslide, as into sin
32 Bible times, today
33 Garden feature, maybe
34 Washington figure (abbr.)
35 Pre-game stretches (hyph.)
37 Lake youngster

41 Mined matter
42 You are "_____ of the earth" (Matt. 5:13)
43 Pharisee's tithed herb
44 You have "more _____ than" sparrows
   (Luke 12:7)
47 With 48 Across: _____ those who _____ you
48 Opposite of 47 Across
49 Declare, as one's beliefs
50 Shepherd's staff
51 Group of Roman families
52 Smoke, as used by Native Americans
54 Dr. Zhivago's flame
56 Droop
57 Stockings
59 Roman road needs
63 Jesus _____ with sinners
64 Devil's_____ desire
65 Christmas morning cry (2 words)
66 Moses _____ Israelites from Egypt
67 They who will inherit the earth
68 One who persecutes

DOWN

1 Investment pro's credential
2 Achan _____ loot under tent
3 Sodom ember
4 Wool gatherers
5 Merciful obtain it
6 Possessive pronoun
7 Earning salvation not _____
8 Poet Dickinson
9 Wicked not "_____ to rise" (Ps. 36:12)
10 Totals (2 words)
11 Prepares to pray
12 Not put under a bushel (Matt. 5:15)
14 Jesus made the blind to _____
21 Above ankles
23 "They _____ be filled" (Matt. 5:6)

24 Biblical narrative, e.g.
25 "_____ in spirit" (Matt. 5:3)
27 Quirky
29 Jesus came to fulfill it
30 "My _____ is in thee" (Ps. 39:7)
31 Jesus came to save the _____
33 "_____ in heart" see God (Matt. 5:8)
34 Bronze serpent site
36 Those who _____ receive comfort
37 Pilate's need at Jesus' trial, maybe
38 Est.'s realm, today
39 Biblical edibles
40 "Golly!"
42 Jesus, God's _____
44 Serf

45 Pilot

46 Rough-_____ hawk, Arctic flyer

47 TV collie

48 25 Down reward

50 Garlic segment

51 Holy Land vine

53 "Pssst!"

55 GI's address

58 Antlered animal

60 Belonging to (suffix)

61 Lip, as of a cup

62 Prodigal son's milieu

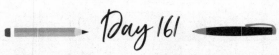

LEAH: THE UNLOVED WIFE

ACROSS

1 Likely in Leah's heart because Jacob did not love her (Gen. 29:30)

5 Rachel would ___ with Jacob over her barrenness (Gen. 30:1)

9 Transport for Leah and the family (Gen. 31:17) (sing.)

14 White fruit

15 ___ Major, Big Dipper locale

16 Leah thought she would ___ herself to Jacob (Gen. 29:32)

17 Laban and Jacob agreed not to cross a boundary "for ___" (Gen. 31:52)

18 Andrew's tools (Matt. 4:18)

19 Feelings Jacob believed Esau had (Gen. 33:1) (abbr./slang)

20 Leah's father-in-law (Gen. 25:26)

22 Leah did not ___ around Rachel's feelings (Gen. 30:15)

24 "Ye have made it a ___ of thieves" (Matt. 21:13)

25 Martha certainly put one on the table (John 12:2)

27 Strap for 9 Across

31 Mongolian desert

32 Bilhah's son (Gen. 35:25)

34 African antelope

35 "Who is a ___ man?" (James 3:13)

38 Transparent sheet (abbr.)

40 Jacob, when he discovered Laban's trick (Gen. 29:25)

42 Awry (Scot.)

44 Rhoda answered Peter's (Acts 12:13)

46 "Noses have they," but they won't smell these (Ps. 115:6)

47 Their covenant was meant to ___ the bitterness between them (Gen. 31:44)

48 "Scatter thou the people that delight in ___" (Ps. 68:30)

50 Stake

51 Luau dish

52 Leah's feelings to know she was not loved (Gen. 29:31)

55 Where Paul would have debarked in Perga (Acts 13:13)

57 They made Leah's heart glad (Gen. 30:20)

59 Of Laban's daughters, Jacob would ___ Rachel (Gen. 29:18)

61 Government dept.

64 Perhaps Leah's was pale (Gen. 29:17)

66 Chocolate substitute

68 Leah's dad (Gen. 29:16)

71 Leah's were weak (Gen. 29:17)

73 Pilate's 13

74 Buckinghamshire village

75 It was sown among the wheat (Matt. 13:25)

76 "If ye ___ to them of whom ye hope to receive" (Luke 6:34)

77 Describes Pharaoh when he refused to let Israel go (Ex. 5:2)

78 "Give me children, or ___ I die" (Gen. 30:1)

79 Jacob was on ___ to see Esau coming (Gen. 33:1)

DOWN

1 Rose bug

2 "We. . .do not ___ to pray for you" (Col. 1:9)

3 "Of ___ are we" (Gen. 29:4)

4 Writer Bombeck

5 In Joseph's dream, it bowed before him (Gen. 37:9)

6 Jacob thought Rachel ___ than Leah (Gen. 29:17–18)

7 Active

8 Perhaps Job did this as he groaned (Job 23:2)

9 "See ya!" in Assisi

10 Leah responded with this when Rachel requested the mandrakes (Gen. 30:15)

11 Pharaoh's cup, maybe (Gen. 40:11)

12 "To ___ from the words of knowledge" (Prov. 19:27)

13 Name for one of Daniel's denizens, maybe (Dan. 6:16)

21 Head honcho

23 Oolong

26 TV network

28 Laban would ___ Jacob with the promise of Rachel (Gen. 29:26–27) (2 words)

29 Jesus was this in the storm (Mark 4:37–38)
30 "Rebekah their sister, and her ___" (Gen. 24:59)
31 Computer expert (slang)
33 Intelligence agency (abbr.)
35 Summer stingers
36 Ice house
37 "The sons of Jacob came upon the ___, and spoiled the city" (Gen. 34:27)
39 The Ten Commandments
41 Twelfth month (Est. 3:7)
43 KJV "yea"
45 Some home decorators
49 ___-rac, zigzag trim (var.)
53 Communication method (abbr.)
54 Do not do this to one word of Scripture! (Rev. 22:19)

56 Series ender, often (abbr.)
58 Spies on (arch.)
60 Crown of life receivers must be this (Rev. 2:10)
61 Cooking method for fish
62 "Thou hast now done foolishly in so ___" (Gen. 31:28)
63 Laban to Jacob: "___ with me" (Gen. 29:19)
65 Green Gables girl
67 Shaft
68 Acid (abbr.)
69 One of the ship's hairy passengers (1 Kings 10:22)
70 Rachel's last, for short (Gen. 35:24)
72 Philip to Nathanael: "Come and ___" (John 1:46)

LUKE: THE BELOVED PHYSICIAN

ACROSS

1 Sinai desert climate
5 "Let us go forth therefore unto him without the ____" (Heb. 13:13)
9 "God. . .raised up Jesus, whom ye ___" (Acts 5:30)
13 Way you can memorize Bible verses
14 Philip's preaching, e.g. (Acts 8:35)
15 *Aida* is one
16 First gardener
17 Bloody river (Ex. 7:17)
18 "____ stood up in the midst of the disciples" (Acts 1:15)
19 Luke wrote so readers would do this (Luke 1:1)
21 "All they which dwelt in ____ heard the word" (Acts 19:10)
23 Legume
24 Greek goddess
25 Matthew collected this (Matt. 9:9)
29 Simon tried to ____ the apostles with money (Acts 8:18)
30 Paul's sermons were more than just one of these
32 Paul warned the voyage would ____ the ship not just a little (Acts 27:10)
33 Painter Richard
36 Explore thoroughly
37 Dessert choice
38 He follows Luke
39 "Through the wrath of the LORD of hosts," people are these (Isa. 9:19)

40 Luke was one, for short
41 Perga to Derbe (dir.)
42 Lucre descriptor (1 Tim. 3:3)
43 To some, the first Christians belonged to these
44 Today, Paul and Luke might use this for their journeys
45 Giant of folklore
46 "Thou shalt. . .bring forth a ___" (Luke 1:31)
47 Elijah "made a ____ about the altar" (1 Kings 18:32)
49 Health org.
50 Joseph would pay one in Bethlehem (Luke 2:5)
53 One of these asked Jesus, "What shall I do to inherit eternal life?" (Luke 10:25) (abbr.)
55 47 Across was not this, but around the altar (1 Kings 18:35)
57 Texas tourist site
60 Shopping area
62 Jesus to His followers
63 Seed sower (Luke 8:5)
64 What 63 Across wanted from his labor
65 Craftsman would do this to the four wooden pillars (Ex. 36:36)
66 Tools for 63 Across
67 Luke's second treatise
68 Laodicea, known for its eye salve, may have had a cure for one (Rev. 3:18)

DOWN

1 Some were present at Pentecost (Acts 2:11)
2 Event near 57 Across, perhaps
3 Where Julius planned to take Paul (Acts 27:1)
4 Half (prefix)
5 Joseph and Mary would have traveled in one for protection on the road in Luke 2:4
6 Ram in the sky
7 Not good, (prefix)
8 Paul demanded to take his to Caesar (Acts 25:11)
9 Jesus was pierced with one (John 19:34)
10 Agrippa would have ____ Paul go had he not demanded to see Caesar (Acts 26:32)

11 Poet's "before"
12 "What king, going to make ____ against another king, sitteth not down first?" (Luke 14:31)
15 Vinegar given to Jesus on the cross may have acted slightly like this (John 19:29)
20 Snaky fish (pl.)
22 What a sword does (Luke 2:35)
26 The wind would ____ the ship toward Clauda (Acts 27:15–16)
27 "Men ought always to pray, and not to ___" (Luke 18:1)
28 Some people are choked with these and "bring no fruit to perfection" (Luke 8:14)

29 Writing tool

30 "Ye should. . .not have loosed from ___" (Acts 27:21)

31 Mary said, "He that is mighty hath done. . .great things; and ___ is his name" (Luke 1:49)

33 It took ten plagues before Pharaoh would ___ the Israelites (Ex. 12:31)

34 Threat to whales, often

35 "___ was in the days of Herod" (Luke 1:5)

36 What Daniel heard, maybe (Dan. 6:22)

39 Pharisees: "Let us not ___ against God" (Acts 23:9)

40 What Simon Peter might have drawn today (John 18:10)

42 Luke (Col. 4:14)

43 The young man found the ___ of discipleship too steep (Matt. 19:20–22)

46 The hairy ___ of willful sinners will be wounded (Ps. 68:21)

48 Listings in Matthew 10:2

49 Joshua would ___ land to tribes (Josh. 18:10)

50 "Every tree is known by his own ___" (Luke 6:44)

51 When the women went to Jesus' tomb (Luke 24:1)

52 Jesus would ___ those that would "take him by force, to make him a king" (John 6:15)

54 Christian community org.

56 Prophecy: "As one gathereth ___ that are left, have I gathered all the earth" (Isa. 10:14)

57 Burnt offerings residue

58 WC in London

59 Luke's feeling toward Jesus' ministry (Acts 1:1–4)

61 Shape of God's promise to Noah (Gen. 9:16)

OLD TESTAMENT PLANTS

ACROSS

1 Baby Esau called Isaac, slangily
5 Ancient Indian
10 Unclean rodent
13 Warning
15 Body of Christ
16 Satan's was large
17 Absurd
18 Remove lid
19 Small gulf
20 "Yet in my flesh shall I __ God" (Job 19:26)
21 Depend
23 Egypt to Red Sea was one
25 Volcano
26 Skirt type
28 Crop's home (2 words)
31 Brush off
32 The Word of God
33 Lubricants
34 Diet Coke precursor
37 Shield (var.)
38 Jesus said, "__ I tell you" (Luke 23:33)
40 Sin, slangily (hyph.)

41 Hallucinogen (abbr.)
42 "He...is greater __ he who is in the world" (1 John 4:4)
43 Debates (arch.)
44 One sheltered Jonah
45 Egyptian food
46 Pacify
49 Date grower
50 Bible land legumes
51 Part of ark window, maybe
52 Expression of surprise
55 Smack
56 Statement of faith
59 Wilderness resting spot
61 "The voice of __ crying in the wilderness" (John 1:23)
62 Time period
63 Artist Andrew
64 Type of 24 Down
65 Kings' Joshua 9 trick: don __ clothes
66 "My yoke is __...my burden is light" (Matt 11:30)

DOWN

1 Adam, Jacob, et. al. slangily
2 Healing plant
3 Palm fruit
4 "Are," KJV-style
5 Bird claw part
6 Buffoonish
7 __-tac-toe
8 Seventh letter in Corinth alphabet
9 Bible land tree
10 Disprove
11 Ephod stone
12 Played
14 Evergreen tree
22 Alpha/omega, beginning/__
24 Acorn producer

25 Snaky fish
26 Short epistle (abbr.)
27 __ of the Valley
28 Cain's brother
29 Bible land fruits
30 As previously cited (Lat.)
31 God will heal every __
34 Working implement
35 Negative (prefix)
36 Pear type
38 One of two crucified with Jesus
39 "Lips that speak knowledge are a __ jewel" (Prov. 20:15 NIV)
40 Criterion
42 Bread crisper

43 Bible land flowering herb
44 Weapon
45 Ruth or Mary, e.g. (slang)
46 Loathe
47 Paris river
48 Filled
49 Spongy

51 Christianity, at first
52 Galilee is one (2 words)
53 Punches
54 Like Sodom and Gomorrah
57 Group dealing with Mph (abbr.)
58 "And forget ___ all His benefits" (Ps. 103:2)
60 Sailors' "yes"

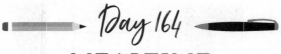

MEALTIME

ACROSS

1 New England state (abbr.)
5 Paul shipwreck site
10 Food energy (abbr.)
13 Shepherd "guides me __ the right paths (Ps. 23:3 NIV)
15 "I will __ thee, O Lord" (Ps. 30:1)
16 Trinity: three-in-__
17 Naaman became one (2 Kings 5:1)
18 Data transfer device
19 Isaac: son of Sarah's old __
20 Enemy of Israel
21 After a while, to Shakespeare
23 Wicked's fate: __ darkness
25 Baths
26 Jacob gave Esau some (Gen. 25:34 NIV)
28 Grain
31 Typographic character
32 Sandwich cookies brand
33 Unclean ocean dweller
34 Resort hotel
37 Lump
38 Play part

40 Number of Ezek.'s living creatures
41 "Let us __ aside every weight" (Heb. 12:1)
42 Particle
43 For better or __
44 Do-__
45 Genealogies record these
46 Jesus "is __ at the right hand of the throne of God" (Heb. 12:2) (2 words)
49 Land of __ and honey
50 Frenchman's Tuesday
51 Promised Land fruits
52 Sheep mom
55 First cook
56 Transferred image
59 Type of oil
61 Downwind
62 Music used as practice
63 Lowest point
64 Hallucinogen (abbr.)
65 Palm fruits
66 Bird of peace

DOWN

1 Prodigal's dinner
2 Tub spread
3 No
4 Joppa to Nineveh (dir.)
5 Short notes
6 Nerve fiber
7 Ford model
8 Anointed digit
9 Nut types
10 Raccoonlike animal
11 Heavenly messenger
12 Jeers
14 See 51 Across
22 3 Down, KJV-style
24 Colorado tribe

25 Slit
26 Legal claim
27 Pronoun for Est. (Fr.)
28 Pottage holder
29 Cyrus's was Persia
30 "My God on whom I can __" (Ps. 59:17 NIV)
31 Swarms
34 Noah loaded "two of every __" (Gen. 7:9)
35 Force
36 War god at Corinth
38 Savory dish
39 Cob vegetable
40 Utensil
42 Evaded, as in 1 Samuel 18:11
43 Comedian Flip

44 Mismatched

45 Describes 8 Down

46 Isaac knew Esau by this

47 Temple roofs (1 Kings 7:9 NIV)

48 At bay

49 "Go with them two __" (Matt. 5:41 NIV)

51 Deteriorate

52 Prank

53 Tel __

54 Meager

57 Terminal abbr.

58 Sliced

60 "Male child," KJV-style

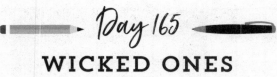

WICKED ONES

ACROSS

1 Like David vis-à-vis Goliath, for short
6 What partridge sits on in Jeremiah 17:11
10 What Alpine yodels do
14 Wicked one
15 Ark man
16 Jezebel's greedy spouse
17 Lord "set _____" godly for himself (Ps. 4:3)
18 1970s rock band from Ohio
19 "Redeeming the _____...days are evil" (Eph. 5:16)
20 IT guy, maybe
21 Potiphar's wife falsely accused him
23 "Yea" opposite in Matt. 5:37
24 "Forever and _____. Amen"
26 Nutty pie ingredients
28 Evil _____, insanity diagnosis
31 Repeated writing-on-wall word
32 Dampen
33 12 Down plot stopper
36 Gain whole world "and _____ himself" (Luke 9:25)
40 Raised

42 Adam's Eden tool, maybe
43 False witness' words in Proverbs 6:19
44 "_____ fell among thorns" (Mark 4:7)
45 Set of five
48 It's lost when you stand
49 Herodias' nemesis
51 Jael, Esther, and Martha descriptor
53 Rattling gourd
56 Lot's wife's pillar
57 Many a Psalm
58 Bargainer
61 Applaud
65 Ananias lied about its amount
67 God restores and makes _____
68 Make a ruffle
69 Breastplate, as of faith
70 "He died unto sin _____" (Rom. 6:10)
71 Old photo tone
72 Religious offshoot
73 "It shall bruise thy _____" (Gen. 3:15)
74 Epistle

DOWN

1 Ocean Spray drink starters
2 "Hypocrite's _____ shall perish" (Job 8:13)
3 Seaweed substance
4 Nathan accused David of it
5 Fido or Fluffy
6 OT witch site
7 Leaves
8 Jesus _____ his life for sin
9 58 Across, maybe
10 Eve would _____ forbidden fruit
11 Good dishes
12 33 Across plotter
13 Righteous one _____ God's commandments
21 JFK landers
22 "As a _____ gathereth" her chicks (Matt. 23:37)
25 Contend

27 Electronic device
28 Canaan to Egypt (dir.)
29 Instant hot beverage
30 Object
31 "Rich and poor _____ together" (Prov. 22:2)
34 ". . ._____ would I fly away" (Ps. 55:6)
35 Sweetie, for short
37 Anointing fluids
38 Jesus' judgment _____
39 Discern
41 _____ vu
45 Plagued leader
46 "Why standest thou _____ off?" (Ps. 10:1)
47 Keyboard key (abbr.)
50 Reformation Day mo.
52 Yens

53 Exodus figure
54 Proverbs quote
55 Saint's bone, maybe
56 What Dorcas did
59 Jesus' grandmother, traditionally
60 Ten (prefix)
62 "Flattering _____ and...double heart" (Ps. 12:2)

63 Oratorio section
64 "_____, lest ye enter into temptation" (Luke 22:46)
66 KJV verb ending
68 Tyre to Jerusalem (dir.)

Day 166

LIFE IS GOOD

ACROSS

1 "_____porridge hot"
6 Government edibles watchers (abbr.)
9 Lion feature
13 God would _____Adam and Eve
14 Knock
15 We are _____through faith
16 Shock
17 Tres minus dos
18 "O come, let us _____him!"
19 Jesus' Jerusalem ride
20 God will _____to prayer
22 Jesus _____victory on the cross
23 Belonging to (suffix)
24 Dash partner
25 Joseph's coat had many
27 Organic compound
29 Tasks
33 "World without _____. Amen"
34 Praying Pharisee had a big one
35 Crow cousin
36 Cana pots were filled to their _____
39 Water wall
40 Land of milk and _____

41 50-plus org.
42 Mule's mouth need of Psalm 32:9
43 God sent His only _____
44 Disciples' number, (plural)
46 "Unto us a _____" of rivers (Isa. 33:21)
49 Storied star site
50 "_____the truth" (Prov. 23:23)
51 Drag
53 Serenity site, maybe
56 Beehive State dweller
58 Eve "conceived, and _____Cain" (Gen. 4:1)
59 Rest for the heavy _____, as in Matthew 11:28
61 "Beaten with _____stripes" (Luke 12:48)
62 Israelites' first priest
63 God sets godly _____for himself
64 Jesus _____5,000
65 Ungodly "men _____in unawares" (Jude 4)
66 Ravens don't need one in Luke 12:24
67 Like Judas
68 Colorado park

DOWN

1 "LORD will bless. . .with _____" (Ps. 29:11)
2 God's light will _____evil
3 Words fitly spoken comparison (Prov. 25:11)
4 Christ sits on his judgment _____
5 Church addition, maybe
6 3 Down category
7 Jacob's son, and others
8 Pithy, instructive saying, as in Prov.
9 KJV "demon-possessed"
10 God would _____His promise repeatedly
11 Wicked Roman emperor
12 13 Across site
15 Less 9 Down
20 Title for Jesus

21 Vacation cash, maybe
24 Dan.'s captivity site, and others
26 Tenerife town
28 "LORD is in his holy _____" (Ps. 11:4)
30 Negative prefix
31 Deer
32 KJV "firmament"
34 "Man did _____angels' food" (Ps. 78:25)
36 Cave dweller
37 Uncooked
38 God shows _____against sin
39 Tools used for spinning, as in Prov. 31:19
40 God sends His _____Spirit to us
42 "Covet...the _____gifts" (1 Cor. 12:31)

43 What Prov. 31:19 woman did

45 Praying Pharisee would _____ himself

47 French red table wine

48 21 Down spending site

50 Sacrilegious

52 Men, for short

53 Sacrificial offering altar

54 Adam to Abel

55 Esther's month

57 "Thou shalt bruise his _____" (Gen. 3:15)

58 "Cut in sunder _____ of iron" (Isa. 45:2)

60 European sea eagle

62 Pro

MARK: THE EVANGELIST

ACROSS

1 Elisabeth and Mary's needs (Luke 1:41–42)
6 Jesus: "This cup is the new testament in my blood, which is ___ for you" (Luke 22:20)
10 Judas carried one (John 12:6)
13 There was one between Paul and Barnabas about Mark (Acts 15:39–40)
15 East Indian dress
16 Forbidden fruit eater
17 Paul felt this about Mark (Acts 15:37–38)
18 "We know that thou art ___" (Mark 12:14)
19 "Pssst!"
20 Jesus fed many with two (Mark 6:38)
22 Mark highlights these in his Gospel
24 Butcher's hook
26 Eject
28 Swerve
29 Offspring of the beast "like to a bear" (Dan. 7:5)
30 What might have been in Mark's mother's home
31 Tooth-leaved tree
32 Spherical body
33 Pinch
34 "If I should ___ with thee, I will not deny thee" (Mark 14:31)
35 Jesus made great calm on this (Mark 4:39)
37 Mark wanted to show that Jesus was this (Mark 1:1) (2 words)

41 Ananias told one (Acts 5:3)
42 Abode
43 Santa's helper
44 Goliath does this to the army of Saul (1 Sam. 17:8)
47 Former Italian magistrate
48 Crucifixion need (John 20:25) (sing.)
49 Fencing sword
50 One may have been thrown over the colt Jesus rode (Mark 11:7)
51 El ___, TX
52 Mark wrote of Jesus' resurrection to prove His ___ over death
54 Jesus would ___ His disciples "what things should happen unto him" (Mark 10:32)
56 Describes the morsels in Psalm 147:17
57 Paul's vote on taking Mark on a second journey (Acts 15:39)
59 "___ were gathered" (Acts 4:26)
63 The disciples ___ the colt to Jesus (Mark 11:7)
64 God came ___ the mount Sinai (Ex. 19:20)
65 Pilot Earhart
66 Direction Mark traveled from Perga to Jerusalem
67 Pre-Easter season
68 Taken by Samson from Gaza (Judg. 16:3)

DOWN

1 One might be at your desk (abbr.)
2 Perhaps Mark: what the naked young man did (Mark 14:52)
3 Modern job opportunity for Matthew (Matt. 9:9)
4 Features of many coastlines
5 Stems of letters (sing.)
6 Boomer
7 Scribes and Pharisees did this to Jesus frequently
8 Sound of two who "shall come to poverty," perhaps (Prov. 23:21)
9 Both those mentioned in Proverbs 23:21 had a bad one

10 KJV: "look!"
11 Route
12 One of the "fountains of the great deep," perhaps (Gen. 7:11)
14 KJV "yea"
21 What cannot stand if divided (Mark 3:25)
23 "Multitude of ___" (Ps. 97:1)
24 Jesus, to some followers
25 Shorten
27 Response to manna kept overnight, as in Exodus 16:20
29 Paul's port on the way to Tyre (Acts 21:1) (var.)

30 Mark might have run one, naked (Mark 14:51–52)

31 Assistant

33 Paul may have stood on one to preach

34 Feature of many cathedrals

36 King Solomon had one in 1 Kings 9:26

37 Paul to Barnabas: I'll ____ someone more reliable than Mark! (Acts 15:37–39) (2 words)

38 Sailed by Mark to reach Perga

39 Hodgepodge

40 Sports assoc.

42 What one of "them ye may eat" might do (Lev. 11:22)

44 Mark relates how Jesus "cast out many ____" (Mark 1:34)

45 Tops of Sinai and Ararat, e.g.

46 After Barnabas takes Mark, they ____ from the narrative

47 Ohio city

48 Chili brand

50 Some hearers at Pentecost were from here (Acts 2:11)

51 Seven cows looking like this emerged from the river (Gen. 41:2)

53 Speedway shape

55 Time of the early Church was one

58 Paul would ____ for Silas in place of Mark (Acts 15:39–40)

60 Building addition

61 Tigris, e.g. (Sp.)

62 ____ Leandro, CA

MARTHA: THE SERVER

ACROSS

1 Wise men saw one (Matt. 2:1–2)
5 Martha did this to meet Jesus (John 11:20)
9 Martha to Jesus: "Bid her . . .____ me" (Luke 10:40)
13 Clearly, an attribute of Martha
14 Beautiful Helen's city
15 Crippling disease
16 Martha's sister's choice (Luke 10:42)
17 Martha to Jesus: "I know that he shall ____ again" (John 11:24)
18 In 9 Across, Martha was this. . .
19 . . .and this
21 Martha to Jesus: "My brother had not ____" (John 11:21)
23 Couldn't Martha's sister ____ the problem?
24 Martha's sister wouldn't lift one ____ finger!
25 Potato brand
29 Martha's motto: Don't just think about it, ____!
30 Bluish-white metal
32 Calais negative
33 Gear for the Bahamas
36 Physicist Marie
37 Pull
38 Jesus was not telling Martha's sister one of these
39 ____ boom

40 Was Martha's kitchen this?
41 Like Martha, it's busy (Prov. 30:25)
42 Actress Day
43 Head covering
44 Blemish
45 Ski destination
46 Temperature in Martha's kitchen, perhaps
47 Blood part
49 Sower's medium (Luke 8:8)
50 San Diego winter hour (abbr.)
53 Martha to Jesus: "Dost thou not ____?" (Luke 10:40)
55 Outspoken Martha didn't do this with words (2 words)
57 Ran wild in the desert (Job 24:5)
60 The transfiguration took place____ a high mountain (Mark 9:2)
62 Martha's sister wiped Jesus' feet with this (John 11:2)
63 Martha said Lazarus's body would do this (John 11:39)
64 Aaron used one to fashion an idol (Ex. 32:4)
65 "They cried out all at ____" (Luke 23:18)
66 Belly (Scot.)
67 Pop
68 Martha wanted to ____ her sister into action

DOWN

1 Long stories
2 Cut of beef
3 How Martha felt in the kitchen (Luke 10:40)
4 Martha needed to ____ her to-do list (Luke 10:42)
5 Wall ____
6 Martha probably took this in her housekeeping
7 Goddess known to 14 Across
8 Describes the rich man's garments (Luke 16:19)
9 Crowd

10 Antlered animal
11 Devil is its father (John 8:44)
12 Spacecraft detachment
15 "A sword shall ____ through thy own soul also"(Luke 2:35)
20 Christian community org.
22 Paul would have seen these kinds of columns in Athens
26 The Jews would ____ Lazarus in a cave (John 11:38)
27 Elijah would ____ God's altar with water (1 Kings 18:33–34)

28 What Martha probably suffered concerning what she would serve Jesus

29 Bible patriarch, for short

30 American Indian tribe

31 Rhizome riser

33 One of what a philatelist collects

34 Dug around God's altar, as in 1 Kings 18:35

35 Extreme (prefix)

36 Org.

39 Describes "the greater light to rule the day" (Gen. 1:16)

40 "Martha. . .went and ____ him" (John 11:20)

42 Fabric used in interior decorating

43 Soma

46 Sounds like a lot of this when Lazarus died (John 11:19)

48 Martha's sister caused one anointing Jesus' feet (John 12:3)

49 "Chief priests and scribes ____ and vehemently accused him" (Luke 23:10)

50 Organ substitute in some churches

51 Adhere

52 Martha, her sister, and brother

54 Martha, perhaps: Everyone ____ well at my place!

56 Thump

57 Though Martha came out, Jesus needed to____ for Mary (John 11:28)

58 Prodigal son's workplace (Luke 15:15)

59 Martha's sister chose to do this and listen to Jesus (Luke 10:39)

61 Martha's lesson for us: It's possible to be ____ busy (Luke 10:41)

OLD TESTAMENT PLACES

ACROSS

1 Cut
5 Pharaoh's daughter walked __ the riverbank
10 Cedar's "blood"
13 Sound when Elisha raised boy
15 Jonah's under-gourd attitude
16 Number of ribs to make Eve (Sp.)
17 Razorlike
18 Saying
19 African antelope
20 May be clay or bronze
21 Esau's land
23 "__ up a child in the way he should go" (Prov. 22:6)
25 Tiny ark flyer
26 Taught
28 The Promised Land
31 Church governing group
32 Holds 20 Across
33 Bearded or Dutch
34 Prompt
37 Ear or liver part
38 Belief

40 Tang promoters (abbr.)
41 Israel split into __ kingdoms
42 28 Across city
43 Sky flyers
44 Philosopher Rousseau
45 Berate (2 words)
46 Large weapon
49 Est.'s garden party
50 More adept
51 Pet.'s catch
52 Ephod decoration
55 "Is any thing __ hard for the Lord?" (Gen. 18:14)
56 Lombard's love
59 Wear away
61 Small dwelling
62 Colder
63 Small kin to 46 Across
64 Swine's home
65 Treed (2 words)
66 Nuance

DOWN

1 Door fastener
2 Sound heard in ruins
3 "__ is man, that thou art mindful of him?" (Ps. 8:4)
4 Neither's partner
5 Wicked land of Amos 1:13
6 Weaver's need
7 Choose
8 51 Across need
9 Machpelah, et. al. (poet.)
10 Cane product
11 Orphaned redhead
12 British currency
14 Musical productions
22 Lion's home
24 Pole

25 Get smaller
26 Hiram's land
27 Dimension
28 Jesus' Palm Sunday ride
29 Promise (2 words)
30 With 31 Down, biblical mounts
31 See 30 Down
34 Comedian Reiner
35 Meat-grading org.
36 Magi's starting point
38 Target of 46 Across
39 Post-exile prophet
40 Egyptian river
42 Peach State
43 Jacob's altar site (Gen. 35)

44 Garden of Eden tool

45 Ruth's answer to Boaz

46 OT measures

47 Regarding

48 Polish monetary unit

49 Describes wilderness serpents

51 Pet tormenter

52 Sixties dancer (hyph.)

53 Mankind's first home

54 "How can __ mortals prove their innocence before God?" (Job 9:2 NIV)

57 May be violence or kindness

58 Shirt protector

60 Groove

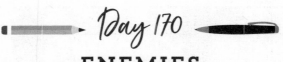

ENEMIES

ACROSS

1 Spinning toy (2 words)
5 Burt offering, a sweet __
10 Situps target (abbr.)
13 Venomous snake
15 Empties, as in Amos 5:8 NIV
16 Nehemiah shook as a sign
17 Town __, announcer of old
18 You do not receive, because you ask __
19 Frozen water
20 First letter of tabernacle
21 City paired with 65 Across
23 Alaskan territory
25 Voucher for a small debt
26 Eden deceiver
28 Incite, as in Amos 6:14 NIV (2 words)
31 Fertile desert area
32 Lowest point
33 Cocooned insect
34 Cooking measure (abbr.)
37 Gideon's Midianite foe
38 Meat offering frequency

40 Secure, as in Esther 8:8
41 Constrictor snake
42 Swiss capital
43 End, as in Ezra 5:5
44 Be holy and without __
45 Fought Asa in 1 Kings 15
46 Lion descriptor
49 More's opposite
50 Persian king
51 "Your redemption draweth __" (Luke 21:28)
52 Prefix meaning "daughter of" (Heb.)
55 __ Fool's Day (abbr.)
56 Job's foe
59 "Let us make man in our __" (Gen 1:26)
61 "Is anything __ hard for the Lord?" (Gen. 18:14)
62 Excite
63 Abigail's husband
64 Jezreel to Samaria (dir.)
65 City paired with 21 Across
66 David used to soothe Saul

DOWN

1 Ledger (abbr.)
2 Grieving, Jacob __ his clothes
3 Off-Broadway award
4 Before (prefix)
5 Separate
6 Israel's oppressor
7 French "yes"
8 Sarah to Abraham (abbr.)
9 Jonah's destination
10 Similar
11 Breakfast meat
12 Used
14 Camelot's king
22 Shrill bark
24 Delivery service (abbr.)
25 Manger, as Job 39:9

26 Israel's first king
27 Caleb sent to "__ out the land" (Josh. 14:7)
28 Stuck-up person
29 Tropical edible root
30 Notion
31 State as an opinion
34 Chamomile, Green, e.g.
35 Priestly garment piece
36 Supplication
38 Do with, as in Ruth 1:17 NIV
39 David's fighting force
40 Red, Galilee, e.g.
42 "The Lord __ his people with peace" (Ps. 29:11 NIV)
43 Redeem (2 words)
44 Heat measurement (abbr.)

45 Plead, as in Esther 4:8 NIV
46 Gets out
47 Misspellings, etc.
48 Jehoram slain with one
49 Fine fabric
51 Multi-national military alliance (abbr.)

52 Moses, Samuel, e.g.
53 Another name for Sinai
54 From a distance (comb. form)
57 Forty Thieves' guy __ Baba
58 Later apostle, to friends
60 Last OT book (abbr.)

GOD: THE FATHER

ACROSS

1 Solomon's visitor's home
6 Talk back
10 Field caller, for short
13 Fuel
15 Via Dolorosa sight
16 "Raven" author
17 Parable rich man's pride
18 Tropical edible root
19 God's created light
20 God gave "breath of _____" (Gen. 2:7)
22 Jesus' Jordan experience
24 Life stories, for short
26 Wound
28 Thought
29 God _____ His Son
30 "_____, Father!"
31 God is _____ with evildoers
32 Horse tidbit
33 Eastern cartel (abbr.)
34 Cheerleader's cheer
35 More shaded
37 God _____ Himself in Scripture

41 God's mercies "ever of _____" (Ps. 25:6)
42 God _____ His only son
43 Sodom fleer
44 KJV "cleave unto his wife"
47 Sluggard's examples of Proverbs 6:6
48 God's attribute in Proverbs 3:19
49 First murder victim
50 Dog food brand
51 Antifreeze brand
52 Unit of luminous intensity
54 Voting choices
56 Chemical suffix
57 "I will not _____ to speak" (Rom. 15:18)
59 Board band, as on a house
63 God makes all things _____
64 TV award
65 Pharisees' looks toward others
66 Eden serpent sound
67 Place for jewels in Isaiah 3:21
68 Tidbit

DOWN

1 Canaan to Egypt (dir.)
2 One of many in Joseph's coat
3 DFW data
4 Voter's need
5 Those against
6 Jesus _____ at Jacob's well
7 Sinai site
8 "Go away!"
9 Merchant's milieu
10 God may turn our plans _____ down
11 Barn cat
12 Baruch was Jer.'s (Jer. 36:4)
14 High frequency (abbr.)
21 Sodom sight
23 Offering to God

24 Godly ones _____ good fruit
25 God brings us "_____ a large place" (Ps. 18:19)
27 Outline letters
29 Weep
30 Imitated
31 God will _____ His people
33 God's _____ Son, Jesus
34 Pastors, for short
36 God's creation
37 Tattle (2 words)
38 Wicked "prophesy _____ unto you" (Jer. 29:21) (2 words)
39 God seeks the _____
40 Holy woman in France (abbr.)

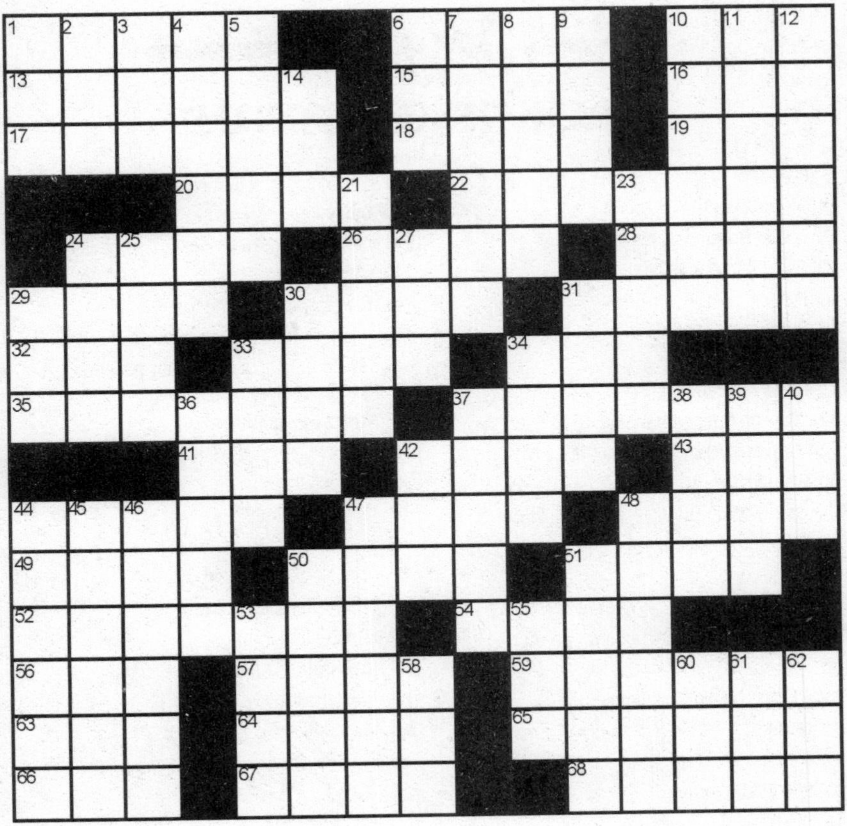

42 Economic indicator (abbr.)
44 Georgia city, and others
45 Humiliates
46 God ______ repentant souls
47 OT trumpet calls, at times
48 Kitchen oil
50 Remembered Texas site
51 God ______ prayers
53 God's garden
55 Not "on"
58 God has His ______ on you
60 Lake purity law (abbr.)
61 Business ender (abbr.)
62 God invites us to ______ Him

NAMES OF JESUS

ACROSS

1 Metric measure
5 Jesus: Bright and morning _____
9 Jesus' cloak was one
13 Risqué
14 Jesus: _____ vine
15 Leaf gatherer
16 Black
17 "Why do the heathen _____?" (Ps. 2:1)
18 Man created in _____ of God
19 Jesus: Seed of _____
21 Jesus: "I am the _____" (John 10:9)
23 Dross of Ezekiel 22:18
24 Shrill bark
25 Devil tries to _____ Gospel
29 Royal Observatory measure (abbr.)
30 Step
32 _____ Times, Rev. topic
33 Never _____ to Jesus' words (2 words)
36 Jesus: _____ of Life
37 Playground game
38 Jesus: _____ of lords
39 Israelite's threshing place

40 Horse hair
41 Lyons affirmative
42 Circus figure
43 Drags or draws forcibly
44 "_____ not vain repetitions" (Matt. 6:7)
45 "Weep and _____ for your miseries" (James 5:1)
46 Wise virgins number
47 Jesus: _____ of nations
49 Legume
50 _____ of Galilee
53 Traveler's need, maybe
55 Mythical king of Thebes
57 Breastplate, as of faith
60 Sunrise
62 Indonesian island
63 Eucharist vessel
64 Iowa university city
65 Tea choice
66 States
67 Jesus' mother
68 Sinai descriptor

DOWN

1 Jesus: _____ Shepherd
2 Jesus: _____, teacher
3 Squirrel's dinner
4 Indian starling
5 "Enter ye at the _____ gate" (Matt. 7:13)
6 Hobo
7 Summer mo.
8 "Bruised _____ shall he not break" (Isa. 42:3)
9 Toyota model
10 Wanted poster letters
11 Hook
12 How long "_____ they believe me?" (Num. 14:11)
15 What some did after Paul's sermon
20 Sunday song

22 Movie award
26 23 Across, e.g.
27 Witless
28 "Sharp sword with two _____" (Rev. 2:12)
29 Jesus: Son of _____
30 Devil will _____, seeking victims
31 Big number of years
33 "Yea, I will sing _____" (Ps. 59:16)
34 Quench
35 Red Sea _____ up for Israelites
36 "God shall _____ the trumpet" (Zech. 9:14)
39 Ice sheets
40 Jesus: Son of _____
42 Messiah
43 Jesus: _____ of the Church

46 Mustard seed descriptor
48 Some New England universities
49 Jesus: _____of God
50 "I gave her _____to repent" (Rev. 2:21)
51 Swiss mathematician
52 Whisper, sometimes

54 Jesus: Second _____
56 Pond wader
57 Med. research organization
58 OT or NT, e.g.
59 Peter or Paul, e.g. (slang.)
61 Physicians' org.

MARY: THE VIRGIN MOTHER

ACROSS

1 Most women's response to the plague of frogs, as in Exodus 8:3

4 Mary's pregnancy came ____ of a relationship with a man (Luke 1:34)

9 Jesus said, "Thou shalt not ____ the Lord thy God" (Matt 4:7)

14 ____ chi, martial art

15 What Jacob could have served Esau's pottage with (Gen. 25:30)

16 Single

17 "Mary kept ____ these things, and pondered them" (Luke 2:19)

18 One was sent to Mary (Luke 1:26–27)

19 What Mary's song of praise was, in a way (Luke 1:46–55)

20 Ships are shifted with a very small one (James 3:4)

22 Mary may have had plans, but accepted God's ____ (Luke 1:38)

24 "The mote that is in thy brother's ____?" (Luke 6:41)

25 "____ Gabriel" (Luke 1:19) (2 words)

27 Shape of each ruling light God created (Gen. 1:16)

29 French brandy

32 Pharisees had high, though misplaced, ones (Luke 11:42)

35 Dance

36 Certain roofs

38 The angel appeared to Joseph in one (Matt. 1:20)

40 Mary and Joseph's child is theirs ____, too (Luke 2:23)

42 Comforter

44 The Gospel of Matt. opens with this

45 Usually followed by ruin

47 Ointment ran down Aaron's (Ps. 133:2)

49 Without children, Elisabeth certainly was this (Luke 1:7)

50 Element of Mary's song (Luke 1:46–55)

52 John: unworthy to ____ Jesus' shoes (Luke 3:16)

54 What Lazarus of Jesus' parable did (Luke 16:20)

55 Card game

56 One-sixtieth of a minute (abbr.)

59 It must have been hard for Mary to fully ____ Gabriel's message

63 Apprehends

67 Hosea ____ Israel with sweet words (Hos. 2:14)

69 Likely shape of some of the gems in Exodus 28:18–19

71 There was one in the garden (Song 6:11)

72 Joseph "____, and took the young child" (Matt. 2:21)

73 David's harp playing soothed Saul's (1 Sam. 16:23)

74 Bethlehem to Jerusalem (dir.)

75 "The ____ of the Highest shall overshadow thee" (Luke 1:35)

76 The flight to Egypt was to ____ Herod (Matt. 2:13)

77 Member of a disbelieving generation (Matt. 23:33)

DOWN

1 Beehive State

2 One wouldn't disturb the house built on rock (Matt. 7:25)

3 "Mary. . .went into the ____ country" (Luke 1:39)

4 ____ carte (2 words)

5 Mary's description of herself (Luke 1:38)

6 Joseph was on the ____ of leaving Mary (Matt. 1:19)

7 Beverages at Belshazzar's feast (Dan. 5:2–3)

8 Corned beef on rye source

9 The angel's message might have made Mary's face do this (Luke 1:34) (2 words)

10 Egypt to Nazareth (dir.)

11 Spice

12 What 64 Down did in the Temple (Luke 2:37)

13 Mary had the ____ of trust we should desire (Luke 1:38)

21 Soviet-era fighter plane

23 "With ____ nothing shall be impossible" (Luke 1:37)

26 "Go to the ___" (Prov. 6:6)
28 Psalmist, in a way
29 Mary would have entered the Temple's (Luke 2:22)
30 Big name in daytime TV
31 Associations
32 Card player's statement (2 words)
33 Borrower's option (Prov. 22:7)
34 Jesus' tempter (Matt. 4:10)
35 What the wise men would do (Matt. 2:11)
37 Adam's helpmeet
39 Describes 60 Down's son
41 Wound covering
43 Mary felt this way at Gabriel's greeting (Luke 1:29)
46 One who works with dough
48 Baptized into Christ, do this with Christ (Gal. 3:27)

51 Soviet-era police
53 Mary's baby (Luke 1:31)
56 Servants would ___ Jesus with their hands (Mark 14:65)
57 Continental coin
58 "Before the cock ___, thou shalt deny me thrice" (Matt. 26:34)
60 Father to Jesus: my son "___ vexed" (Matt. 17:15)
61 Track shape
62 Prego's competition
64 She praised Mary's baby (Luke 2:36–38)
65 Hamburger rolls
66 The Lord directs this (Prov. 16:9) (sing.)
68 Emmaus to Jerusalem (dir.)
70 Nazareth to Jerusalem (dir.)

MARY MAGDALENE: FIRST AT THE TOMB

ACROSS

1 "[Jesus] appeared ____ to Mary Magdalene" (Mark 16:9)
6 Illegal drug (abbr.)
9 Droops
13 Nice farewell
14 What's easy to see in another's eye (Matt. 7:3)
15 Fake butter
16 What someone was when soldiers bet for Jesus' clothes
17 ____ "the first day of the week" Mary came to the tomb (John 20:1)
18 Pale sherry
19 Brew
20 "He is ____" (Matt 28:6)
22 Could have been used to start fire for breakfast (John 21:9)
23 Synonym for Aramaic *Raca*, as in Matthew 5:22
24 The Israelites burned offerings under this tree (Hos. 4:13)
26 KJV "no"
27 Skateboard with a handle
30 How some may have responded to Mary before Jesus cast out her demons (Mark 16:9)
32 Created on fourth day (Gen. 1:16)
33 Connect
36 "Many women were there beholding ____ off" (Matt 27:55)
40 The curtain being torn in two was a good one (Luke 23:45)
41 Jesus came to ____ for our sins (Heb. 2:17)
42 Jerusalem to Jericho (dir.)
43 "I write not these things to shame you, but as my beloved sons I ____ you" (1 Cor. 4:14)
44 Despot
45 Cabbage cousin
46 "Why make ye this ____, and weep?" (Mark 5:39)
48 Saul never ____ to be king of Israel (1 Sam. 9:21)
51 Executive director
54 Km/h
56 "The ____ person will speak villany" (Isa. 32:6)
57 What Mary saw at tomb (Matt. 28:2)
59 La Scala is famous for it
61 "Absalom spake. . .neither good nor ____" (2 Sam 13:22)
64 Others thought Mary's words were "____ tales" (Luke 24:11)
65 The women Mary was with had had "____ spirits" (Luke 8:2)
66 A headdress of the ancient Persians, like Queen Est.
68 "Earth shall ____" (Isa. 24:20)
69 Allows
70 One touched Isaiah's lips (Isa. 6:6–7)
71 Chances of winning
72 Seraphim do this (Isa. 6:6)
73 "Therefore ____ I to them in parables" (Matt. 13:13)

DOWN

1 Syllables used in songs (2 words)
2 Baal was one (Judg. 2:13)
3 Jesus told His followers He'd ____
4 Angel to Mary: "Come, ____ the place" (Matt. 28:6)
5 Little tower
6 Elisha did this to pull ahead of Ahab (1 Kings 18:46)
7 Mary saw the angel roll this from the tomb (Matt. 28:2)
8 Jesus accused merchants of turning the temple into a "____ of thieves" (Mark 11:17)
9 A divan is one kind
10 The Magi chose to ____ their journey with a star (Matt. 2:9)
11 Birthplace of Columbus
12 Describes those who mourned in sackcloth and ashes
14 Aquatic rodents
21 Cain felt this about Abel (Gen. 4:5)
22 Madagascar franc (abbr.)
23 Another woman with Mary at Jesus' tomb (Luke 24:10)
25 Pear-shaped instrument

27 The angel Mary saw wore clothes as "white as ___" (Matt 28:3)

28 Cause of unconsciousness

29 "Sitting ___ against the sepulchre" (Matt. 27:61)

31 Handkerchief, for short

34 Type of serpent

35 Jesus' appearance to Mary ___ the mystery of the empty tomb (Mark 16:9)

37 The angel told Mary, "___ not ye" (Matt 28:5)

38 Jesus was ___ to cast seven devils from Mary (Mark 16:9)

39 Put in Jesus' hand instead of a scepter (Matt. 27:29)

41 Gideon built an altar ___ the place of Baal's (Judg. 6:28)

47 Measure of volume (abbr.)

49 Mary addressed risen Jesus, "___" (John 20:15)

50 Silver ones were brought from Tarshish (Jer. 10:9)

51 Egyptian capital

52 Mary thought Jesus' life ___ on the cross (Matt. 27:55–61)

53 David did this to Bathsheba (2 Sam. 11:2)

55 Where widow lived, perhaps (1 Kings 17:12)

58 Snaky fish (pl.)

60 Jonah felt this for a gourd (Jonah 4:10)

61 "Ye shall find the ___ wrapped in swaddling clothes" (Luke 2:12)

62 Palestine, e.g.

63 "Cometh Mary Magdalene early, when it was yet ___" (John 20:1)

65 Fairy

67 Mythical demon, whereas the ones that tormented Mary were real

NAMES OF GOD

ACROSS

1 Annapolis, US Naval __ (abbr.)
5 Opposed
9 Spicy condiment
14 Esther's banquet
15 __ of the woman
16 Animal's nose
17 Blind guides "strain at a __" (Matt. 23:24)
18 Unclean hopper
19 Heron
20 "__has sent me" (Ex. 3:14) (2 words)
21 Airport landing area
23 Nile whirlpool
24 Hebrew name for God
26 Jonathan to David (slang)
28 "The Lord our God is __"
29 Sacrificial lamb would not have one
31 Latin greeting
34 Write later time
37 Female horses
39 __ of the host of the Lord (abbr.)
40 Mighty __

41 Time Jesus was crucified
42 Tend to, as in Genesis 2:15
44 Where birds fly
47 __ Commandments
48 Encourage
50 Billion years
51 Egypt to Israel (dir.)
52 "Abba, __"
56 Waltons creator Hamner
59 Dot __ printer
63 First woman
64 Baton action
66 Weapon metal
67 Modern name for Persia
68 Sins (slang) (2 words)
69 Trick, as in Joshua 9:4 NIV
70 Traveled by camel
71 Chilly
72 Samuel and Zadok role
73 Him who __ no sin

DOWN

1 Ephod stone (slang)
2 Irrigation ditch
3 "Remember the __"
4 Music storage format (abbr.)
5 Guilty, as in Psalm 25:2
6 Draw __ to God
7 Time in office
8 Thought
9 Megiddo to Samaria (dir.)
10 __ of the Lord
11 King of kings, __ of lords
12 Took to court
13 Lawyer (abbr.)
21 Color
22 Bean counter (abbr.)
25 Lord of __

27 The Lord redeems with His (Ex. 6:6)
29 Cooking area
30 Surrender
31 Opera solo
32 Peddle
33 Samaria to Jerusalem (dir.)
34 Cut, as in Deuteronomy 21:12
35 He shall __ ; none shall shut
36 Aghast
38 Concerning
39 Texas summer time zone (abbr.)
43 __ of Righteousness
45 His fire purifies
46 69 Across synonym
49 Sleep type (abbr.)
51 God who sees (Heb.) (2 words)

53 Wading bird
54 Circumvent
55 "__a right spirit within me" (Ps. 51:10)
56 Italian volcano
57 Mil. absence
58 Status symbol in Bible times

60 Ventilates
61 He is Faithful and __
62 __ of Sharon
65 Psychotropic drug (abbr.)
67 Annoy

MESSIAH

ACROSS

1 Copied
5 Buccaneers city
10 "Before," KJV-style
13 Lion of __
15 Ad
16 "The eyes of the Lord __ to and fro" (2 Chron. 16:9)
17 Having wings
18 Aging
19 Card game
20 LP speed
21 "Let him __ himself, and take up his cross" (Matt. 16:24)
23 Molded salad
25 Leer at
26 Unyoke oxen
28 OT prophet
31 Describes Bible lands people
32 Improve
33 Steered Galilee craft
34 Canaan to Egypt (dir.)
37 Priestly leader
38 Describes Ehud

40 Lotion ingredient
41 Mozart's "__ Giovanni"
42 Horse command
43 Messiah's is fruitful (Isa. 10:18)
44 Messiah rose this day
45 Totter
46 "Do not be wise in your own __" (Rom. 12:16 NKJV)
49 Give
50 Sculpture types
51 "Into thine __ I commit my spirit" (Ps. 31:5)
52 Santa's helper
55 Baseball stat
56 Prep dough
59 __ Lauder cosmetics
61 "__, though I walk through the valley of the shadow of death" (Ps. 23:4)
62 Pursue, as in 1 Pet. 3:11
63 Esau's color (Fr.)
64 Part of a min.
65 "The Word was made flesh, and __ among us" (John 1:14)
66 Book of Numbers contains many (sing.)

DOWN

1 It will hold widow's oil (2 words)
2 Fruit interior
3 Dutch cheese
4 Recording medium (abbr.)
5 Steak type
6 Partner
7 Blindness "cure" (John 9:6 NIV)
8 Before (prefix)
9 OT patriarch
10 Burst out
11 Having a secret meaning
12 Prophet who walked with God
14 Protected, as in Psalm 139:5 NKJV
22 First letter of Lam.
24 Transgression

25 Swine's "hello"
26 Wields
27 Egypt river
28 Messiah raised from the __
29 David's army need (slang)
30 Light-producing gas
31 "After I have risen, I will go __ of you into Galilee" (Mark 14:28 NIV)
34 Messiah's blood was __
35 Jacob, "First __ me your birth right." (Gen. 25:31 NIV)
36 Way to cross Jordan River
38 Buckeye State
39 Messiah was __ of a virgin
40 Messiah pierced here

42 Carried away
43 Manger "food"
44 Holy Spirit power like (abbr.)
45 __ Commandments
46 "Whoever __ your word will never taste death" (John 8:52 NIV)
47 Make into sauce
48 Jacob's father

49 Trainee
51 Drag, as in John 21:6 NIV
52 Decorative needle case
53 Messiah's were not broken
54 Messiah's were pierced
57 Masada to Bethlehem (dir.)
58 Jerusalem to Bethlehem (dir.)
60 Wise king, to friends

WHAT TO WEAR?

ACROSS

1 FDR's terrier
5 "I am _____ and Omega" (Rev. 21:6)
10 "Women... _____ goats' hair" (Ex. 35:26)
14 Wading bird
15 Swine "ran...down a _____ place" (Luke 8:33)
16 "Delight thyself _____ in the LORD" (Ps. 37:4)
17 Zacharias's wife, for short
18 False witnesses _____ one's name
19 "Though I be _____ in speech" (2 Cor. 11:6)
20 Disciples were _____ in Gethsemane
22 With 53 Across, fine robe recipient
24 "Foundation of God standeth _____" (2 Tim. 2:19)
26 Gene letters
27 When repeated, it means to threaten, intimidate
30 Pet.'s catch
32 Cascades mount
37 Swiss mount
38 David's stone proved _____ to Goliath
40 Bethlehem shiner
41 Seamless garment wearer

43 Fig leaf wearer
44 John the Baptist's garments
45 Baker's need
46 Some would _____ angrily to Jesus' claims
48 Boaster has a big one
49 Good News _____ through centuries
52 Squabble
53 See 22 Across
54 Pull
56 Former Russian ruler
58 Curtain, often
63 King's palace dweller of Proverbs 30:28
67 Repeated, Jesus' cross cry
68 Church doctrine
70 Stem joint
71 Ephod measure of Exodus 39:9
72 Org.
73 Valley
74 Large purse
75 "Children of the _____ of Abraham" (Acts 13:26)
76 "Here am I; _____ me" (Isa. 6:8)

DOWN

1 Liar's tales
2 43 Across son
3 Dieter's word
4 Worn with sackcloth
5 Ancient Israel foe
6 New "lol" in messaging
7 Soft sound
8 "He _____ my voice" (Ps. 18:6)
9 Paul's healing garments (Acts 19:12)
10 Indian garment
11 You might pull it
12 Food safety org.

13 Christmas
21 Huffs go-with
23 Dit's partner
25 Organic compound
27 Military rank
28 Pain relief brand
29 Jonah was _____ at gourd's loss
31 High-earners, e.g.
33 "_____, and it shall be given" (Matt. 7:7)
34 22 Across workplaces
35 It takes two to do it
36 Malicious burning
39 What healed lame man did

42 Spanish list starter
44 Israelite's sandal part
47 Priest's garment
50 British business ender (abbr.)
51 Joppa garment maker
55 Most evil
57 Ephod add-ons
58 "Covet...the _____ gifts" (1 Cor. 12:31)
59 Fido's food

60 Joseph's had many colors
61 Cattle of Pharaoh's dream
62 Mexican money
64 Pineapple brand
65 43 Across home
66 "_____ your heart," not garments (Joel 2:13)
69 Short title for Luke

GODLY GIFTS

ACROSS

1 "My _____ is glad" (Ps. 16:9)
6 God is not _____ off, as in Jeremiah 23:23
10 Dashboard information
13 Stick to, as God's laws
15 Greedy man _____ God, as in Malachi 3:8
16 "Ye _____ my friends" (John 15:14)
17 Devil, often
18 Ukraine capital
19 Zero
20 Wedding miracle site
22 "One Lord, one faith, one _____" (Eph. 4:5)
24 Land of Israel did _____ Judah
26 "Is there no _____ in Gilead?" (Jer. 8:22)
28 Herb brought to Jesus' tomb
29 Bent in prayer, often
30 Sewing machine inventor Elias
31 "_____ us thy salvation" (Ps. 85:7)
32 Possessive pronoun
33 Jesus will _____ the lost, as in Matthew 18:11
34 Ermine
35 Sodium _____
37 Cricket cousin

41 Psalm 23 subject
42 Satan's Eden's noise
43 "How long..._____ they believe?" (Num. 14:11)
44 Dales
47 "Thy _____ shall not stumble" (Prov. 3:23)
48 God's _____ for you is good
49 Jesus _____ from the tomb
50 Goodness... "all the _____" of life (Ps. 23:6)
51 Where Jesus raised widow's son
52 Finish faster and better
54 Ship feature
56 _____ Dolorosa, Jerusalem site
57 Christmas
59 Medals
63 KJV verb ending
64 Center
65 Godly will _____ from sin
66 "Taste and _____ that" God is good (Ps. 34:8)
67 God: "there is none _____" (Isa. 45:5)
68 Suspicious

DOWN

1 Halo, maybe
2 Nigerian city
3 "Gotcha!"
4 "Lord..._____ my soul" (Ps. 35:17)
5 Indulgence
6 Noah's float
7 Shortcoming
8 "_____ is in thine own eye" (Matt. 7:4) (2 words)
9 Invitation abbreviation
10 Philippines capital
11 Paul and Silas prayed in one
12 "Take the _____ of salvation" (Eph. 6:17)
14 Sea eagle

21 God in heaven _____
23 "_____ ye here, and watch" (Mark 14:34)
24 Against
25 "Covet...the _____ gifts" (1 Cor. 12:31)
27 "Stand in _____, and sin not" (Ps. 4:4)
29 Mary and Elizabeth relationship
30 "What I _____, that do I" (Rom. 7:15)
31 Daring
33 Prunes, as unfruitful branch
34 Religious activity, maybe
36 God will _____ the repentant soul
37 Stall, often retail
38 Sandwich source, for short
39 Esther's realm, today

40 Daniel's prison
42 Pirate's attention-getting cry
44 OT sites of idol worship, often
45 Alberta lake
46 He "remembers us in our low _____"
(Ps. 136:23)
47 Wolves in sheep's clothing, for example
48 Herod's abode
50 Slobber

51 Stairway post
53 Christ died _____ for sin
55 "Give _____ to my words, O Lord" (Ps. 5:1)
58 Robert E.
60 KJV "deer"
61 Boss (Abbr.)
62 Judas descriptor

MATTHEW: THE TAX COLLECTOR

ACROSS

1 "By ___ are ye saved" (Eph. 2:8)
6 Elijah was making one for the benefit of Baal's prophets (1 Kings 18:27)
10 Part of a doorway
14 What some Jews felt a taxman, like Matthew, was
15 Matthew learned "the Son of man is Lord ___ of the sabbath day" (Matt. 12:8)
16 Mary's ointment filled the house with this (John 12:3) (var.)
17 "___ in me" (John 15:4)
18 Matthew was one of the "twelve Jesus ___ forth" (Matt. 10:5)
19 Pharaoh was a royal ___ to Moses and God's people
20 "As ___ children" (Eph. 5:1)
21 Dawn
23 School group (abbr.)
24 Chances of winning
26 Matthew did this in Jesus' name (Matt. 10:7)
28 Protrusion of an organ
31 God would ___ out Laodicea (Rev. 3:16) (var.)
32 Passenger on ships from Tarshish (2 Chron. 9:21)
33 Like a leaky faucet
36 Fifth book of the NT
40 "Ye have ___ of all these things" (Matt. 6:32)

42 Government spy org.
43 Past times
44 Restaurant
45 "Brother of low ___" (James 1:9)
48 Eve's beginning (Gen. 2:21)
49 Glided
51 Sins
53 In 1 Samuel 17:49, David ___ Goliath with a slingshot
56 "___ the sick" (Matt. 10:8)
57 Number of Bible books by Matthew
58 Tradition says Matthew was one
61 Jesus healed the ___ (Matt. 11:5)
65 "Throughout all ___" (Eph. 3:21)
67 Most Bible scholars believe the wife of Alphaeus ___ Matthew, aka Levi (Luke 5:27)
68 Matt. was in this because of Jesus (Matt. 26:56)
69 Kate ___, model
70 Lazarus "had ___ in the grave" (John 11:17)
71 Joseph "turned ___ into the parts of Galilee" (Matt. 2:22)
72 Esau sold his birthright for this (Gen. 25:30–33)
73 Writer Bombeck
74 Riding a white ___ (Rev. 19:11)

DOWN

2 How Matthew felt after Jesus rose from the dead (John 20:20)
2 The one Jesus was given was scarlet (Matt. 27:28)
3 The Holy Spirit stopped Paul from preaching here (Acts 16:6)
4 Brook Matthew crossed toward Gethsemane (John 18:1)
5 "Come down ___ my child die" (John 4:49)
6 Matthew and the disciples did "as ___ commanded" (Matt. 21:6)
7 "Ye shall not have gone ___ the cities of Israel, till the Son of man be come" (Matt. 10:23)
8 Beano

9 This did not happen to Jesus in the tomb (Ps. 16:10)
10 Regarded as Bible's oldest book
11 Matthew would ___ life of an itinerate preacher (Matt. 10:14)
12 ___ Carlo
13 Disciples forgot this (Matt. 16:5)
21 Twelfth Jewish month (Est. 3:7)
22 "Blessed ___ the poor in spirit" (Matt. 5:3)
25 "The disciples ___ as Jesus had appointed them" (Matt. 26:19)
27 "Will ye also go ___?" (John 6:67)
28 "Dippeth his ___ with me in the dish" (Matt. 26:23)

29 Fencing sword

30 To draw in

31 Box

34 Type of tea

35 Host for demons (Matt. 8:32)

37 Matthew ate this on the Sabbath (Matt. 12:1)

38 Mathematical study of triangles (abbr.)

39 Emmaus to Bethlehem (dir.)

41 God said via the prophets, "I will wipe Jerusalem as a man wipeth a ___" (2 Kings 21:13)

45 Break

46 Perhaps used to fill jars with water at a wedding (John 2:7)

47 Epoch

50 Memory of things long past

52 Ishmael was Abraham's ___ son (Gen. 17:18–19)

53 Fizzes

54 Metal bar

55 Long-necked fowl (pl.)

56 African scavenger

59 "The young lions ___ after their prey, and seek their meat from God" (Ps. 104:21)

60 In Jesus' parable, the virgins awake and ___ their lamps (Matt. 25:7)

62 Canal

63 A disciple, like Matthew, could be regarded as one to Jesus

64 After Jesus' arrest, "all the disciples forsook him, and ___" (Matt. 26:56)

66 Jericho to Bethlehem (dir.)

68 Abraham, Isaac, and Jacob, e.g.

NATHANAEL CAME AND SAW

ACROSS

1 David's dad, for short (Ruth 4:17)
5 "The ___ priests answered" (John 19:15)
10 "___ to teach" (1 Tim. 3:2)
13 Dunkable sandwich cookies
15 Island nation
16 Sticky black substance
17 Eastern religion
18 Some believe "Bartholomew" may be Nathanael's ___
19 Jesus stirred this up in many of the Pharisees
20 Even filled with 153 fish, Nathanael's didn't break (John 21:11)
21 Nathanael's friend's ___ was Philip (John 1:45–46)
23 Shampoo brand
25 Peter swam to shore, but Nathanael came "in a little ___" (John 21:8)
26 Eluded
28 Billy ___, evangelist
31 Moses brought water forth from this kind of rock (Deut. 8:15)
32 Nathanael's net was pushed to this in John 21:11
33 Breathing need
34 Metric capacity measure (abbr.)
37 Jesus told Nathanael, "Ye shall see heaven ___" (John 1:51)
38 Canned chili brand
40 Disobeying God would be one

DOWN

1 Only Gospel Nathanael is mentioned in
2 Canal
3 "Father hath ___ me" (John 20:21)
4 "Jacob ___ pottage" (Gen. 25:29)
5 Rocky Balboa
6 Sound physical condition
7 Caesar's trio
8 Airport info
9 "I go a ___" (John 21:3)
10 Tipped
11 Analyze

41 What Jacob called his youngest son, for short? (Gen. 35:18)
42 Jesus told Nathanael he'd see angels going up and ___ (John 1:51)
43 More pallid
44 David's sling stones come from one (1 Sam. 17:40)
45 Squirted
46 Stays
49 Nathanael saw one when he came ashore (John 21:9)
50 Women should "___ themselves in modest apparel" (1 Tim. 2:9)
51 "God took one of his ___" (Gen. 2:21)
52 Jetted tub
55 Guileless Nathanael wouldn't do this to anyone (slang)
56 Capital of Afghanistan
59 "Many ___ signs truly did Jesus" (John 20:30)
61 "Out of whose womb came the ___?" (Job 38:29)
62 Socially superior
63 Judas resorted to using one (Matt. 27:5)
64 "That which groweth of ___ own accord" (Lev. 25:5)
65 Side of the ship Jesus told Nathanael and his friends to throw the net over (John 21:6)
66 Dogs, cats, birds, e.g.

12 "Behold, I give unto you power to ___ on serpents and scorpions" (Luke 10:19)
14 Nathanael could have used this while fishing (2 words)
22 What David did before letting the stone from his slingshot fly
24 None of the disciples asked Jesus, "Who ___ thou?" (John 21:12)
25 Lower leg
26 Counterfeit coin
27 Nathanael told Jesus, "Thou art the ___ of Israel" (John 1:49)

28 Lump

29 "The harvest of the earth is ___" (Rev. 14:15)

30 Last word in the Bible

31 Side

34 Foolish person

35 "At the name of Jesus every ___ should bow" (Phil. 2:10)

36 When Nathanael came ashore, he knew the stranger "was the ___" (John 21:12)

38 "How ___ is the fig tree withered away!" (Matt. 21:20)

39 How animals were grouped for the ark

40 How Philip referred to his friend, perhaps

42 KJV's "drunkard"

43 "He that deviseth to do evil shall be called a mischievous ___" (Prov. 24:8)

44 "I will break also the ___ of Damascus" (Amos 1:5)

45 Fore-and-aft sail

46 More than one radius

47 One went out from Caesar Augustus (Luke 2:1)

48 "We have found him, of whom ___ in the law ...did write" (John 1:45)

49 ___ mignon

51 Naomi's daughter-in-law (Ruth 2:22)

52 "The kinsman said unto Boaz, Buy it for thee. So he drew off his ___" (Ruth 4:8)

53 Unwanted insect

54 Greek god of war

57 Boxer Muhammad

58 Jesus' resurrection was this kind of news to Nathanael

60 "The veil of the temple was rent in twain from the ___ to the bottom" (Mark 15:38)

ANSWERS

DAY 1

```
CHEEK  ACHE  ALT
HEARER CLAY  TEE
ANTONY VINE  TAR
   DYES  FORGIVE
IDEA  HIFI  ORES
GOOD  MENS  FAENA
OWE  SEEN  BLT
BARKEEP COASTAL
LET  SHIP  SEA
FREUD FOOL  MARY
LENT  SINK  GARY
AMAZING  ETUI
MAM  SOUL  LIMBER
EKE  LORE  CLEAVE
DEL  EPEE  EDGED
```

DAY 2

```
BRA  WIDOW  SAMBA
REF  ADOBO  ILIAD
EAR  LETIN  GOADS
ALASKA  DONE
CLIP  OWED  SITE
HYDE  GUARD  SIN
   CENTS  BALED
JAIRUS  WEEPER
WATER  HINDI
OPT  ATONE  EMUS
KEYS  RAGE  CANA
   INKS  FUELED
ADAGE  SAGAS  LAD
LIGHT  EXAMS  ESE
BRATS  LEPER  TEN
```

DAY 3

```
TRA  ALGIN  CLUBS
OIL  FARSI  RITAS
MVP  FOIST  USARE
BEHOLDNOWISTHE
RADII  IRA
   ACCEPTEDTIME
CEO  TEAR  EASED
RAHS  ARING  MILE
ISONE  MORE  GEN
BEHOLDNOWISTHE
   BIA  ECO
DAYOFSALVATION
BELOW  SNOOP  RUE
ALAKE  ENSUE  ATE
SEWED  REESE  MAD
```

DAY 4

```
AHARD  SCAT  BAY
SEDER  ELAH  AGE
PLANE  AIRE  ROT
PRESERVEMEO
   SAC  EAMES
SAME  THOR  RELY
APILE  WAS  TON
GODFORINTHEEDO
ELI  NOR  ERRED
SLAT  DAMS  ASAS
TONIC  AID
IPUTMYTRUST
WIT  PAID  ONEAS
ACE  ILEA  NITRO
YES  DENY  ETHAN
```

DAY 5

```
BIT  ACRES  ALAMB
ADO  CHARY  PETER
REM  SATAN  LOOSE
BABE  RESCUE  PAW
   XII  NNW
BOTTOM  MOTORS
CAL  STONE  YOUTH
IBID  SLOTS  FRAU
SEVEN  DREAM  ARM
LEPERS  SNAILS
   TWO  BOM
HAH  NESTER  PALM
IMAGE  EATUP  MIA
DOLES  ATONE  ERR
ENOLS  TENOR  NAY
```

DAY 6

```
CHAS  LASH  SCROD
HOBO  TREE  PROBE
OURS  DIVA  ROBIN
ISAAC  DELAYS
REM  PENNED  SAPS
   LOVE  DON  RAT
ACTE  ESS  APACE
REIGN  STE  BABEL
EATON  DAM  USDA
ASH  WEB  SOIL
SEES  LESION  ACE
   TAIWAN  NIGHT
PETER  AMEN  NOAH
SPLAT  ROSE  TRIO
TACKY  EAST  OARS
```

DAY 7

```
BIAS  AQUA  WASP
IDLE  LUST  HAILSA
RATE  BEAT  OTTER
CHANCEL  YALE
HOR  OIL  MIRIAM
   GMT  DAME  NBE
ARGUE  SAGAS  URN
LION  LINEN  BRAD
PSI  ZINCS  POEMS
HEN  URGE  SLY
ANGORA  BTU  ALA
   RISE  ARMADAS
ISAAC  SAME  BOTH
BERTH  ABBA  ERIE
MAKE  URIM  LENS
```

DAY 8

```
NABAL  CPS  FOOL
EBONY  HAY  WORSE
ALONE  AIR  HEALS
TOTE  STRIFE  IOT
HOE  SOS  NOAH
MEALY  GOLIATH
   CIA  LED  GLEE
SHEEP  PAS  SHEAR
PORT  MEW  ATE
APRICOT  BURMA
   CORN  EBB  EMU
WPM  DEADLY  MAON
IRATE  MOO  TENET
FOUND  ESP  ALIBI
EMIT  SEE  IDEAL
```

DAY 9

```
SCALP  LAVA  CDS
TIDIED  AVIS  HOE
MADMAN  WILE  RUN
   BRAG  ANANIAS
PAUL  LARA  OSLO
BEGS  MARY  ALTAR
ORE  RACK  FCA
TURBINE  WITNESS
EON  SINS  RIO
SPURT  SODS  SILL
TUNE  LENO  BENT
ELEAZAR  WORD
EPA  ERMA  WEAKEN
DIS  AGON  NATION
STY  LENT  DENSE
```

ANSWERS

DAY 10

```
A H A | J U N T A | A T A L E
B E G | U S I N G | L E P E R
I R E | D E L T A | M E R G E
D E I C E R |     | B A S T
E T N A | S M U G | H I G H
D O G E | P A S S E | B O A
    S C O U T |   | O D I U M
C H A P E L | A C C O S T
M O O R S | P L A T O
O I L | H A S T Y | D A S H
O N Y X | O N T O | A R I A
    E S P Y | A N D R E W
A C U R A | W E D G E | E R A
R U F U S | A N N A S | S R I
C R O S S | Y E A R S | T A I
```

DAY 11

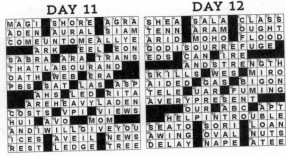

```
M A G I | S H O R E | A G R A
A D E N | A U R A L | S I A M
C O M E U N T O M E A L L Y E
    A R K |   E E L | E O N
S A B R A | A R A | T R A N S
T H A T L A B O U R A N D
O A T H | W E B | E R A
P B S | S A T | L A S | A S P
    A H S | L E D | R I T A
A R E H E A V Y L A D E N
C O S T S | V P I | V I E W S
H U I | A V O |   M O M
A N D I W I L L G I V E Y O U
I C E S | A V E I L | N E W S
R E S T | L E D G E | T R E E
```

DAY 12

```
S H E A | S A L A | C L A S S
T E N N | A R A M | O U G H T
A R I D | M O H O | F L O O D
G O D I S O U R R E F U G E
E D S | C A N | I R E
    A N D S T R E N G T H
S K I L L S | W E S | M I R O
A I D E D | G A S | B I G O N
T E L E | U A R | F U M I N G
A V E R Y P R E S E N T
    O U R | A B C | A P T
H E L P I N T R O U B L E
S E A T O | S O R I | L O A N
A W I N G | O V A L | N U T S
D E L A Y | N A P E | A T E E
```

DAY 13

```
B A N J O | S E E R | H A S P
A F O O T | U R G E | E M I R
T R E S S | S A I L | N O N O
S O L E | M A S S I F | N A B
    P L A N |   | V E G G I E
E S T H E R | H E D Y
Z O O | E X O D U S | P E C K
R U T H | P A L | S P A N
A L O E | D E P L O Y | I L E
    A M E N | M U S C L E
S C U L P T |   | L A L A
A L T | H E S T O N | M A R S
V O T E | C H A R | A S C O T
E V E R | T O L D | C O M M A
S E R E | S E E S | S N E E R
```

DAY 14

```
A W A S H | C A P O | T I M
C A S P E R | F L A X | E N E
E X P I R E | L I C E | A D S
    D O V E | G E N E S I S
E D E N | M E N S | B E A R
P O O R | B E E S | C O R N S
A N T | H U N G | D O N
L E O P A R D | B I C Y C L E
    E R N | L E A K | O I L
C R A N E | F O A L | C L E F
R E I N | B A G S | T U T U
A C R Y L I C | T I E R
V I M | I B I S | I T S E L F
A P E | O L E O | I R O N E D
T E N | N E S T |   | A R D O R
```

DAY 15

```
A B S | H I K E | L E S S O R
B I T | E D E N | E X H A L E
R O E | L A N D | E X I T E D
A T R O P H Y | S O N
M I N I | O A R S | N A H O R
C A L I | E L F | E M U
    E O S | F A O | M A I D
S P U R T E R | B U R E T T E
L E S S | E E L | L A X
O R E | D I E | M I F F
B U R N T | N E B E | C O R E
    O U R | I G N O R E D
C A T T L E | M A Y O | M S G
O R A C L E | A L P S | A C E
B E T H E L | M Y T H | L A D
```

DAY 16

```
B O B B Y | S C A B | A R A B
A D O R E | P U R L | D A L I
B O N E S | E R I E | S T I R
A R E A | U N E A S E | E N D
T E N D |   | S N O R E S
E T C H E D | S E E D
A H A | L O G G E D | D R A B
C O L A | O U T | S O U L
H U L L | M A Y H E M | A T E
A B E L | Y A R R O W
C U R S E D | S E M I
E V E | T U L I P S | T H E M
D U S T | S I D E | S U E D E
A L T O | A F E W | P A R E R
R A S P | S E A S | A L O N E
```

DAY 17

```
P E A L | C A G E | A S I A
L A N E | L A M B | C L I C K
E G G S | I N T O | A T S E A
B L E S S E D | N A D A
E E L | N N W | L E R O U X
    H O T | W E P T | N N E
S C R E W | H I G H S | S I R
H O A R | G E N O A | P E T E
E B B | F L A G S | B I T E S
E R A | O A R S | D O T
P A T M O S | N E W | O A T
    A L S O | A P L E N T Y
S M O K E | P A V E | A T O P
T A P E D | E D E N | T O N E
E Y E S | C O L D | S P E D
```

DAY 18

```
B L A B | S T Y E | P H I L
L I F E | T H A T | C R E T E
O M I T | R E S T | R I N S E
A B R A H A M | A G E S
T O E | E Y E | R O M A N S
    R E S | G O A L | L A W
S I S A L | B R A C E | T I E
A D A M | C R A T E | L O V E
M O N | T R U T H | U P S E T
O L D | I O T A | E R N
A S S E T S | B U G | M S T
    A L S O | E R E M I T E
A W A R E | U M B O | A L A N
G I F T S | C O O P | R A G S
E T C H | H O P E | K N E E
```

ANSWERS

DAY 19

DAY 20

DAY 21

DAY 22

DAY 23
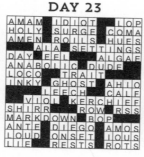

DAY 24

DAY 25

DAY 26

DAY 27

ANSWERS

DAY 28

DAY 29

DAY 30

DAY 31

DAY 32

DAY 33

DAY 34

DAY 35

DAY 36

ANSWERS

DAY 37

DAY 38

DAY 39

DAY 40

DAY 41

DAY 42

DAY 43

DAY 44

DAY 45

ANSWERS

DAY 46

DAY 47

DAY 48

DAY 49

DAY 50

DAY 51

DAY 52

DAY 53

DAY 54

ANSWERS

DAY 55

DAY 56

DAY 57

DAY 58

DAY 59

DAY 60

DAY 61

DAY 62

DAY 63

ANSWERS

DAY 64

DEN SHRUB SPURT
EVE HOUSE ERROR
VET ANGST MONEY
ONTIME TWIX
ILLS TREE YMCA
DYER AWARD EON
AESOP ESSAY
SHELLS ACTUAL
CHALK AURAL
ION LORRY TRAP
ADDS IDEA RAGE
EPEE PSYCHE
ALEVE SHEEP HAL
LEPER SUGAR ESE
BEANO ANGRY LTD

DAY 65

BILK PACT BEAN
ERIE ALAR FROWN
GAGE SOLO AISLE
ATHLETE YARD
NET SOS SMELLS
APR LICE YEA
PALSY FUROR SAT
LEAK DEMIT POSE
ARM LEAPS BELTS
SIB AIRS ROW
MESSRS NOD UPS
HYMN ABYSSAL
WIDEN APSE EURO
ANNEX WEAR RASP
SNAP SALT FLEE

DAY 66

GRASP TAPS AFC
OUTPUT WILL CEO
DESIRE OREO TIM
RIND BAPTISM
GRIM ROAD BOTA
SEAT HANG TONYS
LEG HOPE NUN
UKULELE BOREDOM
LAY NEON EGO
SAVOR CYAN FARM
TRAY PUCK LIFE
AIRDROP SAUL
PSI EWOK ICICLE
LEE SELL DRAWER
END TRAM ELATE

DAY 67

DNAS SCAMS BASE
RIPE HAVOC ARAN
ACHE AGORA BOLD
WHILEWEWEREYET
SEDER SHELL
DIES SLOPES
FAT ELIAS NOAH
OUR SINNERS USE
ARAB ADMIT RED
LAYEST ITIF
STEAL FLARE
CHRISTDIEDFORUS
ROAD RONDO ROMS
OPIE ARENO ISEE
WINS SEDAN DENS

DAY 68

DOES DOMY HERAS
OSLO OREO ADORE
THANKSBEUNTOGOD
EATEN STAY MESA
SIR ATAT TEN
ASS TAR ECHO
NEAR FOR KARATE
NEGEV BAD TAMAR
ANODES HIS LOLL
STEM NOD SEE
AMP OLES PAD
BOAS META TARES
UNSPEAKABLEGIFT
TETON OGLE OSTE
STATE FEED NEST

DAY 69

SARAH ADAM ECHO
AROMA DAME THEN
GETON OVER HURT
ASCENT INCA ZOO
BARED ILIAD
ABRAHAM EAT
HOE MOSES EYED
OREO TAR MARY
YELL DEPOT LIE
EVE DECREED
SPOOL BERRA
NOR WISE MICHAL
EDIT LOGO SHIRE
ROME AFAR EERIE
OMEN HATE SLEDS

DAY 70

ERAS SPED STEW
DINE MARY MANNA
EPIC ANNE ENTER
MUSTARD SALT
APE MMA LOAVES
HEY EBON ORT
AVION BEEFS CIA
MINT CARAT RACK
MST FRUIT PULSE
ATE RODE POE
NARROW OLD FFA
ANDY LASSOES
SPLIT UNIT ILLS
BEANS LOVE NILE
EGGS EDEN GOAT

DAY 71

LADEN EBBS PINT
AGORA LOLL AREA
TOPAZ INTO LAWS
ENE ACAD GDANSK
PROS AKC
SCARED DANGERS
PLAIT FOGS EPA
AARGH ERE ASAIL
TWO PAID VODKA
SNIPERS SAWYER
SON SAIS
BARREN PHIL ELM
APIA ASEA INDIA
ISLE NEAR NIGER
TELL TALK GLENS

DAY 72

TIFF ATTIC ELLE
AIDE FAUNA BIOS
BIRTHRIGHT OBOE
COO ATONE
SIGHT FALLS RED
ION REDEEM IRE
SUPPLIED ISAAC
ROOD TRUE
HANOI AROMATIC
ICE TRIPOD ABR
DEW EASED BARMY
SERVO SIR
ALMS AMPHIBIANS
LEAP GETAT SHOO
BONY ERASE EATS

ANSWERS

DAY 73

DAY 74

DAY 75

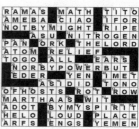

DAY 76

DAY 77

DAY 78

DAY 79

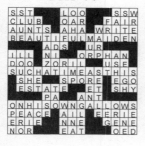

DAY 80

DAY 81

ANSWERS

DAY 82

DAY 83

DAY 84

DAY 85

DAY 86

DAY 87

DAY 88

DAY 89

DAY 90

ANSWERS

DAY 91

DAY 92

DAY 93

DAY 94

DAY 95

DAY 96

DAY 97

DAY 98

DAY 99

ANSWERS

DAY 100

DAY 101

DAY 102

DAY 103

DAY 104

DAY 105

DAY 106

DAY 107

DAY 108

ANSWERS

DAY 109

```
COMBS  ACAD   ABBA
AGORA  BABA   SLUR
BLOOD  RICH   KERI
SENT MAN   ODESSA
    HARM   AMIDST
DEFERS   TIES
USURP  BERYL  MEN
MANSE  LEE  OVATE
BUD  GRAND  YARNS
   GUMS   PARKAS
  FAMINE  MALI
NATION  SUM  AGAR
ALAS  IBIS  GNOME
ISLE  NOAH  ACRID
LEER  GAMY  DEEDS
```

DAY 110

```
APPAL  ALPO   CRIB
CRANE  LIEU   LANE
MOTTO  GNAT   OVEN
EPEE  DIE  DIVERT
    LEAD   RODENT
IDIOCY   SHOE
RASPS  OPERA  RPM
ISLET  BAT  TIARA
SHE  AVERT  INGOT
   TUSK   LOCUST
  AWHILE  MENU
DIRECT  RAT  BEAR
ODOR  UNIT  SAMBA
VETO  ROTE  ATILT
EDEN  EWER  CERES
```

DAY 111

```
SBE   START   BOB
LAVA  CURIE  SOLA
ICED  UNION  ENDS
THROBBED  OGRESS
    EAR    REV
DADA  SIN  LECH
SONATA  VET  HOG
HIGH  SHOWS  RANI
ANE  PAR  AMENDS
GLAD  GYM  ALTO
   GOD   EEL
BOBOLI  ALMIGHTY
ADAR  NABOB  EURO
ARIA  ELUDE  TEAR
LET  SATYR  DYE
```

DAY 112

```
ALTAR  BEDS   REST
MARRY  ADAM   ONTO
OVATE  KITE   IRON
SEMI  METALS  ONE
   SAAR   TITLES
PALTRY   GENE
UNO  KAISER  APES
MORE  DAM  MOPE
ANDY  SENSOR  SEE
   ETNA   WASHER
NEEDLE   INTO
ADD  CAMELS  CLAY
AGES  KERI  ACURA
CAMP  EMMA  PETER
PRAY  ROAD  TREAD
```

DAY 113

```
UTAH   SOL   CLEF
MIRE  SQUIB  HEEL
PLEA  TUTEE  ONLY
LATVIA   SMARTS
   HERTZ   ADD
WAFER  SAD  SALAD
ORANGE  PAS  LEVI
ORE  ESTONIA  TAN
DONE  EAT  PURINA
SWANK  REF  TENTH
   TIM   CAROB
  ISRAEL  JOSEPH
FREE  LICIT  KEEP
LAMA  TENTS  ASIA
UNIT  USA  HORN
```

DAY 114

```
ALIAS  AGORA   SEE
DEVIL  BRAUN   TNT
AFIRE  BURNT   ASH
MTV  SNOB  ISSUE
   GIFT  BROTHER
SCHOOL   SAUCY
ORION  WITH  MOB
FORD  TEETH  PIPE
APE  MATE  TONAL
   MOUNT  TOKILL
ATLANTA  BONY
HEIRS  CLEG  PSI
ERN  TABLE  UPEND
ARE  ELIAS  EERIE
DAD  RENDS  PUPA
```

DAY 115

```
PSALM  FOOD   STYE
TABOO  RUDE   AHOY
SLEPT  USES   LAKE
DEL  OMIT  CITIES
   BRAT   EVE
ADJOIN  TINYDOG
TEENS  WEST  ROB
OCTET  HAL  FUGUE
MAT  GAME  USAGE
LYCEUMS   PLANES
  ORE   WOLF
THORNS  COIN  EPA
HERR  SAAR  EATUP
AREA  EVIL  SPURS
TOOL  SEND  STILE
```

DAY 116

```
ORBS   ORALB   USA
PILAF  RECUR   MON
EDEMA  DIEGO   BUG
NEW  TEEN  TERSE
   CHAR  ISHMAEL
MOTHER   ADIEU
AMOUR  PEAR  WAG
LAMB  ABRAM  TOGO
ENE  PERO  SEOUL
   HERON  LOADED
POMELOS   WELL
APART  SEED  LED
RED  IRATE  ERASE
ERA  NAKED  RIVAL
RAM  GNAWS  MAUI
```

DAY 117

```
POSSE  BOSC   TOTS
OATHS  EMIR   EZRA
SHEEP  VINE   NOEL
HUMP  BET  STONES
   HULL   ATONES
SAFEST   EPEE
AFORE  BANDS  TWO
LAUDS  ATE  OCHER
ERR  ATSEA  RHINE
   CHIN  BEASTS
  ASSAIL  BUST
WATERS  ROD  TASK
IRAN  THAN  TITLE
FOND  LORD  ONTOP
ENDS  EYES  EGYPT
```

ANSWERS

DAY 118

```
CLAP  COIN    THEE
HOPE  OGRE  ARENA
AGAR  ELSE  SOWER
FORGIVE   DICT
FST  BAD  DESPOT
     AIL  BLIN  ERA
ANTIS  BROOD  TAR
FOUR  FLOAT  METE
OIL  PROOF  CARES
USS  LOCK  JOY
LEAVEN  DIR  SAG
     EATS  IGNITER
CLUES  AMOS  RAGE
CARPE  NADA  ARIA
OWNS  DREW  NEST
```

DAY 119

```
STAR  TEST  UNFED
COLA  ODOR  SIEVE
AWAY  BEMA  ESTEE
REM  MANAMA  SEND
FROLIC      SKI
     INC  ACHE  TSP
DIGIORNO  GRACE
NOSH  AGE  OMAN
BOLTS  REDEEMER
FRE  USER  FDA
     PEA   FINEST
BABA  DESPOT  ATE
ALARM  REAR  PROX
SORTS  MAST  ETNA
SEEST  AMOS  THEN
```

DAY 120

```
FFA  ABLE  CUPFUL
LAD  BAIT  UNEASE
ERR  ETNA  SCARED
SCOTTIE   SAC
HEIR  KNEW  PERCH
STOP  YEA   OUI
     USA  EAR  IMPS
ALLTIME  RAWNESS
LIES  EVE  BAT
ACV  NIP  CALM
SEISM  LAND  COAT
     PEA  ORATORY
AFIELD  FLUX  TIP
TOILED  BANE  ENE
EXILES  INKS  RED
```

DAY 121

```
PAS  JACOB  DANTE
ENE  EXUDE  ONION
ODD  SLEET  OGLED
PRAISE   HOME
LETS  ADEN  RUSE
EWER  AGILE  REV
     ASPEN  EAGLE
SWEETS   CARMEL
VIOLA  SHIRE
ALL  BROAD  LEAH
TOFU  LENT  INCA
     PITA  HIATUS
TEMPO  LAPIN  RAT
ASSET  THANK  ATE
TETRA  YARDS  PEN
```

DAY 122

```
SBW  CLIMB  ABASH
LEE  LUNAR  VERSA
EAT  ACCRA  IRKED
UNTIDY   NAVY
TIES  ARCH  LAMB
HERR  OMAHA  GEL
     AARON  CHEAT
REEVES   PRIEST
TABLE  REPAY
ORB  CHASM  DATE
MESA  AIDT  AREA
     GOLD  BUYING
ALTAR  DUELS  SOL
CASTE  ENSUE  ERE
TYPES  NOTED  SST
```

DAY 123

```
KATE  TROD   GRAF
ODOR  HOLY  SAUTE
ROAM  RODE  TUNED
ABSALOM   SMOG
HET  ANY  ANEMIA
     USE  BANE  URN
FAITH  SIGNS  TAG
ROSE  BEREA  PETE
ERA  CLADS  YODEL
ETA  HEMS  AWE
RACERS   ARC  TEE
     GIST  LEADERS
SONYS  ALAN  ERRS
ADOPT  LIRA  AREA
DEBT  KEYS  LADY
```

DAY 124

```
PAPA  COBRA  ART
OUTGO  ADLIB  DOW
ONSET  ROTOR  OBI
LTD  HEAR  AARON
     PERT  ATHLETE
RETURN  AXIAL
USERS  GERM  ROW
MANE  PRIDE  SAGA
PUT  PAUL  CHILD
CARNE  PHONES
RIPOSTE  BOOT
EGYPT  HEIR  GAL
ELL  OTTER  ALAMO
LOO  REALM  LEPER
SON  SNIPS  TEND
```

DAY 125

```
SOAP  LYNX  THORN
AUTO  LANE  RAMIE
ACTS  AMEN  ASIDE
RHYTHMS  OMITTED
     PEA   PITY
IDOLS  SHE  DEL
DRONE  STONE  ESE
EATEN  NAB  SALTS
ATE  AFORE  CRIES
RED  EWE  CURSE
     CREW  ADO
CHERITH  CLOGGED
AURAS  IDOL  AERO
PLANE  TAME  NAIL
EASES  EYED  TREE
```

DAY 126

```
LIFE  AMEBA  SBW
OSAKA  EATEN  ALI
ALIEN  STAGG  TEN
DEI  SPOT  USING
     SWAP  FRIENDS
HOSTEL   SOUSE
INCUR  HIGH  BCG
RYAN  HEELS  BOIL
EXT  PERO  AORTA
PERIL   DRONED
ZAPOTEC   NECK
ELATE  RICH  DYE
STY  RAVEN  ENEMY
TEE  EXIST  DANCE
ARE  DEATH  PTAS
```

ANSWERS

DAY 127

DAY 128

DAY 129

DAY 130

DAY 131

DAY 132

DAY 133

DAY 134

DAY 135

ANSWERS

DAY 136

DAY 137

DAY 138

DAY 139

DAY 140

DAY 141

DAY 142

DAY 143

DAY 144

ANSWERS

DAY 145

DAY 146

DAY 147

DAY 148

DAY 149

DAY 150

DAY 151

DAY 152

DAY 153

ANSWERS

DAY 154

DAY 155

DAY 156

DAY 157

DAY 158

DAY 159

DAY 160

DAY 161

DAY 162

ANSWERS

DAY 163

```
DADA  AZTEC  RAT
ALARM LAITY  EGO
DOTTY UNCAP  BAY
SEE RELY   ROUTE
   ETNA PLEATED
AFIELD WHISK
BIBLE  OILS TAB
EGIS TRULY  NONO
LSD THAN  MOOTS
  GOURD GARLIC
ASSUAGE  PALM
BEANS  SILL  AHA
HIT TENET  OASIS
ONE EPOCH  WYETH
RED RATTY   EASY
```

DAY 164

```
CONN  MALTA  CAL
ALONG EXTOL  ONE
LEPER MODEM  AGE
FOE ANON   OUTER
   SPAS LENTILS
BARLEY TILDE
OREOS  EELS  SPA
WELT SCENE  FOUR
LAY ATOM  WORSE
  OVERS BIRTHS
SETDOWN MILK
MARDI  FIGS  DAM
EVE DECAL  OLIVE
LEE ETUDE  NADIR
LSD DATES  DOVE
```

DAY 165

```
CHAMP  EGGS  ECHO
ROGUE  NOAH  AHAB
APART  DEVO  TIME
NERD JOSEPH  NAY
   EVER  PECANS
SPIRIT  MENE
WET ESTHER  LOSE
BRED  HOE   LIES
SOME PENTAD  LAP
  JOHN  FEISTY
MARACA  SALT
ODE TRADER  CLAP
SALE ANEW  SHIRR
EGIS ONCE  SEPIA
SECT HEAD  ESSAY
```

DAY 166

```
PEASE  FDA  MANE
EXPEL  RAP  SAVED
APPAL  UNO  ADORE
COLT LISTEN  WON
ESE DOT  HUES
ESTER  ERRANDS
  END  EGO ROOK
BRIMS DAM  HONEY
AARP  BIT  SON
TWELVES  PLACE
  EAST BUY  LUG
SPA UTAHAN  BARE
LADEN  FEW  AARON
APART  FED  CREPT
BARN   SLY  ESTES
```

DAY 167

```
CRIBS  SHED  BAG
PARLEY SARI  EVE
UNSURE TRUE  HEY
  FISH ACTIONS
GAFF OUST  SLUE
CUBS  RUGS  ALDER
ORB DASH  DIE
SURFACE GODSSON
  LIE HOME  ELF
DARES DOGE  NAIL
EPEE  CAPE  PASO
VICTORY TELL
ICE VETO  RULERS
LED ATOP  AMELIA
SSE LENT  PYLON
```

DAY 168

```
STAR  SPED  HELP
ABLE TROY  POLIO
GOOD RISE  IRKED
ANNOYED  DIED
SEE WEE  ORE IDA
  ACT ZINC  NON
SCUBA CURIE  TUG
TALE SONIC  MESS
ANT DORIS  BERET
MAR ALPS  HOT
PLASMA  SOD  PST
  CARE TOYWITH
ASSES ATOP  HAIR
STINK TOOL  ONCE
KYTE  SODA  POKE
```

DAY 169

```
HEWN  ALONG  SAP
ACHOO MOPER  UNO
SHARP MOTTO  GNU
POT EDOM   TRAIN
  WREN TUTORED
CANAAN  SYNOD
OVENS  IRIS  CUE
LOBE TENET  NASA
TWO GAZA  BIRDS
  HENRI YELLAT
BAZOOKA  FETE
ABLER  FISH  GEM
TOO GABLE  ERODE
HUT ICIER  LUGER
STY ATBAY  TONE
```

DAY 170

```
ATOP  AROMA  ABS
COBRA POURS  LAP
CRIER AMISS  ICE
TEE TYRE   YUKON
  CHIT SERPENT
STIRUP OASIS
NADIR  PUPA  TSP
OREB DAILY  SEAL
BOA BERN  CEASE
  BLAME BAASHA
STATELY  LESS
CYRUS  NIGH  BAT
APR SATAN  IMAGE
TOO ELATE  NABAL
SSW SIDON  LYRE
```

DAY 171

```
SHEBA  SASS  UMP
BUTANE ARCH  POE
WEALTH TARO  SUN
  LIFE BAPTISM
BIOS MAIM  IDEA
SENT ABBA  STERN
OAT OPEC  RAH
BROWNER  REVEALS
  OLD GAVE  LOT
MARRY ANTS  WISE
ABEL ALPO  HEET
CANDELA  NOES
OSE DARE  FASCIA
NEW EMMY  FROWNS
SSS NOSE  SNACK
```

ANSWERS

DAY 172

DAY 173

DAY 174

DAY 175

DAY 176

DAY 177

DAY 178

DAY 179

DAY 180

MORE GREAT BIBLE PUZZLES!

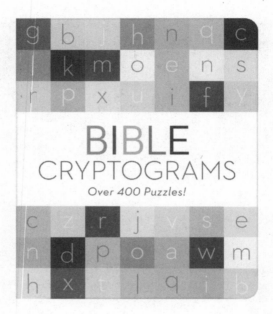

Drawn from the King James Version, these 404 cryptograms each provide a brief passage featuring substituted letters that you'll need to decode to solve the verse. Covering the people, places, things, and ideas of scripture, *Bible Cryptograms* will entertain and educate you, delivering important Bible truths in an enjoyable puzzle package.

Paperback / 978-1-64352-733-8 / $12.99